PRESENT DAY ISSUES
IN PHILOSOPHY

PRESENT DAY ISSUES IN PHILOSOPHY

by

Robert Elias Abu Shanab
Florida State University

and

G. Jay Weinroth
Cleveland State University

Cover credit: **Sondra Weinroth** *and* **Margret Shanab**

KDH

KENDALL/HUNT PUBLISHING COMPANY
DUBUQUE, IOWA

Contents

v

The design of this book of readings has been animated by the goal of making available a variety of substantive commentaries on some of today's critical issues. With this end in mind, materials have been included for their ability to make clear what the issues are, and not merely because they express the viewpoints of some currently prominent authors or social groups.

Thus, for example, the collection of material on the topic "What is education?" is intended to introduce the reader to various reports of the experiences and efforts of educators, so that the reader may better establish for himself what are the relevant empirical premises in arguments concerning education. The reports, criticisms and proposals included on this topic present to the reader a variety of challenges to the commonsense assumption that we hardly need bother to ask the question—"What is education?" Indeed, the gap between the critical attitude of these challenges and the commonsense attitude is so great that being introduced to these sorts of critical arguments is virtually the same thing as being introduced to the meaningfulness of the question ("What is education?"). The consensus of these critical arguments is that, when we arrive at a good answer as to what is indeed education, it becomes clear that what we *call* "education" is not that at all. According to these critics, what we call "education" might be described with more accuracy as fitting people to jobs in corporations, or replacing creativity with regimentation.

The five issues which have been selected for examination in this book are not primarily the issues currently most discussed in a conscious way. On the contrary, we would argue that these issues are among the most important issues currently facing humanity, but that they are not as often discussed in a conscious way as are other issues because people are not very clear as to the nature of these issues. Again, concerning the first topic (What is education?), people dispute hotly the questions of what should be taught and who should control the schools, but they seldom face the fact that they really do not know why we should bother to have schools at all. The schools are there, and they are taken for granted. Our authors, by contrast, probe deeply into the question of why we should bother to have schools at all. Similarly, the existence of philosophies of protest (topic II) is something that is thus far poorly understood. Within this broad topic, to raise the subordinate issue of the contrast between a spirit of community and a basic system of class oppression is, for many persons, to present a totally new set of categories for cognizing the social world. It is not that the average person has decided where he or she stands on the issue of community versus class oppression. Rather, the case, apparently, is that many persons have never thought of the issue at all. In topic III (the search for freedom in national liberation movements) the reader is again introduced to a fundamental concept which may well have been missing from his or her conceptual repertoire. The political world today is perhaps focally revolving about the phenomenon of the national liberation movements while in our civilization the existence of this phenomenon appears to be hardly understood at all. Topic IV (man versus technology) has perhaps received more popular discussion than the first three topics. Nevertheless, it is hardly a topic that is firmly understood by all. Its import, according to some of the authors whose works we include, is that man is about to be overwhelmed not so quickly by environmental pollution as he is by the freedom-crushing effects of his own technology. Lastly, in topic V (The good life), we have a selection of attempts concerning what is in fact the good sort of thing for us to seek, rather than merely talking about the fact that people do seek the good in various ways.

Since the material which we have selected here is intended in every instance to be educational—i.e. to make a valuable contribution to one's understanding of the issues involved—and not merely to provoke discussion, our introductions to the material are often written in the same educational manner. That is, much of the introductory material attempts to emphasize, to make clear, what is in fact being said in the various selections. The study questions at the end of each topic are meant to assist the student in reflecting upon what he has read.

Finally, we should note one further underlying idea that helped determine the structure of this book. That idea is the hope and the design that an introduction to philosophy may be an exciting intellectual experience, and one of immediate interest to the student. There are a great many important technical issues in more advanced philosophical studies, and perhaps they cannot be approached in the manner which we have chosen for this book—at least not without some difficulty. Frankly, however, for an introduction to philosophy these more technical sorts of considerations often constitute something of a great bore for the student and teacher alike. Such boredom can be ill afforded in a time of cultural crisis, and we have endeavored to avoid it by the approach taken herein.

We wish to acknowledge the assistance of our students, William Hains, Hartmut Ramm and J. Runkle. Also, we would like to thank Sondra Weinroth and Margaret Ann Abu Shanab for their help, patience and understanding.

It is to Margaret, Sondra, Joel, Steve, Elias and Jonathan that we dedicate this book.

REAS
GJW
June 1971

Acknowledgements

Plato, "Self-Knowledge in Education," is taken from *Republic*, translated by Benjamin Jowett, 3rd edition.

John Dewey, "Education for Peaceful Change." From *Human Nature and Conduct* by John Dewey. Copyright 1922 by Holt, Rinehart and Winston, Inc. Copyright 1950 by John Dewey. Reprinted by permission of Holt, Rinehart and Winston.

Erich Fromm, "Man for Himself." From *Man for Himself* by Erich Fromm. Copyright 1947 by Erich Fromm. Reprinted by permission of Holt, Rinehart and Winston, Inc.

Christopher Jencks, "The Future of American Education." This article first appeared in *Dissent* March/April 1966, and is reprinted by permission. Also reprinted by permission of the author.

Jonathan Kozol, "Death at an Early Age." From *Death at an Early Age*. Copyright © 1967 by Jonathan Kozol. Reprinted by permission of the publisher, Houghton Mifflin Company.

Paul Goodman, "Freedom and Learning: The Need for Choice." Copyright 1968 *Saturday Review*, Inc. Reprinted by permission of the publisher and the author.

James Ridgeway, "The Closed Corporation," From *The Closed Corporation*, by James Ridgeway, Copyright © 1968 by James Ridgeway. Reprinted by permission of Random House, Inc.

Noam Chomsky, "The Student Movement." This article first appeared in the *Humanist* September/October 1970, and is reprinted by permission. Also reprinted by permission of the author.

Plato, "The Obligation of a Citizen," is taken from *Crito*, translated by Benjamin Jowett, 3rd edition.

Henry D. Thoreau, "An Essay on Civil Disobedience," in *The Portable Thoreau*, edited by Carl Bode, Viking Press, 1947.

Kahlil Gibran, "The Criminal," from *A Treasury of Kahlil Gibran*, edited by Martin L. Wolf, published by Philosophical Library Publishers. Reprinted by permission of the publishers.

Aristotle, "Social Systems," taken from the *Politics*, translated by Benjamin Jowett.

Karl Marx and Friedrich Engels, "The Communist Manifesto," M. Eastman (editor), Capital, *The Communist Manifesto and Other Writings*, Random House, 1959. Reprinted by permission of Random House, Inc.

Huey P. Newton, "Functional Definition of Politics." Reprinted by permission of the Black Panther Party from "The Black Panther."

Students, Philosophy and Relevancy

Robert Elias Abu Shanab and Jay Weinroth

A story was going around the other day about a very large class in Introduction to Philosophy. The professor for the course had been lecturing for about ten minutes when a student in the back row of the auditorium stood up and requested permission to make a comment. The professor replied, "I am sorry, but I must ask that you hold your comments until the end of the lecture." "But sir," the student protested, "what I have to say is of great importance to everyone here." The professor removed his glasses with a characteristic motion, laid them on the lecturn, and asserted in what was intended to be a polite but firm manner, "It is my responsibility to judge what is of importance in this course." The student protested more frantically: "But sir, what I'm trying to tell you is that the auditorium is on fire!" Unruffled, the professor replied: "Really, I must remind you that this is a class in philosophy, not current events. I am afraid that your remarks are simply not relevant to the subject of today's lecture. Now, as I was saying . . ." As the narrator of the story would have it, students began fleeing the burning auditorium at this point, but the professor lectured on to the end, although it is not clear whether the end of the class period or some other end was meant.

While this story has its obvious element of poking fun, at the same time it symbolizes the existence of a serious problem in the teaching of philosophy today. Speaking symbolically, our society is much like the burning auditorium and the professor who lectures on despite the stampeding students and the crackling flames is much like academic enterprise in general when it steadfastly pursues its own internally defined purposes, indifferent to whatever may be happening in the society at large. Under ordinary circumstances it *may* be proper to argue that the purpose of philosophy courses is indeed to pursue the arguments of Descartes and Spinoza on the existence of God or the nature of substance, regardless of the existence of other pressing human problems. On this argument, philosophy is somewhat like pure science, which is not intended to turn out products for immediate use but is rather designed to pursue ends of more long range significance for mankind. However, if the symbolic building, i.e. the society, is indeed on fire and we all likely to perish in the flames unless we take some remedial action, then it is a bit odd to declare that there is *any* context of discussion to which the topic of putting out fires is irrelevant. There is obviously something wrong in an emphasis on long range discoveries when we are rather uncertain that there will be any human beings left alive to enjoy these discoveries in the future.

In discussing these matters, we find ourselves obviously in the midst of a consideration of the notion of relevance. The professor in the anecdote defined relevance in a rigid, restrictive way. This may well be a mistake in any circumstances. However, when the term "relevance" arises these days with respect to the subject of education, it is frequent to hear the comment that if students only want to talk about what is already of direct interest to them then they might as well not come to school in the first place. What is often assumed in comments of this sort is that the notion of "relevance" necessarily implies a focus on the problems of young love, the food in the cafeteria, and whether John Smith will be drafted this year. I.e., it is assumed that when someone objects that a university course is irrelevant, he necessarily means that the course neglects considerations of this rather pedestrian sort. Hence it is assumed that "relevance" in this context is used to refer only to relevance in the pedestrian sense.

There is, however, another quite different sense of the notion of "irrelevance." This is the sense in which the logician or professional philosopher would use the term. For example, an argument is structurally unsound—invalid—if the statements which it asserts as premises are not related to the conclusion which the argument would produce; i.e. there is no adequate connection between premises and conclusions. Thus a convincing demonstration from the given premise that murder is a dastardly crime does not prove that John Smith did in fact murder James Jones.

It may well be in this professional sense that someone wishes to say that much of what we do in the university is in fact irrelevant. How would this apply to philosophy in particular? It would appear to apply most particularly in the sense that philosophy as an activity, as a discipline, has generally been considered to have responsibility for asking certain kinds of questions. Critics may feel that some current approaches in philosophy are neglecting this professional responsibility. Since the earliest recorded philosophical arguments, philosophers have been asking certain sorts of questions more often than anyone else. What is the difference between a true belief and false belief ? Does the world cease to exist when I close my eyes? What is the relation between mind and body? What is really the nature of my moral duty? Are the actions that people in my society happen to regard as one's moral duty really good actions, or are they merely indifferent or bad actions that people in my society have been taught to approve? Is the psychological theory of human behavior that happens to be believed in my society really a scientifically accurate theory, or is it merely the sort of theory that people are currently accustomed to call "scientific"? Do machines think?

Considering that such is in fact the professional tradition of philosophy—viz. asking these sorts of questions—it appears entirely in keeping with the philosopher's responsibility to ask just those sorts of questions that are often derided today as "not relevant to academics." Do our public officials make a regular practice of deceiving us? Has something gone fundamentally insane in our culture? Is our educational system becoming a farce? It is precisely in philosophy that we are able to raise, and are responsible for raising, such questions. Do the officials, the scientists, the educators, really know what they are doing? Are they being true to the requirements of their respective disciplines? What are these requirements and when are they fulfilled?

The material for the readings in this book has been primarily chosen for its emphasis on *relevant* issues that are outside the traditional area of philosophy. From this point of view what is unique to philosophy is its capacity as a discipline for criticism of what we usually take for granted. Philosophy has made a science of asking discomforting questions. The content of the selections which follow should serve to demonstrate that it is well worth the effort to ask such questions. The answers are usually surprising, and indicative of the fact that we are not doing nearly as well in attaining our various objectives as we think we are.

It should also be noted that philosophy as a critical discipline is thus naturally associated with attempts at social change. What would appear to be the truth is that change is a natural process in life, but a process which is morally unacceptable to the leaders and followers of established social institutions. From this point of view philosophy is the discipline which aids us in establishing standards governing the need for change. In this sense the practice of philosophy is rather unique among social institutions. While most social institutions are inherently conservative, philosophy appears to be "inherently" a force for change.

PRESENT DAY ISSUES IN PHILOSOPHY

Part 1

WHAT IS EDUCATION?

Introduction

The selections included on this topic raise a number of questions that are of great importance in current public controversy. What are the goals of education? Why should we try to educate at all? What constitutes genuine success in seeking to educate? If what we call "education" does not serve goals or ends appropriately belonging to what really is education, then what goals or ends are we in fact serving?

People often appear accustomed to consider themselves "educated" when they mean little or nothing more than that they can say and do the kinds of things that will gain them more wealth and favor in their society. At the present time, debates are raging throughout U.S. communities concerning the way in which the public schools and the universities ought to be conducted. Where this process of debate involves the public schools, protagonists identify themselves as "parents," "taxpayers," or "educators," and are busily engaged in publishing and orally presenting arguments about "the quality of our children's education." Seldom, if ever, do these arguments state what it is that one ought to want, *as a student,* or a parent, or taxpayer, or educator. Is education the ability to use correct grammar, read two foreign languages, and solve problems in trigonometry? Is education a list of grades earned? Is education a high score on the college entrance exams and an admission to Harvard University? Many people who talk extensively in public about education appear to have nothing in mind as criteria for "quality education" other than just these sort of things.

What are some alternative criteria for identifying what we perhaps ought to have in mind when we discuss education? To answer this question in an intelligent fashion, we must presumably begin from the consideration that it is human beings who are to be educated. Thus we must consider what are probably the important needs of human beings

1

for self-fulfillment. Presumably we shall want to pay some attention to the behavior of people in various educational settings and thus to learn what appears beneficial to students and what appears to be useless or even harmful to them.

When we extend our considerations about education to the college or university level, similar questions arise. As a student or teacher (or both), what do I really want to know (that is, if someone will let me ask the questions)? What am I after, as a person? What am I doing here, and what am I getting, or giving, in the guise of "education"?

The writers whose arguments are examined here have been in search of answers to just these sorts of questions. Plato, writing in the 4th century B.C. in ancient Greece, argued that knowledge in the fullest sense of the word is something to be acquired only after rigorous mental preparation, e.g. the study of mathematics, philosophical reasoning, the sciences, literature. After years of this sort of preparation, whereby the mind is trained to focus on the abstract and the form of things—as opposed to the mere appearances of things to the senses—the person may be fortunate enough to experience, one day, a leap of insight into the world of true knowledge. Plato argues that one can understand things as they really are only after one has attained a vision of knowledge—the true, the good, the beautiful—as a good in itself. Plato's commentary on one hand, emphasizes the importance of self-knowledge for education in general. On the other hand, Plato assumes the importance of a fixed world of knowledge independently of considerations of the interests of the individual learner.

Writing half a century ago, John Dewey emphasized that the true purpose of education can only be to enable the student to grow to be the sort of person who will continue to educate himself throughout the rest of his life. "Education" is discussed by Dewey in this broader sense as the on-going activity of benefitting from and enriching one's life as a result of intelligently understood experience. "Education" in the proper sense of the term, for Dewey, indicates an activity of self-discovery and discovery of the world. Thus, he reasons, it is a wrong view of education which sets up goals outside of the students' own range of interests. Dewey sees wrong approaches to education as focusing on what adults want children to learn, rather than upon what children themselves want to learn. He appears to attribute much of the origin of wrong approaches to education to the influence of cultures whose social structures have been of a master-slave nature rather than of a democratic variety. As Dewey sees the matter, a good approach to education benefits not only the students but the society as a whole. Education, which does *not* impose goals from outside the educational experience, does succeed in promoting creative responses in coping with humanity's problems in survival in the world.

In an approach which strongly supports Dewey's views, Erich Fromm stresses that the proper meaning of the term "education" is literally shown in its Latin root, "educere," which means "to lead forth." I.e., genuine education, as Fromm sees it, amounts to an encouragement of those individual tendencies of skill-development and expression that the particular child wishes to manifest. The very opposite of education is a predetermined plan to mold the child so that he will learn primarily what is expected of him. We try to mold people, Fromm argues, because our economic system demands that employees fit whatever requirements the market or personnel office may demand. Such an educational approach, however, expresses an utter lack of faith in the value of human beings for themselves.

A proposal for radical reform of the public school system is offered by Christopher Jencks. Jencks argues that the public school system is primarily regarded in our society as a means for upward social mobility, i.e. a good education is seen as the crucial step toward getting a good job. However, what actually happens is that the expenditure of public funds for schooling is so manipulated that the least privileged social groups get the least benefit from the schools while more privileged groups are able to increase the advantage they already have. Jencks' solution is that we turn over to each family the amount of money that the state supposedly spends on their children for education, with the understanding that they may then enroll their children in any public school which they feel is acceptable to them and pay this money to the school as tuition. Jonathan Kozol was fired from the Boston Public School system because he persisted in doing things such as giving the children art material which they enjoyed but which "The Art Teacher" insisted they were not able to appreciate. His commentary is primarily about ghetto schools, but it would seem to have a clear applicability to our public school system in general. Kozol sees "education" defined all too often by other teachers as a process in which the children adopt the manners of speaking, writing, and judging that the teachers have. In Kozol's school, defensive, white teachers, in a dilapidated building, with outdated textbooks, regarded the culture of the black community as merely a set of bad habits. The response of the students, predominantly black and poor, was an understandable apathy. By contrast, Kozol introduced the children to exercises in looking, listening, and writing about their daily experiences, which produced dramatic responses of understanding and enthusiasm.

Mary Greenfield teaches a special education class for hand-

icapped children who are formally classified by the school system as
"learning problems." However, in many cases, these children are better
described as too emotionally disturbed to be in ordinary classrooms.
Greenfield's discussion of her work is a valuable form of commentary
on the educational process, especially in her description of the quality
of the children's experiences.

Paul Goodman's commentary on our educational system combines
a scathing criticism of the system as largely harmful with a very concrete proposal for replacing the current system with, e.g. inexpensive,
store-front schools. Goodman argues that the average school or university curriculum, by its irrelevance to the average child or young adult,
is responsible for stultifying the intellectual abilities of the students. He
suggests that the causes of this irrelevance is to be seen in the fact that
a great portion of the budget for schools goes to supervisory personnel
and equipment which are similarly irrelevant to the process of genuine
education. Goodman's proposal for reform of the school system is thus
considerably more radical than that offered by most other commentators. It would, for one thing, replace the centrally controlled school
system with autonomous smaller schools in which neighborhood residents could seek genuine education for their children and themselves,
rather than organized stultification.

Turning to considerations of education in the university, James
Ridgeway gives a startling exposé of the ways in which numerous U.S.
universities have literally served as front for the corporate profit
manipulations of trustees, friends of trustees, and financially-minded
professors. Ridgeway shows that major universities are heavily involved
with profit-making activities that are divorced from the educational
activities of these institutions. He argues that, in fact, many of our
universities' administrators and senior faculty are mainly or exclusively
in the business of increasing profits and power for the military, for
industry, and for themselves. He argues further that this situation has
clearly caused our typical major university to degrade the importance
and quality of teaching and learning to a tenth-rate level, that the mere
pretense of education is all that is wanted so that the private business
of the money-makers can go on behind the front of the public institution. Ridgeway ends his argument with a series of proposals for change
in the modern university, including democratic management, elimination of degree requirements for teachers and students, and a re-empha-
sis on personal contact between teacher and student.

Noam Chomsky takes up the hotly debated issue of the nature of
recent campus uprisings and of the student protest movement in general. Chomsky strongly defends the student protest movement against

accusations directed at it by "liberals" in the teaching profession. He offers friendly criticism of the tactics and the arguments used by the student movement, arguing simply that they have not chosen effective means for their purposes. His major criticism, however, is directed against what he finds to be a great hypocrisy employed by some professors who have condemned student radicals as a threat to freedom on the campus. As Chomsky sees the matter, the only freedoms on which student radicals are infringing is the freedom of teachers to evade responsibility to their students and the freedom of these teachers to instead spend their time on personally profitable activity that has turned the university into a research and propaganda agency of the government and military industry. It is rank hypocrisy, Chomsky argues, to protest the "politicization" of the university by radicals when it is already thoroughly politicized by conservatives. Chomsky proposes, however, that concerned students spend less time painting verbal images of every university administrator as a direct tool of Wall Street and more time in the concrete work of turning the university into a center of truly objective scholarship, which would normally turn out to be radical scholarship.

Jay Weinroth and Robert Shanab, in collaboration with a small group of university students from a class in Introduction to Philosophy, present some on-the-scene impressions of students concerning self-directed education versus the usual educational process. This material focuses graphically on the contrast between work done in a university class because that is what you do in order to get a grade, and the experience of defining your own educational goals.

Self-Knowledge in Education

And now, I said, let me show in a figure how far our nature is enlightened or unenlightened:—Behold! human beings living in an underground den, which has a mouth open towards the light and reaching all along the den; here they have been from their childhood, and have their legs and necks chained so that they cannot move, and can only see before them, being prevented by the chains from turning round their heads. Above and behind them a fire is blazing at a distance, and between the fire and the prisoners there is a raised way; and you will see, if you look, a low wall built along the way, like the screen which marionette players have in front of them, over which they show the puppets.

I see.

And do you see, I said, men passing along the wall carrying all sorts of vessels, and statues and figures of animals made of wood and stone and various materials, which appear over the wall? Some of them are talking, others silent.

You have shown me a strange image, and they are strange prisoners.

Like ourselves, I replied; and they see only their own shadows, or the shadows of one another, which the fire throws on the opposite wall of the cave?

True, he said; how could they see anything but the shadows if they were never allowed to move their heads?

And of the objects which are being carried in like manner they would only see the shadows?

Yes, he said.

And if they were able to converse with one another, would they not suppose that they were naming what was actually before them?

Very true.

And suppose further that the prison had an echo which came from the other side, would they not be sure to fancy when one of the passers-by spoke that the voice which they heard came from the passing shadow?

No question, he replied.

To them, I said, the truth would be literally nothing but the shadows of the images.

That is certain.

And now look again, and see what will naturally follow if the prisoners are released and disabused of their error. At first, when any of them is liberated and compelled suddenly to stand up and turn his neck round and walk and look towards the light, he will suffer sharp pains; the glare will distress him, and he will be unable to see the realities of which in his former state he had seen the shadows; and then conceive some one saying to him, that what he saw before was an illusion, but that now, when he is approaching nearer to being and his eye is turned towards more real existence, he has a clearer vision,—what will be his reply? And you may further imagine that his instructor is pointing to the objects as they pass and requiring him to name them,—will he not be perplexed? Will he not fancy that the shadows which he formerly saw are truer than the objects which are now shown to him?

Far truer.

And if he is compelled to look straight at the light, will he not have a pain in his eyes which will make him turn away to take refuge in the objects of vision which he can see, and which he will conceive to be in reality clearer than the things which are now being shown to him?

True, he said.

And suppose once more, that he is reluctantly dragged up a steep and rugged ascent, and held fast until he is forced into the presence of the sun himself, is he not likely to be pained and irritated? When he approaches the light his eyes will be dazzled, and he will not be able to see anything at all of what are now called realities.

Not all in a moment, he said.

He will require to grow accustomed to the sight of the upper world. And first he will see the shadows best, next the reflections of men and other objects in the water, and then the objects themselves; then he will gaze upon the light of the moon and the stars and the spangled heaven; and he will see the sky and the stars by night better than the sun or the light of the sun by day?

Certainly.

Last of all he will be able to see the sun, and not mere reflections of him in the water, but he will see him in his own proper place, and not in another; and he will contemplate him as he is.

Certainly.

He will then proceed to argue that this is he who gives the season and the years, and is the guardian of all that is in the visible world, and in a certain way the cause of all things which he and his fellows have been accustomed to behold?

Clearly, he said, he would first see the sun and then reason about him.

And when he remembered his old habitation, and the wisdom of the den and his fellow-prisoners, do you not suppose that he would felicitate himself on the change, and pity them?

Certainly, he would.

And if they were in the habit of conferring honours among themselves on those who were quickest to observe the passing shadows and to remark which of them went before, and which followed after, and which were together; and who were therefore best able to draw conclusions as to the future, do you think that he would care for such honours and glories, or envy the possessors of them? Would he not say with Homer, 'Better to be the poor servant of a poor master,' and to endure anything, rather than think as they do and live after their manner?

Yes, he said, I think that he would rather suffer anything than entertain these false notions and live in this miserable manner.

Imagine once more, I said, such an one coming suddenly out of the sun to be replaced in his old situation; would he not be certain to have his eyes full of darkness?

To be sure, he said.

And if there were a contest, and he had to compete in measuring the shadows with the prisoners who had never moved out of the den, while his sight was still weak, and before his eyes had become steady (and the time which would be needed to acquire this new habit of sight might be very considerable), would he not be ridiculous? Men would say of him that up he went and down he came without his eyes; and that it was better not even to think of ascending; and if any one tried to loose another and lead him up to the light, let them only catch the offender, and they would put him to death.

No question, he said.

This entire allegory, I said, you may now append, dear Glaucon, to the previous argument; the prison-house is the world of sight, the light of the fire is the sun, and you will not misapprehend me if you interpret the journey upwards to be the ascent of the soul into the intellectual world according to my poor belief, which, at your desire, I have expressed—whether rightly or wrongly God knows. But, whether true or false, my opinion is that in the world of knowledge the idea of good appears last of all, and is seen only with an effort; and, when seen, is also inferred to be the universal author of all things beautiful and right, parent of light and of the lord of light in this visible world, and the immediate source of reason and truth in the intellectual; and that this is the power upon which he who would act rationally either in public or private life must have his eye fixed.

I agree, he said, as far as I am able to understand you.

Moreover, I said, you must not wonder that those who attain to this beatific vision are unwilling to descend to human affairs; for their souls are ever hastening into the upper world where they desire to dwell; which desire of theirs is very natural, if our allegory may be trusted.

Yes, very natural.

And is there anything surprising in one who passes from divine contemplations to the evil state of man, misbehaving himself in a ridiculous manner; if, while his eyes are blinking and before he has become accustomed to the surrounding darkness, he is compelled to fight in courts of law, or in other places, about the images or the shadows of images of justice, and is endeavouring to meet the conceptions of those who have never yet seen absolute justice?

Anything but surprising, he replied.

Any one who has common sense will remember that the bewilderments of the eyes are of two kinds, and arise from two causes, either from coming out of the light or from going into the light, which is true of the mind's eye, quite as much as of the bodily eye; and he who remembers this when he sees any one whose vision is perplexed and weak, will not be too ready to laugh; he will first ask whether that soul of man has come out of the brighter life, and is unable to see because unaccustomed to the dark, or having turned from darkness to the day is dazzled by excess of light. And he will count the one happy in his condition and state of being, and he will pity the other; or, if he have a mind to laugh at the soul which comes from below into the light, there will be more reason in this than in the laugh which greets him who returns from above out of the light into the den.

That, he said, is a very just distinction.

But then, if I am right, certain professors of education must be wrong when they say that they can put a knowledge into the soul which was not there before, like sight into blind eyes.

They undoubtedly say this, he replied.

Whereas, our argument shows that the power and capacity of learning exists in the soul already; and that just as the eye was unable to turn from darkness to light without the whole body, so too the instrument of knowledge can only by the movement of the whole soul be turned from the world of becoming into that of being, and learn by degrees to endure the sight of being, and of the brightest and best of being, or in other words, of the good.

Very true.

And must there not be some art which will effect conversion in the easiest and quickest manner; not implanting the faculty of sight, for that exists already, but has been turned in the wrong direction, and is looking away from the truth?

Yes, he said, such an art may be presumed.

And whereas the other so-called virtues of the soul seem to be akin to bodily qualities, for even when they are not originally innate they can be implanted later by habit and exercise, the virtue of wisdom more than anything else contains a divine element which always remains, and by this conversion is rendered useful and profitable; or, on the other hand, hurtful and useless. Did you never observe the narrow intelligence flashing from the keen eye of a clever rogue—how eager he is, how clearly his paltry soul sees the way to his end; he is the reverse of blind, but his keen eye-sight is forced into the service of evil, and he is mischievous in proportion to his cleverness?

Very true, he said.

But what if there had been a circumcision of such natures in the days of their youth; and they had been severed from those sensual pleasures, such as eating and drinking, which, like leaden weights, were attached to them at their birth, and which drag them down and turn the vision of their souls upon the things that are below—if, I say, they had been released from these impediments and turned in the opposite direction, the very same faculty in them would have seen the truth as keenly as they see what their eyes are turned to now.

Very likely.

Yes, I said; and there is another thing which is likely, or rather a necessary inference from what has preceded, that neither the uneducated and uninformed of the truth, nor yet those who never make an end of their education, will be able ministers of State; not the former, because they have no single aim of duty which is the rule of all their actions, private as well as public; nor the latter, because they will not act at all except upon compulsion, fancying that they are already dwelling apart in the islands of the blest.

Very true, he replied.

Then, I said, the business of us who are the founders of the State will be to compel the best minds to attain that knowledge which we have already shown to be the greatest of all—they must continue to ascend until they arrive at the good; but when they have ascended and seen enough we must not allow them to do as they do now.

What do you mean?

I mean that they remain in the upper world: but this must not be allowed; they must be made to descend again among the prisoners in the den, and partake of their labours and honours, whether they are worth having or not.

But is not this unjust? he said; ought we to give them a worse life, when they might have a better?

You have again forgotten, my friend, I said, the intention of the legislator, who did not aim at making any one class in the State happy above the rest; the happiness was to be in the whole State, and he held the citizens together by persuasion and necessity, making them bene-factors of the State, and therefore benefactors of one another; to this end he created them, not to please themselves, but to be his instru-ments in binding up the State.

True, he said, I had forgotten.

Observe, Glaucon, that there will be no injustice in compelling our philosophers to have a care and providence of others; we shall explain to them that in other States, men of their class are not obliged to share in the toils of politics: and this is reasonable, for they grow up at their own sweet will, and the government would rather not have them. Being self-taught, they cannot be expected to show any gratitude for a culture which they have never received. But we have brought you into the world to be rulers of the hive, kings of yourselves and of the other citizens, and have educated you far better and more perfectly than they have been educated, and you are better able to share in the double duty. Wherefore each of you, when his turn comes, must go down to the general underground abode, and get the habit of seeing in the dark. When you have acquired the habit, you will see ten thousand times better than the inhabitants of the den, and you will know what the several images are, and what they represent, because you have seen the beautiful and just and good in their truth. And thus our State, which is also yours, will be a reality, and not a dream only, and will be adminis-tered in a spirit unlike that of other States, in which men fight with one another about shadows only and are distracted in the struggle for power, which in their eyes is a great good. Whereas the truth is that the State in which the rulers are most reluctant to govern is always the best and most quietly governed, and the State in which they are most eager, the worst.

Quite true, he replied.

And will our pupils, when they hear this, refuse to take their turn at the toils of State, when they are allowed to spend the greater part of their time with one another in the heavenly light?

Impossible, he answered; for they are just men, and the commands which we impose upon them are just; there can be no doubt that every one of them will take office as a stern necessity, and not after the fashion of our present rulers of State.

Yes, my friend, I said; and there lies the point. You must contrive for your future rulers another and a better life than that of a ruler, and then you may have a well-ordered State; for only in the State which offers this, will they rule who are truly rich, not in silver and gold, but in virtue and wisdom, which are the true blessings of life. Whereas if they go to the administration of public affairs, poor and hungering after their own private advantage, thinking that hence they are to snatch the chief good, order there can never be; for they will be fighting about office, and the civil and domestic broils which thus arise will be the ruin of the rulers themselves and of the whole State.

Most true, he replied.

And the only life which looks down upon the life of political ambition is that of true philosophy. Do you know of any other?

Indeed, I do not, he said.

And those who govern ought not to be lovers of the task? For, if they are, there will be rival lovers, and they will fight.

No question.

Education as a Force for Peaceful Change

... The plasticity of the young presents a temptation to those having greater experience and hence greater power which they rarely resist. It seems putty to be molded according to current designs. That plasticity also means power to change prevailing custom is ignored. Docility is looked upon not as ability to learn whatever the world has to teach, but as subjection to those instructions of others which reflect *their* current habits. To be truly docile is to be eager to learn all the lessons of active, inquiring, expanding experience. The inert, stupid quality of current customs perverts learning into a willingness to follow where others point the way, into conformity, constriction, surrender of scepticism and experiment. When we think of the docility of the young we first think of the stocks of information adults wish to impose and the ways of acting they want to reproduce. Then we think of the insolent coercions, the insinuating briberies, the pedagogic solemnities by which the freshness of youth can be faded and its vivid curiosities dulled. Education becomes the art of taking advantage of the helplessness of the young; the forming of habits becomes a guarantee for the maintenance of hedges of custom.

Of course it is not wholly forgotten that habits are abilities, arts. Any striking exhibition of acquired skill in physical matters, like that of an acrobat or billiard-player, arouses universal admiration. But we like to have innovating power limited to technical matters and reserve our admiration for those manifestations that display virtuosity rather than virtue. In moral matters it is assumed that it is enough if some ideal has been exemplified in the life of a leader, so that it is now the part of others to follow and reproduce. For every branch of conduct, there is a Jesus or Buddha, a Napoleon or Marx, a Froebel or Tolstoi, whose pattern of action, exceeding our own grasp, is reduced to a practicable copy-size by passage through rows and rows of lesser leaders.

The notion that it suffices if the idea, the end, is present in the mind

14

of some authority dominates formal schooling. It permeates the unconscious education derived from ordinary contact and intercourse. Where following is taken to be normal, moral originality is pretty sure to be eccentric. But if independence were the rule, originality would be subjected to severe, experimental tests and be saved from cranky eccentricity, as it now is in say higher mathematics. The regime of custom assumes that the outcome is the same whether an individual understands what he is about or whether he goes through certain motions while mouthing the words of others—repetition of formulæ being esteemed of greater importance, upon the whole, than repetition of deeds. To say what the sect or clique or class says is the way of proving that one also understands and approves what the clique clings to. In theory, democracy should be a means of stimulating original thought, and of evoking action deliberately adjusted in advance to cope with new forces. In fact it is still so immature that its main effect is to multiply occasions for imitation. If progress in spite of this fact is more rapid than in other social forms, it is by accident, since the diversity of models conflict with one another and thus give individuality a chance in the resulting chaos of opinions. Current democracy acclaims success more boisterously than do other social forms, and surrounds failure with a more reverberating train of echoes. But the prestige thus given excellence is largely adventitious. The achievement of thought attracts others not so much intrinsically as because of an eminence due to multitudinous advertising and a swarm of imitators.

Even liberal thinkers have treated habit as essentially, not because of the character of existing customs, conservative. In fact only in a society dominated by modes of belief and admiration fixed by past custom is habit any more conservative than it is progressive. It all depends upon its quality. Habit is an ability, an art, formed through past experience. But whether an ability is limited to repetition of past acts adapted to past conditions or is available for new emergencies depends wholly upon what kind of habit exists. The tendency to think that only "bad" habits are disserviceable and that bad habits are conventionally enumerable, conduces to make all habits more or less bad. For what makes a habit bad is enslavement to old ruts. The common notion that enslavement to good ends converts mechanical routine into good is a negation of the principle of moral goodness. It identifies morality with what *was* sometime rational, possibly in some prior experience of one's own, but more probably in the experience of some one else who is now blindly set up as a final authority. The genuine heart of reasonableness (and of goodness in conduct) lies in effective mastery of the conditions which *now* enter into action. To be satisfied with repeating, with traversing the ruts which in other conditions led to good, is the surest way of creating carelessness about present and actual good.

Consider what happens to thought when habit is merely power to repeat acts without thought. Where does thought exist and operate when it is excluded from habitual activities? Is not such thought of necessity shut out from effective power, from ability to control objects and command events? Habits deprived of thought and thought which is futile are two sides of the same fact. To laud habit as conservative while praising thought as the main spring of progress is to take the surest course to making thought abstruse and irrelevant and progress a matter of accident and catastrophe. The concrete fact behind the current separation of body and mind, practice and theory, actualities and ideals, is precisely this separation of habit and thought. Thought which does not exist within ordinary habits of action lacks means of execution. In lacking application, it also lacks test, criterion. Hence it is condemned to a separate realm. If we try to act upon it, our actions are clumsy, forced. In fact, contrary habits (as we have already seen) come into operation and betray our purpose. After a few such experiences, it is subconsciously decided that thought is too precious and high to be exposed to the contingencies of action. It is reserved for separate uses; thought feeds only thought not action. Ideals must not run the risk of contamination and perversion by contact with actual conditions. Thought then either resorts to specialized and technical matters influencing action in the library or laboratory alone, or else it becomes sentimentalized.

Meantime there are certain "practical" men who combine thought and habit and who are effectual. Their thought is about their own advantage; and their habits correspond. They dominate the actual situation. They encourage routine in others, and they also subsidize such thought and learning as are kept remote from affairs. This they call sustaining the standard of the ideal. Subjection they praise as team-spirit, loyalty, devotion, obedience, industry, law-and-order. But they temper respect for law—by which they mean the order of the existing status—on the part of others with most skillful and thoughtful manipulation of it in behalf of their own ends. While they denounce as subversive anarchy signs of independent thought, of thinking for themselves, on the part of others lest such thought disturb the conditions by which they profit, they think quite literally *for* themselves, that is, *of* themselves. This is the eternal game of the practical men. Hence it is only by accident that the separate and endowed "thought" of professional thinkers leaks out into action and affects custom.

For thinking cannot itself escape the influence of habit, any more than anything else human. If it is not a part of ordinary habits, then it is a separate habit, habit alongside other habits, apart from them, as isolated and indurated as human structure permits. Theory is a possession of the theorist, intellect of the intellectualist. The so-called separation of theory and practice means in fact the separation of two kinds of practice, one taking place in the outdoor world, the other in the study. The habit of thought commands some materials (as every habit must do) but the materials are technical, books, words. Ideas are objectified in action but speech and writing monopolize their field of action. Even then subconscious pains are taken to see that the words used are not too widely understood. Intellectual habits like other habits demand an environment, but the environment is the study, library, laboratory and academy. Like other habits they produce external results, possessions. Some men acquire ideas and knowledge as other men acquire monetary wealth. While practising thought for their own special ends they deprecate it for the untrained and unstable masses for whom "habits," that is unthinking routines, are necessities. They favor popular education—up to the point of disseminating as matter of authoritative information for the many what the few have established by thought, and up to the point of converting an original docility to the new into a docility to repeat and to conform.

Yet all habit involves mechanization. Habit is impossible without setting up a mechanism of action, physiologically engrained, which operates "spontaneously," automatically, whenever the cue is given. But mechanization is not of necessity *all* there is to habit. Consider the conditions under which the first serviceable abilities of life are formed. When a child begins to walk he acutely observes, he intently and intensely experiments. He looks to see what is going to happen and he keeps curious watch on every incident. What others do, the assistance they give, the models they set, operate not as limitations but as encouragements to his own acts, reinforcements of personal perception and endeavor. The first toddling is a romantic adventuring into the unknown; and every gained power is a delightful discovery of one's own powers and of the wonders of the world. We may not be able to retain in adult habits this zest of intelligence and this freshness of satisfaction in newly discovered powers. But there is surely a middle term between a normal exercise of power which includes some excursion into the unknown, and a mechanical activity hedged within a drab world. Even in dealing with inanimate machines we rank that invention higher which adapts its movements to varying conditions.

All life operates through a mechanism, and the higher the form of the life the more complex, sure and flexible the mechanism. This fact alone should save us from opposing life and mechanism, thereby reducing the latter to unintelligent automatism and the former to an aimless splurge. How delicate, prompt, sure and varied are the movements of a violin player or an engraver! How unerringly they phrase every shade of emotion and every turn of idea! Mechanism is indispensable. If each act has to be consciously searched for at the moment and intentionally performed, execution is painful and the product is clumsy and halting. Nevertheless the difference between the artist and the mere technician is unmistakeable. The artist is a masterful technician. The technique or mechanism is fused with thought and feeling. The "mechanical" performer permits the mechanism to dictate the performance. It is absurd to say that the latter exhibits habit and the former not. We are confronted with two kinds of habit, intelligent and routine. All life has its élan, but only the prevalence of dead habits deflects life into mere élan.

Yet the current dualism of mind and body, thought and action, is so rooted that we are taught (and science is said to support the teaching) that the art, the habit, of the artist is acquired by previous mechanical exercises of repetition in which skill apart from thought is the aim, until suddenly, magically, this soulless mechanism is taken possession of by sentiment and imagination and it becomes a flexible instrument of mind. The fact, the scientific fact, is that even in his exercises, his practice *for* skill, an artist uses an art he already has. He acquires greater skill because practice *of* skill is more important to him than practice *for* skill. Otherwise natural endowment would count for nothing, and sufficient mechanical exercise would make any one an expert in any field. A flexible, sensitive habit grows more varied, more adaptable by practice and use. We do not as yet fully understand the physiological factors concerned in mechanical routine on one hand and artistic skill on the other, but we do know that the latter is just as much habit as is the former. Whether it concerns the cook, musician, carpenter, citizen, or statesman, the intelligent or artistic habit is the desirable thing, and the routine the undesirable thing:—or, at least, desirable and undesirable from every point of view except one.

Those who wish a monopoly of social power find desirable the separation of habit and thought, action and soul, so characteristic of history. For the dualism enables them to do the thinking and planning, while others remain the docile, even if awkward, instruments of execution. Until this scheme is changed, democracy is bound to be perverted in realization. With our present system of education—by which something much more extensive than schooling is meant—democracy multiplies occasions for imitation not occasions for thought in action. If the visible result is rather a messy confusion than an ordered discipline of habits, it is because there are so many models of imitation set up that they tend to cancel one another, so that individuals have the advantage neither of uniform training nor of intelligent adaptation. Whence an intellectualist, the one with whom thinking is itself a segregated habit, infers that the choice is between muss-and-muddling and a bureaucracy. He prefers the latter, though under some other name, usually an aristocracy of talent and intellect, possibly a dictatorship of the proletariat. . . .

In the case of the young it is patent that impulses are highly flexible starting points for activities which are diversified according to the ways in which they are used. Any impulse may become organized into almost any disposition according to the way it interacts with surroundings. Fear may become abject cowardice, prudent caution, reverence for superiors or respect for equals; an agency for credulous swallowing of absurd superstitions or for wary scepticism. A man may be chiefly afraid of the spirits of his ancestors, of officials, of arousing the disapproval of his associates, of being deceived, of fresh air, or of Bolshevism. The actual outcome depends upon how the impulse of fear is interwoven with other impulses. This depends in turn upon the outlets and inhibitions supplied by the social environment.

In a definite sense, then, a human society is always starting afresh. It is always in process of renewing, and it endures only because of renewal. We speak of the peoples of southern Europe as Latin peoples. Their existing languages depart widely from one another and from the Latin mother tongue. Yet there never was a day when this alteration of speech was intentional or explicit. Persons always meant to reproduce the speech they heard from their elders and supposed they were succeeding. This fact may stand as a kind of symbol of the reconstruction wrought in habits because of the fact that they can be transmitted and be made to endure only through the medium of the crude activities of the young or through contact with persons having different habits.

For the most part, this continuous alteration has been unconscious and unintended. Immature, undeveloped activity has succeeded in modifying adult organized activity accidentally and surreptitiously. But with the dawn of the idea of progressive betterment and an interest in new uses of impulses, there has grown up some consciousness of the extent to which a future new society of changed purposes and desires may be created by a deliberate humane treatment of the impulses of youth. This is the meaning of education; for a truly humane education

consists in an intelligent direction of native activities in the light of the
possibilities and necessities of the social situation. But for the most part,
adults have given training rather than education. An impatient, premature mechanization of impulsive activity after the fixed pattern of adult
habits of thought and affection has been desired. The combined effect
of love of power, timidity in the face of the novel and a self-admiring
complacency has been too strong to permit immature impulse to exercise its reorganizing potentialities. The younger generation has hardly
even knocked frankly at the door of adult customs, much less been
invited in to rectify through better education the brutalities and inequi-
ties established in adult habits. Each new generation has crept blindly
and furtively through such chance gaps as have happened to be left
open. Otherwise it has been modeled after the old.

We have already noted how original plasticity is warped and
docility is taken mean advantage of. It has been used to signify not
capacity to learn liberally and generously, but willingness to learn the
customs of adult associates, ability to learn just those special things
which those having power and authority wish to teach. Original modifi-
ability has not been given a fair chance to act as a trustee for a better
human life. It has been loaded with convention, biased by adult convenience. It has been practically rendered into an equivalent of non-
assertion of originality, a pliant accommodation to the embodied
opinions of others.

Consequently docility has been identified with imitativeness, instead of with power to re-make old habits, to re-create. Plasticity and
originality have been opposed to each other. That the most precious
part of plasticity consists in ability to form habits of independent judgment and of inventive initiation has been ignored. For it demands a
more complete and intense docility to form flexible easily re-adjusted
habits than it does to acquire those which rigidly copy the ways of
others. In short, among the native activities of the young are some that
work towards accommodation, assimilation, reproduction, and others
that work toward exploration, discovery and creation. But the weight
of adult custom has been thrown upon retaining and strengthening
tendencies toward conformity, and against those which make for varia-
tion and independence. The habits of the growing person are jealously
kept within the limit of adult customs. The delightful originality of the
child is tamed. Worship of institutions and personages themselves lacking in imaginative foresight, versatile observation and liberal thought,
is enforced.

Very early in life sets of mind are formed without attentive
thought, and these sets persist and control the mature mind. The child

learns to avoid the shock of unpleasant disagreement, to find the easy way out, to appear to conform to customs which are wholly mysterious to him in order to get his own way—that is to display some natural impulse without exciting the unfavorable notice of those in authority. Adults distrust the intelligence which a child has while making upon him demands for a kind of conduct that requires a high order of intelligence, if it is to be intelligent at all. The inconsistency is reconciled by instilling in him "moral" habits which have a maximum of emotional empressment and adamantine hold with a minimum of understanding. These habitudes, deeply engrained before thought is awake and even before the day of experiences which can later be recalled, govern conscious later thought. They are usually deepest and most unget-at-able just where critical thought is most needed—in morals, religion and politics. These "infantilisms" account for the mass of irrationalities that prevail among men of otherwise rational tastes. These personal "hangovers" are the cause of what the student of culture calls survivals. But unfortunately these survivals are much more numerous and pervasive than the anthropologist and historian are wont to admit. To list them would perhaps oust one from "respectable" society.

And yet the intimation never wholly deserts us that there are in the unformed activities of childhood and youth the possibilities of a better life for the community as well as for individuals here and there. This dim sense is the ground of our abiding idealization of childhood. For with all its extravagancies and uncertainties, its effusions and reticences, it remains a standing proof of a life wherein growth is normal not an anomaly, activity a delight not a task, and where habit-forming is an expansion of power not its shrinkage. Habit and impulse may war with each other, but it is a combat between the habits of adults and the impulses of the young, and not, as with the adult, a civil warfare whereby personality is rent asunder. Our usual measure for the "goodness" of children is the amount of trouble they make for grownups, which means of course the amount they deviate from adult habits and expectations. Yet by way of expiation we envy children their love of new experiences, their intentness in extracting the last drop of significance from each situation, their vital seriousness in things that to us are outworn.

We compensate for the harshness and monotony of our present insistence upon formed habits by imagining a future heaven in which we too shall respond freshly and generously to each incident of life. In consequence of our divided attitude, our ideals are self-contradictory. On the one hand, we dream of an attained perfection, an ultimate static goal, in which effort shall cease, and desire and execution be once and for all in complete equilibrium. We wish for a character which shall be steadfast, and we then conceive this desired faithfulness as something immutable, a character exactly the same yesterday, today and forever. But we also have a sneaking sympathy for the courage of an Emerson in declaring that consistency should be thrown to the winds when it stands between us and the opportunities of present life. We reach out to the opposite extreme of our ideal of fixity, and under the guise of a return to nature dream of a romantic freedom, in which *all* life is plastic to impulse, a continual source of improvised spontaneities and novel inspirations. We rebel against all organization and all stability. If modern thought and sentiment is to escape from this division in its ideals, it must be through utilizing released impulse as an agent of steady reorganization of custom and institutions.

While childhood is the conspicuous proof of the renewing of habit rendered possible by impulse, the latter never wholly ceases to play its refreshing rôle in adult life. If it did, life would petrify, society stagnate. Instinctive reactions are sometimes too intense to be woven into a smooth pattern of habits. Under ordinary circumstances they appear to be tamed to obey their master, custom. But extraordinary crises release them and they show by wild violent energy how superficial is the control of routine. The saying that civilization is only skin deep, that a savage persists beneath the clothes of a civilized man, is the common acknowledgment of this fact. At critical moments of unusual stimuli the emotional outbreak and rush of instincts dominating all activity show how superficial is the modification which a rigid habit has been able to effect.

When we face this fact in its general significance, we confront one of the ominous aspects of the history of man. We realize how little the progress of man has been the product of intelligent guidance, how largely it has been a by-product of accidental upheavals, even though by an apologetic interest in behalf of some privileged institution we later transmute chance into providence. We have depended upon the clash of war, the stress of revolution, the emergence of heroic individuals, the impact of migrations generated by war and famine, the incoming of barbarians, to change established institutions. Instead of constantly utilizing unused impulse to effect continuous reconstruction, we have waited till an accumulation of stresses suddenly breaks through the dikes of custom.

It is often supposed that as old persons die, so must old peoples. There are many facts in history to support the belief. Decadence and degeneration seem to be the rule as age increases. An irruption of some uncivilized horde has then provided new blood and fresh life—so much so that history has been defined as a process of rebarbarization. In truth the analogy between a person and a nation with respect to senescence and death is defective. A nation is always renewed by the death of its old constituents and the birth of those who are as young and fresh as ever were any individuals in the hey-day of the nation's glory. Not the nation but its customs get old. Its institutions petrify into rigidity; there is social arterial sclerosis. Then some people not overburdened with elaborate and stiff habits take up and carry on the moving process of life. The stock of fresh peoples is, however, approaching exhaustion. It is not safe to rely upon this expensive method of renewing civilization. We need to discover how to rejuvenate it from within. A normal perpetuation becomes a fact in the degree in which impulse is released and habit is plastic to the transforming touch of impulse. When customs are flexible and youth is educated as youth and not as premature adulthood, no nation grows old.

Man for Himself

In our time the marketing orientation has been growing rapidly, together with the development of a new market that is a phenomenon of the last decades—the "personality market." Clerks and salesmen business executives and doctors, lawyers and artists all appear on this market. It is true that their legal status and economic positions are different: some are independent, charging for their services; others are employed, receiving salaries. But all are dependent for their material success on a personal acceptance by those who need their services or who employ them.

The principle of evaluation is the same on both the personality and the commodity market: on the one, personalities are offered for sale; on the other, commodities. Value in both cases is their exchange value, for which use value is a necessary but not a sufficient condition. It is true, our economic system could not function if people were not skilled in the particular work they have to perform and were gifted only with a pleasant personality. Even the best bedside manner and the most beautifully equipped office on Park Avenue would not make a New York doctor successful if he did not have a minimum of medical knowledge and skill. Even the most winning personality would not prevent a secretary from losing her job unless she could type reasonably fast. However, if we ask what the respective weight of skill and personality as a condition for success is, we find that only in exceptional cases is success predominantly the result of skill and of certain other human qualities like honesty, decency, and integrity. Although the proportion between skill and human qualities on the one hand and "personality" on the other hand as prerequisites for success varies, the "personality factor" always plays a decisive role. Success depends largely on how well a person sells himself on the market, how well he gets his personality across, how nice a "package" he is; whether he is "cheerful," "sound," "aggressive," "reliable," "ambitious"; furthermore what his family background is, what clubs he belongs to, and whether he knows the right people. The type of personality required depends to some degree on the special field in which a person works. A stockbroker, a salesman, a secretary, a railroad executive, a college professor, or a hotel manager must each offer different kinds of personality that, regardless of their differences, must fulfill one condition: to be in demand.

The fact that in order to have success it is not sufficient to have the skill and equipment for performing a given task but that one must be able to "put across" one's personality in competition with many others shapes the attitude toward oneself. If it were enough for the purpose of making a living to rely on what one knows and what one can do, one's self-esteem would be in proportion to one's capacities, that is, to one's use value; but since success depends largely on how one sells one's personality, one experiences oneself as a commodity or rather simultaneously as the seller *and* the commodity to be sold. A person is not concerned with his life and happiness, but with becoming salable. This feeling might be compared to that of a commodity, of handbags on a counter, for instance, could they feel and think. Each handbag would try to make itself as "attractive" as possible in order to attract customers and to look as expensive as possible in order to obtain a higher price than its rivals. The handbag sold for the highest price would feel elated, since that would mean it was the most "valuable" one; the one which was not sold would feel sad and convinced of its own worthlessness. This fate might befall a bag which, though excellent in appearance and usefulness, had the bad luck to be out of date because of a change in fashion.

Like the handbag, one has to be in fashion on the personality market, and in order to be in fashion one has to know what kind of personality is most in demand. This knowledge is transmitted in a general way throughout the whole process of education, from kindergarten to college, and implemented by the family. The knowledge acquired at this early stage is not sufficient, however; it emphasizes only certain general qualities like adaptability, ambition, and sensitivity to the changing expectations of other people. The more specific picture of the models for success one gets elsewhere. The pictorial magazines, newspapers, and newsreels show the pictures and life stories of the successful in many variations. Pictorial advertising has a similar function. The successful executive who is pictured in a tailor's advertisement is the image of how one should look and be, if one is to draw down the "big money" on the contemporary personality market. . . .

Thinking as well as feeling is determined by the marketing orientation. Thinking assumes the function of grasping things quickly so as to be able to manipulate them successfully. Furthered by widespread and efficient education, this leads to a high degree of intelligence, but not of reason.[1] For manipulative purposes, all that is necessary to know is the surface features of things, the superficial. The truth, to be uncovered by penetrating to the essence of phenomena, becomes an obsolete concept—truth not only in the pre-scientific sense of "absolute" truth, dogmatically maintained without reference to empirical data, but also in the sense of truth attained by man's reason applied to his observations and open to revisions. Most intelligence tests are attuned to this kind of thinking; they measure not so much the capacity for reason and understanding as the capacity for quick mental adaptation to a given situation; "mental adjustment tests" would be the adequate name for them.[2] For this kind of thinking the application of the categories of comparison and of quantitative measurement—rather than a thorough analysis of a given phenomenon and its quality—is essential. All problems are equally "interesting" and there is little sense of the respective differences in their importance. Knowledge itself becomes a commodity. Here, too, man is alienated from his own power; thinking and knowing are experienced as a tool to produce results. Knowledge of man himself, psychology, which in the great tradition of Western thought was held to be the condition for virtue, for right living, for happiness, has degenerated into an instrument to be used for better manipulation of others and oneself, in market research, in political propaganda, in advertising, and so on.

Evidently this type of thinking has a profound effect on our educational system. From grade school to graduate school, the aim of learning is to gather as much information as possible that is mainly useful for the purposes of the market. Students are supposed to learn so many things that they have hardly time and energy left to *think*. Not the interest in the subjects taught or in knowledge and insight as such, but the enhanced exchange value knowledge' gives is the main incentive for wanting more and better education. We find today a tremendous enthusiasm for knowledge and education, but at the same time a skeptical or contemptuous attitude toward the allegedly impractical and useless thinking which is concerned "only" with the truth and which has no exchange value on the market. . . . The process of creative thinking in any field of human endeavor often starts with what may be called a "rational vision," itself a result of considerable previous study, reflective

1. The difference between intelligence and reason will be discussed later on, pp. 00ff.
2. Cf. Ernest Schachtel, "Zum Begriff und zur Diagnosis der Persoenlichkeit in 'Personality Tests' [On the concept and Diagnosis of Personality Tests]," *Zeitschrift, fuer Sozialforschung* (Jahrgang 6, 1937), pp. 597-624.

thinking, and observation. When the scientist succeeds in gathering enough data or in working out a mathematical formulation, or both, to make his original vision highly plausible he may be said to have arrived at a tentative hypothesis. A careful analysis of the hypothesis in order to discern its implications and the amassing of data which support it, lead to a more adequate hypothesis and eventually perhaps to its inclusion in a wide-ranging theory.

The history of science is replete with instances of faith in reason and vision of truth. Copernicus, Kepler, Galileo, and Newton were all imbued with an unshakable faith in reason. For this Bruno was burned at the stake and Spinoza suffered excommunication. At every step from the conception of a rational vision to the formulation of a theory, *faith* is necessary: faith in the vision as a rationally valid aim to pursue, faith in the hypothesis as a likely and plausible proposition, and faith in the final theory, at least until a general consensus about its validity has been reached. This faith is rooted in one's own experience, in the confidence in one's power of thought, observation, and judgment. While irrational faith is the acceptance of something as true only *because* an authority or the majority say so, rational faith is rooted in an independent conviction based upon one's own productive observing and thinking.

Thought and judgment are not the only realm of experience in which rational faith is manifested. In the sphere of human relations, faith is an indispensable quality of any significant friendship or love. "Having faith" in another person means to be certain of the reliability and unchangeability of his fundamental attitudes, of the core of his personality. By this I do not mean that a person may not change his opinions but that his basic motivations remain the same; that, for instance, his capacity or respect for human dignity is part of his self, not subject to change.

In the same sense we have faith in ourselves. We are aware of the existence of a self, of a core in our personality which is unchangeable and which persists throughout our life in spite of varying circumstances and regardless of certain changes in opinions and feelings. It is this core which is the reality behind the word "I" and on which our conviction of our own identity is based. Unless we have faith in the persistence of our self, our feeling of identity is threatened and we become dependent on other people whose approval then becomes the basis for our feeling of identity with ourselves. Only the person who has faith in himself is able to be faithful to others because only he can be sure that he will be the same at a future time as he is today and, therefore, to feel and to act as he now expects to. Faith in oneself is a condition of our ability to promise something, and since, as Nietzsche pointed out, man can be defined by his capacity to promise, that is one of the conditions of human existence.

Another meaning of having faith in a person refers to the faith we have in the potentialities of others, of ourselves, and of mankind. The most rudimentary form in which this faith exists is the faith which the mother has toward her newborn baby: that it will live, grow, walk, and talk. However, the development of the child in this respect occurs with such regularity that the expectation of it does not seem to require faith. It is different with those potentialities which can fail to develop: the child's potentialities to love, to be happy, to use his reason, and more specific potentialities like artistic gifts. They are the seeds which grow and become manifest if the proper conditions for their development are given, and they can be stifled if they are absent. One of the most important of these conditions is that the significant persons in a child's life have faith in these potentialities. The presence of this faith makes the difference between education and manipulation. Education is identical with helping the child realize his potentialities. The opposite of education is manipulation, which is based on the absence of faith in the growth of potentialities and on the conviction that a child will be right only if the adults put into him what is desirable and cut off what seems to be undesirable. There is no need of faith in the robot since there is no life in it either. . . .

The Future of American Education

The inability of schools to cure America's social disorders is a continuing source of surprise to almost everyone (with the possible exception of teachers). Americans have always tended to assume that good schools could offset all the defects of American homes, churches, and employers. Our dependence on schools to socialize the young has increased steadily over recent years. The reason for this is not the megalomania of educators. Nor is it the instinctive faith of laymen in educators; on the contrary, such faith has been conspicuously lacking. The reason is that parents, clergymen, and employers have found it harder and harder to meet their traditional responsibilities under modern conditions and, in reluctant desperation, have turned to educators for help.

The inability of the typical American home to prepare its young for adult life needs little documentation. The world is changing too fast for parents to feel confident about imposing the values of their own youth on their children. They look outside the home for guidance; to their neighbors, to the mass media, to Dr. Spock and Margaret Mead, and to the schools. If elementary schools suggest that it is more important for children to get along with one another than to acquire adult virtues, most parents will acquiesce. If high schools sanction cars and cigarettes as normal to adolescent life, most parents will do the same. If colleges take sex and liquor for granted among undergraduates, most parents will protest only feebly, devoting most of their emotional energy to looking the other way.

The parent who would resist this pattern soon discovers that his powers are extremely limited. The days are long gone when parents could or would spend most of their time with the young, either in household or farm work. By the time most students reach adolescence they have become expert in seeming outwardly to conform to parental demands while actually adapting to the less easily evaded expectations of their classmates. They have found, too, that their schools are in fact *ersatz* families, competing with parents for control over the young. The modern "school child" is therefore in many respects just that: the child of an institution. For him the school provides the mirror in which to

29

discover oneself. In large part, moreover, this mirror is the creation of his classmates, not his teachers. If the child is successful by his classmates' standards he becomes confident in a way that he never does if he succeeds only in pleasing his elders. Yet he can seldom be healthy or satisfied unless he also has the skill to make some kind of peace, however fragile or fraudulent, with adult expectations.

The decline of the family as a shaper of the young has been matched by the decline of the churches, and for similar reasons. The geographic mobility which has made it easier for children to anticipate that they will sooner or later be freed from the parental shadow has also made it possible for everyone to change churches more easily, creating a buyer's market in religion. The growing complexity of the economy has created a variety of occupations which rival or surpass the clergy in erudition and breadth of experience, thereby reducing the authority of the pulpit as the arbiter of community morals. There are other factors too complex to enumerate. Suffice it to say that if American churches ever played a major role in shaping the lives of the young, that time is past. As a result education has become a kind of secular religion, and teachers a sort of lay clergy, equipping the young with whatever theology, morality, and spirituality they have. This is as true of public as of parochial schools.

Industry is also eager to transfer responsibility for the socialization and training of prospective employees to the schools. Employers have wanted to put vocational and professional training under public auspices to save themselves money and effort. Labor unions, professional associations, and the like put their training programs in schools and colleges to give their callings status. All have agreed that such a transfer of responsibility would provide more equality of opportunity and more assurance that the young would get high-quality training. The roots of this change go back to the nineteenth century, when schools of medicine, law, and theology were established in the better American universities. In this same era land-grant colleges were set up to provide scientific training for farmers and engineers. Later, with the help of federal grants-in-aid, vocational training won a place in the secondary schools. In recent decades even business and public administration, the last prestigious holdouts against professionalization and academic preparation, have begun to fall into line. Today there is little real debate about the necessity of providing occupational training in classes as well as (and in some measure instead of) on the job. The only serious debate is whether particular kinds of training need be extensive or brief, and at which educational level they should be provided.

It is clear, then, that schools and colleges are being asked to assume a large measure of responsibility for the personalities, attitudes, and competence of the next generation. It is also clear that they are not set up to meet this responsibility. In the first place, America has assigned a comparatively small share of her resources to the task. Expenditures on education are usually reckoned at between 5 and 6 per cent of the gross national product. Less than 3 per cent of the adult population is employed in teaching, and except at the graduate level and in a few colleges this 3 per cent includes only a few of America's most talented men and women. Even our commitment of time may well be inadequate for the tasks we expect to accomplish in the classroom. The average American goes to school only twelve years out of almost seventy, and during those years he is in school only about 180 days out of 365, and usually only about six hours each day. This means he devotes only about 2 per cent of his lifetime to formal education. Academically talented or socially fortunate children are, of course, likely to give more of their lives to educational institutions: often as much as 4 and sometimes even 6 per cent. In some of these cases the impact of what happens in school is so strong that it helps shape the rest of the student's life. But this is the exception. Often enough life outside the school is so much more compelling than life inside that a student is psychologically absent even during the hours he spends in class.

The basic reason why schools and colleges cannot cure our major social disorders is not, however, their lack of resources; it is that they are part of the system which produces the disorders. The resulting limitations are illustrated by looking closely at one of the many problems education is normally expected to solve: poverty.

American society is organized on the assumption that if you want to live comfortably you have to perform some kind of work which society values. Those who cannot perform such work are, with certain exceptions, condemned to live at or below the subsistence level. It is therefore usually assumed that the cure for poverty is an educational system which gives everyone the skills for doing some kind of valuable work. In other words, if everyone were literate, ambitious, and socially poised, everyone could earn a comfortable middle-class living.

Unfortunately, however, skills are not absolute but relative—and hence competitive. If the least adept students are given slightly better instruction, while instruction of the most adept gets substantially better, the competitive position of the least adept will deteriorate rather than improve. If that happens, poverty will grow more widespread. If the schools want to end poverty they must not only improve the position of the poor pupils; *they must improve it faster than they improve the position of the rest of the pupils.* Parents of the better pupils (the middle-class parents by and large) inevitably resist such efforts. They do not, of course, defend giving inept students an inept teacher or poorly equipped classroom. But they do not want talented teachers diverted from work with gifted children to "remedial" or "vocational" work, nor do they want improvement of slum schools given higher priority than the improvement of their own schools. The middle classes realize quite well that American life is competitive and that if their children are to prosper they must get "the best" education. Both "the best" and "the worst" are defined by comparison with the rest. If "the worst" gets better, then middle-class parents will want "the best" improved even more. Given today's political realities, educators can seldom resist such middle-class demands. Nor do most educators have an impulse to resist, even if they could. They typically argue that "the best way to improve the education system is to start at the top." This is probably true. But improving the system in this way will do nothing to eliminate poverty, and may even intensify it. If we want to end poverty we must concentrate not on increasing the absolute educational level of the population but on narrowing the gap between the best educated and the worst educated.

As this example suggests, the social role of education is at bottom a political rather than a technical question. Schools and colleges can play a major role in solving America's social problems only if control over them passes to new individuals and interests who expect to benefit from solving these problems. If the poor, for example, want to narrow the gap between what their children learn in school and what the children of the middle classes learn, they will have to fight for a larger voice in the allocation of personnel and money among competing schools and competing programs within schools.

A radical analysis of American education must, then, begin by focusing on the question of who controls our schools and colleges. At first glance this appears to be a fairly simple question, which can be answered by studying the legislators, philanthropists, and parents who put up most of the money for education, and the boards of education and trustees that nominally control most schools and colleges. This kind of analysis shows quite clearly that education is a virtual monopoly of the middle classes, and that the great conflicts are in large part intra-class conflicts. The battle over church-state relations, for example, is largely a struggle between middle-class Catholics who want "the best" education for their child and don't want to pay for it twice, and the middle-class non-Catholics who think religious separatism a national menace. The battle over racial segregation, too, is largely a struggle between lower-middle-class Negroes who want to escape the ghetto mentality and lower-middle-class whites whose status and self-assurance are too fragile to accept Negroes as equals. (This is not to say that poor Negroes accept segregation willingly. But for the most part they are not ready to organize, and they are more interested in new buildings and good teachers than in integration per se.)

Most conflicts over education are not, however, conflicts among lay interests but between one or another lay group and the professionals. Formally, of course, these battles are fought in the lay arena. Typically there is a "liberal" group which takes its cues from the professionals and supports their demands, and a "conservative" group which opposes the dominant professional opinion on the subject. The classic example of this pattern is the perennial struggle over educational finances, in which the educators ask for more money, the "liberals" support the demand, and the "conservatives" oppose it. Another recurrent example is the struggle for "academic freedom," a term which can mean almost anything but is generally used in debates about the political, theological, or moral content of a teacher's classes or reading lists. Again, the pattern is one in which the "liberals" support professional autonomy while the "conservatives" argue for the layman's right to decide what goes on in a school or college. With the major exceptions of racial and religious questions, this pattern characterizes almost the full range of educational politics. Sooner or later (mostly later) victory in such struggles usually goes to the liberals. The result is that the educators have more and more control both over their own affairs and over their students'. The reasons for this trend deserve careful attention, for until they are understood it is impossible to map a realistic program of educational reform, radical or otherwise.

. . . .

What is an appropriate radical response to these developments—assuming I have predicted them accurately? First, it seems to me the radical must ask how such a system of education is going to affect the character of the larger society. Will changes of the kind I have predicted cure any of the present diseases of American society? Will they stimulate new ones? Second, a radical must ask whether the emerging system of education will be good in its own right, i.e., will those who teach and learn and live within the system find it more satisfying than they find the present system?

The impact of the emerging system of education on American society is far from clear, but at least in some respects trouble appears likely. We seem to be headed for a world in which everyone will spend more time in the classroom and related activities, in which performance in these activities will be more important for success elsewhere, and in which the larger society will increasingly mirror the values and organization of the classroom. This may not be such a bad thing; certainly it is better than a society which demands and values physical brawn or the right ancestors. But educational institutions also have important limitations. At least as presently and prospectively organized, they keep students largely passive and dependent. The student, at whatever level, is not encouraged to discover and define reality for himself. Rather, he is encouraged to accept the definitions and demands of others and is rewarded according to his ability and willingness to adapt to these demands. Such schools and colleges provide appropriate socialization for the corporate or governmental civil service and for many professions. But a society cannot be wholly run by organization men. Somewhere it must have men who initiate new activities, who take the lead in responding to new problems and to a changing environment. Whether any educational system can encourage and reward this kind of talent, or can help young people who have such talents find appropriate roles in adult society, is an open question. Nevertheless it seems clear that efforts in this direction must be made.

If everyone is to spend a substantial part of the years between five and twenty-five in educational institutions, the definition of such institutions must somehow become more flexible. Already this is happening in some measure: from elementary school to graduate school, the definition of institutional responsibilities and possibilities has been enormously broadened since 1900, and further expansion seems likely. As academics become more involved in the affairs of society, their assumptions about what young apprentices should be doing also seem to become somewhat broader. Scholars who commute to Washington as consultants, for example, often listen sympathetically to those who propose that graduate or undergraduate students should gain political experience as part of their education. At the other end of the spectrum, elementary schoolteachers who are also mothers want to expose their pupils to the full range of activities that they offer their own children, from trips to the zoo to individual reading or tinkering projects. The result of all this is that while it becomes harder for the young to escape the embrace of educational institutions, the range of activities possible within this embrace is much wider than it was a generation or two ago. This applies not only to the diversification of "credit" courses but to the growing flexibility of the role of the "student." A generation ago young people almost never mixed marriage with study. Comparatively few responsible employed adults were also students. Today both mixtures are becoming more common, and the role of the "student" is far more open-ended and potentially satisfying to late adolescents and young adults of dissimilar temperaments.

The present trend will probably continue. But it is by no means certain that the role of the student will be diversified as fast as it should be when you consider the increasing proportion of the population which is being forced into this role for ever longer periods of time. Even more important, although the role of the student is fairly flexible when viewed in a national context, it is often extremely rigid in the particular school or college he is forced to attend.

There are, of course, exceptions to this pattern of uniformity. A big state university, for example, is likely to have a variety of student subcultures, and a student is likely to have considerable freedom to join whichever he finds congenial. This is true to a lesser extent of some big comprehensive high schools. Nevertheless there are very few schools or colleges which include the full range of possible responses to such youthful realities as ignorance and curiosity, loneliness and sexuality, powerlessness and irresponsibility. In the great majority of institutions there is one dominant style, and all other possibilities are looked down on. If a student is not comfortable with the style which dominates his institution, if he does not find that the attitudes and talents of its leading crowd complement his own, he must either go underground or go elsewhere. In most cases he can go underground only at great cost to himself, and elsewhere only at great cost to his parents. As a result many young people spend years in institutions they hate, learn very little, and drop out too soon to have much chance of realizing their potential as adults.

What can be done to remedy this situation? One possibility is to try to make schools and colleges more pluralistic, encouraging faculty to teach in more ways and students to create more subcultures within each institution. Once educators have got done denying that the problem doesn't exist, they usually make suggestions of this kind to solve it. As a practical matter, however, pluralism within institutions has both limitations and drawbacks.

The limitations derive from the fact of central administration and from the desire of most teachers to work with colleagues who differ from themselves along only a few dimensions. The consequences of central administration vary, of course, according to the administrative system and the philosophy on which it operates. University administrators are usually readier than school administrators to allow a variety of distinctive or even conflicting enterprises within their bailiwick; but it is almost impossible to find administrators at any level who can take responsibility for actively promoting a wide variety of contradictory programs. The most one can hope for is an administrator who will hire subordinates of quite different outlooks and then let them ride off in all directions. Even this is rare.

The power of a single organization to move in diverse directions is usually limited not only by the top man but by the staff. Especially in colleges and universities, where the faculty expect to play a major role in choosing their colleagues, there is normally great resistance to establishing new programs which will bring radically different sorts of instructors into the club. Indeed, there is often strong resistance even to allowing faculty who are already in the club to undertake radically new programs which seem to constitute an indictment of the status quo. A college professor has a great deal of freedom to teach *what* he pleases, and a schoolteacher has some, but neither is free to decide *how* to teach —whether in large groups or small, in departmentalized courses or others, one day a week or five. The limits are as often imposed by colleagues anxious to preserve "standards" and "continuity" as by administrators. There is nothing like as much freedom to organize teaching projects in an idiosyncratic way as there is with research projects.

Even if these problems could be solved the drive for pluralism would entail major sacrifices. The most important problem is size. If an institution wants to be all things to all people, it must be large. At the college level, a small, manageable student body will not usually have enough students interested in politics to sustain a group of left- or right-wing activists. If it does, there will not be enough journalists to put out a good newspaper or enough squares to sustain the fraternities. Similarly, a small junior high school will not have enough bookish students to sustain an intellectual subculture (nor will it have enough potential junkies to support a narcotics salesman).

Size has many advantages, especially for the student with unusual talent, energy, or interests, who can master a complex environment. But for many students bigness is an invitation to passivity and *anomie.* One reason is that, while increased enrollment brings an increase in the number and variety of student activities, the latter never increase in proportion to the former. No matter how big the place gets, there is only one student paper, one band, one football team, one valedictorian, and so forth. Competition for these slots therefore grows more intense as size increases. The quality of performance in each activity is better, but fewer students participate actively. Many students must gain whatever satisfaction they can from watching classmates they scarely know perform with skill they cannot equal. In a large student body, no matter how carefully selected, many individuals find they have no special contribution to make, no well-defined role to give them a sense of being valued, and every reason to assume that they are regarded as expendable.

Size tends to affect not only the relationship among students but that between students and adults. As student subcultures grow more diverse and encompass more of the students' lives, their dependence on adults seems in some respects to diminish. This may be fine from the students' viewpoint, but it frees them for foolish as well as wise experiments. The anonymity of a large institution can lead to tragedy as well as emancipation. Indeed, it is perhaps the possibility of the former which encourages the latter. For the many youngsters who are born tragedy-prone, such as educational setting is a mistake.

For all of these reasons, an educational system which aspires to offer the young both a manageable environment and a wide range of choice should not try to make each of its enterprises all things to all people. Instead, a system with such aims must try to establish a wide variety of somewhat specialized and distinctive institutions, each following its unique path, each doing only what its staff can do well, each attracting its own constituency and serving that constituency in its own way. Some of these institutions should be large, others small, but in each case the aim should be to determine size according to the needs of the teachers and students rather than on the basis of administrative convenience or logistic pressure.

The first step toward the establishment of such an educational system would be to abandon the tradition that education should be rooted in geography. According to this venerable notion, the best educational system is one in which everyone who lives in a particular area attends school or college with everyone else living in that area. This assumption is now firmly established in the elementary schools, largely dominant in the secondary schools, and for reasons already indicated is spreading to the colleges. Its justification is twofold. First, it is cheap and convenient. Transportation costs are cut to a minimum for the young, and even college students are spared the expense of living away from home. Second, certain communities have a wide spread of incomes and personalities. This means that schools and colleges rooted in these communities seem very "democratic." We are, however, more and more an urban people, whose rich live in suburbs and whose poor live in slums. There are fewer communities in which a "local" school or college is heterogeneous and more in which it is economically and/or ethnically homogeneous. This pattern is extremely obvious in elementary education, increasingly so in junior and senior highs, and has begun to appear even in higher education. Efforts to provide government scholarships which would give such students a wider range of choice have come to little.

What is the alternative? First, every effort must be made to ensure that students and parents have complete freedom to choose among all the various schools and colleges in the nation. This means that a child living in one part of town must be allowed to apply for a school in another part on precisely the same basis as a child who lives around the corner from the school in question. It means that a student who wants to attend a university which is two hundred (or two thousand) miles from his home should be given as much assistance as he needs to pay his room and board bills rather than being forced by poverty to attend a junior college to which he can commute. Perhaps most important, it means that a student who wants to attend a private school or college should get the same subsidy from the state as a student who wants to attend a public school or college, so long as the private institution meets minimal criteria established by the state.

The essential principle of such an educational system would be that the needs of individual students have primacy over the needs of institutions, public or private, and that subsidies will be spent on the kinds of education parents and students want, not on the kind politicians want and control. This principle could be realized either by making all subsidies take the form of tuition grants or by paying public funds to schools and colleges according to the number, level, and perhaps the incapacity to pay of their students. The essential point in either case would be to use the market mechanism to ensure that the allocation of resources among competing schools and colleges was in the hands of students and parents.

The value of such a system depends, of course, on the amount of real diversity it creates. Little will be gained by providing more choice if this turns out to be among hundreds of virtually identical institutions. To avoid this we must make a real effort to promote experimentation and to create specialized schools catering to various minority tastes. In part, of course, the proposed reorganization of the academic market place will do this, for if a special-purpose school, either public or private, can draw from all social classes and all geographic areas its chances of finding and retaining a stable constituency will be much greater than today. If we want to go very far in this direction, however, the administration of the public sector of the educational economy must be reorganized. If students have a choice about whether or not they attend a particular school, it should become politically possible to free the principal and staff of the school from many of the restrictions which now hem them in. If a principal wants to recruit a staff and set up a Montessori school, and if he can find parents who want to send their children to such a school, he should be free to follow his vision. If another principal wants to use McGuffey's reader, and if enough teachers and parents support this quaint notion, they should be free to do that too. If a school wants to recruit teachers without regard to the number of education courses they have taken, and if parents find the resulting program suits their children, this should be possible. If a public university wants to hire fewer professors and pay higher salaries than its competitors, it should be free to take that approach so long as it can live within a standard allocation of money for each student. Public institutions, in other words, should wherever possible have the same kinds of autonomy that private institutions now have. At every level an effort should be made to reduce the distinction between the public and private sectors, encouraging them to compete on equal terms for students and allocating funds among them according to the number of students they attract.

In its pure form, the system I am advocating would give the professional educators absolute freedom to establish any kinds of schools and colleges they see fit, while giving parents and students absolute freedom to choose among these schools and colleges as they see fit. As a practical matter, however, this purity would have to be diluted in certain respects.

First, the public must be protected against fraud. This means that any school which receives public funds should be open to public inspection, and that the results of such inspection should be publicly available. An educational "consumers' union" would be useful in this context, and if millions of parents were suddenly free to choose among a variety of schools and colleges, such a union would probably spring up.

A second limitation emerges from the fact that in many parts of the country there is only one school within bussing distance of most families. If such families don't like the nearest school their only alternative is a boarding school. While this solution ought to be more widely available than it is, particularly to Negroes in the Deep South, it is not an appealing alternative to many families. In sparsely settled areas and in smaller towns geography will have to remain one of the organizing principles of education. In such settings the professional educators' freedom to experiment will continue to be limited by what the local board of education judges acceptable to the community.

A third limitation is that there are some parents whose educational preferences do not deserve to be indulged, even if educators can be found to indulge them. Parents who want their children to attend all-white schools should not be allowed to use public funds to pursue this preference. Other restrictions would inevitably be imposed by the courts and by legislators. The courts would presumably hold, for example, that public funds could not go to a school or college which discriminated in favor of Catholics. They might also hold that public funds could not go to a school or college which held religious services on its premises—though this latter seems unlikely. Politicians in some areas might well feel that public funds should not be used to support and promote academic elitism, at least among the young. In that case they might require that a school receiving public support be open to all comers, regardless of IQ or academic record. This should not, in my view, prevent a school from setting up a strictly academic program geared to hard-working and talented children; but there is much to be said for leaving the decision about whether to enter such a school to parents and students rather than to testers and teachers. (Teachers will no doubt disagree.)

With the safeguards outlined, a system of free choice could have an enormously beneficial effect on the American educational scene. The market mechanism is not, of course, foolproof; in areas where mass production or national advertising is vitally important, a "free" market tends to produce oligopoly or monopoly, and the customer is often left with no real choice among products. But education does not appear to be an industry with such a propensity to concentration. Rather, it is an industry in which the small entrepreneur can often do his job as well as, or better than, the big-time operator. Competition can and does flourish when the government does not rig the market. In such a market the consumer has a reasonable hope of getting what he wants—*if* the government gives him enough money to pay for it. A free market would, of course, reduce enrollment in publicly controlled schools and increase enrollment in privately controlled schools. But that is not in itself an argument against change. There is no inherent virtue in public administration of the schools any more than in public administration of universities, post offices, or the telephone system. One must judge by results, and today's largely public system of administration has produced neither an equitable nor an efficient and imaginative deployment of educational resources.

I have suggested that the major change now taking place in the educational system is the growing power of the professional educators, and I have argued that this will do little to solve the problems of most students. If we want a radical change in the present system, a mechanism must be found for offsetting the power of the profession. Sporadic reassertions of political control are not likely to turn the trick; indeed, many of the more common sorts of intervention by boards of laymen are likely to make matters worse. The only alternative that I can see is to establish a freer market and thus give more direct power to parents and students.

Death at an Early Age

A young teacher without powerful connections or impressive affiliations does not last long in the Boston school system unless he learns
to remain relatively silent about the things that he sees. It is a different
story with a teacher who is simply incompetent. Teachers who are
senile, physically degenerate, mentally unstable, have been kept on
often for months, in some cases for years, before the school system has
begun to address itself effectively to the question of whether or not they
were really teaching anything. This was the situation with the Fourth
Grade teacher in my school, neither senile nor degenerate, but certainly unstable to the point of being a considerable threat to the mental
health and education of a class of children. Beginning in the autumn,
his presence within that classroom had brought little to the children
beyond unending noise and chaos, yet all of the complaints of children
and parents and even the stated dissatisfaction of the Principal had not
been able to effect a change. Now at last, somehow, after about five
months, he was leaving. But, in his place, the school system did not have
the wisdom to send in anyone more qualified. Instead of a confident or
experienced instructor, there arrived first a bashful and terrified young
lady and then, after her departure, a string of substitute teachers who
seemed at times truly to have been dragged off the street at seven-
thirty, handed a twenty-dollar bill, and shipped over to our school-
house in a taxi. Some of them were nice people but few had any kind
of apparent qualification. Anyone who looked once into that hectic
classroom and then at these hapless teachers would have said in an
instant that it was not likely to work out. Sending these teachers in here
was as unthought-about, as uncalculated, as unplotted, as wholly whim-
sical, as unplanned, as it had been to send me into a school for discipline
problems during my first weeks of teaching and without bothering to
tell me the nature of the school.

So, in this case, the children were beginning to get some very strange specimens: one day a fellow who did not even arrive until about ten-thirty or eleven because he had been out driving a cab the night before and who announced, within about forty-five minutes, that he would certainly not be coming back. The consequence of all of this, in academic terms, was an overall retardation of almost the entire class of children, the few exceptions being those who were essentially being educated by their parents outside school. There was a chart on the wall that gave some measure of this by keeping a record of math and spelling grades. It was apparent from this that the math average of the children for weeks had remained, almost without exception, below the point of failing—and, for certain stretches of time, as much as thirty points below. Their spelling and their writing had fluctuated around the Third Grade level. Reading levels were a year, in many cases two years, behind the national norm. All of these were major tragedies because, in many respects, and for a number of the children, the stunting of their learning at such an early age was likely to prove almost irreversible. But the math and reading and spelling and writing, in one respect, were not as devastating setbacks for them as their work in social studies. For at least in the basic subject areas, and no matter how poorly they were doing, the children in that class had had some continuity of material and had done pretty much the same thing every day. In geography and history, there had not even been continuity, but rather a frantic and endless shifting of subject area, and consequently in those areas the children in the class were hopelessly mixed up.

One day a substitute teacher, groping for a way to kill an hour, would have the children read aloud to him about India. The next day, another teacher—not knowing or asking what had been done the day before, and maybe having a special fondness for another country, Holland perhaps—would tell the class to flip back a hundred pages and read about dikes and wooden shoes. Then someone would appear long enough to get some help from one of the full-time teachers and maybe the children would get two or three abortive sessions on the desert, but the day after that suddenly they would be doing India all over again, then off to Lima, Peru, suddenly to American cotton production, or the "corn belt" or "coal production"—or then, with the arrival of a new teacher, back to dikes and wooden shoes again. It is not surprising that, with a crazy arrangement of this sort, the children would frequently start out by lying to a new substitute and would do their best to destroy him and to break him down. Nor is it surprising that, after the course of such a year, their sense of place and time and even of self-localization would have been disastrously confused. They had no idea at all of the real relationships of different areas of the earth and could make no distinction, even in the most tentative and general manner, between a city, a town, a state, a country—or even a continent or island. Words like Yangtse River, Hemisphere, Nile, Himalayas, Pyramid, Ganges, Nomad, or Colorado were all inextricably mixed up in their minds. A question about what you can get from rushing streams in Switzerland might elicit such an answer as "population" or "migration" and a question about what "self-evident" means or "created equal" could easily bring back from the class such answers as "Red Coats," "transportation" or "white coal."

Seven different teachers in the course of ten days became the final catastrophe of this classroom. The children became wild, and the atmosphere from day to day grew more disturbing to the rest of the school. At this point, on the morning of the sixth of May, the Principal called me in to her office and asked me if I would agree to move across the hall and take that room. The idea was for one of the older teachers to take my own pupils and for me to take over the class of children who had been having such a time. With the assurance that my students would not be getting a string of substitutes, I agreed to make the transfer and I stayed up very late that night and the next day I went in to start with my new class.

I had a difficult time with that class of children for the first four or five days. It was almost as confusing and chaotic as the first days I had spent in the discipline school. Some of those mornings, I thought of myself as a row-boat going under in mid-ocean, the ocean being noise and cries and movements on all sides of me and all at almost the same time. During those days, I am sure I must have yelled and shouted at the children in that room as much as any teacher had ever done before and I probably scared some of them more than I should have. The point, though, is that I really did survive with them, and that I survived, in the end, in what I know now to have been the only good way: by which I mean that I saw the *class* survive and saw them not merely calm down but genuinely come to life again. I know, moreover, that it was not creating fear and shouting which did it, although that may have helped me to get through those first few days, but that it was something far more continuous and more important. The real reason that I was able to get on with those children in the state in which I found them is that I came into that room knowing myself to be absolutely on their side. I did not go in there with even the littlest suggestion that what had been going on that year was even one-fiftieth their fault. If I had done that, I am convinced that things would have been hopeless. I went in there, on the contrary, and in a manner that they soon detected, with loyalty only to them for their nerve and for their defiance and with an obvious and openly expressed dissatisfaction with the stupidity of a school system that had cheated them.

The first writing assignment that they passed in emphasized what many of those children were thinking and feeling. The assignment was to describe the way they felt about their school. As an alternative I said that, if they wanted, they could write about the street they lived on or about the whole neighborhood or about any other part of town. Because of the miserable state their writing was in, and out of a fear that they might not write anything at all if they felt they were going to be lambasted, I said that I wouldn't be looking at grammar or spelling or syntax in the beginning but that I would be looking for two things: (1) the richness and specificity of details and (2) the openness and courage with which they would put their own most private feelings down. Although I have taught all kinds of writing classes since then, I don't think that I ever again will receive such a trusting and wide-open reponse.

"In my school," began a paper that was handed back to me a few days later, "I see dirty boards and I see papers on the floor. I see an old browken window with a sign on it saying, Do not unlock this window are browken. And I see cracks in the walls and I see old books with ink poured all over them and I see old painting hanging on the walls. I see old alfurbet letter hanging on one nail on the wall. I see a dirty fire exit I see a old closet with supplys for the class. I see pigons flying all over the school. I see old freght trains throgh the fence of the school yard. I see pictures of contryies hanging on the wall and I see desks with wrighting all over the top of the desks and insited of the desk."

Another paper that was passed in to me said this: "There is a torn up house I live near and the stairs are broken down. The windows are boarded up too. One day I saw a little boy and his dog on the third floor. I don't know how they got up there but they were. The doors are pushed in and there is trash in the house dirt for it hasn't been clean for a long time. Everything is boarded up. The railing on the porch looks like it is going to fall off. One of the steps are about to fall off. Some children even go into the yard and on the porch of the house. The yard has glass, paper, rocks, broken pens and pencils, a torn dress, some pants, in it. It is the junkiest yard Ive ever seen. There is always a black cat in the yard too I never go near it though. I don't go into the yard but I look over my fence and I look into the house and yard."

Another child told me this: "I see lots of thinings in this room. I see new teachers omots every day. I can see flowers and children books and others things. I like the 100 papers I like allso cabnets. I don't like the drity windows. And the dusty window shallvalls ..."

A little girl wrote this: "I can see old cars with gas in it and there is always people lighting fires old refrigartor an wood glass that comes from the old cars old trees and trash old weeds and people put there old chairs in there an flat tires and one thing there is up there is wood that you can make dog houses and there are beautiful flowers and there are dead dogs and cats ... On some of the cars the weel is of and wisey bottles beer cans car seats are all out cars are all tip over and just the other day there was a fire and it was just blasting and whew in the back there is a big open space where Girl Scouts could mabe cook ... this feild was a gas staition and the light pole is still up."

This was one more: "I see pictures in my school. I see pictures of Spain and a pictures of Portofino and a pictures of Chicago. I see arithmetic paper a spellings paper. I see a star chart. I see the flag of our Amerrica. The room is dirty ... The auditorium dirty the seats are dusty. The light in the auditorium is brok. The curtains in the auditorium are ragged they took the curtains down because they was so ragged. The bathroom is dirty sometime the toilet is very hard. The cellar is dirty the hold school is dirty sometime ... The flowers are dry everything in my school is so so dirty."

When these essays were passed in, I showed one of them to the Reading Teacher. She became very angry. Her first reaction, which was expressed soon after I had handed her the essay, was to accuse me of having somehow concocted or coaxed this writing out of the child, whoever it was, who had composed it. "You must have induced it," she said, or "suggested it" or "invited it" or something like that, which was a way of disqualifing totally the independent intelligence and perception of the child who did the writing, at the same time that it discredited the impartiality and honesty of the teacher who could have allowed such thoughts to find their way to paper. What she said to me, essentially, was that I must have planted such gloomy word-pictures in the minds of the children or else they could not conceivably have written such things down. I was, on the contrary, very happy and quite proud of the children's essays because they were so direct and open and also so much filled with details. It was, I suppose, correct that in a sense I *had* induced this writing by telling the class to really go out and look at things and not write about their neighborhood or their school or about anything as if it were identical with the ingredients of the world or neighborhood that was often depicted in the pictures of their books. The Reading Teacher also was probably correct in saying that the children wouldn't have written those essays if I hadn't said what I did because, as I have already shown, the great majority had been thoroughly disciplined into the same kind of pretense which the teachers themselves had adopted for self-comfort; and this was a pretense which did not allow for broken cars and boarded windows. Another of the children's essays just started off and announced that in September they had begun with such and such a teacher and then had had so and so, and then so and so, and then so and so, and right on through a list of about eight or nine teachers ending up finally with me. It was cold-blooded, factual, showed a good memory and was shatteringly effective simply by rattling off almost the entire list without making any pointed comments. This again she may or may not have done if she hadn't been told she *could* do it, because the general atmosphere at school militated against a photographic frankness of that sort.

The Reading Teacher was upset by this, by whichever of the essays it was that I showed her, but rather than coming to terms with it by moving toward the center of the problem and by asking how the curriculum and tone of the school program fitted in with such a picture of this child's life, the Reading Teacher instead was able to handle the child's honesty by pointing out to me that I had probably angled for this, or induced it or coaxed it or had been looking for it anyway—the last of which charges possibly held a grain of truth but did not have a thing to do with the problems that the essays posed for her. The crux of it, I suppose, is that this woman, like many other teachers, had worked hard to develop and to solidify a set of optimistic values. To perpetrate the same views upon her pupils therefore was not to lie to them (for her), at least not consciously, but to extend to them, to attempt really to "sell" to them, her own hard-earned hopes about the world. During a long career she had had a great deal of apparent success in inducing the children she taught to write cheery and pastel little letters and stories and book reports to correspond to her own views. The reason the essays written by my pupils were bound to be disturbing to her was that she either deeply knew, or at least faintly feared, that they were true.

There was another example of something like this at one point a little earlier in the year. On one wall of the section of the auditorium where the Reading Teacher took her pupils, there was a list which I once took the time to copy down. What the list amounted to was a collection of suggested adjectives for the children to try to use when they were doing book reports. I remember that I studied the list and later discussed it with the Reading Teacher because there was something quite remarkable about it: All of the adjectives were laudatory. Everything that they implied was something nice. "Humorous" and "interesting" and "comical" and "adventurous" were typical of the words which were recommended to the children by virtue of being included in this list. There wasn't one that left room for even partial criticism. As these were the adjectives which the children were being asked to use, the consequence, except in the case of a rare intellectual accident, would have had to be a book report that spoke only in terms of various kinds of "good." Since we know that not all books are good, and in fact that many books are bad, and since we know in particular that many of the books at school were poor, that some were really rotten and that only a handful, probably only a very slim minority were books of any real quality at all, and since, beyond that (and this seems much more important) even a book that seems good to one person, to a teacher or to one pupil, may very likely seem poor to another pupil, and be poor for him, and for some very good reason too—for all of these reasons I was curious about the effect of this list of laudatory adjectives which had faded upon the wall from what I believe to have been many years of use.

I remember a day when I was reading in the auditorium with a small group of children. We were reading, out of the phonics book *Wide Doors Open,* a story which none of them seemed to like very much and several were yawning the whole while. The Reading Teacher's manner of handling this would have been to attempt to "sell" it to the children, to call it wonderful and to sweep over them with a wave of persuasive enthusiasm in order to make up for their resistance to the work. I did not see why I ought to do this or why I ought to try to force upon them an appreciation of a type of story which they did not like. The story that we were reading was for some good reason of no importance to them and I was not going to try to persuade them it was terrific when they did not feel it. When we were done with the story I asked them whether they had liked it, and the thing that astonished me was that almost every one of them pretended that he *had.* I said: "What did you think of it? How would you describe it? What kind of story was it?" The answers came back: "Interesting"—"humorous"—"colorful"—"adventurous"—and all of the rest of the words on the Reading Teacher's list.

I twisted my head and I looked up at the list in the back of the room. There they all were. The words thay they had given me were all up in neat order on the permissible list. They had not even begun thinking. They had not even started responding. They had simply assumed that, because I had asked the question, one of those words must be the right answer. The terrible thought that there *was* a right answer and that I already *knew* it and that it remained only for them to *guess* it was most disheartening of all. I remember that when they suggested each adjective it was not in a voice which said "I think it was humorous"—or "I think it was adventurous"—or "I think it was interesting"—or any other kind of definitive assertion of opinion. Rather, it was all phrased as a kind of guessing-game to which there was one answer: "Humorous?"

"Adventurous?" "Interesting?" "Comical?" It was all in the interroga-
tive and the effort was all to find out what I, their teacher, had already
decided to be true. Finally, irritated and a little angry, I asked them
flatly: "What are you telling me? You've all been yawning and twisting.
Why didn't you pay attention if all of those wonderful things were so?"

One boy answered me simply, as if there were no contradiction
between this and the use of the other words: "Because it was so baby-
ish." Then how on earth could they have used all of the words on the
Reading Teacher's list? Another boy said: "It was so boring." So there
the real answer was. It seemed obvious why they had lied to me in the
beginning. The Reading Teacher had taught them that those were the
only things you were supposed to say about a book. One of them, one
of those adjectives, was "correct" and the only problem for them was
to find out which one it was. The word, all too clearly, had been divorced from the world, and the application of the correct pat adjective
need have nothing in particular to do with the child's idea about the
book.

I felt troubled enough about this to relate it later to the Reading
Teacher. Just as with the essays by the children that I had shown her,
I felt she was immediately disturbed by what she was hearing but I also
recognized that she was very quick to cancel it out. She seemed troubled for a moment but then, instead of saying that it was a pity, or that
it was funny but regrettable, or too bad that they had reacted in such
a manner, or anything else at all that might have brought her doubt or
pause, she said only this:

"At least it shows that they know the words on the list."

What I felt when she said that, was that knowing all those big words
on the list would not be of any use. It would not be of any use because
they could not work with them but could only "supply" them, fetch
them out literally from their place on the list, in much the same manner
that a young dog fetches a thrown stick. By reassuring herself that at
least the children had gotten down those big words for future use, the
Reading Teacher was able to rise above the painful matter that she had
effectively taught them to be good liars and in fact had equipped them
with a set of tools to keep themselves at as far as possible a distance from
the truth.

Rather than learn those ten-dollar words, the introduction of which
into their book reports might win them such rewards as gold stars and
extra points, the children would have gained greatly from having been
invited to search their own barrel of modifiers, containing such words
as "boring," "horrible," "terrible," "great," "pathetic," "idiotic," "terrific," "marvelous" or "dumb." These are the kinds of strong words

which are looked for by good college English instructors in their efforts at erasing the use of the kinds of cliché terms listed above. But what process of education is it which would inculcate these very unnatural "cultured words" at the age of ten only to have to define their artificiality and point up their lack of vitality and attempt in many cases to root them out only ten years later?

I remember the Reading Teacher on one occasion asking a child for the antonym of "fat" and getting "skinny." The Reading Teacher's response was something on this order: "Oh let's see if we can't find a nicer word than skinny"—and getting "thin" and "slender" in its place. A decade later, if that child made it to college, I thought, her English teacher would work his heart out trying to get "skinny" back again.

At one point later in the spring, the Deputy Superintendent, Miss Sullivan, went on record as indicating that she held it a key goal of the Boston Public Schools to break the children of Roxbury of what she called their "speech patterns." There is no way to be absolutely certain of what she intended, but if the Deputy Superintendent meant by this process the replacement of words like "skinny" by such a word as "thin" or "slender," then I think that she may very well succeed in enabling some of the children to speak more like herself but I do not believe that she will have helped them toward expressing themselves richly or with any kind of honesty or strength. Honest writing and private feeling seem to me to be the only possible starting-points for everything else in teaching English and one of the first places where the world outside and the word within the classroom ought to eloquently coexist. To bring about this kind of a meeting would not be easy in much of the present Boston school system, but it would be education.

. . . .

Perhaps a reader would like to know what it is like to go into a new classroom in the same way that I did and to see before you suddenly, and in terms you cannot avoid recognizing, the dreadful consequences of a year's wastage of real lives.

You walk into a narrow and old wood-smelling classroom and you see before you thirty-five curious, cautious and untrusting children, aged eight to thirteen, of whom about two-thirds are Negro. Three of the children are designated to you as special students. Thirty per cent of the class is reading at the Second Grade level in a year and in a month in which they should be reading at the height of Fourth Grade performance or at the beginning of the Fifth. Seven children out of the class are up to par. Ten substitutes or teacher changes. Or twelve changes. Or eight. Or eleven. Nobody seems to know how many teachers they have had. Seven of their lifetime records are missing: symptomatic and emblematic at once of the chaos that has been with them all year long. Many more lives than just seven have already been wasted but the seven missing records become an embittering symbol of the lives behind them which, equally, have been lost or mislaid. (You have to spend the first three nights staying up until dawn trying to reconstruct these records out of notes and scraps.) On the first math test you give, the class average comes out to 36. The children tell you with embarrassment that it has been like that since fall.

You check around the classroom. Of forty desks, five have tops with no hinges. You lift a desk-top to fetch a paper and you find that the top has fallen off. There are three windows. One cannot be opened. A sign on it written in the messy scribble of a hurried teacher or some custodial person warns you: DO NOT UNLOCK THIS WINDOW IT IS BROKEN. The general look of the room is as of a bleak-light photograph of a mental hospital. Above the one poor blackboard, gray rather than really black, and hard to write on, hangs from one tack, lopsided, a motto attributed to Benjamin Franklin: *"Well begun is half done."* Everything, or almost everything like that, seems a mockery of itself.

Into this grim scenario, drawing on your own pleasures and memories, you do what you can to bring some kind of life. You bring in some cheerful and colorful paintings by Joan Miro and Paul Klee. While the paintings by Miro do not arouse much interest, the ones by Klee become an instantaneous success. One picture in particular, a watercolor titled "Bird Garden," catches the fascination of the entire class. You slip it out of the book and tack it up on the wall beside the doorway and it creates a traffic jam every time the children have to file in or file out. You discuss with your students some of the reasons why Klee may have painted the way he did and you talk about the things that can be accomplished in a painting which could not be accomplished in a photograph. None of this seems to be above the children's heads. Despite this, you are advised flatly by the Art Teacher that your naïveté has gotten the best of you and that the children cannot possibly appreciate this. Klee is too difficult. Children will not enjoy it. You are unable to escape the idea that the Art Teacher means herself instead.

For poetry, in place of the recommended memory gems, going back again into your own college days, you make up your mind to introduce a poem of William Butler Yeats. It is about a lake isle called Innisfree, about birds that have the funny name of "linnets" and about a "bee-loud glade." The children do not all go crazy about it but a number of them seem to like it as much as you do and you tell them how once, three years before, you were living in England and you helped a man in the country to make his home from wattles and clay.

The children become intrigued. They pay good attention and many of
them grow more curious about the poem than they appeared at first.
Here again, however, you are advised by older teachers that you are
making a mistake: Yeats is too difficult for children. They can't enjoy it,
won't appreciate it, wouldn't like it. You are aiming way above their
heads . . . Another idea comes to mind and you decide to try out an easy
and rather well-known and not very complicated poem of Robert Frost.
The poem is called "Stopping By Woods on a Snowy Evening." This
time, your supervisor happens to drop in from the School Department.
He looks over the mimeograph, agrees with you that it's a nice poem,
then points out to you—tolerantly, but strictly—that you have made
another mistake. "Stopping By Woods" is scheduled for Sixth Grade. It
is not "a Fourth Grade poem," and it is not to be read or looked at
during the Fourth Grade. Bewildered as you are by what appears to be
a kind of idiocy, you still feel reproved and criticized and muted and
set back and you feel that you have been caught in the commission of
a serious mistake.

On a series of other occasions, the situation is repeated. The children are offered something new and something lively. They respond to
it energetically and they are attentive and their attention does not
waver. For the first time in a long while perhaps there is actually some
real excitement and some growing and some thinking going on within
that one small room. In each case, however, you are advised sooner or
later that you are making a mistake. Your mistake, in fact, is to have
impinged upon the standardized condescension on which the entire
administration of the school is based. To hand Paul Klee's pictures to
the children of this classroom, and particularly in a twenty-dollar
volume, constitutes a threat to this school system. It is not different from
sending a little girl from the Negro ghetto into an art class near Harvard
Yard. Transcending the field of familiarity of the administration, you
are endangering its authority and casting a blow at its self-confidence.
The way the threat is handled is by a continual and standardized under-
rating of the children: They can't do it, couldn't do it, wouldn't like it,
don't deserve it . . . In such a manner, many children are tragically and
unjustifiably held back from a great many of the good things that they
might come to like or admire and are pinned down instead to books the
teacher knows and to easy tastes that she can handle. This includes,
above all, of course, the kind of material that is contained in the Course
of Study.

Try to imagine, for a child, how great the gap between the outside
world and the world conveyed within this kind of school must seem: A
little girl, maybe Negro, comes in from a street that is lined with car-

carcasses. Old purple Hudsons and one-wheel-missing Cadillacs represent her horizon and mark the edges of her dreams. In the kitchen of her house roaches creep and large rats crawl. On the way to school a wino totters. Some teenage white boys slow down their car to insult her, and speed on. At school, she stands frozen for fifteen minutes in a yard of cracked cement that overlooks a hillside on which trash has been unloaded and at the bottom of which the New York, New Haven and Hartford Railroad rumbles past. In the basement, she sits upon broken or splintery seats in filthy toilets and she is yelled at in the halls. Upstairs, when something has been stolen, she is told that she is the one who stole it and is called a liar and forced abjectly to apologize before a teacher who has not the slightest idea in the world of who the culprit truly was. The same teacher, behind the child's back, ponders audibly with imagined compassion: "What can you do with this kind of material? How can you begin to teach this kind of child?"

Gradually going crazy, the child is sent after two years of misery to a pupil adjustment counselor who arranges for her to have some tests and considers the entire situation and discusses it with the teacher and finally files a long report. She is, some months later, put onto a waiting-list some place for once-a-week therapy but another year passes before she has gotten anywhere near to the front of a long line. By now she is fourteen, has lost whatever innocence she still had in the back seat of the old Cadillac and, within two additional years, she will be ready and eager for dropping out of school.

Once at school, when she was eight or nine, she drew a picture of a rich-looking lady in an evening gown with a handsome man bowing before her but she was told by an insensate and wild-eyed teacher that what she had done was junk and garbage and the picture was torn up and thrown away before her eyes. The rock and roll music that she hears on the Negro station is considered "primitive" by her teachers but she prefers its insistent rhythms to the dreary monotony of school. Once, in Fourth Grade, she got excited at school about some writing she had never heard about before. A handsome green book, brand new, was held up before her and then put into her hands. Out of this book her teacher read a poem. The poem was about a Negro—a woman who was a maid in the house of a white person—and she liked it. It remained in her memory. Somehow without meaning to, she found that she had done the impossible for her: she had memorized that poem. Perhaps, horribly, in the heart of her already she was aware that it was telling about her future: fifty dollars a week to scrub floors and bathe little white babies in the suburbs after an hour's streetcar ride. The poem made her want to cry. The white lady, the lady for whom the maid was working, told the maid she loved her. But the maid in the poem wasn't going to tell any lies in return. She know she didn't feel any love for the white lady and she told the lady so. The poem was shocking to her, but it seemed bitter, strong and true. Another poem in the same green book was about a little boy on a merry-go-round. She laughed with the class at the question he asked about a Jim Crow section on a merry-go-round, but she also was old enough to know that it was not a funny poem really and it made her, valuably, sad. She wanted to know how she could get hold of that poem, and maybe that whole book. The poems were moving to her . . .

This was a child in my class. Details are changed somewhat but it is essentially one child. The girl was one of the three unplaced special students in that Fourth Grade room. She was not an easy girl to teach and it was hard even to keep her at her seat on many mornings, but I do not remember that there was any difficulty at all in gaining and holding onto her attention on the day that I brought in that green book of Langston Hughes.

Of all of the poems of Langston Hughes that I read to my Fourth Graders, the one that the children liked most was a poem that has the title "Ballad of the Landlord." This poem may not satisfy the taste of every critic, and I am not making any claims to immortality for a poem just because I happen to like it a great deal. But the reason this poem did have so much value and meaning for me and, I believe, for many of my students, is that it not only seems moving in an obvious and immediate human way but that it *finds* its emotion in something ordinary. It is a poem which really does allow both heroism and pathos to poor people, sees strength in awkwardness and attributes to a poor person standing on the stoop of his slum house every bit as much significance as William Wordsworth saw in daffodils, waterfalls and clouds. At the request of the children later on I mimeographed that poem and, although nobody in the classroom was asked to do this, several of the children took it home and memorized it on their own. I did not assign it for memory, because I do not think that memorizing a poem has any special value. Some of the children just came in and asked if they could recite it. Before long, almost every child in the room had asked to have a turn.

All of the poems that you read to Negro children obviously are not going to be by or about Negro people. Nor would anyone expect that all poems which are read to a class of poor children ought to be grim or gloomy or heart-breaking or sad. But when, among the works of many different authors, you do have the will to read children a poem by a man so highly renowned as Langston Hughes, then I think it is important not to try to pick a poem that is innocuous, being like any other poet's kind of poem, but I think you ought to choose a poem that is genuinely representative and then try to make it real to the children in front of you in the way that I tried. I also think it ought to be taken seriously by a teacher when a group of young children come in to him one morning and announce that they have liked something so much that they have memorized it voluntarily. It surprised me and impressed me when that happened. It was all I needed to know to confirm for me the value of reading that poem and the value of reading many other poems to children which will build upon, and not attempt to break down, the most important observations and very deepest foundations of their lives.

Teaching Children with Special Needs *

This article is an account of a teacher's experiences and efforts in her work with a class of children who have been excluded from ordinary public school kindergarten because they are not able to fit into the standard school program. The implications of these considerations, however, go far beyond the experiences of one teacher. Here are children abused and neglected by various institutions of our society to the point where they are unable to do "ordinary school work" because they are in need of such things as hearing aids and psychotherapy. The city school system's apparatus of teachers, specialists, administrators and equipment does next to nothing of value for these children. More than anything else, the school system as a whole reinforces the rejection experienced by the children, by formally labeling them as too dumb to be in regular classes. In this context, through the pre-primary curriculum, dedicated teachers and assistants have transformed the lives of these children. They have accomplished what the school and social system as a whole could not accomplish, largely because they wanted to help the children and the system did not. This account of the experiences of children, teacher, and assistants suggests that in general genuine education and helping children to become themselves are very much related.(Editors)

I teach a pre-primary class of "kindergarten exclusions." Pre-primary is a federally funded, experimental program in special education, set up under Titles I and VI of the 1965 Elementary and Secondary Education Act. My students come from several public and private school Kindergartens. They are Kindergarten failures for a variety of reasons: they do not learn in a standard classroom setting, they may

*The children's names in this essay have all been changed in order to protect the identity of the individuals.

have developmental lags which cause "learning problems," or they display emotional upset, physical handicaps, brain damage or mental retardation.

Until the start of this program, excluded children were kept home for a year. Often they went back the next year still unable to fit in and "adjust themselves" to the school curriculum. The result was that at eight years of age they were already turned off to school through continued failure, frustration, and repeated exclusions and they still displayed the original learning problems often complicated by their situation. Now they could be placed in a special class for slow learning children. By this time, the children are behind, yet may not be "slow learners" by nature. Valuable years for intervention therapy in learning are wasted in this way.

The school where I teach has two buildings. The newer building is the main structure, containing offices and regular classrooms. The other used to be the school several years ago but is now designated as "the Annex." The Annex is referred to by most students at the school as the "dumb building." It contains all the special classes; two upper and one intermediate, and pre-primary. Morale among the teachers in the Annex is low. Communication between pre-primary and the "new" school is minimal. When the doctor examined one of my pre-primary children she commented to the assistant principal on the child's ability to read and draw so perceptively in spite of severe cataracts. "I don't know much about those children," he replied, "we just house them here."

What are the children like? First of all, they're children, and like all children they have as their main occupation the task of understanding their world. They are thinking, feeling individuals who do learn, though often with interference. Or they learn the wrong things and then must go through a more complicated process of unlearning and relearning correctly.

Sammy Turner has been in Pre-primary since the center's inception in April, 1969. When he first entered he was uncommunicative and sad. At five, he had a wizened face and stooped shoulders, wistful blue eyes and blond hair which was usually shaved every time it dared start to curl.

Sammy is moderately neglected and sometimes abused at home. Home is at best chaotic, definitely not secure and often not a safe place to be. His father is in jail and his stepfather has presented a fear and confusion to Sammy about himself. When someone asked his name, Sammy would shout, "Sam." If further questioned, "Sam, what?" he would lower his head and voice and whisper "Sam Arthur." To "Sam Arthur, what?" he would close his eyes as if to its reality and in a barely audible voice whisper "Turner." Sometimes he would come up to me and say ruefully, "My mother's name is Alver, my little brother's name is Alver, and my sister's name is Alver." Again, down to his chest his head would bow, and in a resigned but shamed voice he'd finish "but I'm a Turner."

Sammy had been in Pre-primary about a month when I suspected he might not hear well. It took several months to set up a hearing test at school, and when he was examined the results were inconclusive. Around this time a circus was in town. My assistant and I took several children to an evening performance, since it was not a school function. Sammy was sitting on my lap. I whispered something in his right ear about the tight rope walker. He jerked around and in an exasperated voice said "Not that ear. I can't hear you in there. Tell me in the other one!"

I called Sammy's mother to tell her that my suspicions about his hearing seemed well-founded. She could recall several incidents which may have caused the loss. His father had mistreated him when he was a baby—he'd dropped him on his head, stuck small objects into his ears and treated him generally in a rough manner. When he was not quite three, he'd fallen and banged his head, causing his ear to bleed. "But," his mother went on, "I never figured he was deaf. He gets the strap when it seems like he doesn't listen to us."

It took six months from the time of this initial discovery before Sammy was finally taken to an ear specialist, and it took another two months after he had been diagnosed as totally deaf in one ear and partially deaf in the other before a hearing aid was prescribed. During the examination, it was determined that he also needed glasses, so the aid was attached to his frames. It was hard for Sammy to get accustomed to the new addition to his face. He kept taking his glasses off and "forgetting" them. During a home visit one Monday I found that he wasn't wearing his glasses at all, except during schooltime, to "save the batteries from wearing out." No wonder Sammy could not adjust to the glasses and aid properly; he was not wearing them often enough.

I explained to his mother that taking the glasses away from Sammy was like taking away his eyes and ears, leaving him in a blurred and confusing world. She said she couldn't help it; the batteries were supplied by the welfare department. "They give me just so many a month, but if I let him wear them all day, the batteries are used up in less than two weeks. So I save them so at least he'll have them at school." A call to the welfare department in January by the Title I Speech Therapist resulted in a promise to supply more batteries. To date this promise has not been fulfilled.

Sammy's relationship with the other children was a tentative one. During self-chosen periods of activity he would run up to one child after another and push them, poke, shove and tease them as his main method of communication. Then one day in the middle of a story, Sam pulled a button-on-a-string out of his pocket, shoved it around hurriedly at the other children and quickly stuck it back into his pocket. The other children were disconcerted, so, story temporarily interrupted, I asked Sammy to show us what he had. Slowly, head hanging, he produced the well worn button-on-a-string. Patiently, he showed how to make the button spin on the string. After he demonstrated this procedure he patiently showed each child how to do it, and without outside suggestion, allowed each child to have a turn. It was a very personal interaction between Sam and each child. When he'd finished, he put the home made toy safely away in his pocket. The other children made comments about how nice it was, or how much fun, and "thanks Sam, I like you."

Sam was so proud when he finished he burst into tears. It was hard for Sammy to express his feelings in words. He scorned attempts to talk about feelings as "sissy stuff." Yet a male volunteer in the class helped change Sam's attitude. Sam had never known a young man like the college student who came to be his good friend. At first Sam made fun of his friend's "weird pants" and "long hair." But Sam had never been told that his work was "really extraordinarily good" by a man before. And he'd never had a grown male admire even his tries at things, as well as his successes. With the help of this friend, Sam began to express himself through his paintings. With all eight basic tempora colors and a large easel Sammy could paint happy or sad. Sometimes he'd paint "tough, mad" pictures and on in-between days his paintings were "sleepy." One day he painted a nightmare in black and brown, with a big red splotch in the center. He flicked white droplets of paint from his brush onto the finished picture and as they dripped down the paper he described them as "those tears I wanted to cry in my dream, but couldn't." Gradually, Sammy became the most eloquent spokesman of feelings. One day during a group discussion Sammy told about holding his genitals at night. "When I'm afraid, and I touch me, I'm not afraid no more."

After he'd had his hearing aid and glasses a few months he began to grow at a mental age twice that of normal chronological growth. He had a lot of catching up to do. He is learning rapidly and with the additional strength of his newly developed sensitivity. After he began to recognize that letters make words, he joined the few others in the class who were also learning to read by making their own word cards. This rough-and-tumble, overactive and aggressive child's words the first week, which he thought up himself, spelled out and wrote down were: flowers, pineapple, butterfly, and grass. He is going to the first grade in September. Hopefully he will be able to continue to develop all facets of himself.

Rebecca Finch spends a good part of her mornings in the doll corner. She is role playing. Sometimes she takes the part of mommy and daddy and child simultaneously. She acts out her frightened, distorted world dramatically and by storytelling. "I'll tell you a story," she'll whisper to my assistant or to me. That's a signal that something is disturbing her. The stories usually deal with death and sickness. She told me about her uncle Herman and her grandmother's death.

When she came into the program Becky could not take alternating steps up and down stairs. She also could not take the last step from stair to floor. The change from steps to a flat surface threw off her sense of balance. It took many trials from carrying her off the step, to her stepping down while holding on to my hands, to stepping without assistance. She had a poor spatial orientation signified by excessive fear of falling. Even as she walked across the room, she kept her arms out like a tightrope walker trying to maintain her balance. She cried just watching other children turn somersaults on the mat. The slightest implication that she might try one herself caused her to panic and scream.

A shy child, Rebecca had a hard time reacting appropriately to the other children. She misinterpreted friendly gestures as threats. For example, once when Roderick Hamilton tried to help her put her jacket on as they were getting ready to go home, she began to struggle as if he were there to hurt her. Roderick did not talk at the time, so he tried to gesture what he wanted to do. Finally, he took her arm to stick it into the arm of the jacket. Becky fell to the floor crying that he broke her arm. Roderick stood bewildered for a minute, holding the jacket. Then he bleated his tongue at her, dropped the jacket and went to get his own coat from the hook.

I explained to a tearful Becky that he only meant to help her. "He didn't mean to hurt me, huh?" she asked, still crying. "No, he didn't know you were frightened when he touched you." "He didn't know I say he'd hurt me." "You thought he might hurt your arm when he touched it." "I thought he'd hurt me." "He was trying to help you put on your jacket." "He was going to help me, but it was an accident and I cried."

Becky could not stand to be touched. On rare occasions the teachers and volunteers could put a hand on her shoulder or touch her face. Usually this was when we were down at her eye level, and had been talking with her awhile. Sometimes while telling her stories she would sit on my lap. She had to be the one to initiate this. If I reached out to her it might frighten her into flailing her arms hysterically or running away. If this happened she would be furious and upset. It would take time and a good deal of talking to calm her down. If the behavior were ignored she would begin to grumble about what had happened and from there delve into many other subjects which frightened and upset her. She talked to no-one in particular, but just walked around, hands on hips, muttering. She rejected any suggestion to work with any materials. If guided to one, she would sit with it but still brood aloud. Usually I sat with her and reflected back on what she was saying.

Becky was disturbed by things that happened at home. Her mother had a habit of going back to bed after Becky went to school. Often times she would not hear the bus driver beep his horn as he brought her home at noon. The door would be locked and the driver would bring the terrified little girl back to school. "My mommy didn't come to the door," she cried. Sometimes she stayed until my afternoon class was nearly over before her mother or father would come to pick her up. Every day for months after she would ask, when getting ready to go home, "Will my mommy be there today?"

After she was brought back to school more than a dozen times, the police women's bureau was brought in on the case. Two policewomen spoke to Rebecca's parents. The child welfare department was notified of possible neglect but has not followed through. Unwashed and unkempt, Becky learned to wash her face and hands and arms at school. At one time, she had running sores on her arms and legs from not being kept clean. In the summer I washed her hair and tied it back in two pigtails. During the winter her hair, which was usually matted and disheveled, combed only lightly over the tangles, was a source of discomfort and upset to her. She kept pulling on it and hitting the back of her head. She allowed me to look at it and touch it, and with a shock I realized that at the nape of her neck were two balls of matted, sticky braid. The braids I had made during the summer had never been taken out!

Becky's progress at school, despite these emotional factors, has been steady. She has gained enough motor balance to run and attempt to skip. She does her work slowly, almost as if in slow motion. She needs lots of reassurance. She is sometimes fearful of attempting to do something new. She'll try to avoid it by saying it's silly, or she can't do it because it will hurt her. Often with repeated directions or a demonstration, and enough time to work at her own pace she can and does finish many projects and attempted tasks. She will need further help in handling her fears. Thus, though she is intellectually ready for first grade she will attend a class for emotionally disturbed children next fall, if her parents consent to it.

Tommy Bennett is fascinated by the force of the small magnet attached to a string. He goes fishing all over the room to see what he can "catch." He is a handsome child with curly hair, large bright brown eyes and a clear complexion. It was not always so. In the program for a year and a half, Tommy has been transformed in front of my eyes. There is no other way to describe him, but to contrast him then to what he is now.

In December 1969, Tommy's face and neck and arms were covered with scratch marks inflicted by himself. He would also bite himself, pinch himself black and blue, flip over backwards and run into walls. He seemed off in another world much of the time. He could sit immobile and silent for hours at a time. He was unaware of other people around him. He would respond to situations which did not occur, except inside himself, and react inappropriately to that which did happen. He might laugh hysterically or cry pathetically while sitting alone on the floor. He remained passive and unresponsive to an invitation to play.

I spent a good deal of time trying to establish any kind of relationship with Tommy. Down on the floor beside him I would talk and talk to him. He sat gazing innocently about, as if unaware of my presence. Sometimes he smiled very briefly, but not in response to anything I said. He had one toy down on the floor with him; a small blue car. He would push it back and forth tirelessly. The only life he seemed to notice was that of insects. He caught a fly once, held it and examined it and let it go. He caught it again later and repeated the examination, laughing. He tried flying occasionally, taking off from his position of half-sitting, half-laying on the floor. Arms spread like wings, he would flit here and there, then "land" again back in his spot and resume his still and silent position. Down on the floor beside him I talked about the parts of his body. I pointed to my own eyes and ears and touched his. Sometimes another child would come over and join us, and show that he, too, had those body parts.

After he was in the class for about two weeks, Tommy flew over to me and let his fingers gently pass over me. It was as if he were touching a piece of furniture absent-mindedly as he went past. But later, down on the floor, he reached up and took my face very briefly between his two hands. His eyes, which rarely focused on one object, looked directly into mine. Then he flitted away like a butterfly and landed six feet or so from me. Later as he was standing outside at the sink washing his hands I heard him giggle. I looked out and as the water ran over his outstretched hands he wiggled his fingers, saying, "fin-gers." Then he laughed and wiggled them more. "Fin-gers. Fingers!" That was the beginning. He started touching me oftener. We compared hands and feet and heads and hair. He liked to play with my hair. He would spread it out from my ears and watch it fall back against them. A few weeks later a college student volunteering in the class was able to develop a close relationship with him, too. He had started using words, and he called her extra long hair her "wings."

Tommy became very affectionate over a long period of time. He was ecstatic over close physical contact. He would open his arms and say "Pi' u' me." (Pick up me.) When held, he would feel my eyes and nose and ears and mouth and neck, and stroke my hair. Then he'd laugh, and this time I could share his laughter.

Soon after he began relating to people as people, he started having temper tantrums. He would fall off his chair as if he had suddenly lost his skeletal support. Thrashing around on the floor, he shook his head, flapped his arms and screamed. We ignored this behavior except to be sure he didn't hurt himself. After trying unsuccessfully to get our attention this way, he'd creep bonelessly around on the floor a few minutes, then slink back into his chair. It was a cue that he needed extra support and encouragement. We tried to show him in other ways that we recognized his needs and feelings rather than by responding to these outbursts.

He identified strongly with others now, and began to react to their experiences as if they were his own. Yet he was often unable to feel things or recognize incidents that happened to him. For example, another child bumped her eye, and Tommy, seeing this, went around for a good two weeks with his hand over his own eye. He cried, "my eh, my eh," blinking it and rubbing it in comic exaggeration.

Another time a classmate came in with a new pair of shoes. Tommy showed everyone *his* new "soos." He pushed and patted at them, and spit on them to make them shine, although the soles were flapping. When he received new tennis shoes for school, it had to be pointed out that these were indeed his new shoes, and didn't they look nice. He would respond "yeah" and forget about them until about the fourth day of being reminded they were his, they were new, they were nice. Then he began showing off his new "tenny soos." But it was exciting to see him do it, because it showed an awareness of others and their activities he had never shown before. He was beginning to see himself in relation to other people. Tommy's favorite part of the morning was snack. He was not yet ready for other activities—if asked to sit with the group for story or music he would fall on the floor or pretend to be hurt. He'd wait for a chance to escape and run or "fly" away. If this didn't work, he might try laughing loudly, waving his arms, or babbling incoherently.

Tommy really responded to any request immediately before snack. After refreshments were over with, so was Tommy's day. He just went back to the floor and pushed his car. One day I asked him if he would play some "candy games" with me. He came readily. I used m & m's as an immediate reward to his responses as I showed him a series of picture cards and asked him to identify them. From there we went to colors, and shapes, and counting. He worked patiently up to twenty minutes a sitting or as long as the m & m's held out. Then we changed to jelly beans. I didn't give out as many since they were bigger than the m & m's, so he had to do a little more to earn one. He cut and pasted, colored and painted, learned names of things, made popsicle stick triangles and frosting for a cake. All with one eye on the "j.b.'s," as he called them.

From there he graduated to cookies. If he could sing songs with the other children he could have a cookie. If he watched the film-strip story and could remember what it was about, enough to tell me after, he could have a cookie. It was bribery of sorts, yes. But that's the idea behind stimulus-response theory, and the basis of behavior modification. I don't recommend it as a method applicable to all children, yet in cases like Tommy's, where ego strength is minimal, it was an important motivational technique. At the same time I gave him the cookies I gave him verbal praise and encouragement which I gradually substituted more and more for the sweet rewards. But praise was not sufficient until it became more meaningful to him than the sweets. When it did it was supplied in large measure.

Tommy is at the point now where he does not need a cookie or candy as a reinforcement. He still enjoys snack, but during the rest of the morning he is motivated more from his own satisfaction at doing his work well than for any other reason, including praise. Yet he still requires a large amount of verbal recognition and if he feels he is not receiving his share he'll burst out, "teacher, you don' li' me." Usually a hug or a pat from me is what he wants. Sometimes a smile is enough. He'll catch it and smile back—and it really is enough. He can go on confidently. It's been nearly half a year since his scratching and biting went away. There's not a mark on him. He expresses anger sometimes by stamping his foot, but more often verbally. Once or twice he has cried in frustration. But he has found alternatives to frustration. He is able to ask another child to help him, or the teacher or assistant or volunteer tutor. Now more often, he finds he can handle it.

Postscript on Greenfield's Article by Jay Weinroth and Robert Elias Abu Shanab

The children who have been or are in the special class discussed here, and other children who are or have been in similar learning environments, are comparatively fortunate in their opportunities to enter such environments. It is ironic to call these children "fortunate," yet they are indeed fortunate in comparison with children who experience similar misfortunes and who are not able to enter classes like the one described here. For children unable to enter such a class, and for children who have passed the age limit for continued enrollment in the Kindergarten Exclusion program (eight years of age is the limit), what alternatives await? Our typical public school program has no place for and no interest in these children, because they cannot learn the three R's in the standard classroom context. They cannot sit quietly. They cannot recite. They cannot obey unquestioningly when told to put their heads down on their desks. They cannot restrain themselves from hitting out at teachers who browbeat them because they are different in a variety of ways.

One may wonder just what it is that children receive as benefits when they are able to fit into our standard public school context and remain there for twelve or thirteen years. Judging from a recent Presidential Commission's report on education in the U.S., there is not much that is missed by not going through these twelve or thirteen years. However, for children who cannot manage to remain in the standard educational context, the most likely alternative is apparently that they will be placed in some other institutional context where they are treated as mentally retarded. Unless parents are wealthy and enlightened enough to find a good therapeutic or learning environment for their child, the child in our society is most often presented with the limited alternatives of thirteen years of obedience and boredom or else with quasi-imprisonment in some institution. This is the situation in a society which has split the atom, placed men on the moon, transplanted human hearts, and spent hundreds of billions in dollars in the last two decades for military weapons and an undeclared war in Southeast Asia.

At the same time, most of what the teacher and assistants have been doing in this special class would seem to be the kind of thing that ought to be done with children who do *not* have special problems. If these children with special problems were able to remain in this sort of learning/therapy context for as long a time as they need to remain there, would they not probably emerge as better able to live creative lives than the child who enters the standard public school with no special handicaps and emerges with a life-orientation of boredom and disinterest? Dare we hope that in the future we may see the spread of humanistic, freedom oriented attitudes toward children, that our society will use its vast resources to provide ample learning/therapy environments for all children?

Freedom and Learning: The Need for Choice

The belief that a highly industrialized society requires twelve to twenty years of prior processing of the young is an illusion or a hoax. The evidence is strong that there is no correlation between school performance and life achievement in any of the professions, whether medicine, law, engineering, journalism, or business. Moreover, recent research shows that for more modest clerical, technological, or semi-skilled factory jobs there is no advantage in years of schooling or the possession of diplomas. We were not exactly savages in 1900 when only 6 per cent of adolescents graduated from high school.

Whatever the deliberate intention, schooling today serves mainly for policing and for taking up the slack in youth unemployment. It is not surprising that the young are finally rebelling against it, especially since they cannot identify with the goals of so much social engineering —for instance, that 86 per cent of the federal budget for research and development is for military purposes.

We can, I believe, educate the young entirely in terms of their free choice, with no processing whatever. Nothing can be efficiently learned, or, indeed, learned at all—other than through parroting or brute training, when acquired knowledge is promptly forgotten after the examination—unless it meets need, desire, curiosity, or fantasy. Unless there is a reaching from within, the learning cannot become "second nature," as Aristotle called true learning. It seems stupid to decide a priori what the young ought to know and then to try to motivate them, instead of letting the initiative come from them and putting information and relevant equipment at their service. It is false to assert that this kind of freedom will not serve society's needs—at least those needs that should humanly be served; freedom is the only way toward authentic citizenship and real, rather than verbal, philosophy. Free choice is not random but responsive to real situations; both youth and adults live in a nature of things, a polity, an ongoing society, and it is

65

these, in fact, that attract interest and channel need. If the young, as they mature, can follow their bent and choose their topics, times, and teachers, and if teachers teach what they themselves consider important—which is all they can skillfully teach anyway—the needs of society will be adequately met; there will be more lively, independent, and inventive people; and in the fairly short run there will be a more sensible and efficient society.

It is not necessary to argue for free choice as a metaphysical proposition; it is what is indicated by present conditions. Increasingly, the best young people resolutely resist authority, and we will let them have a say or lose them. And more important, since the conditions of modern social and technological organization are so pervasively and rigidly conforming, it is necessary, in order to maintain human initiative, to put our emphasis on protecting the young from top-down direction. The monkish and academic methods which were civilizing for wild shepherds create robots in a period of high technology. The public schools which did a good job of socializing immigrants in an open society now regiment individuals and rigidify class stratification.

Up to age twelve, there is no point to formal subjects or a prearranged curriculum. With guidance, whatever a child experiences is educational. Dewey's idea is a good one: It makes no difference *what* is learned at this age, so long as the child goes on wanting to learn something further. Teachers for this age are those who like children, pay attention to them, answer their questions, enjoy taking them around the city and helping them explore, imitate, try out, and who sing songs with them and teach them games. Any benevolent grownup—literate or illiterate—has plenty to teach an eight-year-old; the only profitable training for teachers is a group therapy and, perhaps, a course in child development.

We see that infants learn to speak in their own way in an environment where there is speaking and where they are addressed and take part. If we tried to teach children to speak according to our own theories and methods and schedules, as we try to teach reading, there would be as many stammerers as there are bad readers. Besides, it has been shown that whatever is useful in the present eight-year elementary curriculum can be learned in four months by a normal child of twelve. If let alone, in fact, he will have learned most of it by himself.

Since we have communities where people do not attend to the children as a matter of course, and since children must be rescued from their homes, for most of these children there should be some kind of school. In a proposal for mini-schools in New York City, I suggested an elementary group of twenty-eight children with four grownups: a licensed teacher, a housewife who can cook, a college senior, and a teen-age school dropout. Such a group can meet in any store front, church basement, settlement house, or housing project; more important, it can often go about the city, as is possible when the student-teacher ratio is 7 to 1. Experience at the First Street School in New York has shown that the cost for such a little school is less than for the public school with a student-teacher ratio of 30 to 1. (In the public system, most of the money goes for administration and for specialists to remedy the lack of contact in the classroom.) As A. S. Neill has shown, attendance need not be compulsory. The school should be located near home so the children can escape from it to home, and from home to it. The school should be supported by public money but administered entirely by its own children, teachers, and parents.

In the adolescent and college years, the present mania is to keep students at their lessons for another four to ten years as the only way of their growing up in the world. The correct policy would be to open as many diverse paths as possible, with plenty of opportunity to backtrack and change. It is said by James Conant that about 15 per cent learn well by books and study in an academic setting, and these can opt for high school. Most, including most of the bright students, do better either on their own or as apprentices in activities that are for keeps, rather than through lessons. If their previous eight years had been spent in exploring their own bents and interests, rather than being continually interrupted to do others' assignments on others' schedules, most adolescents would have a clearer notion of what they are after, and many would have found their vocations.

For the 15 per cent of adolescents who learn well in schools and are interested in subjects that are essentially academic, the present catch-all high schools are wasteful. We would do better to return to the small preparatory academy, with perhaps sixty students and three teachers—one in physical sciences, one in social sciences, one in humanities—to prepare for college board examinations. An academy could be located in, and administered by, a university and staffed by graduate students who like to teach and in this way might earn stipends while they write their theses. In such a setting, without dilution by nonacademic subjects and a mass of uninterested fellow students, an academic adolescent can, by spending three hours a day in the classroom, easily be prepared in three or four years for college.

Forcing the nonacademic to attend school breaks the spirit of most and foments alienation in the best. Kept in tutelage, young people, who are necessarily economically dependent, cannot pursue the sexual, adventurous, and political activities congenial to them. Since lively youngsters insist on these anyway, the effect of what we do is to create a gap between them and the oppressive adult world, with a youth subculture and an arrested development.

School methods are simply not competent to teach all the arts, sciences, professions, and skills the school establishment pretends to teach. For some professions—e.g., social work, architecture, pedagogy —trying to earn academic credits is probably harmful because it is an irrelevant and discouraging obstacle course. Most technological know-how has to be learned in actual practice in offices and factories, and this often involves unlearning what has been laboriously crammed for exams. The technical competence required by skilled and semiskilled workmen and average technicians can be acquired in three weeks to a year on the job, with no previous schooling. The importance of even "functional literacy" is much exaggerated; it is the attitude, and not the reading ability, that counts. Those who are creative in the arts and sciences almost invariably go their own course and are usually hampered by schools. Modern languages are best learned by travel. It is pointless to teach social sciences, literary criticism, and philosophy to youngsters who have had no responsible experience in life and society.

Most of the money now spent for high schools and colleges should be devoted to the support of apprenticeships; travel; subsidized browsing in libraries and self-directed study and research; programs such as VISTA, the Peace Corps, Students for a Democratic Society, or the Student Nonviolent Coordinating Committee; rural reconstruction; and work camps for projects in conservation and urban renewal. It is a vast sum of money—but it costs almost $1,500 a year to keep a youth in a blackboard jungle in New York; the schools have become one of our major industries. Consider one kind of opportunity. Since it is important for the very existence of the republic to countervail the now over-whelming national corporate style of information, entertainment, and research, we need scores of thousands of small independent television stations, community radio stations, local newspapers that are more than gossip notes and ads, community theaters, high-brow or dissenting magazines, small design offices for neighborhood renewal that is not bureaucratized, small laboratories for science and invention that are not centrally directed. Such enterprises could present admirable opportunities for bright but unacademic young people to serve as apprentices.

Ideally, the polis itself is the educational environment; a good community consists of worthwhile, attractive, and fulfilling callings and things to do, to grow up into. The policy I am proposing tends in this direction rather than away from it. By multiplying options, it should be possible to find an interesting course for each individual youth, as we now do for only some of the emotionally disturbed and the troublemakers. Voluntary adolescent choices are often random and foolish and usually transitory; but they are the likeliest ways of growing up reasonably. What is most essential is for the youth to see that he is taken seriously as a person, rather than fitted into an institutional system. I don't know if this tailor-made approach would be harder or easier to administer than standardization that in fact fits nobody and results in an increasing number of recalcitrants. On the other hand, as the Civilian Conservation Corps showed in the Thirties, the products of willing youth labor can be valuable even economically, whereas accumulating Regents blue-books is worth nothing except to the school itself.

(By and large, it is not in the adolescent years but in later years that, in all walks of life, there is need for academic withdrawal, periods of study and reflection, synoptic review of the texts. The Greeks understood this and regarded most of our present college curricula as appropriate for only those over the age of thirty or thirty-five. To some extent, the churches used to provide a studious environment. We do these things miserably in hurried conferences.)

We have similar problems in the universities. We cram the young with what they do not want at the time and what most of them will never use; but by requiring graded diplomas we make it hard for older people to get what they want and can use. Now, paradoxically, when so many are going to school, the training of authentic learned professionals is proving to be a failure, with dire effects on our ecology, urbanism, polity, communications, and even the direction of science. Doing others' lessons under compulsion for twenty years does not tend to produce professionals who are autonomous, principled, and ethically responsible to client and community. Broken by processing, professionals degenerate to mere professional personnel. Professional peer groups have become economic lobbies. The licensing and maintenance of standards have been increasingly relinquished to the state, which has no competence.

In licensing professionals, we have to look more realistically at functions, drop mandarin requirements of academic diplomas that are irrelevant, and rid ourselves of the ridiculous fad of awarding diplomas for every skill and trade whatever. In most professions and arts there are important abstract parts that can best be learned academically. The natural procedure is for those actually engaged in a professional activity to go to school to learn what they now know they need; re-entry into the academic track, therefore, should be made easy for those with a strong motive.

Universities are primarily schools of learned professions, and the faculty should be composed primarily not of academics but of working professionals who feel duty-bound and attracted to pass on their tradition to apprentices of a new generation. Being combined in a community of scholars, such professionals teach a noble apprenticeship, humane and with vision toward a more ideal future. It is humane because the disciplines communicate with one another; it is ideal because the young are free and questioning. A good professional school can be tiny. In *The Community of Scholars* I suggest that 150 students and ten professionals—the size of the usual medieval university—are enough. At current faculty salaries, the cost per student would be a fourth of that of our huge administrative machines. And, of course, on such a small scale contact between faculty and students is sought for and easy.

Today, because of the proved incompetence of our adult institutions and the hypocrisy of most professionals, university students have a right to a large say in what goes on. (But this, too, is medieval.) Professors will, of course, teach what they please. My advice to students is that given by Prince Kropotkin, in "A Letter to the Young": "Ask what kind of world do you want to live in? What are you good at and want to work at to build that world? What do you need to know? Demand that your teachers teach you that." Serious teachers would be delighted by this approach.

The idea of the liberal arts college is a beautiful one: to teach the common culture and refine character and citizenship. But it does not happen; the evidence is that the college curriculum has little effect on underlying attitudes, and most cultivated folk do not become so by this route. School friendships and the community of youth do have lasting effects, but these do not require ivied clubhouses. Young men learn more about the theory and practice of government by resisting the draft than they ever learned in Political Science 412.

Much of the present university expansion, needless to say, consists in federal-and-corporation-contracted research and other research and has nothing to do with teaching. Surely such expansion can be better carried on in the Government's and corporations' own institutes, which would be unencumbered by the young, except those who are hired or attach themselves as apprentices.

Every part of education can be open to need, desire, choice, and trying out. Nothing needs to be compelled or extrinsically motivated by prizes and threats. I do not know if the procedure here outlined would cost more than our present system—though it is hard to conceive of a need for more money than the school establishment now spends. What would be saved is the pitiful waste of youthful years—caged, daydreaming, sabotaging, and cheating—and the degrading and insulting misuse of teachers.

It has been estimated by James Coleman that the average youth in high school is really "there" about ten minutes a day. Since the growing-up of the young into society to be useful to themselves and others, and to do God's work, is one of the three or four most important functions of any society, no doubt we ought to spend even more on the education of the young than we do; but I would not give a penny to the present administrators, and I would largely dismantle the present school machinery.

The Closed Corporation

THE MACHINE

"The function of college is not to prepare you for life," the philosopher Paul Weiss said. "It is to prepare you to be a man, and when you are a man you can face life, whatever the conditions."

In all likelihood most Americans believe, like Weiss, that universities are places where professors teach students. They are wrong. In fact, the university looks more like a center for industrial activity than a community of scholars.

The general citizenry may be surprised to learn that they pay such high prices for medicines partly because the universities ganged together and lobbied Congress in behalf of the drug companies; that the professor of medieval history at Princeton University runs from his classes to the Central Intelligence Agency, where he helps straighten out the spies; and that Yale University hawks about a mutual fund.

In the *Notes on the Post Industrial State,* Daniel Bell makes it plain enough: "The university, which is the place where theoretical knowledge is sought, tested and codified in a disinterested way, becomes the primary institution of the new society. Perhaps it is not too much to say that if the business firm was the key institution of the past one hundred years because of its role in organizing production for the mass creation of products, the university will become the central institution of the next hundred years because of its role as the new source of innovation and knowledge."

This book is an inquiry into the different sorts of relationships universities and professors have with the rest of society, carried forward in large part to find out what their impact is and whether there is anything to the notion that the university is central to industrial activity.

The university industry basically consists of 2200 institutions, with total annual revenues of $10 billion and a growth rate of some 10 percent. The business employs half a million people as instructors, and holds 6.7 million students. The shape of the industry changes, depending as it does on the shifting alliances with government, which supplies much of the money for research, and on business, which makes the products resulting from the research.

It is difficult to gain any clear understanding of the university because it remains as one of the few large secret organizations within the nation. One can find out more about the activities of a public corporation than about a university. The trustees of private universities are invariably self-perpetuating bodies of businessmen who meet in private and do not publish accounts of their activities. In public institutions, where there are more apt to be periodic open meetings of the regents and trustees who are elected or appointed by the state governor, the real business goes on behind the scenes in executive sessions, and the minutes of these back-room deals are either nonexistent or never made public. Institutions of higher learning are tax exempt, yet unlike the foundations which enjoy the same status but are required by the Internal Revenue Service to make public certain financial information, universities are not subject to such provisions. And so far as the private colleges are concerned, the government allows them to operate in total secrecy if they desire. Many of the large private universities do publish financial reports to reassure their alumni, but this is not a standard practice. Columbia University will make available on request a list of its securities investments but refuses to disclose real estate holdings, a delicate matter since some of them are located in slum areas. The University of Chicago will not disclose any of its investments. Even though Long Island University, a private university, is chartered by the state of New York and numbers among its trustees a U.S. congressman, Ogden Reid, it refused to provide a financial report to a state legislative committee investigating its activities. The University of California, a public institution—the largest university in the world—with a budget of nearly $1 billion, steadfastly refused to disclose its holdings, and even the members of the regents committee which invests the money have expressed their ignorance of where it goes. At the University of Maryland the budget is figured with the administration by a planning bureau, which will not even make known the full details to different academic departments, on the general theory that if one department doesn't know what the others are getting, it won't be likely to argue about the course of university expansion.

While it is usual to distinguish between private and public universities, this can be misleading. Two thirds of American students go to public institutions, and the government spends large amounts of money in both types of schools, so much so that Clark Kerr, former president of the University of California, calls the modern university the "Federal Grant University."

In the Northwest Ordinance of 1787, the federal government set forth its intention of encouraging education, but as a practical matter this meant little until the passage of the Morrill Act of 1862 and subsequent legislation which provided land for public institutions and funds for instruction in agriculture. This led to the establishment of university-operated agricultural extension programs and farm experiment stations. In World War I the government spent a little money at universities for research in improving aircraft and established the ROTC programs for training officers. By the 1930's it was spending money for research in cancer through the creation of the National Cancer Institute. During the depression the universities assisted the government with New Deal public-works measures.

The U.S. government's involvement with the universities had a distinctly utilitarian bent, tied for the most part to industrial or military ends; by contrast, the European universities had become research centers. Consequently, many of the great scientists in the United States during the early part of the century were schooled abroad. Because of the demands of the second world war, the scientists and the military formed a working partnership which resulted first in dramatic scientific breakthroughs leading to the atomic bomb, and subsequently widened into the present pervasive relationship between government and all segments of the Academic Community.

The first controlled chain reaction which led to the development of the atomic bomb was achieved in laboratories at the University of Chicago. Johns Hopkins ran the Applied Physics Laboratory which developed the self-deteriorating proximity fuse. The Radiation Laboratory at MIT was the main center for radar research. During the period of the cold war the ties between university scientists and the government broadened and solidified. Many of the studies which led to the development of the hydrogen bomb were made by university scientists who spent their summers at Los Alamos; the father of the bomb, Edward Teller, of course, is from the University of California. The Lincoln Labs at MIT carried forward work on radar defense warning systems, as well as on missile guidance systems. The Jason Division of the Institute for Defense Analysis, a think tank run for the Defense Department by twelve universities, made studies for the military on missile re-entry problems, counter-insurgency and tactical uses of nuclear warfare in Southeast Asia. Professors at Harvard and MIT worked on building clever communications systems for the military, and others worked secretly during the summers on breaking codes. It was during the 1950's that the CIA began its covert financing through universities. It was interested in building up anti-communist student movements at home and creating anti-communist labor unions abroad.

Today more than two thirds of the university research funds come from the Department of Defense, the Atomic Energy Commission or the National Aeronautics and Space Administration, all closely concerned with defense matters. Much of this money is channeled to a small number of well-known universities. A congressional study in 1964 indicated that of 2100 universities, ten received 38 percent of the federal funds for research and development. (They are the University of California, MIT, Cornell, Columbia, University of Michigan, Harvard, Illinois, Stanford, Chicago and Minnesota.) This money often accounts for large portions of the universities' total budgets. Thus, 80 percent of MIT's funds are estimated to come from the government; Columbia and Princeton get about 50 percent of their money from Washington. In addition, there has been widespread covert funding by the CIA of university projects through front foundations.

The universities' growing liaison with the defense agencies over the past decade has coincided with the expanding importance of the Defense Department, which under Robert McNamara wandered rather far afield from military matters. The Defense Department, which bought the professors' expertise, helped shape the aerospace industry, then laid the groundwork for and supported the new education business. As a hedge against disarmament, the Defense Department encouraged the electronics firms which relied on it for business to get into other fields, one of which was to develop the computer for use in teaching children. The Defense planners also were leaders among those who pointed out that there might be businesses in slum rebuilding, water and air pollution abatement. The Defense Department helped write the poverty program, and when under the stewardship of Sargent Shriver it failed to meet expectations, McNamara sent along efficiency experts to restore order. McNamara's assistants were put in the Department of Health, Education and Welfare, where they remodeled it in imitation of the Pentagon. As they moved from one endeavor to the next, McNamara's staff towed along professors to add their expertise.

In a good many instances the liaisons between the defense agencies and the universities were accomplished through the federal contract research centers. There are forty-seven of them; the centers do $1.2 billion worth of research and development work annually, almost all of it sponsored by the Defense Department or the Atomic Energy Commission. Nearly half the money goes to centers managed by universities. The center idea has provided a convenient way for inveigling bright scientists into defense work. The government can pay the scientists higher wages by hiring them through universities, thereby getting around the civil service pay scales. As for the scientists themselves, they appear more distinguished to their colleagues as members of the faculty of some great university than if they were working on bomb sites in some dingy Pentagon office. And the centers give the universities a bit of prestige and a management fee. (Johns Hopkins gets $1 million annually in fees for administering the $50 million budget of the Applied Physics Laboratory.)

In theory, the government gets the best independent scientific advice in this manner, but in fact, what happens is that the major universities become first captive and then active advocates for the military and para-military agencies of government in order to get more money for research. This leads to bizarre situations; last spring Senator Fulbright, the chairman of the Senate Foreign Relations Committee, announced he had been denied certain information concerning the war in Vietnam, prepared for the Defense Department by the Institute for Defense Analysis, although the presidents of the sponsoring universities had access to it.

During the presidency of John Kennedy the Defense Department civilians were important in fashioning and implementing schemes for limited war and counter-insurgency, which resulted in the army's being viewed as an instrument of foreign policy in Southeast Asia and Latin America. Previously it had been widely assumed that the conduct of foreign affairs was the job of the State Department. Whereas during past wars the military relied on relatively straightforward methods of pitting armies against one another, during the Kennedy and early Johnson periods the civilians in the Defense Department got excited about the possibilities of using propaganda devices to manipulate the internal policies of foreign countries, and this in turn led to financing grandiose projects by university social scientists to study the behavior of the enemy, and involving foreign universities in the same work through grants. In 1968, the military will be spending approximately $50 million for projects related to developments in U.S. foreign policy. While there is some pressure within the Congress for stopping these projects, it is more likely that they will instead be expanded, for the social scientists have lately been smitten with what the Defense Department calls "Peacefare," ways of transposing the ideas and machinery employed by the military for civilian uses, such as counter-insurgency tactics in the ghetto, or teaching blacks to behave themselves by putting them all in the army, where, as Patrick Moynihan argues, they may learn a trade before being packed into a coffin in Vietnam.

It was through the Defense Department that the universities and business first worked together in consortia arrangements to develop complicated weapons systems. This troika arrangement is slowly evolving into a new sort of corporate machine, or more precisely, machine parts which engage or disengage depending on the job to be done. Basically, the parts consist of the university, where products or processes are conceived, the government, which finances their development, and private business, which makes and sells the finished item.

The emerging forms of corporate organization are very much in flux, but the professor entrepreneurs, who dart back and forth from university to government to business, help shape corporate structures and policies.

The theory is that the activities of the corporations can be planned and set in motion by scholars who scheme together at their innards. Other scholars within the government make sure the goals of production are worthy, and to control the activity of the corporations, they ring changes through the economic machinery, as, for example, in the late Senator Robert Kennedy's slum rehabilitation plan. Its central feature is to bring outside economic support into the ghetto and yet promote the illusion of black control. In fact, the control remains with the large corporations, which in return for widening their power base are slightly more beneficent, hiring some blacks but passing on the cost of the involvement to the consumers through higher prices.

So the scholars dash back and forth, building the new economic and political machinery. They see themselves as renaissance men, the proprietors of the new factories.

. . . .

CONCLUSION

The idea that the university is a community of scholars is a myth. The professors are less interested in teaching students than in yanking the levers of their new combines so that these machines will grow bigger and go faster. The university has in large part been reduced to serving as banker-broker for the professors' outside interests. The charming elitism of the professors has long since given way to the greed of the social and political scientists whose manipulative theories aim only at political power. Meanwhile the undergraduate students lie in campus holding pens, while graduate apprentices read them stories. The stories are boring, and students turn to making their own "free universities" or spend their time hatching political revolutions on the outside.

There are certain structural changes of a democratic bent that might assist universities in regaining the interest of their professors and students in education, and if some of these were taken up, then at least it would be possible to advantageously discuss the politics of these institutions.

The principle that should govern higher education, and all education in America, surely is simple enough: Since educational institutions are generally regarded as serving a public function, and financed to a large extent by the general citizenry, they ought to be responsible to the public. The different institutions should be run by students, teachers and administrators who are concerned with education. And they should be free to all.

This would require some changes in the manner in which these institutions now function. For one thing, no college or university whose members of its governing board are self-perpetuating should be eligible for public funding. Because of the present method of governing institutions of higher learning, there is an opportunity for a small group of men to use a university for their own ends. Since these institutions bear public responsibilities and receive much of their money from government they should be made responsible to the public and trustees should be elected—for terms of perhaps four to six years—by the students, alumni, faculty and other members of the immediate university community.

Trustees should not be selected because their private business interests may be useful to the college, but rather because of their views toward education. One way to move in this direction would be to prohibit members of the board of trustees from transacting any business with the university. Business dealings should be made at arm's length, and not by members of some club. To make it possible for younger people and poor people to become university trustees, there might well be a stipend for this work, and the trustees should have an expert staff so that, in fact, they can understand and intelligently criticize the work of the administration.

Meetings of the governing boards of a university should be public. So should the meetings of other groups whose decisions bear on the conduct of the university (i.e., faculty and student meetings). A reporter should be present during all of these gatherings, to make verbatim records, which can then be transcribed and published. In dealing with especially delicate matters, which would entail the trustees' holding executive sessions, the transcript of these sessions should receive timely publication. Disclosure is one way to protect the public's interests. If this sort of procedure had been in practice during Columbia's negotiations for the cigarette-filter patent, or during its land grab on 125th Street, there at least would have been a chance to alert people to what was going on. Surely these modest provisions should be in effect before any public official takes on the role of trustee in a private university. Among the trustees at Columbia is Frank Hogan, the district attorney of the City of New York, who in the case of the Piers renewal project placed himself in the position of being party to a real estate deal pending before New York City in behalf of a private corporation. He has no business being involved in such deals. Neither does Frederick Van Pelt Bryan, a federal district judge, who is also a trustee of Columbia University.

Moreover, the federal government should require all universities to issue publicly each quarter a detailed financial report, including an investment portfolio, showing any and all changes in holdings of securities, real estate and other types of investments. Each year the trustees and officers of universities should be required to furnish additional public statements that show their business affiliations, stock and property holdings. Harvard University's relations with the State Street Investment Corporation ought to be broken off, and so should all others like it. The Congress should block investment companies from profiting by combining their assets with those of tax-exempt educational institutions in seeking market leverage. Educational institutions are not meant to control industrial organizations. Yale University does not receive public funds to enhance its position as an educational institution so that it might better promote a mutual fund; its investment company should be disbanded. In general, McGeorge Bundy's proposal that the universities play the stocks more shrewdly is not wise, for the result is merely to involve them more intimately in the market, which in turn makes them more dependent on the profits of large companies and less inclined to criticize their activities.

University administrators, in particular their presidents, should be directed to run the affairs of the university; they are paid well to do so. They should be prohibited from sitting on the boards of directors of any company, foundation, government agency, or any other group. As Kingman Brewster observed, these relationships are more apt to raise competing interests and are a waste of time.

Professors are paid by the university to teach students, not to lobby. If they want to work for the CIA or some soap company, then they should quit and do so. If they enter into consulting arrangements with government or business, these should be disclosed, along with the fee, if one is paid.

As for professors who have articles published in university publications, law journals and reviews, Justice William O. Douglas suggests, "I propose an editorial policy that puts in footnote number one the relevant affiliations of the author. If the article is paid for, I would not necessarily require the disclosure of the amount of the fee; the fact that there was a fee would be sufficient. If there is no fee, but a client's interest was reflected in the article, I would want disclosure of that client's identity. If the author was a free-lancer in a particular field, I would want a general statement that his professional interest lay in the direction of certain types of litigation."

While the members of the Congress may consider it a matter of amusement that this or that professor appears before them without disclosing that he has in fact been retained by some company or other interested party, this should not be taken lightly. The testimony is often printed and distributed around the country and may well mislead public opinion. It should be made doubly clear to witnesses before the Congress that they must disclose any connection with the matter at hand.

The undergraduate students, who now have little or no say in how the university should be run, would, as suggested above, be included in the community that selects the governors. They might also insist on granting bodies of student government the veto power over major university decisions, such as admissions and finances. The typical argument against giving students a voice in running a university is that they are transient and young. In fact, they are no more transient than a member of the House of Representatives, who serves a two-year term. As for their youth, it was the students, not the faculty or administrators, who raised and kept after the war research issue. What is unusual about the student revolts is that the undergraduates have displayed so much interest in attempting to get the universities back to teaching. When one considers that all they got for their trouble was the creation, one after the other, of deadly independent investigatcry commissions controlled by the faculty proprietors and headed by labor mediators, their patience and good sense seem extraordinary.

Prying open the universities by changing around their organizational framework does not necessarily mean that their politics will also change. It is often dimly understood by the administrators of these places that the radicals who demand more of a say for the students are not representative of the great mass of undergraduates, many of whom are conservative. Nonetheless, at the very least a change in structure opens the possibility of influencing the shape of the policies through a democratic process, and the students will be a little better off for knowing a bit more about the operations of the institutions.

One may hope that the country will pursue the idea that a university is a place where great teachers and students are brought together. It doesn't really matter whether this occurs on the campus of some quaint Ivy League college or in the streets of Harlem, and surely the impedimenta which are used by the faculty guilds to stifle decent teachers ought to be done away with. What difference does it make whether the instructor has a degree, or how many books and honors he has to his name? It really is not especially important whether the student comes along for two or four or six years, or whether he gets a diploma, or for that matter whether he meets the entrance standards some psychologist has laid out for him to meet. One of the most useful endeavors in higher education would be to get rid of the bachelor's degree entirely, thereby doing away with a false admissions slip into the upper middle classes, and into the dreary academic guilds.

Secret research, whether it is performed as proprietary work for a company or the government, has no place in a university. It stands between the institution and a free society. This is not to say that the universities should not undertake controversial projects. People might now be alive had Cornell used its information about cars to challenge large corporations, rather than lying down meekly before the automobile makers and taking their money in exchange for silence.

In the case of the large city universities, it may well prove useful for the residents of the neighborhoods in which they exist to view these institutions for what they are, sort of de facto governments; and in exchange for suffering their presence, wring some concessions. The deals will differ depending on the locale. But it may make good sense for the residents of Hyde Park in Chicago or Morningside Heights in New York to insist on electing the presidents, respectively, of the University of Chicago and Columbia. They may also want guarantees of certain unskilled jobs, including those in the social science research projects, and receive free college education for their children. In the case of the University of Chicago, Columbia, Harvard or MIT, this would mean that the professors would find it necessary to spend a certain amount of their time in the streets teaching ignorant people. But this wouldn't hurt them. In recent years the clergy has found it a bracing experience to rediscover the parish, and the teacher may find it equally refreshing to meet some students.

The Student Movement*

GROWING OPPOSITION TO STUDENT ACTIVISM

The student movement today is the one organized, significant segment of the intellectual community that has a real and active commitment to the kind of social change that our society desperately needs. Developments now taking place may lead to its destruction, in part through repression, in part through what I think are rather foolish tactics on the part of the student movement itself. I think this would be a great, perhaps irreparable, loss. And I think if it does take place the blame will largely fall on the liberal enlightened community that has permitted a situation to arise in which the most committed, sincere, and most socially active of young people are perhaps working themselves into a position at the end of a limb, from which they may be sawed off at great cost to all of us and to society as a whole.

One development that makes me feel that this matter is of crucial importance right now is the rise on the campuses of a growing movement that I think is quite ill-conceived and that may lead to repression of student activism and destruction of what I deem the few possibilities for significant social change. I have in mind a letter (which I did not receive, though a number of my colleagues did) from the Coordinating Center for Democratic Opinion headed by Sidney Hook and a number of other people. [The organization is now called University Centers for Rational Alternatives.] The letter calls upon people to join this organization, the goals of which "will be to defend academic freedom against extremism, to promote the activism of nonextremists in all aspects of civic affairs, to foster rational treatment of contemporary problems, and to combat attacks on the democratic process," particularly "terrorist attacks and multiple varieties of putschism" such as at San Francisco

---

*The above article is a slightly edited version of a talk given at the New York Ethical Culture Society in February, 1969.

State, and also "many other extremist resorts to disruption, intimidation and violence," all of which amount to a "new McCarthyism of the left." The letter speaks of the dangers of appeasing this movement, pointing out that appeasement is both "morally intolerable and practically disastrous." And it says that "the main thrust" of the new organization is to be "to protect and advance the freedom and democratic integrity of academic life," to struggle against the "extremist challenge," "to support the university as an open center of free thought and speech—as a meeting house of many viewpoints—not as an enclave of enforced conformity or a totalitarian beachhead in a democratic society."

It would be very difficult to find anyone who would reject these goals. It would be difficult to find anyone who would be in favor of a university that would be an "enclave of enforced conformity" or who would oppose the view that the university should be "an open center of free thought and speech." But in another and more serious sense it represents, I think, an extremely dangerous, even perhaps vicious development; no doubt inadvertently, but I think objectively. When I see things of this sort, what immediately comes to mind is some advice that A. J. Muste gave to pacifists about a half century ago. He said that their task is to

> ... denounce the violence on which the present system is based and all the evil, material and spiritual, this entails for the masses of men throughout the world. So long as we are not dealing honestly and adequately with this 90 per cent of our problem, there is something ludicrous—and perhaps hypocritical—about our concern over the ten per cent of violence employed by the rebels against oppression.

I think that's a sensible remark. And in fact, even if the criticism of "McCarthyism of the left" contained in this letter and similar statements were entirely accurate, still I think Muste's words would be quite appropriate. It would be surprising that that much attention should be given to this miniscule element in the problems of society and the problems of the university.

I want to apologize in advance because later I am going to do something, in Muste's words, "ludicrous and perhaps hypocritical"; namely, spend part of this discussion on an infinitesimal part of the problems that face American society and in particular the universities: tendencies in the student movement that strike me as irrational and objectionable and probably ultimately suicidal. My reason for doing this is precisely because I think that the student movement does have a historic mission, and I think it would be a great tragedy if the tendencies to which I have referred were to lead it into such disaster that this mission will not be fulfilled. There's no other force in society that I see from which one can hopefully expect that a comparable achievement will come.

MILITARY DOMINANCE

But before turning to this important though marginal aspect of our present social problems, let me refer, obviously inadequately, to what seem to me the real problems. The basic problem is indicated by the fact that since World War II, our society has devoted something over a trillion dollars to what is euphemistically called "defense" and unknown additional amounts to subversion. We have intervened with military force to overthrow governments that we admit were popular and legally constituted and to maintain in power repressive dictatorships throughout the world that are willing to subordinate themselves to our interests. And furthermore we have at least once certainly, and perhaps several times, brought the world perilously close to nuclear destruction. Worse still, we continue to accept as legitimate the principles on the basis of which those decisions were made. So we can expect the situation to recur.

It's remarkable that liberals and conservatives alike, just about all those in the mainstream of opinion, applaud this splendid performance. There is very little serious criticism of the decisions that were made, let us say, during the Cuban missile crisis, when we did bring the world very close to total destruction in order to establish the principle that we have a right to have missiles on the borders of the Soviet Union while they do not have the same right to have missiles on our border. One finds little criticism of that principle, little mention of the criminal insanity of those willing to risk nuclear war to defend such a principle, within the mainstream of opinion. What you find rather are statements like those of Presidential historian Thomas Bailey, who refers to this as a high point of the Kennedy Administration: when Kennedy showed that he knew how to play "nuclear chicken."

The dangers of nuclear war and its consequences are obviously immense and require no comment. But the problem of repression, of the institution of dictatorial forms, is one that definitely can be talked about and is very serious. For example, last year there was a good deal of reporting in the papers about political developments in Thailand. But there were a number of things that were not mentioned in these reports. In particular there was a long report in the New York *Times* about the sudden reappearance in Peking of a man named Pridi Phanomyong, who was simply identified as a Communist Thai leader who had suddenly come into some prominence in China. There is an interesting background, not reported in the story, to his appearance in Peking.

If one looks into the history of these developments, one finds some important things. In 1932 Pridi Phanomyong was leader of the liberal reform movement that tried to introduce parliamentary institutions into Thailand and overthrew the absolute monarchy. He himself was overthrown shortly afterward, then during World War II fought together with the American OSS in the "Free Thai" guerrilla movement against the Japanese, while Thailand was under the rule of a basically fascist dictator who had an alliance with Japan. In 1946–7 Pridi led a liberal parliamentary reform movement and won Thailand's only more-or-less free election in history. But he received almost no support from the United States and was quickly overthrown in a coup. By 1948 the fascist dictator who had been a collaborator with the Japanese was back in power. He was immediately recognized by the United States and given very substantial military and economic aid to develop Thailand as one of the supposed bastions of freedom in Southeast Asia.

In fact, Thailand developed into one of the most bloody, repressive, vicious dictatorships in the world. Its enormous crimes are reported in such historical documents as a book by a Kennedy liberal named Frank Darling (one of the signers of the Hook Committee's statement, incidentally) who goes to great length to detail the repression and the role of the United States in instituting it during this post-war period after the coup. And he points out something that the *Times* did not bother to mention; namely, after Pridi was overthrown by a coup that was supported immediately by the United States, he remained in Thailand for a few years and then escaped to China, so that by 1954 the liberal reformer who had been fighting against the Japanese, with the Americans, was in Communist China, and the fascist dictator who had been allied with the Japanese, and had declared war on us, was ruling in Thailand, now an authoritarian military dictatorship with substantial American military support. This, Mr. Darling says, was "ironic"! He then concludes and summarizes this situation as follows:

> the vast material and diplomatic support provided to the military leaders by the United States helped to prevent the emergence of any competing groups who might check the trend toward absolute political rule and lead the country back to a more modern form of government.

The last phrase is interesting: "lead the country *back* to a more modern form of government." But it is quite accurate because the Thais had a more modern form of government in 1946-7 under the leadership of a liberal reformer who is now in Communist China; and it was American military aid that very largely created a situation in which one now hopes they might move back to this more modern form of government.

This is a fairly typical example of the American impact on the less developed countries. If we can escape nuclear war, then the prospects for peace are really prospects for the peace of the prison or the peace of the graveyard, if present tendencies continue. It is interesting that Darling, though he deplores the consequences of our actions in Thailand, nevertheless urges that we continue about as before. He thus expresses the predominant voice in American society: What follows from our actions is deplorable, but it is not our fault, we have no choice, we must continue. Now of course this is not quite the predominant voice because Frank Darling is liberal, a CIA analyst and basically a Kennedy liberal.

There is another voice in the mainstream of American opinion that is becoming more dominant: the voice of people like Melvin Laird, who has called for a "first strike" if the situation requires it. This makes us as far as I know, the only country in the world where the Minister of War has come out in favor of "preventive war" if "our interests" demand it. And he is supported—I suppose again this makes us the only country in the world where this is true—by the leading military spokesman in the press, Hanson Baldwin, who has come out in favor of first use of nuclear weapons for what he refers to as "defensive purposes"; specifically, bolstering weak governments against subversion and aggression—where we decide, of course unilaterally, when this is taking place—as in Vietnam in 1964, when it appears a decision was made perhaps even prior to the 1964 election campaign to escalate the war and to attack North Vietnam. One recalls the rhetoric during the election campaign. This decision, whenever it was actually made, was secret and private. It was a conspiracy, an illegal conspiracy to carry out acts of war that then were put in effect in February, 1965. This conspiracy has not been challenged in the courts although it is one of very great significance, not only to the people of Vietnam but to ourselves, and although it violates domestic law insofar as international treaties are part of that law.

What is investigated in the courts are other sorts of "conspiracies"; for example, the "conspiracy" by Dr. Spock and others to challenge the illegal acts of the government. It is striking that the government made clear what it regards as the basis of the Spock conspiracy. It made this even more clear at the appeals level than it did during the trial by giving a list of "co-conspirators," of whom I am one. The criterion that identifies this set of co-conspirators is precise; the people tried at the Spock trial and the co-conspirators happen to be exactly the group that appeared at a press conference, independently, to speak their minds, to say what they thought about the war and resistance. Many of them never met before or since. This was the only link between the people named as "conspirators" in the Spock trial.

I believe this indicates what is the real peril not only to academic freedom, but to the freedoms provided by the Bill of Rights. Even if one were to agree with everything said in criticism of the student movement, this criticism would, in proper perspective, be quite insignificant.

The dominant voice in American society, the mainstream opinion, is bracketed by people like Frank Darling, on the one side, and by people like Melvin Laird and Hanson Baldwin, on the other. This voice is one that was made explicit by Barrington Moore in an article in the *Proceedings of the Academy of Political Science* in early 1960:

> You may protest in words as loud as you like. There is but one condition attached to the freedom we would like very much to encourage. Your protests may be as loud as possible so long as they remain ineffective. Though we regret your sufferings very much and would like very much to do something about them—indeed we have studied them very carefully and have already spoken to your rulers and immediate superiors about these matters—any attempt by you to remove your oppressors by force is a threat to civilized society and the democratic process. Such threats we cannot and shall not tolerate. As you resort to force we will, if need be, wipe you from the face of the earth by the measured response that rains down flame from the skies.

I think if you observe American society, you find that this is its predominant voice. It's a voice that expresses clearly the needs of the socioeconomic elite; it expresses an ideology that is adopted and put forth with varying degrees of subtlety by most American intellectuals and that gains a substantial degree of adherence on the part of a majority of the population, which sees itself as entering or already having entered the affluent society.

APATHY TOWARD ATROCITIES

This predominant voice is supported by a predominant attitude of almost total apathy that makes it possible for any atrocity to appear in the front pages as long as it is directed against alleged "communists" or landless peasants or something of the sort. And it arouses virtually no response, certainly no response commensurate with what is described. This attitude is developed from the very earliest years.

I've become more aware of that since my children have been in school. Let me give you one example that I came across. I have a daughter in the Lexington, Massachusetts, Public School. Lexington is a very progressive, professional, largely upper-middle-class community that prides itself on its outstanding school system. My daughter had a social science reader that talked about the marvelous New England heritage. The protagonist in this reader is a young fellow named Robert, who is being told about the wonders of the colonial past, including the following:

> Captain John Mason made plans to capture the Pequot fort where the Rhode Island Colony and the Connecticut Colony met. His little army attacked in the morning before it was light and took the Pequots by surprise. The soldiers broke down the stockade with their axes and rushed inside and set fire to the wigwams. They killed nearly all the braves, squaws and children and burned their corn and other food. There were no Pequots left to make more trouble. When the other Indian tribes saw what good fighters the white men were they kept the peace for many years.
> "I wish I were a man and had been there," thought Robert.

And this is his last thought on the subject.

There is no doubt that if the Germans had won World War II, little Hans would be reading similar stories about Lidice, and he would also be wishing that he were a man and had been there. But this is the fare that is fed our children from earliest school experience, that is reinforced by the mass media, and that certainly goes a long way toward accounting for the fact that it's possible to have a story exactly like this in the newspapers—where one replaces "Pequots" by "Vietnamese" and "stone axes" by "B-52's"—and to find the zombie-like reaction that permits any kind of atrocity to take place with nothing said about it. Now my daughter is not being exposed to some of the more remarkable statements by New England intellectuals at the time; for example, Cotton Mather, who described that very same incident as follows: "It was supposed that no less than 600 Pequot souls were brought down to hell that day." Mather goes on to talk about the diseases that decimated the Indians after the Mayflower landing, saying, "The woods were almost cleared of these pernicious creatures to make room for a better growth."

This is a part of our tradition that people ought to be exposed to, and they ought to be shown how it relates and compares to what is happening today. In such circumstances it might be possible to maintain peace—if the oppressed peoples of the world were silent and quiet, if they were willing to continue to play the role that was once described by Philippine nationalist Jose Rizal in castigating his countrymen because their aspirations were "dreams of a slave who asks only for a bandage to wrap the chain so that it may rattle less and not ulcerate his skin." But of course, those days are over. The slaves are no longer just calling for a bandage to wrap the chains, and that is the major reason for the disorder around the world, and the resulting disorder on American campuses.

EROSION OF LIBERTIES

It is hardly necessary to emphasize that the very same predominant voice is heard with reference to domestic issues. A look at the files of the New York Civil Liberties Union will explain very clearly what "law and order" means to the poor. What it means is permanent harassment by the forces of justice. You get a very clear picture of this in books by Algernon Black, for example, or Paul Chevigny in *Police Power,* where he discusses no real atrocities but just the low-level, day-to-day harassment that defines the life of poor people in their relation to the forces of order. He does not mention events like the murder of students, events which lead to a great deal of sympathetic clucking of tongues, but do not lead to the formation of any national committees to defend the rights of students.

I might mention that the hypocritical role of the government in the civil rights movement is evident to everyone who had anything to do with it. My own involvement was not very great, but it was enough to make clear what was going on. The federal government does have the authority under the United States Code to use force to defend the rights of citizens against state authorities. It has not done so. Everyone, many other people much more than I, has seen incidents of brutal violence carried out by state authorities against citizens, with F.B.I. agents standing there taking notes when they have the right, the duty in fact, to intervene to prevent this—if they are given the appropriate orders, which they're seldom given.

Let me turn to another area. Ralph Nader has pointed out that in the state of Pennsylvania 2,000 miners die each year of so-called "black lung." This is not a cost that is calculated by business or by professional economists when they talk about the health of the economy. And we can be quite certain that if these miners were, let's say, to seize the mines, if they were to insist that reasonable standards be imposed, or to be more exact, that reasonable standards be enforced to prevent this, then we can be quite sure that there would be a movement to prevent "left fascism" from taking over American society; and any impoliteness or violence that would result would be blamed on the miners and headlined on the front pages, as the troops are called in to repress these "multiple forms of putschism," as they were by Franklin D. Roosevelt 30 years ago.

There are more subtle but equally pernicious forms of violence. The Hook letter quoted earlier mentions San Francisco State. The letter did not mention that San Francisco is a city that is 20 per cent black, and that its college is there to serve the urban community. San Francisco State College last year had 3.6 per cent black students, down from 11 per cent seven years before, in a city that is 20 per cent black.

According to an article by Professor A. K. Bierman of San Francisco State, a bill to provide funds to help disadvantaged students to enter college passed the state legislature but was vetoed by Governor Reagan, who may well have been trying to set up a confrontation for political reasons. No national committees were formed to investigate this particular situation, let alone to deplore it; and the facts that I just mentioned are not referred to in the discussion of the "putschism" that took place on the San Francisco campus, though they surely have something to do with it. This kind of omission makes one seriously question the judgment of people who are putting together this kind of ultimately repressive movement. I need not mention that a college degree is a certificate of entry to the affluent society.

Personally I would entirely agree with the people I quoted who deplore the acts of those who shout down speakers at public meetings. Thus I deplore the acts of the "responsible" students who during the years 1965 and 1966 helped to break up public meetings against the war, to deface churches in which public meetings were taking place, and so on. In Boston in 1965 and early 1966, it was impossible to hold a public meeting on the Boston Common to oppose the bombing of North Vietnam, because it would be broken up by force—by M.I.T. students, for example, who would march over from the fraternities, with many others. And the Arlington Street Church was pelted with tomatoes and tin cans when the meetings were shifted indoors. This was all headlined on the front pages of the newspapers. In the *Boston Globe* on October 16, 1965, the entire front page was taken up by a description of the events that happened the day before, and the radio ran constant and detailed reports. And of course the commentators were very indignant about what was happening. They were indignant about the peaceful demonstrators who by what they were saying were inciting this reaction on the part of the responsible, short-haired students. And they were joined by liberal Senators like Mike Mansfield, who also spoke against the irresponsibility of the demonstrators for making statements that he himself was to endorse when the time came two years later. Perhaps he might even admit that, had he done so earlier, the world would be a slightly better place. Again, there were no national committees formed to protect the right of free assembly in the face of this kind of violence.

POLITICIZATION OF UNIVERSITIES

Let's turn to the matter of politicization of the universities, which is a matter that Professor Hook's committee is much concerned with and that he himself has spoken about quite eloquently many times. Professor Hook has argued that there is a prima facie case that Communist Party members should not be granted the rights of academic freedom, the normal rights, because of the fact that they belong to an organization that by its own statements endorses limitations on free speech and urges its members not to tell the truth under certain circumstances. There are also other organizations that have behaved in such fashion; for example, the United States Government, which urges and in fact enjoins participants in its programs not to tell the truth on many subjects. Arthur Sylvester, director of information for the Defense Department a few years ago, said in a fit of anger that anyone who believes a word said by spokesmen for the government should have his head examined, or words approximately to that effect. Quite apart from such outbursts, it is clear that people with access to classified information are required by law to withhold relevant information, or even to lie, with respect to matters that may very well be related to their teaching and research supervision.

Now by Professor Hook's argument, it should follow that in the case of people who are involved in work for the American government, there is also a prima facie case that they should be denied the opportunity to teach. Putting aside Hook's argument, which I do not for a moment accept, their involvement in teaching, in fact their dominance of it in fields like engineering or the social sciences, would certainly suggest a high degree of a very dangerous sort of politicization of the universities. For example, in Cambridge, Massachusetts, there are two major universities, Harvard and M.I.T. Each has an outstanding department of government and political science. The chairmen of both departments are deeply involved in the Indochina war. One is chairman of a Council on Vietnamese Studies that is ultimately responsible to the State Department. The other supervises three-quarters of a million dollars of research outside the university on such topics as counterinsurgency and pacification in Vietnam. This is not untypical, and it does indicate a high degree of politicization of the universities. We need not

ask how many projects there are in which political scientists and tech-
nologists work on the question of how poorly armed guerrillas might
better defend themselves against an overwhelming military force from
10,000 miles away, or how many social science projects there are to deal
with the problems of, say, revolutionary development of Third World
societies in anything like an objective or sympathetic manner.

Those who are sympathetic to revolution are treated rather differently. For example, Staughton Lynd was denied an appointment at
Roosevelt University, a very liberal university in Chicago. The history
department voted to appoint Lynd, and this decision was simply over-
turned by the administration. At San Francisco State, according to the
information that I have been able to obtain, in one of the acts that
initiated the disorders there, George Murray was suspended without
due process by the Regents for statements that he was alleged to have
made. He had made some statements of which they disapproved. He
was apparently suspended by the trustees over the objection of the
president of the University, the mayor of San Francisco, and the police
chief of San Francisco in what appears to have been another attempt
to make political capital by setting up a confrontation on the campus.
These are matters that ought to be explored, but no national committees are set up to defend academic freedom in the face of instances of
this sort, which might be enumerated at considerable length.

SUBVERSION OF SCIENCE, TECHNOLOGY, AND SCHOLARSHIP

Let me turn now to the other aspect of the problem of combatting
the politicization of the universities, the dominant and overwhelming
element of which results from the national psychosis that has developed
during the Cold War, with the subversion of science and technology
and scholarship as they devote themselves to the goals expressed by the
"predominant voice" in American society. This is the real problem of
the universities. Professor Hook's group I think is right in much of what
it deplores; but it is talking about a speck at the margin of the problem.
It is ignoring the real problems of politicization. It is remarkable that
if one wants to find a critique of the subversion of the universities, the
betrayal of the public trust by the universities, if one wants to hear a
real voicing of this critique, one turns not to the civil libertarians but
rather to Senator Fulbright or Admiral Rickover or General Eisenhower, all of whom have spoken quite correctly about the dangers to
a free society when the university associates itself with powerful social
institutions. It's remarkable that a critique of this development, which

is fundamental and significant, has to come primarily from such sources.

I have up to now been discussing "the violence on which the present system is based," to use Muste's words. How about the other aspect, the 10 per cent, or more accurately, the 1 per cent or less of the violence? George Orwell once described political thought, especially on the left, as a kind of masturbation fantasy where the world of facts hardly matters. Unfortunately, there is a good deal of truth to that characterization. One of the Movement newspapers once carried an article by a very distinguished professor at Harvard, an old friend of mine who has become deeply involved in radical politics lately and who says that the "goal of university agitation should be to build anti-imperialist struggles in which the university administration is a clear enemy." Now this man knows American universities very well, and in particular he knows Harvard very well. It's very difficult for me to believe that he really thinks of Nathan Pusey as the representative of imperialism on the Harvard campus. In fact if that were true, things would be very easy. All you would have to do would be to sit in at the administration building and you would have struck a blow at imperialism. But it doesn't work like that. The problem is far deeper. This is almost a pure fantasy.

The real problem is that those who call for freedom in the universities are calling for something that exists but that is very badly misused. The universities are relatively free, fairly decentralized institutions in which the serious decisions, those that actually relate to the interrelation between student and faculty, to the curriculum, to what a person does with his life, the kind of work he does—those decisions are very largely made by the faculty and very largely at the departmental level. At least this is true at the major universities I am familiar with.

Of course, the temptations are very strong to make certain decisions rather than others. For those who choose to put their talents to the service of the powerful institutions of the society, there are many rewards—or what might be thought to be rewards. There's power, prestige, and affluence—a share in the great project of designing an integrated world system dominated by American power, which many feel to be a reward. Those who make different choices can confidently expect a good deal of abuse and recrimination, perhaps the destruction of their professional careers. Hence, in one sense the choice is hardly free. In fact, the choice is approximately as outlined by General Hershey in one of his most famous statements; namely, this is the American or indirect way to insure compliance.

But in a much more important sense the choice really *is* free. And the fact of the matter is, and I think one has to face this, that the politicization of the universities and the subversion of science and scholarship, which is quite real, is the result of a relatively free choice by students and by faculty who have been unwilling to resist the temptations and to face the real difficulties of standing outside the mainstream and of rejecting the rewards, if such they are, that are offered for compliance.

Consider the problem of developing radical scholarship in the universities. This is a category I do not believe adequately exists. I personally believe that objective scholarship will very often lead to radical conclusions in the social sciences, as in every other field. One takes for granted in fields outside the social sciences that objective scholarship will often challenge the predominant framework of thinking. Only in the social sciences is this considered somehow the mark of an alienated intellectual who has to be dealt with by psychiatric means. But the fact of the matter is that the task of developing objective scholarship free from the constraints imposed by the American political consensus is a quite real one, and I personally believe that it will lead to radical conclusions.

The burden of proof is obviously on someone like me, who makes that assertion, who believes that objective research will support conclusions of a radical nature. And this is exactly the point that I want to stress. The failure to develop what might be misleadingly called radical scholarship, the failure to build it into the curriculum, this is by no means the result of decrees by college administrators or by trustees. Rather it results directly from the unwillingness of the students and the faculty to undertake the very hard and serious work that is required and to face calmly and firmly the kind of repression, or at least recriminations and abuse, that they are likely to meet if they carry out this work in a serious way. I would expect these to come not from the administration but rather more from the faculty, which may feel that its guild structure, the professional structure on which its security rests, is being threatened. Particularly in the social and behavioral sciences, where theoretical content is virtually nonexistent and intellectual substance is slight, the pretense of professional expertise is very often used as a defense against quite legitimate criticism and analysis. Here I think can be found one source of the abuse of academic freedom; namely, the restricting of those who try to develop objective academic scholarship that will challenge the prevailing framework of thinking in the professions and the conclusions that are often reached.

Suppose that these barriers are overcome—the barriers being, I think, the unwillingness of students to do the hard work required and the fear of the faculty that their guild structure will be threatened. Suppose that these barriers are overcome. Then it might be that the trustees and the administration would step in to erect new barriers against the implementation of study and research and teaching that leads to radical conclusions and the action programs that ought to flow from honest, serious research. However, this is only speculation. We do not know that the universities will not tolerate programs of this sort, both as teaching programs and programs of research and action as well, because the effort has barely been made. There are cases of administrative interference and they are deplorable, but it would be a great mistake to think that they constitute the heart of the problem. They do not.

I think it crucial that the effort be made. I think we very much need understanding of contemporary society, of its long-range tendencies, of the possibilities for alternative forms of social organization and a reasoned, serious analysis, without fantasy, of how social change can come about. I have no doubt that objective scholarship can contribute to that understanding. But it is hard work and it has to be conducted in an open-minded and honest fashion. Furthermore, I think work of that sort has a political content almost at once and can strike directly at repressive institutions. To cite one example, there's a group of graduate students and junior faculty in Asian studies at Harvard and other universities who have formed a Committee of Concerned Asian Scholars that is attempting to develop—I can only describe it in value-laden terms—a more objective and hence more humane and more sympathetic treatment of the problems of the developing Asian societies. If this attempt on their part succeeds—and I think it may, if it consists of solid and well-grounded work—it may seriously weaken one foundation stone of the national psychosis that plays a major role in promoting the garrison state with its enormous commitment of resources to destruction and waste, and its continual posing of the threat of nuclear war.

SCIENCE AND THE MILITARY

Let me mention perhaps a more important example, the problem of organizing scientists to refuse military work. For example, consider the matter of the ABM. Most scientists know that the ABM is a catastrophe, that it will not increase our security but in fact will probably endanger it by increasing international instability and tensions. But it is quite predictable that having given their lectures to the Senate committees, many of these very same scientists have gone to work to build it, knowing what they are doing. There is no law of nature that dictates that this must be the case. They can refuse individually; they can refuse collectively. They can organize to refuse. I think the real point is that lectures on the irrationality of the ABM, though quite amusing, are basically beside the point if in fact the ABM is motivated not so much by the search for security as by the need to provide a subsidy for the electronics industry. And I think there's very good evidence that that's true. The fact of the matter is that—if I may quote from a paper given at the December, 1967, meeting of the American Economics Association—

> ... the current proposal for an ABM system has been estimated to involve 28 private contractors with plants located in 42 states and 172 congressional districts. Given the political reality of such situations and the economic power of the constituencies involved, there is little hope that the interaction of special interest groups will somehow cancel each other out and that there will emerge some compromise that serves the public interest.

These interest groups are further specified as "the Armed Services, the contractors, the labor unions, the lobbyists who speak of free enterprise while they are getting a government subsidy, the legislatures who for reasons of pork or patriotism vote the funds," and so on. These are the political realities; they have not got much to do with whether there might be an accidental nuclear explosion or the chances of shooting down one of those Chinese missiles that Melvin Laird is worried about. Incidentally, I might add that the electronics industry itself is quite aware of all of this. For example, there is a study of the Electronic Industries Association that discusses prospects for the future. It states that "arms control agreements during the next decade are unlikely. The likelihood of limited war will increase and thus for the electronics firms the outlook is good in spite of the end of hostilities in Vietnam."

Scientists can organize to refuse cooperation with such projects, and they can also try to organize and to take part in the mass politics that provides the only hope in the long run for countering and ultimately dispelling the nightmare that they are creating. I think that if an organization of scientists to refuse military work develops on any significant scale, then precisely because of the role that this work plays in maintaining the so-called "health" of the society, they may find themselves involved in very serious political action. I wouldn't be surprised if they find themselves involved in what is called an "illegal conspiracy," in a kind of resistance. In general, I think one can expect that effective politics—by that I mean politics that really strikes at entrenched interests, that really tries to bring about significant social change—is very likely to lead to repression, hence to confrontation.

CONFRONTATION TACTICS

There is a corollary to this observation: The search for confrontation clearly indicates intellectual bankruptcy. It indicates that one has not developed an effective politics that by virtue of the way it relates to the social realities, calls forth an attempt to defend established interests and perhaps attempts at repression. One who takes his rhetoric at all seriously will work towards serious reforms, perhaps even reforms that have ultimately revolutionary content, and will try to delay confrontations as long as possible, at least until he has some chance of succeeding.

The search for confrontations is a suicidal policy. Now there is an argument for the search for confrontations, and I think one should face it frankly and openly. It's put forward clearly by people like—to quote a past master in this—Daniel Cohn-Bendit. He denies being a leader, but was certainly one of the most articulate spokesmen for the French student actions. He has the following to say about "provocation," about confrontation politics. He says:

> Provocation is not a weapon of war except in special circumstances. It can only be used to arouse feelings that are already present, albeit submerged. In our case [the student case in France] we exploited student insecurity and disgust with life in an alienated world where human relations are so much merchandise to be used, bought and sold in the market place. All we did therefore was to provoke students to express their passive discontent, first by demonstrations for their own sake and then by political action, directly challenging modern society. The justification for this type of provocation is its ability to arouse people who have been crushed under the weight of repression.

That is not an unfamiliar argument and one cannot discount it. But when we talk about the student movement in the United States, we are really not in any serious sense talking about people who have been traditionally crushed under the weight of repression. That's rather hyperbolic. And I think in the actual concrete situation of the student movement the idea of confrontation tactics is often a confession of the inability to develop effective politics or the unwillingness to do the serious and hard work of social reconstruction that can easily be condemned as "reformist," but that any true revolutionary would understand immediately is the only kind of work that could lead to new social forms, which might perhaps even pave the way for a revolutionary or far-reaching change in social organization.

I think that confrontation tactics as they actually evolve are frequently rather manipulative and coercive and really the proper kinds of tactics only for a movement that, inadvertently or not, is aiming toward an elitist, authoritarian structure of a sort that we have had far too much of on the left in the last half-century and that in fact has destroyed what there was of a living, vital left in the Western world.

There is a confusion in all of this talk about tactics that ought to be faced more clearly in the student movement. I am referring to the practice of counterposing "radical tactics" to "liberal tactics." This is a senseless distinction. It makes no sense at all to try to place tactics in a spectrum of political judgment. Tactics are neither radical nor conservative, nor do they lie anywhere else on the political spectrum. They are successful or unsuccessful in achieving certain goals that may be discussed in terms of their political character. But to talk about the tactics as what is "radical" or "liberal" is to make a fundamental error. Part of the style of the student movement is to focus great attention on immediate concerns that are close at hand—what do you do tomorrow, how do you relate to the people near you, and so on. This is nice in some ways. It gives an attractive style to many of the student actions, but it can be politically quite destructive, I think, if it becomes the general framework within which the movement develops.

INTELLECTUALS AND SOCIAL CHANGE

Any serious movement for social change will have to involve many different strata of the population, people who certainly see their needs and goals quite differently, including many groups that are in no position even to articulate their goals and needs, and certainly not to bring them to public attention or to develop political action based on them. I think that these may prove to be related and compatible goals—but of course that has to be shown.

The major task for intellectuals—including the student movement, which in large part has been the cutting edge of a growing movement for social change—is to try to understand and to articulate those goals, to try to assess and to understand the present state of society and how it might change, what alternative forms there are for the future, to try to persuade and to organize and ultimately to act collectively where they can, and individually if it comes to that. On the other hand, it is clear that if the adult community fails to act in some way to meet the real problems of the universities and society, if it contents itself with deploring the occasional absurdities of the student movement and various superficial manifestations of student protests, then I think we can expect with perfect confidence that student unrest will continue. Furthermore it is *right* that it should continue. Those who deplore the forms that it takes, I think might do much better to ask what they can do to eliminate the evils that constitute the core of the problems we face, and then proceed to act in a serious and committed manner to confront these problems.

10.   Jay Weinroth and Robert Elias Abu Shanab

It's Always Best When the
Lights are Off in the Auditorium*

I.

This paper is about grades as a distinct hindrance to the process of
genuine education, and about the experiences of some college students
in a large Introduction to Philosophy class where the instructor substituted an emphasis on student self-evaluation in place of any standardized grading on his part. It is still often the case today that universities
and individual teachers put an emphasis on grades in courses. However,
it is also often the case that individual—teachers and sometimes entire
colleges—have managed to escape this process of punishing students
and themselves by the supposed obligation to attach grades to what
each student happened to do in a particular time period. There is
nothing totally unique today about running a class without grades. On
the other hand, what is of considerable interest about the particular
experimental class to be described here is the way in which the removal
of pre-established grading procedures by the instructor resulted in the
students' becoming conscious of their freedom in the situation, with
various attendant responses of surprise, delight, and fear.

The initial motivation of the instructor of the experimental class,
i.e. his motivation for initiating the experimental conditions, can only
be described as disgust with the procedure of assigning grades altogether. Mr. A, the instructor, thinks that the only proper motive for
people to come to a lecture or otherwise be involved in an educational
class is the motive of interest. Persons who enroll as students in a
university class and who also come to the lectures or other meetings of
that class are not only paying tuition for this privilege but are giving up
their time as well. In Mr. A's view, it is monstrous to add to these
sacrifices a need for the student to gamble that he will not also be
punished for all his effort, by a letter grade which is supposed to indicate

*Written in collaboration with Richard Schultz, Diane Humle, James Petras, Tom Smith,
and Mary Elizabeth Shaff.

poor performance. The question would appear to be—what do grades really have to do with the process of education at all? Does learning take place when a test is given, or before? Surely it is before the test that any learning takes place, if at all. Moreover, Mr. A has concluded from his years of experience in teaching that grades at their best introduce a subtle, destructive element of dishonesty into the teacher-student relationship. No comment of praise or criticism may pass between student and teacher without the lingering suspicion that a bid for an "A" is being made or accepted. At worst, the device of the grade is used by the teacher as an instrument of coercion. It says, 'Do not worry about coming to this class out of interest; come or else!'

With such thoughts in mind, Mr. A set up his class in Introduction to Philosophy, with an enrollment of two hundred students, in such a way that the students were to receive the grades insisted upon by the Registrar's Office with a minimum of the bad side-effects usually associated with the grading process. Individual tests and papers, graded by the instructor, were declared inappropriate as means of expressing the value of the educational experience of the course for the individual student. Instead, the students divided themselves into groups of about ten persons each, each group being charged with the task of devising a better means of expressing the value of the course for each member of the group. The groups met for a minimum of one or two times each week. For other class meetings during each week, Mr. A lectured on various topics in philosophy and he "assigned" readings in the textbooks. Various groups decided upon projects as specific substitutes for the assignments of tests or papers. Some conducted surveys on sexual attitudes, attitudes toward abortion, violence, and so on. Some held on-going discussions on race relations, on the individual members' self-concepts, or on their religious views. One group visited prisoners in the county jail; another interviewed prostitutes; a third ended up imagining themselves as the members of a utopian commune; a fourth got into vehement arguments about the war in Vietnam but ended by investigating the nature of their own hostilities and anxieties as these related to their fears that somehow their disagreements would result in bad grades. Near the end of the term each group's members assigned themselves grades on the basis of the value of each person's contributions to the project, and each group wrote and submitted to the instructor a collective report on the entire activity.

There was still an element of assignment of grades by the instructor though. Mr. A assigned grades to each group report, and averaged the grades on the reports with the grades given by the students to one another. He regarded this as a compromise between what he would like to do and what is usually done. Perhaps it is fortunate that he did adopt such a compromise measure, since even this mild experimental format brought an attack against him from the curiously conservative staff of the campus newspaper. His assessment of the group reports was that he had never before received a set of papers from a university class which were so coherently written and so devoid of nonsense and worthless paraphrasing. With one or two possible exceptions, every one of twenty-four group reports was literally enjoyable to read, along with various sorts of accompanying material, e.g. photos, illustrations, tape-recordings.

The rest of the material in this paper consists of excerpts from one group report. This group was a small one, and one that experienced some hesitancy in conducting a formal project as such. They decided that their experience of interaction was in itself the project, that this was indeed an educational experience of great personal value to each member of the group. Thus their report is about that experience. If it does not violate the spirit of Mr. A's firm belief in freedom in education, it may be noted in passing that at least three of the group's five members have become involved in intensive volunteer work with kindergarten-age children of special needs.

II.

We had met for several weeks during the proper time allotted. Mr. A had lectured and his audience had taken notes, following exact college procedure. During the second week of class he required topics we thought would be interesting to discuss in smaller groups. After much thought we made our choices. The next step was to establish groups. Since our group was comprised of thirty people we had to organize ourselves into smaller sub-groups. This operation was achieved with maximum efficiency: we looked confusingly at one another, mumbled several solutions to the dilemma, became extremely self-conscious because of the uncomfortableness of the situation, gave one another you-tell-him-what-to-do glances, and finally ended up grouped off in different parts of the auditorium wondering with total amazement how the hell this entire disaster had transpired. Well, there we were, all five of us, giving one another the once over. After this gazing ritual, an integral part of any group function, we all introduced ourselves. On the first day we achieved one awful lot of nothing: deciding what to do and how to do it, how to achieve the maximum grade with a minimum amount of work, and thousands of other totally meaningless things usually done during a first group meeting.

Our group clearly showed effects of a disease commonly found in newly-formed groups: lack of informality. For the first several sessions we sat or knelt or slouched or imitated some other type of posture in order to bring on an air of informality. It failed drastically.

At one point in one of our initial discussions we went as far as to trick ourselves into believing we could achieve exceedingly benevolent goals; work together to accomplish some unbelievable task. All absurd! This group fantasizing terminated quickly. We became more of a group of sincere people rather than a group of dedicated students. From that point until now we have achieved nothing. Our work was to no avail. It could not be discussed intellectually. It couldn't be plotted and graphed, set on an over-head projector, laughed at, argued, nor debated. It contained no enlightening facts, nor bore any underlying philosophical ideology. It couldn't be eaten and digested. No concrete here's-my-proof facts. We ask you, Mr. A, not to judge but to experience vicariously.

III.

What started out to be a philosophical discussion on the effects of childhood experiences on adult life flopped. We did not research, we did not delve into the subject; in fact we hardly even scratched it. I can't remember more than two times that the question was ever raised. So what did we do? Did we take advantage of the freedom given us, and abuse this freedom from an overt authority and just fool around for a quarter? Well we did talk about children. I was excited about Summerhill so we talked about it some. We had a couple of good raps about formalized vs. free education yet came to no conclusions. We talked about our own childhood some, about imaginary friends, Santa Claus, guardian angels, first experiences, but we didn't relate them to ourselves now, nor did we attach any more importance to them other than that they were humorous and we kept each other amused. We always got way off the track although there wasn't really a track to be on. We talked of sliding down the steps of the auditorium on cardboard and of cat burgling on halloween at Euclid Beach, of secret islands where we could get away from it all. But even these never became realities. We never went to Euclid Beach or slid down the steps or anything else except sit on the stage and rap and laugh and occasionally worry if we were doing the right thing or not, and then saying the hell with it.

So we failed, right? Wrong. I think we succeeded, in accomplishing something of eminent importance. We formed our own educational experience, lived it and learned it. For instead of discussing children and education we became children in our own educational system. There are three words in the english language which cause some discrepancies; they are "child," "adult," and "mature." One can, I suppose, be all three at once but, to me, "child like" takes on the same connotation that Jesus used when he said "Be like the little children" —be willing to learn, open and sincere. "Adult" can mean worldly, 21 years of age materially and socially but not necessarily spiritually. "Mature" expresses adulthood of the spirit, when the spirit has come of age and has begun to make rational value judgements. I feel that we therefore became children, mature children. Mature in the sense that we made the judgement that a structured format was not what we wanted. That we'd rather risk anarchy than submit to a method of learning that we didn't subscribe to. We were children in that we were open and sincere with one another, willing to learn from each other.

Our new found education system consisted of the interactions of these five mature children. We found that when we were released from the normal pressures of a college course we became much freer. We discovered that people left alone without any overt authority forcing them into a mold will do nothing more than experience each other. But what could be more important? What really is philosophy other than the interworkings of peoples' ideas and ideals? We expressed our ideas and lived them, instead of reading about other people's. We were given a chance to express our own ideas on life and see how others reacted to them. We were five complete strangers but now we are five friends. I guess you could say we had a course in friendship, a course in being rather than accomplishing. A course where people, not subject matter and lesson plans, come first. We acted as children experiencing this new environment, learning and truly becoming educated.

IV.

All of the people in our group have had suburban schooling; either public or parochial school education. When one ponders the thought of a suburban education one is justified in envisioning a highly regimented educational institution. An institution consisting of classrooms and learning materials (not necessarily first in order of priorities although sometimes one would think the structure is more highly esteemed than the faculty or the students), an ultra-efficient faculty, and a student body. The subject matter is related to the student in a consume-regurgitate manner. The student absorbs the most pertinent information. Later the instructor tests the student to evaluate his progress; the more knowledge retained the better the education. Usually these evaluations were of paramount importance to the student. He will initiate any method necessary to obtain a satisfactory evaluation. Fortunately this type of evaluation promotes competition and self-discipline. Unfortunately, it promotes cheating, hatred, envy and other forms of animosity. This process, usually lasting from fifteen to twenty years, terminates with your placement in some job suited to some acquired skill learned in school.

We have just given you an abbreviated description of the American educational process. A process that has a very profound effect on the life style of every individual. When speaking of this philosophy course we decided that the ideas of this course and those of the standard educational process did not correlate. The technique employed and the subject matter discussed were not tools to achieve an end but rather they were distinct in themselves. These methods were not used to prime oneself for a test. We attempted to use them as effective learning experiences in themselves. Furthermore we analyzed the techniques used to relate the subject matter to the students. Our classes for the most part were very informal in presentation. Many times we were diverted away from the original subject matter to pursue some other type of topic or spend time elaborating on some point in the discussion. This type of atmosphere promoted spontaneity. People answered questions more candidly. More people participated in the discussions which, in turn, exposed the students to several points of view. Having a very loosely structured course, we enjoyed the freedom to choose whether or not we would go to class, read the suggested books, etc. It was philosophy taught as it should be taught. Tests were not given. No one coerced you into doing the work. If you enjoyed the subject matter and read the selections, it was usually done because you wanted the knowledge and it became part of you.

V.

How easy it would be for me to describe how great our project is. How easy it would be for me to report how much we accomplished in our group and how diligently we worked together to reach our goal. But that type of BS will not be found here. Because we didn't do any neatly written report compiled from other peoples' ideas. And secondly, we didn't have any specific goal so we didn't turn in a project and say-"Look, see what we did teacher. Do you like it? Do we get a big surprise now?"

When we began our group we were drawn together under the general theme of "children." At our first meeting we got together and tried to decide what would be most beneficial to us and our learning. We were more concerned about what Mr. A wanted to see. Then we began to think and wonder—"Why should we be so structured and concerned about some reward? After all, we all agree that grades are a hindrance to learning. Why don't we just discuss what we want to discuss and forget about that stupid grade?"—We decided that we wanted to be free and go off on tangents and not limit ourselves to just one aspect or just one idea. We did not want to combine our "research" in some helter-skelter way and say—"Here is OUR report."

Our discussions led us to many extremes. Beginning with the topic of children and ending up with *Lady Chatterly's Lover.* I would like to list some of the areas of interest that we touched upon. They are not in order and they don't necessarily relate in any neat and orderly way. I can't tell what I personally got from these topics because some of them didn't touch me at all, while others enabled me to see many new things through four different people's eyes. A partial list of these topics from the group meetings follows: We began discussing the molding of a child's behavior from his earliest years. For instance, a strange feeling comes over the child as he begins to discover the various parts of his own body and is told by his parents not to touch or explore his genitals, because they are dirty. The puzzling predicament a child is put into when his parents tell him to be kind to minority races, and look at them as equals. And then they turn around and tell the kid not to put that penny in his mouth because a "nigger" might have touched it. We discussed the reason for grades and for college itself. Somehow, we got into the television program "Sesame Street" and how they are able to reach children. We talked about how children adopt fads and drop them, including our own experiences with Davey Crockett and Zorro. The problem of the easily distracted pupil was discussed along with the type of society that kids are brought up on today. The trend for people with a strict social conscience to either try to solve the society's problems or just drop out and let someone else worry about them because —"What's the use." The dilemma of letting kids learn what they want to learn or forcing the educational system on them. Must we have money to have "freedom" in this society? We discussed our earliest childhood remembrances. We compared the types of games and toys kids have today with what we had when we were young. In looking at our childhood fantasies, i.e., Santa Claus, Easter Bunny, we realized how today's children are forced to face reality a lot sooner than we were. Along with this, we brought out how they are taught to draw the "correct" way or in other words, to meet the standards of a teacher. We developed anxiety from the process of our group because it was so "abnormal." Must we be forced to learn? We discussed the discontent among some group members because we have nothing to show for what we accomplished in this class. And last but not least we were forced with that inevitable question—"We are being threatened by grades and what should we do?" Maybe our group didn't solve any problems or answer all the questions that were raised, but this group experience enabled me to resolve a few things in my mind. Such things as the reason for me to try to please instructors so I can get a piece of paper at the end of four years which proves that I'm a good BS artist. And how we must remember that children are unique individuals and don't deserve to be molded to what a so-called Establishment wants them to be. These are the things I came away from the group with.

I must now mention that I felt that this group process has been a very enjoyable experience for me. I did not worry about doing my part or reading such and such because I had to. The freedom in these unstructured, informal groups not only allowed me to clarify some of my own ideas about our "sick" educational system but also to meet four fine people with whom I immensely enjoyed talking and joking.

VI. "Grades"

1. For diversity of subject the group must be awarded with the letter A. The subject matter ranged from such heavy subjects as childhood sexual habits to discussions on the nature of God. As for the length of raps, another A is in order for the group consistently ran overtime and even met on days outside of class time. Group participation in rapping merits at least an A+ for many times the various members of the group interrupted each other thus overlapping the rapping of the group, thereby arriving at a greater composite volume of rapping. Fluency and vocabulary used within the raps also merits an A. The raps were fluent unto boisterousness and the vocabulary was rich and sprinkled liberally with cool colloquialisms and favorite expressions of the group members. The composite group grade for rapping is therefore $A \times A \times A \times A = A^4$.

2. Laughter. The laughter of the group was of unusual quality: of deep resonance and full bodied. This laughter was indeed varied. It covered all aspects of the subject ranging from a slight giggle to a guffaw with even an occasional belly laugh. Because of this diversity and high quality it is justifiable in awarding the group with an A in laughter. This laughter often went above and beyond the call of duty of any self righteous laughter. The group in all fairness must recognize the fact that they often laughed when laughter was not called for, this laughter

lasting for long periods of time without any lack of quality or zeal. The group therefore went beyond A work in the field of laughter.

3. As it stands, each of the members failed as individuals but when computed with the group rating each individual's average becomes an $A(A^{5}++=A^{6}\ A^{6}-A^{5}=A^{1})$. Therefore each individual receives an A on his report card. It is not to be overlooked however that, acting on his own, each individual failed as a scholar. None of them accomplished what they set out to do, nor do they have anything to show for their time and effort. In the light of the academic world (which is the brightest light glowing from the eternal fires of knowledge, kept burning by the diligent work of scholars in our fine universities across the nation) the group members have indeed failed. This group is therefore charged with producing highly humanistic actions and holding unconventional and highly irrational values. In essence they acted not as scholars but rather as human beings interacting with one another. In conclusion it can be said that these five highly individualistic people agreed unanimously upon one redeeming and unifying thought. It's always best when the lights are off in the auditorium.

Study Questions

1. Why have education at all? Can you imagine a kind of education which goes on without any formal schools? Why do you suppose that we have developed the formal school system that we do have?
2. What seems to be the source of the antagonism that so many people have toward freedom in education? What is the relation, if any, between freedom and education?
3. What seems to you to be the proper purpose of education for young children, if there is indeed any proper purpose of such education? Should the inherent curiosity of children be intentionally used, as Dewey suggests, to help the child develop his capacities for complex learning? Or, on the contrary, should we carefully avoid suggesting to children that they do anything except what they spontaneously decide that they want to do?
4. What does Greenfield's article imply as to the way in which we treat children in our society? Aren't there supposed to be many tax-financed agencies which see to it that children are well cared for?
5. If Ridgeway's accusations about the university are accurate, is Chomsky wrong, even in his mild criticism of the student Left's argument?
6. What do Kozol's observations suggest about education and miseducation *outside* the ghetto school?

7. How much of the time which you have spent in university courses seems to you to be of value and how much seems to be a waste? What do you think has been responsible for making the valuable experiences indeed valuable, and for making the wasteful experiences indeed wasteful? What do you think can be done, in terms of practical innovations, to reduce the amount of wasted activity in university courses and to increase the amount of valuable experience in university courses?

8. How much of the fundamental structure of our public school system appears to be a waste? How would you run a school if you had a completely free hand in your decision?

9. What studies might constitute Chomsky's curriculum of radical scholarship? In what sense might such studies be called more objective (or less) than those currently pursued?

10. In what ways does your life appear to be governed by the schedule of machines? What would it be like if you set the tempo according to your own schedule?

Part II

PHILOSOPHIES OF PROTEST

Introduction

We can justifiably describe our times as being, among other things, an age of political and social protest. In this section of our readings we are looking for an understanding of some of the basic issues that arise again and again in the current context of political and social protest. We are also interested in trying to understand the phenomenon of political and social protest in itself. What does it signify when a culture finds itself faced with a social and political atmosphere from which public protest is never long absent? The arguments of various philosophers and spokesmen which have been included in this section indicate that the phenomenon of widespread public protest reflects the fact that great numbers of people are now possessed of the new belief that bad social conditions which they once accepted as necessary are in fact both unnecessary and intolerable. Thus, it appears accurate to characterize protest as an awakening, as a surge of self-awareness and awareness of the nature of one's condition and surroundings.

MAN VS. THE STATE

Our first group of selections among philosophers of protest is concerned with the conflict between the human individual and the government and society which expect and usually get the individual's obedience to their rules. However, the nature of this conflict in turn becomes clarified when we ask whether or not the individual must yield to the state solely because the state possesses power which can be used against him if he refuses. Sophocles, in *Antigone,* has given what is quite probably the classic portrayal of a person caught between her allegiance to the values of the state and her allegiance to another, conflicting order of values, in this case, her religion. Sophocles portrays the

111

ruler of the state, Creon, as jealously unable to tolerate any rival in the people's allegiance. Sophocles apparently means to severely criticize such a jealous attitude of authority. He points to the great irony whereby humanity's talents of reason have fashioned a legal situation which here produces the most unreasonable injustice and repression of freedom.

The argument written by Plato for Socrates in the *Crito* gives a more sophisticated treatment to the same sort of issue raised by *Antigone.* Socrates makes clear in the *Crito* that it is the good man's duty to resist the state's demand that he do evil. To aid the officials in executing a fellow citizen without due process of law, or to otherwise publicly show that you believe the officials to be properly following the law when in fact you believe that they are not properly following the law—these are not good actions. On the other hand, it is not a justifiable act to injure another in order to get revenge. It is simply never right to injure another. This is so also where the other "person" is in fact the laws of the state. At the same time, Socrates asserts that the individual does owe a fundamental obligation of obedience to the state by virtue of having been given a home there throughout this life.

Henry David Thoreau's essay on civil disobedience is another classic in its field. Thoreau has given a uniquely explicit examination to the details of a question which is much more often ignored than asked—viz. why should it be assumed that the individual has *any* obligation to the state? Unlike Socrates, Thoreau argues that the state must demonstrate that we owe it anything in particular, and it often cannot really do so. In Thoreau's view, the individual's real moral obligation is to do what he thinks right and resist what he thinks wrong. Thus, the honest, morally concerned person often has a positive obligation to act in a way which will be interpreted by the state as "civil disobedience." Thoreau focuses very specifically on the citizen's strategy of refusal to pay taxes. This refusal forces the tax collector to confront you, as one human being to another, and to consider whether he is willing to go on with his job of doing the state's bidding when you offer him this resistance.

Kahlil Gibran's "The Criminal" forcefully portrays in parable form the phenomenon of protest against injustice as it arises among the poor and ill-treated. An impoverished young man in the story realizes the possibility of using his strength to get by force what he needs and what no one will let him earn. Once this happens, the social situation is totally transformed for him. The loser, Gibran implies, is the society, which forces its talented members to become the greatest criminals of all, i.e. oppressive rulers.

Jay Weinroth argues that, from the contemporary philosopher's perspective, we are already experiencing the politically motivated destruction of language of which George Orwell warned in his *1984.* Along with other devices of control, the super-totalitarian state of Orwell's imaginary future stifles almost all individual protest by eliminating those words and meanings from language which are important for formulating the ideas of protest. Weinroth sees this trend already at work around us when the term "violence" is used by government and corporation officials and their supporters in the public media in such a way that all protest is labeled "violence." Weinroth suggests that ultimately such manipulative tactics will indeed damage the ability of the individual to clearly articulate his protest.

COMMUNITY VS. CLASS OPPRESSION

The two concepts of "community" and "class oppression" are closely related to political issues of a highly volatile nature. On one hand, these two terms—"community" and "class oppression"—are often used today in political argument, and often used with considerable confusion. On the other hand, for many persons in our society the concepts of community and class oppression rarely, if ever, come into conscious use. Thus, to point to these twin concepts is to call attention to what has been neglected in many persons' commonsense view of the world. At the same time, our attending to these concepts may produce some much needed clarification of these terms as they are used by many persons.

The meaning of the two terms, as shown in our reading selections, is made evident by contrasting them. A point of view which stresses these concepts may be presented as follows. We may see various societies as motivated by and characterized by either a spirit of community or else by a system of class oppression. A system of class oppression may be seen as a social system in which some persons are regularly treated in a disadvantageous way, because they are dark-skinned, or young, or female, or poor and uneducated, and so on. Persons are treated by others in such a system according to their social class membership, and one or more social classes are habitually kept at a disadvantage. It is important to realize that the standard mode of class oppression in the society becomes "normal," and is often "explained" by various rationalizations. By contrast, in a society motivated by a spirit of community, persons are treated according to their individual needs, so long as the socio-economic resources are available.

Writing in Athens in the fourth century B.C., Aristotle discussed varieties of social systems in terms of those which are under rule of law and those which are governed only to serve the purposes of a ruling class. In Aristotle's view, the constitution in a society's legal system reflects the actual distribution of political authority and power among the classes of that society. In this respect, Aristotle thinks that there are good constitutions, which reflect the interests of every important group of citizens in the society, and bad constitutions, which give a disproportionate share of power to some groups. The mark of a good constitution, Aristotle argues, is that no single group in the society would prefer a change to a different constitution. The rule of law, Aristotle argues, is an administration of law in fairness to all, as opposed to a government which serves the interest of any one group alone. The result of a rule of law is that citizens aspire to treat one another in the spirit of law. Government in the interest of one class, on the other hand, inspires in citizens the spirit of manipulation and injustice.

Karl Marx and Frederick Engels are world famous for their declaration that all human history up to their time has been the history of the oppression of one social class by another. Marx and Engels clearly mean to emphasize that the systematic oppression of one class—ordinarily the slave or working class—has been so thoroughly built into every major society that such oppression has come to appear normal. Thus the people who do the history-writing for a society (and who usually aspire to belong to or do belong to the upper classes) have often described human history with the remarkable omission of any reference to class oppression at all. However, once we are aware of the phenomenon of class oppression, virtually every event taking place within every cultural institution becomes recognizable as a part of the overall pattern of oppression. In the selection from *The Communist Manifesto* which we include here, Marx and Engels analyze the objections to communism which their opponents have raised. In each instance Marx and Engels point to the way in which, e.g. the nice-sounding argument about the rewards of private property means one thing to the powerful capitalist, and quite another thing to the average person who has no property free-and-clear under the bourgeois system and—as Marx and Engels see it—never will have any property, no matter how hard he works.

Huey P. Newton, Minister of Defense of the Black Panther Party, argues in a political essay that the difference between community self-regulation and regulation of the community by outside political forces is the major thing to understand about current U.S. politics. The police, Newton argues, are supposed to be present in a community to protect the citizens. However, what we see in the ghettos of America, where most of our black people live, is a situation where the police are recruited, paid, and controlled by groups who do not live in the black community and who are class enemies of the black community. The ironic result is that the police force becomes, not a force for protection in the black community, but rather a force for harassing the community if its citizens do not conform to the rules laid down by others outside of the community. Newton concludes that for the black community to have the benefits of genuine law-enforcement, under the present circumstances, the black community alone must be in control of any police force that operates in its neighborhoods.

Karl Llewellyn is a distinguished American legal philosopher whose work has covered a wide variety of theoretical and concrete problems in law. In the selection which we include here from Llewellyn's work, he argues that there is a need for the average citizen or laymen to understand the basic principles of law as it is applied by courts. The layman would then understand the basic purposes of his system's law, and he would be able to articulate his support of or opposition to particular judicial decisions which seek to apply and interpret the rules of the system for particular cases. According to Llewellyn, such a process of understanding would enable the layman and the legal system to work together. As things actually are, however, lawyers have allowed law to become overly technical, so that the average person regards law suspiciously, as only an instrument to be used against him.

VIOLENCE VS. NON-VIOLENCE

The prevalence of discussions today concerning violence and non-violence is eloquent testimony to the predominance of the conscious spirit of protest in our time. This is so because the aims of the many who protest can be fulfilled only by a certain amount of change in the social power structure. And the question of violence versus non-violence is essentially a question of the means to attain this change, since it is an evident fact that the pressures for change meet with initially firm resistance from those who currently inhabit society's positions of advantage.

There are at least two separate sorts of considerations to be kept in mind when studying arguments relating to violence and non-violence. One of these considerations follows directly from the point we have just observed, viz. that questions of violence vs. non-violence are inseparable from questions of protest and change vs. continuation of the social status quo. Thus, there is a great deal of verbal confusion to be observed concerning the term "violence." At times it appears that some

commentators would like to present the alternatives as those of violence vs. doing nothing at all in the interest of change. At times some
commentators are prone to assert that non-violence is a very worthy
strategy *for their opponents,* while ignoring the moral applicability of
such a course of action *for themselves.* Again, at times some commentators show a reluctance to use the term "violence" for any actions except
those of their opponents.

Our second consideration is that philosophies of change by non-
violence and philosophies of change by violence represent the positions
of two more or less specific schools of thought. Each of these two schools
of thought argue that truly effective social change can be attained only
by its specific methods. Accordingly, each of these two schools argues
that violence is or is not justifiable as the means of change, i.e. because
it does or does not produce results which justify the cost. In any case,
however, none of the arguments which we have selected here commits
the confusing error of calling an action "violence" merely because it is
done by your enemy. On the contrary, the question honestly faced by
all of these arguments is—when, if ever, should I commit violence in the
interest of social change?

The Sermon on the Mount is presented to us in the *New Testament*
as a report of a part of the teachings of Jesus of Nazareth. The Sermon
asserts an extensive obligation for the morally righteous person to practice non-violence. The Sermon's various admonitions to the faithful are
now famous clichés—turn the other cheek; love thy enemy; blessed are
the meek; and so on. The general theme of the Sermon is that doing
justice under the conventional law of the community is often insufficient to satisfy the responsibility of the morally righteous person. One
should neither do nor even intend *any* harm to one's fellow human. The
implication of the Sermon is that one simply cannot live a life of acquiring monetary wealth and power without committing a great many
injustices and doing much harm to one's fellow humans. It is the humble
and the poor who shall most easily enter heaven. Every possession of
the rich and powerful is a sign of goods which they have hoarded
instead of shared. As such, these possessions are impediments which
must be discarded to attain righteousness.

Mohandas K. Gandhi is the personal symbol for the advocacy of
non-violence in the modern world. Gandhi asserted the moral superiority of the stance of non-violence, forsaking *any* violent means of
resistance even against a murderous invading enemy army. However,
his noted application of non-violence as an active political strategy
occurred in his leadership of the Indian people's struggle for independence from British colonial rule. As a tactic, non-violence is viewed by

Gandhi as most definitely a form of resistance. Moreover, he sees resistance of bad laws as a moral obligation. One should resist bad law by peaceful non-compliance. Be put in jail but certainly do not obey the law when it is bad. Gandhi further considers non-violence as a sort of force with which one confronts one's opponent, and thus as a peaceful sort of instrument whereby one can morally persuade the opponent to capitulate. He calls this sort of implementation of non-violence by the term "truth-force"—Satyagraha. The reason for this choice of terms is seen in Gandhi's argument that the person who must resort to violent force is the person who is not yet totally unafraid of the truth. Gandhi argues throughout that peaceful happiness can never be won by means of violence, for violence only adds destruction to the world. A full understanding of the truth-force teaches you that no one is important enough to merit the employment of violence against his attacker. There is a choice; violent self-defense is violence all the same.

Bobby Seale, chairman of the Black Panther Party, explains the origin and growth of the Party as a response to a situation of constant threat, harrassment, brutality and killing of persons in the black community by hostile, aggressive policemen. The crucial point, which Seale thinks is demonstrated in the *actions* of the Party, is that the power of the police to thus intimidate the community comes not from any power of law but simply from the fact that the police carry and use guns. The simple fact of the policeman's gun turns the black ghetto resident into a person who does not dare to fight his real enemy and who lives out his life in a pattern of apathy and self-hate. The only remedy, as Seale sees things, is to resort to carrying guns. It is only fair to note that Seale is not advocating the initiation of violence at all. Rather, he asserts that if an oppressed people, such as poor black Americans, are ever to claim their rights as human beings, they must begin by demonstrating in cities that they will shoot *back* at the oppressor's police force *if* the police initiate an attack.

Eldridge Cleaver has attained recent fame as an author and as Minister of Information of the Black Panther Party. On the day of Martin Luther King's assassination, Cleaver addressed himself to the issue of violence vs. non-violence in America. Cleaver argues that it is ultimately impossible to adhere to a policy of protest by non-violence in a thoroughly racist and violence-ridden society such as our own. As Cleaver sees matters, the black militant who advocated use of weapons literally *could not* come to the center of the political stage while Dr. King continued alive in his campaign of non-violent protest. However foolhardy one may have thought Dr. King's position to be, the courageous stance of fighting without weapons could not be effectively criticized so long as Dr. King succeeded in staying alive, i.e. in making his strategy continue to work. Thus, Cleaver argues, non-violence for black Americans died with Dr. King. In killing Dr. King, the white power structure killed *the* symbol in America for non-violence. Now non-violence can never be resurrected in our cultural era. Now the black man will meet the gun with the gun, Cleaver asserts, until "Babylon" is forced by the ensuing havoc "to let the black people go."

Robert Elias Abu Shanab discusses intentional violence as a tactic —viz. terrorism—as this tactic relates to the activities of the Palestinian guerrillas (in particular, the more radical PFLP). Shanab argues that criticism of the PFLP for their acts of terrorism is mostly hypocritical in its neglect of two important considerations. One of these is the great amount of violence perpetrated on Palestinians by the Israeli military. The other is the history of the Zionist occupation of Palestine (now incorporated into Israel) in which Palestinian Arabs were evicted from their homeland and left to exist precariously as refugees. Shanab enumerates the specific sorts of benefits and losses which the PFLP have experienced as a result of their calculated policy of violence. He concludes in effect that, from a realistic point of view, the *response* of violence as a calculated policy is simply to be expected as long as any one party initially persists in such a policy.

A

Man versus the State

Man-Made Laws and Higher Laws

CHARACTERS

Ismene ⎱ *daughters of Oedipus*
Antigone ⎰
Creon, *King of Thebes*
Haemon, *son of Creon*
Teiresias, *a blind prophet*
A Sentry
A Messenger
Eurydice, *wife of Creon*
Chorus *of Theban elders*
King's attendants
Queen's attendants
A boy leading Teiresias
Soldiers

Scene: Before the Palace at Thebes

Enter ISMENE from the central door of the Palace. ANTIGONE follows, anxious and urgent; she closes the door carefully, and comes to join her sister.

ANTIGONE: O sister! Ismene dear, dear sister Ismene!
      You know how heavy the hand of God is upon us;
      How we who are left must suffer for our father, Oedipus.
      There is no pain, no sorrow, no suffering, no dishonour
      We have not shared together, you and I.
      And now there is something more. Have you heard this order,
      This latest order that the King has proclaimed to the city?
      Have you heard how our dearest are being treated like enemies?
ISMENE: I have heard nothing about any of those we love,
      Neither good nor evil—not, I mean, since the death
      Of our two brothers, both fallen in a day.

The Argive army, I hear, was withdrawn last night.
I know no more to make me sad or glad.

ANTIGONE:

I thought you did not. That's why I brought you out here,
Where we shan't be heard, to tell you something alone.

ISMENE:

What is it, Antigone? Black news, I can see already.

ANTIGONE:

O Ismene, what do you think? Our two dear brothers . . .
Creon has given funeral honours to one,
And not to the other; nothing but shame and ignominy.
Eteocles has been buried, they tell me, in state,
With all honourable observances due to the dead.
But Polynices, just as unhappily fallen—the order
Says he is not to be buried, not to be mourned;
To be' left unburied, unwept, a feast of flesh
For keen-eyed carrion birds. The noble Creon!
It is against you and me he has made this order.
Yes, against me. And soon he will be here himself
To make it plain to those that have not heard it,
And to enforce it. This is no idle threat;
The punishment for disobedience is death by stoning.
So now you know. And now is the time to show
Whether or not you are worthy of your high blood.

ISMENE: My poor Antigone, if this is really true,
What more can I do, or undo, to help you?

ANTIGONE:

Will you help me? Will you do something with me? Will you?

ISMENE: Help you do what, Antigone? What do you mean?

ANTIGONE:

Would you help me lift the body . . . you and me?

ISMENE:

You cannot mean . . . to bury him? Against the order?

ANTIGONE:

Is he not my brother, and yours, whether you like it
Or not? *I* shall never desert him, never.

ISMENE:

How could you dare, when Creon has expressly forbidden it?

ANTIGONE: He has no right to keep me from my own.

ISMENE: O sister, sister do you forget how our father
Perished in shame and misery, his awful sin
Self-improved, blinded by his own self-mutilation?

And then his mother, his wife—for she was both—
Destroyed herself in a noose of her own making.
And now our brothers, both in a single day
Fallen in an awful exaction of death for death,
Blood for blood, each slain by the other's hand.
Now we two left; and what will be the end of us,
If we transgress the law and defy our king?
O think, Antigone; we are women; it is not for us
To fight against men; our rulers are stronger than we,
And we must obey in this, or in worse than this.
May the dead forgive me, I can do no other
But as I am commanded; to do more is madness.

ANTIGONE: No; then I will not ask you for your help.
Nor would I thank you for it, if you gave it.
Go your own way; I will bury my brother;
And if I die for it, what happiness!
Convicted of reverence—I shall be content
To lie beside a brother whom I love.
We have only a little time to please the living,
But all eternity to love the dead.
There I shall lie for ever. Live, if you will;
Live, and defy the holiest laws of heaven.

ISMENE: I do not defy them; but I cannot act
Against the State. I am not strong enough.

ANTIGONE: Let that be your excuse, then. I will go
And heap a mound of earth over my brother.

ISMENE: I fear for you, Antigone; I fear—

ANTIGONE: You need not fear for me. Fear for yourself.

ISMENE: At least be secret. Do not breathe a word.
I'll not betray your secret.

ANTIGONE: Publish it
To all the world! Else I shall hate you more.

ISMENE: Your heart burns! Mine is frozen at the thought.

ANTIGONE: I know my duty, where true duty lies.

ISMENE: If you can do it; but you're bound to fail.

ANTIGONE: When I have *tried* and failed, I shall have
failed.

ISMENE: No sense in starting on a hopeless task.

ANTIGONE: Oh, I shall hate you if you talk like that!
And *he* will hate you, rightly. Leave me alone
With my own madness. There is no punishment
Can rob me of my honourable death.

ISMENE: Go then, if you are determined, to your folly.
But remember that those who love you ... love you still.

ISMENE *goes into the Palace.*
ANTIGONE *leaves the stage by a side exit.*

. . .

CHORUS:
Wonders are many on earth, and the greatest of these
Is man, who rides the ocean and takes his way
Through the deeps, through wind-swept valleys of perilous seas
That surge and sway.

He is master of ageless Earth, to his own will bending
The immortal mother of gods by the sweat of his brow,
As year succeeds to year, with toil unending
Of mule and plough.

He is lord of all things living; birds of the air,
Beasts of the field, all creatures of sea and land
He taketh, cunning to capture and ensnare
With sleight of hand;

Hunting the savage beast from the upland rocks,
Taming the mountain monarch in his lair,
Teaching the wild horse and the roaming ox
His yoke to bear.

The use of language, the wind-swift motion of brain
He learnt; found out the laws of living together
In cities, building him shelter against the rain
And wintry weather.

There is nothing beyond his power. His subtlety
Meeteth all chance, all danger conquereth.
For every ill he hath found its remedy,
Save only death.

O wondrous subtlety of man, that draws wondrous subtlety of
man, that draws
To good or evil ways! Great honour is given
And power to him who upholdeth his country's laws
And the justice of heaven.

But he that, too rashy daring, walks in sin
In solitary pride to his life's end.
At door of mine shall never enter in
To call me friend.

(Severally, seeing some persons approach from a distance)

O gods! A wonder to see!
Surely it cannot be—
It is no other—
Antigone!
Unhappy maid—
Unhappy Oedipus' daughter; it is she they bring.
Can she have rashly disobeyed
The order of our King?

> *Enter the SENTRY, bringing ANTIGONE guarded*
> *by two more soldiers.*

SENTRY: We've got her. Here's the woman that did the deed.
We found her in the act of burying him. Where's the King?
CHORUS: He is just coming out of the palace now.

> *Enter CREON.*

CREON: What's this? What am I just in time to see?
SENTRY: My lord, an oath's a very dangerous thing.
Second thoughts may prove us liars. Not long since
I swore I wouldn't trust myself again
To face your threats; you gave me a drubbing the first time.
But there's no pleasure like an unexpected pleasure,
Not by a long way. And so I've come again,
Though against my solemn oath. And I've brought this lady,
Who's been caught in the act of setting that grave in order.
And no casting lots for it this time—the prize is mine
And no one else's. So take her; judge and convict her.
I'm free, I hope, and quit of the horrible business.
CREON:
How did you find her? Where have you brought her from?
SENTRY:
She was burying the man with her own hands, and that's the
truth.
CREON: Are you in your senses? Do you know what you are saying?
SENTRY: I saw her myself, burying the body of the man
Whom you said not to bury. Don't I speak plain?
CREON: How did she come to be seen and taken in the act?
SENTRY: It was this way.
After I got back to the place,
With all your threats and curses ringing in my ears,
We swept off all the earth that covered the body,
And left it a sodden naked corpse again;
Then sat up on the hill, on the windward side,
Keeping clear of the stench of him, as far as we could;

All of us keeping each other up to the mark,
With pretty sharp speaking, not to be caught napping this time.
So this went on some hours, till the flaming sun
Was high in the top of the sky, and the heat was blazing.
Suddenly a storm of dust, like a plague from heaven,
Swept over the ground, stripping the trees stark bare,
Filling the sky; you had to shut your eyes
To stand against it. When at last it stopped,
There was the girl, screaming like an angry bird,
When it finds its nest left empty and little ones gone.
Just like that she screamed, seeing the body
Naked, crying and cursing the ones that had done it.
Then she picks up the dry earth in her hands,
And pouring out of a fine bronze urn she's brought
She makes her offering three times to the dead.
Soon as we saw it, down we came and caught her.
She wasn't at all frightened. And so we charged her
With what she'd done before, and this. She admitted it,
I'm glad to say—though sorry too, in a way.
It's good to save your own skin, but a pity
To have to see another get into trouble,
Whom you've no grudge against. However, I can't say
I've ever valued anyone else's life
More than my own, and that's the honest truth.
CREON *(to ANTIGONE):* Well, what do you say—you, hiding your
     head there:
Do you admit, or do you deny the deed?
ANTIGONE: I do admit it. I do not deny it.
CREON *(to the SENTRY):*
You—you may go. You are discharged from blame.

Exit SENTRY.

Now tell me, in as few words as you can,
     Did you know the order forbidding such an act?
ANTIGONE: I knew it, naturally. I was plain enough.
CREON: And yet you dared to contravene it?
ANTIGONE: Yes.
That order did not come from God. Justice,
That dwells with the gods below, knows no such law.
I did not think your edicts strong enough
To overrule the unwritten unalterable laws
Of God and heaven, you being only a man.
They are not of yesterday or to-day, but everlasting,

Though where they came from, none of us can tell.
Guilty of their transgression before God
I cannot be, for any man on earth.
I knew that I should have to die, of course,
With or without your order. If it be soon,
So much the better. Living in daily torment
As I do, who would not be glad to die?
This punishment will not be any pain.
Only if I had let my mother's son
Lie there unburied, then I could not have borne it.
This I can bear. Does that seem foolish to you?
Or is it you that are foolish to judge me so?

CHORUS: She shows her father's stubborn spirit: foolish
    Not to give way when everything's against her.

CREON: Ah, but you'll see. The over-obstinate spirit
    Is soonest broken; as the strongest iron will snap
    If over-tempered in the fire to brittleness.
    A little halter is enough to break
    The wildest horse. Proud thoughts do not sit well
    Upon subordinates. This girl's proud spirit
    Was first in evidence when she broke the law;
    And now, to add insult to her injury,
    She gloats over her deed. But, as I live,
    She shall not flout my orders with impunity.
    My sister's child—ay, were she even nearer,
    Nearest and dearest, she should not escape
    Full punishment—she, and her sister too,
    Her partner, doubtless, in this burying.
      Let her be fetched! She was in the house just now;
    I saw her, hardly in her right mind either.
    Often the thoughts of those who plan dark deeds
    Betray themselves before the deed is done.
    The criminal who being caught still tries
    To make a fair excuse, is damned indeed.

ANTIGONE:
    Now you have caught, will you do more than kill me?

CREON: No, nothing more; that is all I could wish.

ANTIGONE:
    Why then delay? There is nothing that you can say
    That I should wish to hear, as nothing I say
    Can weigh with you. I have given my brother burial.
    What greater honour could I wish? All these

Would say that what I did was honourable,
But fear locks up their lips. To speak and act
Just as he likes is a king's prerogative.
CREON:
You are wrong. None of my subjects thinks as you do.
ANTIGONE: Yes, sir, they do; but dare not tell you so.
CREON: And you are not only alone, but unashamed.
ANTIGONE: There is no shame in honouring my brother.
CREON:
Was not his enemy, who died with him, your brother?
ANTIGONE:
Yes, both were brothers, both of the same parents.
CREON: You honour one, and so insult the other.
ANTIGONE: He that is dead will not accuse me of that.
CREON: He will, if you honour him no more than the traitor.
ANTIGONE:
It was not a slave, but his brother, that died with him.
CREON: Attacking his country, while the other defended it.
ANTIGONE: Even so, we have a duty to the dead.
CREON: Not to give equal honour to good and bad.
ANTIGONE: Who knows? In the country of the dead that may be the
        law.
CREON: An enemy can't be a friend, even when dead.
ANTIGONE: My way is to share my love, not share my hate.
CREON: Go then, and share your love among the dead.
We'll have no woman's law here, while I live.

Enter ISMENE from the Palace.

CHORUS: Here comes Ismene, weeping
        In sisterly sorrow; a darkened brow,
        Flushed face, and the fair cheek marred
        With flooding rain.
CREON: You crawling viper! Lurking in my house
        To suck my blood! Two traitors unbeknown
        Plotting against my throne. Do you admit
        To a share in this burying, or deny all knowledge?
ISMENE: I did it—yes—if she will let me say so.
        I am as much to blame as she is.
ANTIGONE: No.
        That is not just. You would not lend a hand
        And I refused your help in what I did.
ISMENE: But I am not ashamed to stand beside you
        Now in your hour of trial, Antigone.

ANTIGONE:
>Whose was the deed, Death and the dead are witness.
>I love no friend whose love is only words.

ISMENE: O sister, sister, let me share your death,
>Share in the tribute of honour to him that is dead.

ANTIGONE: You shall not die with me. You shall not claim
>That which you would not touch. One death is enough.

ISMENE: How can I bear to live, if you must die?

ANTIGONE: Ask Creon. Is not he the one you care for?

ISMENE: You do yourself no good to taunt me so.

ANTIGONE: Indeed no: even my jests are bitter pains.

ISMENE: But how, O tell me, how can I still help you?

ANTIGONE: Help yourself. I shall not stand in your way.

ISMENE: For pity, Antigone—can I not die with you?

ANTIGONE:
>You chose; life was your choice, when mine was death.

ISMENE: Although I warned you that it would be so.

ANTIGONE: Your way seemed right to some, to others mine.

ISMENE: But now both in the wrong, and both condemned.

ANTIGONE: No, no. You live. My heart was long since dead,
>So it was right for me to help the dead.

CREON: I do believe the creatures both are mad;
>One lately crazed, the other from her birth.

ISMENE: Is it not likely, sir? The strongest mind
>Cannot but break under misfortune's blows.

CREON: Yours did, when you threw in your lot with hers.

ISMENE: How could I wish to live without my sister?

CREON: You have no sister. Count her dead already.

ISMENE: You could not take her—kill your own son's bride?

CREON: Oh, there are other fields for him to plough.

ISMENE: No truer troth was ever made than theirs.

CREON: No son of mine shall wed so vile a creature.

ANTIGONE: O Haemon, can your father spite you so?

CREON: You and your paramour, I hate you both.

CHORUS:
>Sir, would you take her from your own son's arms?

CREON: Not I, but death shall take her.

CHORUS: Be it so.
>Her death, it seems, is certain.

CREON: Certain it is.
>No more delay. Take them, and keep them within—
>The proper place for women. None so brave

As not to look for some way of escape
When they see life stand face to face with death.

The women are taken away.

. . .

Enter HAEMON.

Son, you have heard, I think, our final judgment
On your late betrothed. No angry words, I hope?
Still friends, in spite of everything, my son?
HAEMON: I am your son, sir; by your wise decisions
My life is ruled, and them I shall always obey.
I cannot value any marriage-tie
Above your own good guidance.
CREON: Rightly said.
Your father's will should have your heart's first place.
Only for this do fathers pray for sons
Obedient, loyal, ready to strike down
Their fathers' foes, and love their fathers' friends.
To be the father of unprofitable sons
Is to be the father of sorrows, a laughing-stock
To all one's enemies. Do not be fooled, my son,
By lust and the wiles of a woman. You'll have bought
Cold comfort if your wife's a worthless one.
No wound strikes deeper than love that is turned to hate.
This girl's an enemy; away with her,
And let her go and find a mate in Hades.
Once having caught her in a flagrant act—
The one and only traitor in our State—
I cannot make myself a traitor too;
So she must die. Well may she pray to Zeus,
The God of Family Love. How, if I tolerate
A traitor at home, shall I rule those abroad?
  He that is a righteous master of his house
Will be a righteous statesman. To trangress
Or twist the law to one's own pleasure, presume
To order where one should obey, is sinful,
And I will have none of it.
He whom the State appoints must be obeyed
To the smallest matter, be it right—or wrong.
And he that rules his household, without a doubt,
Will make the wisest king, or, for that matter,
The staunchest subject. He will be the man

You can depend on in the storm of war,
The faithfullest comrade in the day of battle.
There is no more deadly peril than disobedience;
States are devoured by it, homes laid in ruins,
Armies defeated, victory turned to rout.
While simple obedience saves the lives of hundreds
Of honest folk. Therefore, I hold to the law,
And will never betray it—least of all for a woman.
Better be beaten, if need be, by a man,
Than let a woman get the better of us.

CHORUS: To me, as far as an old man can tell,
It seems your Majesty has spoken well.

HAEMON: Father, man's wisdom is the gift of heaven,
The greatest gift of all. I neither am
Nor wish to be clever enough to prove you wrong,
Though all men might not think the same as you do.
Nevertheless, I have to be your watchdog,
To know what others say and what they do,
And what they find to praise and what to blame.
Your frown is a sufficient silencer
Of any word that is not for your ears.
But *I* hear whispers spoken in the dark;
On every side I hear voices of pity
For this poor girl, doomed to the cruellest death,
And most unjust, that ever woman suffered
For an honourable action—burying a brother
Who was killed in battle, rather than leave him naked
For dogs to maul and carrion birds to peck at.
Has she not rather earned a crown of gold?—
Such is the secret talk about the town.
Father, there is nothing I can prize above
Your happiness and well-being. What greater good
Can any son desire? Can any father
Desire more from his son? Therefore I say,
Let not your first thought be your only thought.
Think if there cannot be some other way.
Surely, to think your own the only wisdom,
And yours the only word, the only will,
Betrays a shallow spirit, an empty heart.
It is no weakness for the wisest man
To learn when he is wrong, know when to yield.
So, on the margin of a flooded river

Trees bending to the torrent live unbroken,
While those that strain against it are snapped off.
A sailor has to tack and slacken sheets
Before the gale, or find himself capsized.
   So, father, pause, and put aside your anger.
I think, for what my young opinion's worth,
That, good as it is to have infallible wisdom,
Since this is rarely found, the next best thing
Is to be willing to listen to wise advice.
CHORUS:
   There is something to be said, my lord, for his point of view,
   And for yours as well; there is much to be said on both sides.
CREON: Indeed! Am I to take lessons at my time of life
   From a fellow of his age?
HAEMON: No lesson you need be ashamed of.
   It isn't a question of age, but of right and wrong.
CREON:
   Would you call it right to admire an act of disobedience?
HAEMON: Not if the act were also dishonourable.
CREON: And was not this woman's action dishonourable?
HAEMON: The people of Thebes think not.
CREON: The people of Thebes!
   Since when do I take my orders from the people of Thebes?
HAEMON: Isn't that rather a childish thing to say?
CREON: No. I am king, and responsible only to myself.
HAEMON: A one-man state? What sort of a state is that?
CREON: Why, does not every state belong to its ruler?
HAEMON: You'd be an excellent king—on a desert island.
CREON: Of course, if you're on the woman's side—
HAEMON: No, no—
   Unless you're the woman. It's you I'm fighting for.
CREON:
   What, villain, when every word you speak is against me?
HAEMON: Only because I know you are wrong, wrong.
CREON: Wrong? To respect my own authority?
HAEMON: What sort of respect tramples on all that is holy?
CREON: Despicable coward! No more will than a woman!
HAEMON: I have nothing to be ashamed of.
CREON: Yet you plead her cause.
HAEMON:
   No, *yours,* and mine, and that of the gods of the dead.
CREON: You'll never marry her this side of death.

HAEMON: Then, if she dies, she does not die alone.
CREON: Is that a threat, you impudent—
HAEMON: Is it a threat
  To try to argue against wrong-headedness?
CREON: You'll learn what wrong-headedness is, my friend, to your
    cost.
HAEMON:
  O father, I could call you mad, were you not my father.
CREON: Don't toady me, boy; keep that for your lady-love.
HAEMON: You mean to have the last word, then?
CREON: I do.
  And what is more, by all the gods in heaven,
  I'll make you sorry for your impudence.
  (Calling to those within)
  Bring out that she-devil, and let her die
  Now, with her bridegroom by to see it done!
HAEMON: That sight I'll never see. Nor from this hour
  Shall you see me again. Let those that will
  Be witness of your wickedness and folly:

                                                        Exit.

                         • • •

          Enter a MESSENGER, from the side of the stage.
MESSENGER: Hear, men of Cadmus' city, hear and attend,
  Men of the house of Amphion, people of Thebes!
  What is the life of man? A thing not fixed
  For good or evil, fashioned for praise or blame.
  Chance raises a man to the heights, chance casts him down,
  And none can foretell what will be from what is.
  Creon was once an enviable man;
  He saved his country from her enemies,
  Assumed the sovereign power, and bore it well,
  The honoured father of a royal house.
  Now all is lost; for life without life's joys
  Is living death; and such a life is his.
  Riches and rank and show of majesty
  And state, where no joy is, are empty, vain
  And unsubstantial shadows, of no weight
  To be compared with happiness of heart.
CHORUS: What is your news? Disaster in the royal house?
MESSENGER: Death; and the guilt of it on living heads.
CHORUS: Who dead? And by what hand?

MESSENGER: Haemon is dead,
      Slain by his own—
CHORUS: His father?
MESSENGER: His own hand.
      His father's act it was that drove him to it.
CHORUS: Then all has happened as the prophet said.
MESSENGER: What's next to do, your worships will decide.

                              The Palace door opens.

CHORUS: Here comes the Queen, Eurydice. Poor soul,
      It may be she has heard about her son.

                    Enter EURYDICE, attended by women.

EURYDICE:
      My friends, I heard something of what you were saying
      As I came to the door. I was on my way to prayer
      At the temple of Pallas, and had barely turned the latch
      When I caught your talk of some near calamity.
      I was sick with fear and reeled in the arms of my women.
      But tell me what is the matter; what have you heard?
      I am not unacquainted with grief, and I can bear it.
MESSENGER:
      Madam, it was I that saw it, and will tell you all.
      To try to make it any lighter now
      Would be to prove myself a liar. Truth
      Is always best.
      It was thus. I attended your husband,
      The King, to the edge of the field where lay the body
      Of Polynices, in pitiable state, mauled by the dogs.
      We prayed for him to the Goddess of the Roads, and to Pluto,
      That they might have mercy upon him. We washed the remains
      In holy water, and on a fire of fresh-cut branches
      We burned all that was left of him, and raised
      Over his ashes a mound of his native earth.
      That done, we turned towards the deep rock-chamber
      Of the maid that was married with death.
      Before we reached it,
      One that stood near the accursed place had heard
      Loud cries of anguish, and came to tell King Creon.
      As he approached, came strange uncertain sounds
      Of lamentation, and he cried aloud:
      'Unhappy wretch! Is my foreboding true?
      Is this the most sorrowful journey that ever I went?

My son's voice greets me. Go, some of you, quickly
Through the passage where the stones are thrown apart,
Into the mouth of the cave, and see if it be
My son, my own son Haemon that I hear.
If not, I am the sport of gods.'
We went
And looked, as bidden by our anxious master.
There in the furthest corner of the cave
We saw her hanging by the neck. The rope
Was of the woven linen of her dress.
And, with his arms about her, there stood he
Lamenting his lost bride, his luckless love,
His father's cruelty.
When Creon saw them,
Into the cave he went, moaning piteously.
'O my unhappy boy,' he cried again,
'What have you done? What madness brings you here
To your destruction? Come away, my son,
My son, I do beseech you, come away!'
His son looked at him with one angry stare,
Spat in his face, and then without a word
Drew sword and struck out. But his father fled
Unscathed. Whereon the poor demented boy
Leaned on his sword and thrust it deeply home
In his own side, and while his life ebbed out
Embraced the maid in loose-enfolding arms,
His spurting blood staining her pale cheeks red.

               EURYDICE goes quickly back into the Palace.

Two bodies lie together, wedded in death,
Their bridal sleep a witness to the world
How great calamity can come to man
Through man's perversity.
CHORUS: But what is this?
    The Queen has turned and gone without a word.
MESSENGER: Yes. It is strange. The best that I can hope
    Is that she would not sorrow for her son
    Before us all, but vents her grief in private
    Among her women. She is too wise, I think,
    To take a false step rashly.
CHORUS: It may be.
    Yet there is danger in unnatural silence
    No less than in excess of lamentation.

MESSENGER: I will go in and see, whether in truth
　　　There is some fatal purpose in her grief.
　　　Such silence, as you say, may well be dangerous.

He goes in.

Enter Attendants preceding the King.

CHORUS: The King comes here.
　　　What the tongue scarce dares to tell
　　　Must now be known
　　　By the burden that proves too well
　　　The guilt, no other man's
　　　But his alone.

Enter CREON with the body of HAEMON.

CREON: The sin, the sin of the erring soul
　　　Drives hard unto death.
　　　Behold the slayer, the slain.
　　　The father, the son.
　　　O the curse of my stubbon will!
　　　Son, newly cut off in the newness of youth,
　　　Dead for my fault, not yours.
CHORUS: Alas, too late you have seen the truth.
CREON: I learn in sorrow. Upon my head
　　　God has delivered this heavy punishment,
　　　Has struck me down in the ways of wickedness,
　　　And trod my gladness under foot.
　　　Such is the bitter affliction of mortal man.

Enter the MESSENGER from the Palace.

MESSENGER: Sir, you have this and more than this to bear.
　　　Within there's more to know, more to your pain.
CREON: What more? What pain can overtop this pain?
MESSENGER:
　　　She is dead—your wife, the mother of him that is dead—
　　　The death-wound fresh in her heart. Alas, poor lady!
CREON: Insatiable Death, wilt thou destroy me yet?
　　　What say you, teller of evil?
　　　I am already dead,
　　　And is there more?
　　　Blood upon blood?
　　　More death? My wife?

The central doors open, revealing the body of EURYDICE.

CHORUS: Look then, and see; nothing is hidden now.

CREON: O second horror!
    What fate awaits me now?
    My child here in my arms ... and there, the other ...
    The son ... the mother ...
MESSENGER: There at the altar with the whetted knife
    She stood, and as the darkness dimmed her eyes
    Called on the dead, her elder son and this,
    And with her dying breath cursed you, their slayer.
CREON: O horrible ...
    Is there no sword for me,
    To end this misery?
MESSENGER: Indeed you bear the burden of two deaths.
    It was her dying word.
CREON: And her last act?
MESSENGER: Hearing her son was dead, with her own hand
    She drove the sharp sword home into her heart.
CREON: There is no man can bear this guilt but I.
    It is true, I killed him.
    Lead me away, away. I live no longer.
CHORUS: 'Twere best, if anything is best in evil times.
    What's soonest done, is best, when all is ill.
CREON: Come, my last hour and fairest,
    My only happiness ... come soon.
    Let me not see another day.
    Away ... away ...
CHORUS: The future is not to be known; our present care
    Is with the present; the rest is in other hands.
CREON: I ask no more than I have asked.
CHORUS: Ask nothing.
    What is to be, no mortal can escape.
CREON: I am nothing. I have no life.
    Lead me away ...
    That have killed unwittingly
    My son, my wife.
    I know not where I should turn,
    Where look for help.
    My hands have done amiss, my head is bowed
    With fate too heavy for me.

Exit.

CHORUS: Of happiness the crown
    And chiefest part

Is wisdom, and to hold
The gods in awe.
This is the law
That, seeing the striken heart
Of pride brought down,
We learn when we are old.

The Obligation of a Citizen

CRITO

PERSONS OF THE DIALOGUE:

SOCRATES.   CRITO.

SCENE:—The Prison of Socrates.

Socrates. Why have you come at this hour, Crito? it must be quite early?

Crito. Yes, certainly.

Soc. What is the exact time?

Cr. The dawn is breaking.

Soc. I wonder that the keeper of the prison would let you in.

Cr. He knows me, because I often come, Socrates; moreover, I have done him a kindness.

Soc. And are you only just arrived?

Cr. No, I came some time ago.

Soc. Then why did you sit and say nothing, instead of at once awakening me?

Cr. I should not have liked myself, Socrates, to be in such great trouble and unrest as you are—indeed I should not: I have been watching with amazement your peaceful slumbers; and for that reason I did not awake you, because I wished to minimize the pain. I have always thought you to be of a happy disposition; but never did I see anything like the easy, tranquil manner in which you bear this calamity.

Soc. Why, Crito, when a man has reached my age he ought not to be repining at the approach of death.

Cr. And yet other old men find themselves in similar misfortunes, and age does not prevent them from repining.

Soc. That is true. But you have not told me why you come at this early hour.

Cr. I come to bring you a message which is sad and painful; not, as I believe, to yourself, but to all of us who are your friends, and saddest of all to me.

Soc. What? Has the ship come from Delos, on the arrival of which I am to die?

Cr. No, the ship has not actually arrived, but she will probably be here to-day, as persons who have come from Sunium tell me that they left her there; and therefore to-morrow, Socrates, will be the last day of your life.

Soc. Very well, Crito; if such is the will of God, I am willing; but my belief is that there will be a delay of a day.

Cr. Why do you think so?

Soc. I will tell you. I am to die on the day after the arrival of the ship.

Cr. Yes; that is what the authorities say.

Soc. But I do not think that the ship will be here until tomorrow; this I infer from a vision which I had last night, or rather only just now, when you fortunately allowed me to sleep.

Cr. And what was the nature of the vision?

Soc. There appeared to me the likeness of a woman, fair and comely, clothed in bright raiment, who called to me and said: O Socrates,

'The third day hence to fertile Phthia shalt thou go.'[1]

Cr. What a singular dream, Socrates!

Soc. There can be no doubt about the meaning, Crito, I think.

Cr. Yes; the meaning is only too clear. But, oh! my beloved Socrates, let me entreat you once more to take my advice and escape. For if you die I shall not only lose a friend who can never be replaced, but there is another evil: people who do not know you and me will believe that I might have saved you if I had been willing to give money, but that I did not care. Now, can there be a worse disgrace than this—that I should be thought to value money more than the life of a friend? For the many will not be persuaded that I wanted you to escape, and that you refused.

Soc. But why, my dear Crito, should we care about the opinion of the many? Good men, and they are the only persons who are worth considering, will think of these things truly as they occurred.

Cr. But you see, Socrates, that the opinion of the many must be regarded, for what is now happening shows that they can do the greatest evil to any one who has lost their good opinion.

Soc. I only wish it were so, Crito; and that the many could do the greatest evil; for then they would also be able to do the greatest good

1. Homer, Il. ix. 363.

—and what a fine thing this would be! But in reality they can do neither; for they cannot make a man either wise or foolish; and whatever they do is the result of chance.

Cr. Well, I will not dispute with you; but please to tell me, Socrates, whether you are not acting out of regard to me and your other friends: are you not afraid that if you escape from prison we may get into trouble with the informers for having stolen you away, and lose either the whole or a great part of our property; or that even a worse evil may happen to us? Now, if you fear on our account, be at ease; for in order to save you, we ought surely to run this, or even a greater risk; be persuaded, then, and do as I say.

Soc. Yes, Crito, that is one fear which you mention, but by no means the only one.

Cr. Fear not—there are persons who are willing to get you out of prison at no great cost; and as for the informers, they are far from being exorbitant in their demands—a little money will satisfy them. My means, which are certainly ample, are at your service, and if you have a scruple about spending all mine, here are strangers who will give you the use of theirs; and one of them, Simmias the Theban, has brought a large sum of money for this very purpose; and Cebes and many others are prepared to spend their money in helping you to escape. I say, therefore, do not hesitate on our account, and do not say, as you did in the court,[2] that you will have a difficulty in knowing what to do with yourself anywhere else. For men will love you in other places to which you may go, and not in Athens only; there are friends of mine in Thessaly, if you like to go to them, who will value and protect you, and no Thessalian will give you any trouble. Nor can I think that you are at all justified, Socrates, in betraying your own life when you might be saved; in acting thus you are playing into the hands of your enemies, who are hurrying on your destruction. And further I should say that you are deserting your own children; for you might bring them up and educate them; instead of which you go away and leave them, and they will have to take their chance; and if they do not meet with the usual fate of orphans, there will be small thanks to you. (No man should bring children into the world who is unwilling to persevere to the end in their nurture and education.) But you appear to be choosing the easier part, not the better and manlier, which would have been more becoming in one who professes to care for virtue in all his actions, like yourself. And indeed, I am ashamed not only of you, but of us who are your friends, when I reflect that the whole business will be attributed entirely to our

2. Cp. Apol. 37 C, D.

want of courage. The trial need never have come on, or might have been managed differently; and this last act, or crowning folly, will seem to have occurred through our negligence and cowardice, who might have saved you, if we had been good for anything; and you might have saved yourself, for there was no difficulty at all. See now, Socrates, how sad and discreditable are the consequences, both to us and you. Make up your mind then, or rather have your mind already made up, for the time of deliberation is over, and there is only one thing to be done, which must be done this very night, and if we delay at all will be no longer practicable or possible; I beseech you therefore, Socrates, be persuaded by me, and do as I say.

Soc. Dear Crito, your zeal is invaluable, if a right one; but if wrong, the greater the zeal the greater the danger; and therefore we ought to consider whether I shall or shall not do as you say. For I am and always have been one of those natures who must be guided by reason, whatever the reason may be which upon reflection appears to me to be the best; and now that this chance has befallen me, I cannot repudiate my own words: the principles which I have hitherto honoured and revered I still honour, and unless we can at once find other and better principles, I am certain not to agree with you; no, not even if the power of the multitude could inflict many more imprisonments, confiscations, deaths, frightening us like children with hobgoblin terrors. What will be the fairest way of considering the question? Shall I return to your old argument about the opinions of men?—we were saying that some of them are to be regarded, and others not. Now were we right in maintaining this before I was condemned? And has the argument which was once good now proved to be talk for the sake of talking—mere childish nonsense? That is what I want to consider with your help, Crito:— whether, under my present circumstances, the argument appears to be in any way different or not; and is to be allowed by me or disallowed. That argument, which, as I believe, is maintained by many persons of authority, was to the effect, as I was saying, that the opinions of some men are to be regarded, and of other men not to be regarded. Now you, Crito, are not going to die to-morrow—at least, there is no human probability of this—and therefore you are disinterested and not liable to be deceived by the circumstances in which you are placed. Tell me then, whether I am right in saying that some opinions, and the opinions of some men only, are to be valued, and that other opinions, and the opinions of other men, are not to be valued. I ask you whether I was right in maintaining this?

Cr. Certainly.

Soc. The good are to be regarded, and not the bad?

Cr. Yes.

Soc. And the opinions of the wise are good, and the opinions of the unwise are evil?

Cr. Certainly.

Soc. And what was said about another matter? Is the pupil who devotes himself to the practice of gymnastics supposed to attend to the praise and blame and opinion of every man, or of one man only—his physician or trainer, whoever he may be?

Cr. Of one man only.

Soc. And he ought to fear the censure and welcome the praise of that one only, and not of the many?

Cr. Clearly so.

Soc. And he ought to act and train, and eat and drink in the way which seems good to his single master who has understanding, rather than according to the opinion of all other men put together?

Cr. True.

Soc. And if he disobeys and disregards the opinion and approval of the one, and regards the opinion of the many who have no understanding, will he not suffer evil?

Cr. Certainly he will.

Soc. And what will the evil be, whither tending and what affecting, in the disobedient person?

Cr. Clearly, affecting the body; that is what is destroyed by the evil.

Soc. Very good; and is not this true, Crito, of other things which we need not separately enumerate? In questions of just and unjust, fair and foul, good and evil, which are the subjects of our present consultation, ought we to follow the opinion of the many and to fear them; or the opinion of the one man who has understanding? ought we not to fear and reverence him more than all the rest of the world: and if we desert him shall we not destroy and injure that principle in us which may be assumed to be improved by justice and deteriorated by injustice;— there is such a principle?

Cr. Certainly there is, Socrates.

Soc. Take a parallel instance:—if, acting under the advice of those who have no understanding, we destroy that which is improved by health and is deteriorated by disease, would life be worth having? And that which has been destroyed is—the body?

Cr. Yes.

Soc. Could we live, having an evil and corrupted body?

Cr. Certainly not.

Soc. And will life be worth having, if that higher part of man be destroyed, which is improved by justice and depraved by injustice? Do we suppose that principle, whatever it may be in man, which has to do with justice and injustice, to be inferior to the body?

Cr. Certainly not.

Soc. More honourable than the body?

Cr. Far more.

Soc. Then, my friend, we must not regard what the many say of us: but what he, the one man who has understanding of just and unjust, will say, and what the truth will say. And therefore you begin in error when you advise that we should regard the opinion of the many about just and unjust, good and evil, honourable and dishonourable.—'Well,' some one will say, 'but the many can kill us.'

Cr. Yes, Socrates; that will clearly be the answer.

Soc. And it is true: but still I find with surprise that the old argument is unshaken as ever. And I should like to know whether I may say the same of another proposition—(that not life, but a good life, is to be chiefly valued?)

Cr. Yes, that also remains unshaken.

Soc. And a good life is equivalent to a just and honourable one— that holds also?

Cr. Yes, it does.

Soc. From these premisses I proceed to argue the question whether I ought or ought not to try and escape without the consent of the Athenians: and if I am clearly right in escaping, then I will make the attempt; but if not, I will abstain. The other considerations which you mention, of money and loss of character and the duty of educating one's children, are, I fear, only the doctrines of the multitude, who would be as ready to restore people to life, if they were able, as they are to put them to death—and with as little reason. But now, since the argument has thus far prevailed, the only question which remains to be considered is, whether we shall do rightly either in escaping or in suffering others to aid in our escape and paying them in money and thanks, or whether in reality we shall not do rightly; and if the latter, then death or any other calamity which may ensue on my remaining here must not be allowed to enter into the calculation.

Cr. I think that you are right, Socrates; how then shall we proceed?

Soc. Let us consider the matter together, and do you either refute me if you can, and I will be convinced; or else cease, my dear friend, from repeating to me that I ought to escape against the wishes of the Athenians: for I highly value your attempts to persuade me to do so, but I may not be persuaded against my own better judgment. And now please to consider my first position, and try how you can best answer me.

Cr. I will.

Soc. Are we to say that we are never intentionally to do wrong, or that in one way we ought and in another way we ought not to do wrong, or is doing wrong always evil and dishonourable, as I was just now saying, and as has been already acknowledged by us? Are all our former admissions which were made within a few days to be thrown away? And have we, at our age, been earnestly discoursing with one another all our life long only to discover that we are not better than children? Or, in spite of the opinion of the many, and in spite of consequences whether better or worse, shall we insist on the truth of what was then said, that injustice is always an evil and dishonour to him who acts unjustly? Shall we say so or not?

Cr. Yes.

Soc. Then we must do no wrong?

Cr. Certainly not.

Soc. Nor when injured injure in return, as the many imagine; for we must injure no one at all?[3]

Cr. Clearly not.

Soc. Again, Crito, may we do evil?

Cr. Surely not, Socrates.

Soc. And what of doing evil in return for evil, which is the morality of the many—is that just or not?

Cr. Not just.

Soc. For doing evil to another is the same as injuring him?

Cr. Very true.

Soc. Then we ought not to retaliate or render evil for evil to any one, whatever evil we may have suffered from him. But I would have to consider, Crito, whether you really mean what you are saying. For this opinion has never been held, and never will be held, by any considerable number of persons; and those who are agreed and those who are not agreed upon this point have no common ground, and can only despise one another when they see how widely they differ. Tell me, then, whether you agree with and assent to my first principle, that neither injury nor retaliation nor warding off evil by evil is ever right. And shall that be the premiss of our argument? Or do you decline and dissent from this? For so I have ever thought, and continue to think; but, if you are of another opinion, let me hear what you have to say. If, however, you remain of the same mind as formerly, I will proceed to the next step.

Cr. You may proceed, for I have not changed my mind.

3. e.g. cp. Rep. i. 335 E.

Soc. Then I will go on to the next point, which may be put in the form of a question:—Ought a man to do what he admits to be right, or ought he to betray the right?

Cr. He ought to do what he thinks right.

Soc. But if this is true, what is the application? In leaving the prison against the will of the Athenians, do I wrong any? or rather do I not wrong those whom I ought least to wrong? Do I not desert the principles which were acknowledged by us to be just—what do you say?

Cr. I cannot tell, Socrates; for I do not know.

Soc. Then consider the matter in this way:—Imagine that I am about to play truant (you may call the proceeding by any name which you like), and the laws and the government come and interrogate me: 'Tell us, Socrates,' they say; 'what are you about? are you not going by an act of yours to overturn us—the laws, and the whole state, as far as in you lies? (Do you imagine that a state can subsist and not be overthrown, in which the decisions of law have no power, but are set aside and trampled upon by individuals?') What will be our answer, Crito, to these and the like words? Any one, and especially a rhetorician, will have a good deal to say on behalf of the law which requires a sentence to be carried out. He will argue that this law should not be set aside; and shall we reply, 'Yes; but the state has injured us and given an unjust sentence.' Suppose I say that?

Cr. Very good, Socrates.

Soc. 'And was that our agreement with you?' the law would answer; 'or were you to abide by the sentence of the state?' And if I were to express my astonishment at their words, the law would probably add: 'Answer, Socrates, instead of opening your eyes—you are in the habit of asking and answering questions. Tell us,—What complaint have you to make against us which justifies you in attempting to destroy us and the state? In the first place did we not bring you into existence? Your father married your mother by our aid and begat you. Say whether you have any objection to urge against those of us who regulate marriage?' None, I should reply. 'Or against those of us who after birth regulate the nurture and education of children, in which you also were trained? Were not the laws, which have the charge of education, right in commanding your father to train you in music and gymnastic?' Right, I should reply. 'Well then, since you were brought into the world and nurtured and educated by us, can you deny in the first place that you are our child and slave, as your fathers were before you? And if this is true you are not on equal terms with us; nor can you think that you have a right to do to us what we are doing to you. Would you have any right to strike or revile or do any other evil to your father or your master, if

you had one, because you have been struck or reviled by him, or received some other evil at his hands?—you would not say this? And
because we think right to destroy you, do you think that you have any
right to destroy us in return, and your country as far as in you lies? Will
you, O professor of true virtue, pretend that you are justified in this?
Has a philosopher like you failed to discover that our country is more
to be valued and higher and holier far than mother or father or any
ancestor, and more to be regarded in the eyes of the gods and of men
of understanding? also to be soothed, and gently and reverently en-
treated when angry, even more than a father, and either to be persuaded, or if not persuaded, to be obeyed? And when we are punished
by her, whether with imprisonment or stripes, the punishment is to be
endured in silence; and if she lead us to wounds or death in battle,
thither we follow as is right; neither may any one yield or retreat or
leave his rank, but whether in battle or in a court of law, or in any other
place, he must do what his city and his country order him; or he must
change their view of what is just: and if he may do no violence to his
father or mother, much less may he do violence to his country.' What
answer shall we make to this, Crito? Do the laws speak truly, or do they
not?

    Cr. I think that they do.

    Soc. Then the laws will say: 'Consider, Socrates, if we are speaking
truly that in your present attempt you are going to do us an injury. For,
having brought you into the world, and nurtured and educated you, and
given you and every other citizen a share in every good which we had
to give, we further proclaim to any Athenian by the liberty which we
allow him, that if he does not like us when he has become of age and
has seen the ways of the city, and made our acquaintance, he may go
where he pleases and take his goods with him. None of us laws will
forbid him or interfere with him. Any one who does not like us and the
city, and who wants to emigrate to a colony or to any other city, may
go where he likes, retaining his property. But he who has experience
of the manner in which we order justice and administer the state, and
still remains, has entered into an implied contract that he will do as we
command him. And he who disobeys us is, as we maintain, thrice wrong;
first, because in disobeying us he is disobeying his parents; secondly,
because we are the authors of his education; thirdly, because he has
made an agreement with us that he will duly obey our commands; and
he neither obeys them nor convinces us that our commands are unjust;
and we do not rudely impose them, but give him the alternative of
obeying or convincing us;—that is what we offer, and he does neither.

    'These are the sort of accusations to which, as we were saying, you,

Socrates, will be exposed if you accomplish your intentions; you, above all other Athenians.' Suppose now I ask, why I rather than anybody else? they will justly retort upon me that I above all other men have acknowledged the agreement. 'There is clear proof,' they will say, 'Socrates, that we and the city were not displeasing to you. Of all Athenians you have been the most constant resident in the city, which, as you never leave, you may be supposed to love. For you never went out of the city either to see the games, except once when you went to the Isthmus, or to any other place unless when you were on military service; nor did you travel as other men do. Nor had you any curiosity to know other states or their laws: your affections did not go beyond us and our state; we were your special favourites, and you acquiesced in our government of you; and here in this city you begat your children, which is a proof of your satisfaction. Moreover, you might in the course of the trial, if you had liked, have fixed the penalty at banishment; the state which refuses to let you go now would have let you go then. But you pretended that you preferred death to exile, and that you were not unwilling to die. And now you have forgotten these fine sentiments, and pay no respect to us the laws, of whom you are the destroyer; and are doing what only a miserable slave would do, running away and turning your back upon the compacts and agreements which you made as a citizen. And first of all answer this very question: Are we right in saying that you agreed to be governed according to us in deed, and not in word only? Is that true or not?' How shall we answer, Crito? Must we not assent?

Cr. We cannot help it, Socrates.

Soc. Then will they not say: 'You, Socrates, are breaking the covenants and agreements which you made with us at your leisure, not in any haste or under any compulsion or deception, but after you have had seventy years to think of them, during which time you were at liberty to leave the city, if we were not to your mind, of if our covenants appeared to you to be unfair. You had your choice, and might have gone either to Lacedaemon or Crete, both which states are often praised by you for their good government, or to some other Hellenic or foreign state. Whereas you, above all other Athenians, seemed to be so fond of the state, or, in other words, of us her laws (and who would care about a state which has no laws?), that you never stirred out of her; the halt, the blind, the maimed were not more stationary in her than you were. And now you run away and forsake your agreements. Not so, Socrates, if you will take our advice; do not make yourself ridiculous by escaping out of the city.

'For just consider, if you transgress and err in this sort of way, what good will you do either to yourself or to your friends? That your friends will be driven into exile and deprived of citizenship, or will lose their property, is tolerably certain; and you yourself, if you fly to one of the neighbouring cities, as, for example, Thebes or Megara, both of which are well governed, will come to them as an enemy, Socrates, and their government will be against you, and all patriotic citizens will cast an evil eye upon you as a subverter of the laws, and you will confirm in the minds of the judges the justice of their own condemnation of you. For he who is a corrupter of the laws is more than likely to be a corrupter of the young and foolish portion of mankind. Will you then flee from well-ordered cities and virtuous men? and is existence worth having on these terms? Or will you go to them without shame, and talk to them, Socrates? And what will you say to them? What you say here about virtue and justice and institutions and laws being the best things among men? Would that be decent of you? Surely not. But if you go away from well-governed states to Crito's friends in Thessaly, where there is great disorder and licence, they will be charmed to hear the tale of your escape from prison, set off with ludicrous particulars of the manner in which you were wrapped in a goatskin or some other disguise, and metamorphosed as the manner is of runaways; but will there be no one to remind you that in your old age you were not ashamed to violate the most sacred laws from a miserable desire of a little more life? Perhaps not, if you keep them in a good temper; but if they are out of temper you will hear many degrading things; you will live, but how?—as the flatterer of all men, and the servant of all men; and doing what?—eating and drinking in Thessaly, having gone abroad in order that you may get a dinner. And where will be your fine sentiments about justice and virtue? Say that you wish to live for the sake of your children—you want to bring them up and educate them—will you take them into Thessaly and deprive them of Athenian citizenship? Is this the benefit which you will confer upon them? Or are you under the impression that they will be better cared for and educated here if you are still alive, although absent from them; for your friends will take care of them? Do you fancy that if you are an inhabitant of Thessaly they will take care of them, and if you are an inhabitant of the other world that they will not take care of them? Nay; but if they who call themselves friends are good for anything, they will—to be sure they will.

'Listen, then, Socrates, to us who have brought you up. (Think not of life and children first, and of justice afterwards, but of justice first, that you may be justified before the princes of the world below.) For neither will you nor any that belong to you be happier or holier or juster in this life, or happier in another, if you do as Crito bids. Now you depart in innocence, a sufferer and not a doer of evil; a victim, not of the laws but of men. But if you go forth, returning evil for evil, and injury for injury, breaking the covenants and agreements which you have made with us, and wronging those whom you ought least of all to wrong, that is to say, yourself, your friends, your country, and us, we shall be angry with you while you live, and our brethren, the laws in the world below, will receive you as an enemy; for they will know that you have done your best to destroy us. Listen, then, to us and not to Crito.'

This, dear Crito, is the voice which I seem to hear murmuring in my ears, like the sound of the flute in the ears of the mystic; that voice, I say, is humming in my ears, and prevents me from hearing any other. And I know that anything more which you may say will be vain. Yet speak, if you have anything to say.

Cr. I have nothing to say, Socrates.

Soc. Leave me then, Crito, to fulfill the will of God, and to follow whither he leads.

13. Henry David Thoreau

An Essay on Civil Disobedience

I heartily accept the motto, "That government is best which governs least"; and I should like to see it acted up to more rapidly and systematically. Carried out, it finally amounts to this, which also I believe—"That government is best which governs not at all"; and when men are prepared for it, that will be the kind of government which they will have. Government is at best but an expedient; but most governments are usually, and all governments are sometimes, inexpedient. The objections which have been brought against a standing army, and they are many and weighty, and deserve to prevail, may also at last be brought against a standing government. The standing army is only an arm of the standing government. The government itself, which is only the mode which the people have chosen to execute their will, is equally liable to be abused and perverted before the people can act through it. Witness the present Mexican war, the work of comparatively a few individuals using the standing government as their tool; for, in the outset, the people would not have consented to this measure.

This American government—what is it but a tradition, though a recent one, endeavoring to transmit itself unimpaired to posterity, but each instant losing some of its integrity? It has not the vitality and force of a single living man; for a single man can bend it to his will. It is a sort of wooden gun to the people themselves. But it is not the less necessary for this; for the people must have some complicated machinery or other, and hear its din, to satisfy that idea of government which they have. Governments show thus how successfully men can be imposed on, even impose on themselves, for their own advantage. It is excellent, we must all allow. Yet this government never of itself furthered any enterprise, but by the alacrity with which it got out of its way. *It* does not keep the country free. *It* does not settle the West. *It* does not educate. The character inherent in the American people has done all that has been accomplished; and it would have done somewhat more,

150

if the government had not sometimes got in its way. For government is an expedient by which men would fain succeed in letting one another alone; and, as has been said, when it is most expedient, the governed are most let alone by it. Trade and commerce, if they were not made of india-rubber, would never manage to bounce over the obstacles which legislators are continually putting in their way; and, if one were to judge these men wholly by the effects of their actions and not partly by their intentions, they would deserve to be classed and punished with those mischievous persons who put obstructions on the railroads.

But, to speak practically and as a citizen, unlike those who call themselves no-government men, I ask for, not at once no government, but *at once* a better government. Let every man make known what kind of government would command his respect, and that will be one step toward obtaining it.

After all, the practical reason why, when the power is once in the hands of the people, a majority are permitted, and for a long period continue, to rule is not because they are most likely to be in the right, nor because this seems fairest to the minority, but because they are physically the strongest. But a government in which the majority rule in all cases cannot be based on justice, even as far as men understand it. Can there not be a government in which majorities do not virtually decide right and wrong, but conscience?—in which majorities decide only those questions to which the rule of expediency is applicable? Must the citizen ever for a moment, or in the least degree, resign his conscience to the legislator? Why has every man a conscience, then? I think that we should be men first, and subjects afterward. It is not desirable to cultivate a respect for the law, so much as for the right. The only obligation which I have a right to assume is to do at any time what I think right. It is truly enough said that a corporation has no conscience; but a corporation of conscientious men is a corporation *with* a conscience. Law never made men a whit more just; and, by means of their respect for it, even the well-disposed are daily made the agents of injustice. A common and natural result of an undue respect for law is, that you may see a file of soldiers, colonel, captain, corporal, privates, powder-monkeys, and all, marching in admirable order over hill and dale to the wars, against their wills, ay, against their common sense and consciences, which makes it very steep marching indeed, and produces a palpitation of the heart. They have no doubt that it is a damnable business in which they are concerned; they are all peaceably inclined. Now, what are they? Men at all? or small movable forts and magazines, at the service of some unscrupulous man in power? Visit the Navy Yard, and behold a marine, such a man as an American government can

make, or such as it can make a man with its black arts—a mere shadow
and reminiscence of humanity, a man laid out alive and standing, and
already, as one may say, buried under arms with funeral accompani-
ments, though it may be,

> "Not a drum was heard, not a funeral note,
>   As his corse to the rampart we hurried;
> Not a soldier discharged his farewell shot
>   O'er the grave where our hero we buried."

The mass of men serve the state thus, not as men mainly, but as
machines, with their bodies. They are the standing army, and the militia, jailers, constables, *posse comitatus,* etc. In most cases there is no
free exercise whatever of the judgment or of the moral sense; but they
put themselves on a level with wood and earth and stones; and wooden
men can perhaps be manufactured that will serve the purpose as well.
Such command no more respect than men of straw or a lump of dirt.
They have the same sort of worth only as horses and dogs. Yet such as
these even are commonly esteemed good citizens. Others—as most
legislators, politicians, lawyers, ministers, and office-holders—serve the
state chiefly with their heads; and, as they rarely make any moral distinctions, they are as likely to serve the devil, without *intending* it, as
God. A very few—as heroes, patriots, martyrs, reformers in the great
sense, and *men*—serve the state with their consciences also, and so
necessarily resist it for the most part; and they are commonly treated
as enemies by it. A wise man will only be useful as a man, and will not
submit to be "clay," and "stop a hole to keep the wind away," but leave
that office to this dust at least:

> "I am too high-born to be propertied,
> To be a secondary at control,
> Or useful serving-man and instrument
> To any sovereign state throughout the world."

He who gives himself entirely to his fellow men appears to them
useless and selfish; but he who gives himself partially to them is pronounced a benefactor and philanthropist.

How does it become a man to behave toward this American government today? I answer, that he cannot without disgrace be associated
with it. I cannot for an instant recognize that political organization as
my government which is the *slave's* government also.

All men recognize the right of revolution; that is, the right to refuse
allegiance to, and to resist, the government, when its tyranny or its
inefficiency are great and unendurable. But almost all say that such is
not the case now. But such was the case, they think, in the Revolution
of '75. If one were to tell me that this was a bad government because

it taxed certain foreign commodities brought to its ports, it is most probable that I should not make an ado about it, for I can do without them. All machines have their friction; and possibly this does enough good to counterbalance the evil. At any rate, it is a great evil to make a stir about it. But when the friction comes to have its machine, and oppression and robbery are organized, I say, let us not have such a machine any longer. In other words, when a sixth of the population of a nation which has undertaken to be the refuge of liberty are slaves, and a whole country is unjustly overrun and conquered by a foreign army, and subjected to military law, I think that it is not too soon for honest men to rebel and revolutionize. What makes this duty the more urgent is the fact that the country so overrun is not our own, but ours is the invading army.

Paley, a common authority with many on moral questions, in his chapter on the "Duty of Submission to Civil Government," resolves all civil obligation into expediency; and he proceeds to say that "so long as the interest of the whole society requires it, that is, so long as the established government cannot be resisted or changed without public inconveniency, it is the will of God . . . that the established government be obeyed—and no longer. This principle being admitted, the justice of every particular case of resistance is reduced to a computation of the quantity of the danger and grievance on the one side, and the probability and expense of redressing it on the other." Of this, he says, every man shall judge for himself. But Paley appears never to have contemplated those cases to which the rule of expediency does not apply, in which a people, as well as an individual, must do justice, cost what it may. If I have unjustly wrested a plank from a drowning man, I must restore it to him though I drown myself. This, according to Paley, would be inconvenient. But he that would save his life, in such a case, shall lose it. This people must cease to hold slaves, and to make war on Mexico, though it cost them their existence as a people. . . .

Unjust laws exist: shall we be content to obey them, or shall we endeavor to amend them, and obey them until we have succeeded, or shall we transgress them at once? Men generally, under such a government as this, think that they ought to wait until they have persuaded the majority to alter them. They think that, if they should resist, the remedy would be worse than the evil. But it is the fault of the government itself that the remedy *is* worse than the evil. *It* makes it worse. Why is it not more apt to anticipate and provide for reform? Why does it not cherish its wise minority? Why does it cry and resist before it is hurt? Why does it not encourage its citizens to be on the alert to point out its faults, and *do* better than it would have them? Why does it always crucify Christ, and excommunicate Copernicus and Luther, and pronounce Washington and Franklin rebels?

One would think, that a deliberate and practical denial of its authority was the only offence never contemplated by government; else, why has it not assigned its definite, its suitable and proportionate, penalty? If a man who has no property refuses but once to earn nine shillings for the State, he is put in prison for a period unlimited by any law that I know, and determined only by the discretion of those who placed him there; but if he should steal ninety times nine shillings from the State, he is soon permitted to go at large again.

If the injustice is part of the necessary friction of the machine of government, let it go, let it go: perchance it will wear smooth—certainly the machine will wear out. If the injustice has a spring, or a pulley, or a rope, or a crank, exclusively for itself, then perhaps you may consider whether the remedy will not be worse than the evil; but if it is of such a nature that it requires you to be the agent of injustice to another, then, I say, break the law. Let your life be a counter-friction to stop the machine. What I have to do is to see, at any rate, that I do not lend myself to the wrong which I condemn.

As for adopting the ways which the State has provided for remedying the evil, I know not of such ways. They take too much time, and a man's life will be gone. I have other affairs to attend to. I came into this world, not chiefly to make this a good place to live in, but to live in it, be it good or bad. A man has not everything to do, but something; and because he cannot do *everything*, it is not necessary that he should do *something* wrong. It is not my business to be petitioning the Governor or the Legislature any more than it is theirs to petition me; and if they should not hear my petition, what should I do then? But in this case the State has provided no way: its very Constitution is the evil. This may seem to be harsh and stubborn and unconciliatory; but it is to treat with the utmost kindness and consideration the only spirit that can appreciate or deserves it. So is all change for the better, like birth and death, which convulse the body.

I do not hesitate to say, that those who call themselves Abolitionists should at once effectually withdraw their support, both in person and property, from the government of Massachusetts, and not wait till they constitute a majority of one, before they suffer the right to prevail through them. I think that it is enough if they have God on their side, without waiting for that other one. Moreover, any man more right than his neighbors constitutes a majority of one already.

I meet this American government, or its representative, the State government, directly, and face to face, once a year—no more—in the person of its tax-gatherer; this is the only mode in which a man situated as I am necessarily meets it; and it then says distinctly, Recognize me; and the simplest, the most effectual, and, in the present posture of affairs, the indispensablest mode of treating with it on this head, of expressing your little satisfaction with and love for it, is to deny it then. My civil neighbor, the tax-gatherer, is the very man I have to deal with —for it is, after all, with men and not with parchment that I quarrel— and he has voluntarily chosen to be an agent of the government. How shall he ever know well what he is and does as an officer of the government, or as a man, until he is obliged to consider whether he shall treat me, his neighbor, for whom he has respect, as a neighbor and well-disposed man, or as a maniac and disturber of the peace, and see if he can get over this obstruction to his neighborliness without a ruder and more impetuous thought or speech corresponding with his action. I know this well, that if one thousand, if one hundred, if ten men whom I could name—if ten *honest* men only—ay, if *one* HONEST man, in this State of Massachusetts, *ceasing to hold slaves,* were actually to withdraw from this copartnership, and be locked up in the county jail therefor, it would be the abolition of slavery in America. For it matters not how small the beginning may seem to be: what is once well done is done forever. But we love better to talk about it: that we say is our mission. Reform keeps many scores of newspapers in it service, but not one man. If my esteemed neighbor, the State's ambassador, who will devote his days to the settlement of the question of human rights in the Council Chamber, instead of being threatened with the prisons of Carolina, were to sit down the prisoner of Massachusetts, that State which is so anxious to foist the sin of slavery upon her sister—though at present she can discover only an act of inhospitality to be the ground of a quarrel with her—the Legislature would not wholly waive the subject the following winter.

Under a government which imprisons any unjustly, the true place for a just man is also a prison. The proper place today, the only place which Massachusetts has provided for her freer and less desponding spirits, is in her prisons, to be put out and locked out of the State by her own act, as they have already put themselves out by their principles. It is there that the fugitive slave, and the Mexican prisoner on parole, and the Indian come to plead the wrongs of his race should find them; on that separate, but more free and honorable, ground, where the State places those who are not *with* her, but *against* her—the only house in a slave State in which a free man can abide with honor. If any think that their influence would be lost there, and their voices no longer afflict the ear of the State, that they would not be as an enemy within its walls, they do not know by how much truth is stronger than error, nor how much more eloquently and effectively he can combat injustice who has experienced a little in his own person. Cast your whole vote, not a strip of paper merely, but your whole influence. A minority is powerless while it conforms to the majority; it is not even a minority then; but it is irresistible when it clogs by its whole weight. If the alternative is to keep all just men in prison, or give up war and slavery, the State will not hesitate which to choose. If a thousand men were not to pay their tax-bills this year, that would not be a violent and bloody measure, as it would be to pay them, and enable the State to commit violence and shed innocent blood. This is, in fact, the definition of a peaceable revolution, if any such is possible. If the tax-gatherer, or any other public officer, asks me, as one has done, "But what shall I do?" my answer is, "If you really wish to do anything, resign your office." When the subject has refused allegiance, and the officer has resigned his office, then the revolution is accomplished. . . .

Some years ago, the State met me in behalf of the Church, and commanded me to pay a certain sum toward the support of a clergyman whose preaching my father attended, but never I myself. "Pay," it said, "or be locked up in the jail." I declined to pay. But, unfortunately, another man saw fit to pay it. I did not see why the schoolmaster should be taxed to support the priest, and not the priest the schoolmaster; for I was not the State's schoolmaster, but I supported myself by voluntary subscription. I did not see why the lyceum should not present its tax bill, and have the State to back its demand, as well as the Church. However, at the request of the selectmen, I condescended to make some such statement as this in writing: "Know all men by these presents, that I, Henry Thoreau, do not wish to be regarded as a member of any incorporated society which I have not joined." This I gave to the town clerk; and he has it. The State, having thus learned that I did not wish to be regarded as a member of that church, has never made a like demand on me since; though it said that it must adhere to its original presumption that time. If I had known how to name them, I should then have signed off in detail from all the societies which I never signed on to; but I did not know where to find a complete list.

I have paid no poll-tax for six years. I was put into a jail once on this account, for one night; and, as I stood considering the walls of solid stone, two or three feet thick, the door of wood and iron, a foot thick, and the iron grating which strained the light, I could not help being struck with the foolishness of that institution which treated me as if I were mere flesh and blood and bones, to be locked up. I wondered that it should have concluded at length that this was the best use it could put me to, and had never thought to avail itself of my services in some way. I saw that, if there was a wall of stone between me and my townsmen, there was a still more difficult one to climb or break through before they could get to be as free as I was. I did not for a moment feel confined, and the walls seemed a great waste of stone and mortar. I felt as if I alone of all my townsmen had paid my tax. They plainly did not know how to treat me, but behaved like persons who are underbred. In every threat and in every compliment there was a blunder; for they thought that my chief desire was to stand the other side of that stone wall. I could not but smile to see how industriously they locked the door on my meditations, which followed them out again without let or hindrance, and *they* were really all that was dangerous. As they could not reach me, they had resolved to punish my body; just as boys, if they cannot come at some person against whom they have a spite, will abuse his dog. I saw that the State was half-witted, that it was timid as a lone woman with her silver spoons, and that it did not know its friends from its foes, and I lost all my remaining respect for it, and pitied it.

Thus the State never intentionally confronts a man's sense, intellectual or moral, but only his body, his senses. It is not armed with superior wit or honesty, but with superior physical strength. I was not born to be forced. I will breathe after my own fashion. Let us see who is the strongest. What force has a multitude? They only can force me who obey a higher law than I. They force me to become like themselves. I do not hear of *men* being *forced* to live this way or that by masses of men. What sort of life were that to live? When I meet a government which says to me, "Your money or your life," why should I be in haste to give it my money? It may be in a great strait, and not know what to do: I cannot help that. It must help itself; do as I do. It is not worth the while to snivel about it. I am not responsible for the successful working of the machinery of society. I am not the son of the engineer. I perceive that, when an acorn and a chestnut fall side by side, the one does not remain inert to make way for the other, but both obey their own laws, and spring and grow and flourish as best they can, till one, perchance, overshadows and destroys the other. If a plant cannot live according to its nature, it dies; and so a man. . . .

The Criminal

A young man of strong body, weakened by hunger, sat on the walker's portion of the street stretching his hand toward all who passed, begging and repeating the sad song of his defeat in life, while suffering from hunger and from humiliation.

When night came, his lips and tongue were parched, while his hand was still as empty as his stomach.

He gathered himself and went out from the city, where he sat under a tree and wept bitterly. Then he lifted his puzzled eyes to heaven while hunger was eating his inside, and he said, "Oh Lord, I went to the rich man and asked for employment, but he turned away because of my shabbiness; I knocked at the school door, but was forbidden solace because I was empty-handed; I sought any occupation that would give me bread, but all to no avail. In desperation I asked alms, but Thy worshippers saw me and said, "He is strong and lazy, and he should not beg."

"Oh Lord, it is Thy will that my mother gave birth unto me, and now the earth offers me back to You before the Ending."

His expression then changed. He arose and his eyes now glittered in determination. He fashioned a thick and heavy stick from the branch of the tree, and pointed it toward the city, shouting, "I asked for bread with all the strength of my voice, and was refused. Now I shall abtain it by the strength of my muscles! I asked for bread in the name of mercy and love, but humanity did not heed. I shall take it now in the name of evil!"

The passing years rendered the youth a robber, killer, and destroyer of souls, he crushed all who opposed him; he amassed fabulous wealth with which he won himself over to those in power. He was admired by colleagues, envied by other thieves, and feared by the multitudes.

His riches and false position prevailed upon the Emir to appoint him deputy in that city—the sad process pursued by unwise governors. Thefts were then legalized; oppression was supported by authority; crushing of the weak became commonplace; the throngs curried and praised.

Thus does the first touch of humanity's selfishness make criminals of the humble, and make killers of the sons of peace; thus does the early greed of humanity grow and strike back at humanity a thousandfold!

The Philosopher's Role in Political Controversies

My concern in this paper is with what appears to me to be a very menacing development in political argument in the U.S. today. The development to which I refer is the tendency to stifle much legitimate protest against the socio-economic and political status quo by *far-fetched* employment of terms like "violence," "disruption," "law and order." Indeed, the employment of these terms by defenders of the established order of things often appears to be nothing less than political manipulation, whether or not such manipulation is done in an entirely conscious way. The situation is one in which the term "violence," like other related terms, is employed often and indiscriminately by public officials and their supporters whenever a radical or economically disadvantaged group undertakes action threatening the status quo. At the same time, actions which would seem to be clear manifestations of violence—e.g. military combat, police attacks on demonstrators—receive little if any description in the public news media *as* acts of violence.

What I propose to do is to demonstrate some of the ways in which the techniques of philosophical analysis may be usefully applied in order to unravel various sorts of ambiguity in the usage of terms like "law and order" and "violence." My focus here is particularly on the term "violence."

The hypocritical use of terms like "violence" and "law and order" at its worst amounts to the claim that an otherwise identical action—e.g. shooting another human being through the head—should be described as "committing violence" on one hand and as "upholding law and order" on the other hand, depending upon whether the person who wields the gun is a Black Panther or a policeman. Such a trend bears frightening resemblance to what we are accustomed to call the reasoning method or moral premises of the authorities in a police state. It resembles also, to some extent, the adage of the master-slave relationship—viz. weapons in the hands of the masters are the sign of an honorable profession; the same weapons in the hands of slaves are a sign of a capital offense.[1] The threat, moreover, to which we in the U.S. today are increasingly subject is that the resentment harbored by the poor in general (especially those in racial minorities), initially founded in the institutionalized social disadvantages they experience, will be provoked by police-state tactics to the point of full-blown revolution with its attendant widespread destruction and death. Thus any success which philosophers may have in clarifying this issue for the general public is certainly more than a matter of mere theoretical nicety.

Opportunities for ambiguity with respect to a term such as "violence" are increased by a tendency in ordinary usage to employ this term in a *personally* biased way. We often fail to identify many events and actions as violent simply because we have become used to ignoring them. They are things that happen to other people in far away places. "Violence," in this limited sense, is only what happens to me or to persons and things for whom I care. *However,* it is clear that responses differ from one person to another once new events and new political groups call upon us to face this complacency. Those who like to use phrases such as "law and order" often act as if they cannot see the point of calling war and police actions forms of violence. Other persons respond with more concern if with some understandable confusion. We seem to be faced with a situation in which new events and new social reformers call upon us to make new—and perhaps ultimately more consistent—extensions of terms like "violence." Simultaneously, political spokesmen for the prerogatives of established property call upon us —covertly, obliquely—to deny extension of the term "violence" to these new areas. Still worse, the latter group of spokesmen also call upon us at the same time to extend the term "violence" in rather overtly bizarre ways; e.g. photographers fallen upon and beaten by policemen somehow become guilty of assaulting policemen!

The process of "doublethink," as George Orwell called it,[2] seems already discernible in a union official's press release opposing the recent wildcat strike by truck drivers: "It's a hell of a day when we have troops riding shotguns on a truck, but somehow we must stop this violence through law."[3]

The statement exhibits a tendency toward doublethink inasmuch as it implies that the terms "law" and "violence" refer to two qualitatively distinct sorts of things, while simultaneously it uses these terms to refer to situations which differ only in that a national guardsman holds the rifle in one case and a wildcat striker holds the rifle in the other case. It would appear, thus, that the meaning of the term "violence" as used by this speaker is indeed "force exercised by someone other than an agent of a government or an agent of property owners." The term "violence" is not to be applied to the possible actions of the national guardsmen. Actually, if the term "violence" were applied in this sentence to the actions of the troops, we would have a very odd statement: " . . . somehow we must stop this violence through violence (!)."

Still, this sort of politically manipulative use of the term "violence" is not as ominous as other forms of distortion of meaning. A worse form of distortion of meaning occurs when even such actions as occupying a building, picketing, or using obscene language are identified as "violence," simply because the actions are clearly challenges against traditionally instituted authority.[4] Here the term "violence" comes to designate and denigrate simply those actions directed against institutional authority. In the same manner the term "law" comes to designate and enshrine those actions carried out by agents of a government or of a property owner. Thus genuinely peaceful demonstrations become violence, while an attack on demonstrators by club-wielding police will simply be law. The phrase "law *and order*" seems quite appropriately invoked here—in a perverse sense—inasmuch as the "order" intended is accurately captured in the sense of the phrase, "the established order."

If this kind of politically biased employment of the term "violence" can be made to prevail, two consequences would follow. (i) There will be no such thing as a justifiable resort to violence, e.g. civil rebellion as in Vietnam. "Violence" will be simply a pejorative term, and prima facie identification of an act which is either criminal or immoral or both. The wrong-doers so identified will never be policemen, soldiers, officials or proprietors. (ii) Policemen, soldiers, officials, and proprietors, by their very identifications, will be incapable of committing violence, at least while on duty. The term will be inapplicable to them.

We may instructively compare this currently developing situation —if it is indeed developing, as I fear—with that described by Thorstein Veblen in 1921 concerning the word "sabotage."[5] The term "sabotage," noted Veblen, initially designated a purposeful slowing down of the work process. As such, it has and ought to be applied not only to the actions of syndicalists but as well to the actions of entrepreneurs when they curtail production for the sake of greater profits. However, the newspaper writers have made a specific point of applying the term only to the actions of workers, and of implying that the action is always violent. Of this intentionally discrediting sort of usage of the term "sabotage," Veblen remarked: "This is unfortunate. It lessens the usefulness of the word by making it a means of denunciation rather than of understanding."[6]

Veblen's point is a very insightful one. The process of distortion underway consists in changing the word from a term of explanation and description, to a term of denunciation. Consequently language suffers in terms of a loss of usefulness. The logically possible extreme of this sort of operation on the meanings of words is portrayed in George Orwell's *1984* in the varieties of the language of Newspeak used in Oceania.[7] In Orwell's projection of the year 1984, the assertion "freedom in slavery" is literally true. Orwell portrays here an extension of the orientation of fascist parties of his time, for whom individual freedom was indeed something bad and subordination to the state a positive good to be sought after by each person. The claims of the Declaration of Independence, Orwell asserts, would be untranslatable into Newspeak, except perhaps as a panegyric on the virtues of absolute dictatorship. In general Newspeak is to function by removing as many words as possible from language, so that "bad" becomes "ungood," "excellent" becomes "plusgood," and so on. Lacking a variety of words, one can produce variations on governmental propaganda with only the greatest effort. Of still greater importance, however, is the elimination, in Newspeak, of the *concept* of freedom in the earlier sense of the word. One can only say, e.g. "The dog is free of lice," but not "The individual person should be free to choose." The latter meaning no longer exists. With the passage of time and the institution of state censorship, the concept of freedom in the old sense becomes literally removed. Now it is not possible to seek freedom, in the old sense, inasmuch as one cannot seek what one cannot cognize.

The situation prevailing in our society today is surely far short of the hopelessness of Orwell's 1984, where the literal meanings of words have already been changed. In 1984 one cannot correctly say, "The officials are using words in the wrong way." Today one can. It is unfortunate that we must conclude, if we would try to speak the truth, that public officials appear to intentionally misuse words in order to justify governmental or corporation actions which violate publicly understood rules while claiming to adhere to these rules. A most recent example is the Defense Department's announcement to the effect that the Air Force is honoring Congress's moratorium on the right of the U.S. military to fly support missions for U.S. supported Cambodian combat troops—honoring this moratorium by *calling* all such combat support missions "interdiction" against enemy action in Cambodia which might effect the welfare of U.S. troops in Vietnam."[8]

I wish to conclude that my examinations clearly show that public officials (government and corporation officials alike) do intentionally use words in the wrong way in order to achieve their desired ends, especially words such as "violence" and "law and order." I think it is intuitively clear that there is something wrong in the way in which these officials use such words, simply inasmuch as they use them in a manipulative way, i.e. pretending that the words have a broad scope but actually giving them a very significantly selected scope. Thus "violence" and "law" would seem, on one level of meaning, to indicate, respectively, "exertion of destructive force" and "publicly agreed-upon official rules for behavior." In actuality, however, as I have argued, the word "violence" is applied indiscriminately to any significant actions of persons who oppose the established order of things, while the word "law" is applied indiscriminately to all actions of officials. In a similar way, what is described as "heroism" when performed by U.S. soldiers or police, or soldiers of our allies, is described as "terrorism" when performed by Viet Cong, Weatherman groups, Black Panthers, Palestinian guerrillas—and so on. There may be some technical distinctions here. E.g. Palestinian guerrillas blow up airliners while Israeli pilots blow up villages. However, it is likely that such distinctions will break down in the long run, and in any case, the general presence of violence in both sorts of cases is what concerns us.

The important issue in all of this, however, is this—*what* is it that constitutes using words 'in the wrong way'? All of the considerations which I have offered in support of my position are considerations about the *consequences* arising from using words in one way as opposed to another. Orwell's account clearly suggests that the importance of extra words is in their capacity to enable us to make extra distinctions. The classical linguist, F. De Sassure, argued that a new word comes into existence in a language when a distinction is needed which the old vocabulary cannot handle with sufficient clarity.[9] The concept of freedom clearly serves the function of enabling people to seek situations corresponding to its content. The concept of violence serves the function of enabling people to reflect upon the fact that suffering, death and destruction are evils in themselves, however much particular circumstances may justify their occurrence—e.g. violent rebellion against a despotic governmental regime. If this concept should be literally removed from applicability to e.g., police actions, then notions of police brutality and civil rights become similarly outmoded.[10]

Is the major part of the notion of right versus wrong usage of terms like "violence" to be found in such considerations? I think so. I realize that this is to assert what will seem strange to many professional philosophers today, viz. that considerations which are at least in part moral ones can serve to determine proper linguistic usage. Nonetheless, it seems to me that this is indeed the case. Nor should this really be surprising, for we are dealing here with borderline or crisis situations in the meanings of words. New situations have given rise to new rifts within the community of users of the language, and to the need for entertaining new questions.

How *should* the word "violence" be used? Is this a moral question, or a technical question, or both? I think it is both. We may compare this sort of question to questions arising within various disciplines. Is James Joyce's *Finnegans Wake* "a novel"? Is segregation according to race a denial of "equal treatment under law," regardless of the fact that separate facilities are technically equal in other respects? The answers to these sorts of questions may be had, presumably, by consulting the users of technical language involved in each case and trying to settle the dispute on the basis of what appears to best serve the long range, publicly understood purposes of the particular discipline involved. E.g. freedom of innovation is a value in aesthetics; acceptability of the social system to citizens of all groups who must be called upon to support that system is a value in law. Other values can be found which compete with these, of course. Perhaps, then, the only way in which to ultimately arrive at an answer is to say that the answer which satisfies the greater portion of participants is the one that must prevail. Unfortunately, in law as in language, a portion of those persons affected by such decisions often have no concept of their right or duty to participate in making these decisions.

What, however, is the long-range purpose of a language system in general, i.e. of everyday language? An answer which is surely correct, but also unsatisfying, is that language in general should serve all the various purposes for which people use language. Perhaps it helps to add that human beings depend to a great extent on language for *survival.* Again, this appears both correct and too vague. A vital clue emerges, however, if we ask, "*Who* decides what is conducive to human survival in a particular society, using a particular language?" Apparently, when we consider such words as "freedom," "democracy," "declared war," "violence," "aggression" and so on, we find ourselves confronted with a very specific political pattern. We find the pattern of an imposition of usage on the bulk of the community, by a controlling minority, for the sake of continuing and extending that control. This is not to say that the majority do not acquiesce in this state of affairs. It is to say that acquiescence is *all* that they do give. They do not reflect, discuss, or contribute to efforts at redefinition. Thus they are easily manipulated.

The final answer I want to give, then, is that proper linguistic usage should be decided, in these critical situations, by a conscious determination on the part of the community of users of the language, based on their understanding of their shared purposes. Philosophers have an important ability, it would seem, to aid in such a process. They are prone, as well as able, to stand partway outside the community's merely accidental usage of the moment, and to point to structural peculiarities therein. This is what I have tried to do with respect to the manipulative use of language on the part of the political right. If I am correct concerning the importance of this sort of task, then surely an entire new field of philosophical activity lies before us. My argument here for the most part only scratches the surface of this new field, in the hope that further investigations will follow.

No doubt some will object that by taking this sort of approach the philosopher thus involves himself in politics. To this I would reply that where the philosopher is uniquely qualified to clarify significant political issues that hinge on linguistic confusion, there is every good reason for the philosopher, in his professional role, to take a political position.

Endnotes

1. See Karl Marx, *The Civil War in France* (1871). Cf. Thorstein Veblen, *The Theory of the Leisure Class* (1899).
2. George Orwell, *1984.*
3. *The Plain Dealer,* April 20, 1970, p. 1.
4. Representative is the comment of Vice President Spiro Agnew, speaking on November 20, 1969 in Montgomery, Alabama, on the topic of student demonstrators: "But they also list in their numbers an arrogant few who march under the flags and portraits of dictators, who intimidate and harass university professors, who use gutter obscenities to shout down speakers with whom they disagree, who openly profess their belief in the efficacy of violence in a democratic society." AP release of the prepared text.
5. Thorstein Veblen, *The Engineers and the Price System,* (1921).
6. *Ibid.,* as reprinted in M. Eastman (ed.), *The Portable Veblen* (N.Y., Viking Press, 1948), p. 431.
7. Orwell, *1984;* see the postscript essay on the techniques of Newspeak.
8. UPI release as printed in *The Cleveland Press,* (Cleveland Ohio; August 7, 1971).
9. Ferdinand DeSassure, *General Course in Lingusitics.*
10. It should be noted that the notion of "police brutality" has a clearly implied usage which is not mere stereotype, but rather a new usage serving an important function. Prior to the introduction of this concept, we lack a significant awareness of the importance of bad behavior on the part of the police. Interestingly enough, as shown by Paul Jacobs, while the notion of police brutality is usually brought up these days with respect to police attacks on demonstrators, the more destructive aspect of police behavior is to be found in the regular practices of terrorizing ghetto residents.

Community versus Class-Oppression

Social Systems

He who would enquire into the nature and various kinds of government must first of all determine 'What is a state?' At present this is a
disputed question. Some say that the state has done a certain act; others,
no, not the state, but the oligarchy or the tyrant. And the legislator or
statesman is concerned entirely with the state; a constitution or government being an arrangement of the inhabitants of a state. But a state is
composite, and, like any other whole, made up of many parts;—these
are the citizens, who compose it. It is evident, therefore, that we must
begin by asking, Who is the citizen, and what is the meaning of the
term? For here again there may be a difference of opinion. He who is
a citizen in a democracy will often not be a citizen in an oligarchy.
Leaving out of consideration those who have been made citizens, or
who have obtained the name of citizen in any other accidental manner,
we may say, first, that a citizen is not a citizen because he lives in a
certain place, for resident aliens and slaves share in the place; nor is he
a citizen who has no legal right except that of suing and being sued; for
this right may be enjoyed under the provisions of a treaty. Even resident aliens in many places possess such rights, although in an imperfect
form; for they are obliged to have a patron. Hence they do but imper-
fectly participate in citizenship, and we call them citizens only in a
qualified sense, as we might apply the term to children who are too
young to be on the register, or to old men who have been relieved from
state duties. Of these we do not say simply that they are citizens, but
add in the one case that they are not of age, and in the other, that they
are past the age, or something of that sort; the precise expression is
immaterial, for our meaning is clear. Similar difficulties to those which
I have mentioned may be raised and answered about deprived citizens
and about exiles. But the citizen, whom we are seeking to define, is a
citizen in the strictest sense, against whom no such exception can be
taken, and his special characteristic is that he shares in the administra-

tion of justice, and in offices. ... When the state is framed upon the principle of equality and likeness, the citizens think that they ought to hold office by turns. In the order of nature every one would take his turn of service; and then again, somebody else would look after his interest, just as he, while in office, had looked after theirs. [That was originally the way.] But now-a-days, for the sake of the advantage which is to be gained from the public revenues and from office, men want to be always in office. One might imagine that the rulers, being sickly, were only kept in health while they continued in office; in that case we may be sure that they would be hunting after places. The conclusion is evident: that governments, which have a regard to the common interest, are constituted in accordance with strict principles of justice, and are therefore true forms; but those which regard only the interest of the rulers are all defective and perverted forms, for they are despotic, whereas a state is a community of freemen.

Having determined these points, we have next to consider how many forms of government there are, and what they are; and in the first place what are the true forms, for when they are determined the perversions of them will at once be apparent. The words constitution and government have the same meaning, and the government, which is the supreme authority in states, must be in the hands of one, or of a few, or of many. The true forms of government, therefore, are those in which the one, or the few, or the many, govern with a view to the common interest; but governments which rule with a view to the private interest, whether of the one, or of the few, or of the many, are perversions. For citizens, if they are truly citizens, ought to participate in the advantages of a state. ... Now, absolute monarchy, or the arbitrary rule of a sovereign over all the citizens, in a city which consists of equals, is thought by some to be quite contrary to nature; it is argued that those who are by nature equals must have the same natural right and worth, and that for unequals to have an equal share, or for equals to have an unequal share, in the offices of state, is as bad as for different bodily constitutions to have the same food and clothing or the same different. Wherefore it is thought to be just that among equals every one be ruled as well as rule, and that all should have their turn. We thus arrive at law; for an order of succession implies law. And the rule of the law is preferable to that of any individual. On the same principle, even if it be better for certain individuals to govern, they should be made only guardians and ministers of the law. For magistrates there must be, —this is admitted; but then men say that to give authority to any one man when all are equal is unjust. There may indeed be cases which the law seems unable to determine, but in such cases can a man? Nay, it will be replied, the law trains officers for this express purpose, and appoints them to determine matters which are left undecided by it to the best of their judgment. Further it permits them to make any amendment of the existing laws which experience suggests. [But still they are only the ministers of the law.] He who bids the law rule, may be deemed to bid God and Reason alone rule, but he who bids man rule adds an element of the beast; for desire is a wild beast, and passion perverts the minds of rulers, even when they are the best of men. The law is reason unaffected by desire. We are told that a patient should call in a physician; he will not get better if he is doctored out of a book. But the parallel of the arts is clearly not in point; for the physician does nothing contrary to reason from motives of friendship; he only cures a patient and takes a fee; whereas magistrates do many things from spite and partiality. . . .

There is a true union of oligarchy and democracy when the same state may be termed either a democracy or an oligarchy; those who use both names evidently feel that the fusion is complete. Such a fusion there is also in the mean; for both extremes appear in it. The Lacedaemonian constitution, for example, is often described as a democracy, because it has many democratical features. In the first place the youth receive a democratical education. For the sons of the poor are brought up with the sons of the rich, who are educated in such a manner as to make it possible for the sons of the poor to be educated like them. A similar equality prevails in the following period of life, and when the citizens are grown up to manhood the same rule is observed; there is no distinction between the rich and poor. In like manner they all have the same food at their public tables, and the rich wear only such clothing as any poor man can afford. Again, the people elect to one of the two greatest offices of state, and in the other they share; for they elect the Senators and share in the Ephoralty. By others the Spartan constitution is said to be an oligarchy, because it has many oligarchical elements. That all offices are filled by election and none by lot, is one of these oligarchical characteristics; that the power of inflicting death or banishment rests with a few persons is another; and there are others. In a well attempered polity there should appear to be both elements and yet neither; also the government should rely on itself, and not on foreign aid, nor on the good will of a majority of foreign states—they might be equally well-disposed when there is a vicious form of government—but on the general willingness of all classes in the state to maintain the constitution. . . .

We have now to enquire what is the best constitution for most states, and the best life for most men, neither assuming a standard of virtue which is above ordinary persons, nor an education which is exceptionally favoured by nature and circumstances, nor yet an ideal state which is an aspiration only, but having regard to the life in which the majority are able to share, and to the form of government which states in general can attain. As to those aristocracies, as they are called, of which we were just now speaking, they either lie beyond the possibilities of the greater number of states, or they approximate to the so-called constitutional government, and therefore need no separate discussion. And in fact the conclusion at which we arrive respecting all these forms rests upon the same grounds. For if it has been truly said in the Ethics that the happy life is the life according to unimpeded virtue, and that virtue is a mean, then the life which is in a mean, and in a mean attainable by every one, must be the best. And the same principles of virtue and vice are characteristic of cities and of constitutions; for the constitution is in a figure the life of the city.

Now in all states there are three elements; one class is very rich, another very poor, and a third in a mean. It is admitted that moderation and the mean are best, and therefore it will clearly be best to possess the gifts of fortune in moderation; for in that condition of life men are most ready to listen to reason. But he who greatly excels in beauty, strength, birth or wealth, or on the other hand who is very poor, or very weak, or very much disgraced, finds it difficult to follow reason. Of these two the one sort grow into violent and great criminals, the others into, rogues and petty rascals. And two sorts of offences correspond to them the one committed from violence, the other from roguery. The petty rogues are disinclined to hold office, whether military or civil, and their aversion to these two duties is as great an injury to the state as their tendency to crime. Again, those who have too much of the goods of fortune, strength, wealth, friends, and the like, are neither willing nor able to submit to authority. The evil begins at home: for when they are boys, by reason of the luxury in which they are brought up, they never learn, even at school, the habit of obedience. On the other hand, the very poor, who are in the opposite extreme, are too degraded. So that the one class cannot obey, and can only rule despotically; the other knows not how to command and must be ruled like slaves. Thus arises a city, not of freemen, but of masters and slaves, the one despising, the other envying; and nothing can be more fatal to friendship and good fellowship in states than this: for good fellowship tends to friendship; when men are at enmity with one another, they would rather not even share the same path. But a city ought to be composed, as far as possible, of equals and similars; and these are generally the middle classes. . . .

The Exploiters and the Exploited

The theoretical conclusions of the Communists are in no way based on ideas or principles that have been invented or discovered by this or that would-be universal reformer.

They merely express, in general terms, actual relations springing from an existing class struggle, from a historical movement going on under our very eyes. The abolition of existing property relations is not at all a distinctive feature of Communism.

All property relations in the past have continually been subject to historical change consequent upon the change in historical conditions.

The French Revolution, for example, abolished feudal property in favor of bourgeois property.

The distinguishing feature of Communism is not the abolition of property generally, but the abolition of bourgeois property. But modern bourgeois private property is the final and most complete expression of the system of producing and appropriating products, that is based on class antagonism, on the exploitation of the many by the few.

In this sense, the theory of the Communists may be summed up in the single sentence: Abolition of private property.

We Communists have been reproached with the desire of abolishing the right of personally acquiring property as the fruit of a man's own labor, which property is alleged to be the groundwork of all personal freedom, activity and independence.

Hard won, self-acquired, self-earned property! Do you mean the property of the petty artisan and of the small peasant, a form of property that preceded the bourgeois form? There is no need to abolish that; the development of industry has to a great extent already destroyed it, and is still destroying it daily.

Or do you mean modern bourgeois private property?

But does wage labor create any property for the laborer? Not a bit. It creates capital, *i. e.,* that kind of property which exploits wage labor,

173

⌐ which cannot increase except upon condition of getting a new ⌐pply of wage labor for fresh exploitation. Property, in its present form, is based on the antagonism of capital and wage labor. Let us examine both sides of this antagonism.

To be a capitalist is to have not only a purely personal, but a social status in production. Capital is a collective product, and only by the united action of many members, nay, in the last resort, only by the united action of all members of society, can it be set in motion.

Capital is therefore not a personal, it is a social power.

When, therefore, capital is converted into common property, into the property of all members of society, personal property is not thereby transformed into social property. It is only the social character of the property that is changed. It loses its class character.

Let us now take wage labor.

The average price of wage labor is the minimum wage, i. e., that quantum of the means of subsistence which is absolutely requisite to keep the laborer in bare existence as a laborer. What, therefore, the wage laborer appropriates by means of his labor, merely suffices to prolong and reproduce a bare existence. We by no means intend to abolish this personal appropriation of the products of labor, an appropriation that is made for the maintenance and reproduction of human life, and that leaves no surplus wherewith to command the labor of others. All that we want to do away with is the miserable character of this appropriation, under which the laborer lives merely to increase capital and is allowed to live only in so far as the interests of the ruling class require it.

In bourgeois society, living labor is but a means to increase accumulated labor. In Communist society accumulated labor is but a means to widen, to enrich, to promote the existence of the laborer.

In bourgeois society, therefore, the past dominates the present; in communist society the present dominates the past. In bourgeois society, capital is independent and has individuality, while the living person is dependent and has no individuality.

And the abolition of this state of things is called by the bourgeois abolition of individuality and freedom! And rightly so. The abolition of bourgeois individuality, bourgeois independence and bourgeois freedom is undoubtedly aimed at.

By freedom is meant, under the present bourgeois conditions of production, free trade, free selling and buying.

But if selling and buying disappears, free selling and buying disappears also. This talk about free selling and buying, and all the other "brave words" of our bourgeoisie about freedom in general have a meaning, if any, only in contrast with restricted selling and buying, with the fettered traders of the Middle Ages, but have no meaning when opposed to the Communistic abolition of buying and selling, of the bourgeois conditions of production, and of the bourgeoisie itself.

You are horrified at our intending to do away with private property. But in your existing society private property is already done away with for nine-tenths of the population; its existence for the few is solely due to its non-existence in the hands of those nine-tenths. You reproach us, therefore, with intending to do away with a form of property, the necessary condition for whose existence is the non-existence of any property for the immense majority of society.

In one word, you reproach us with intending to do away with your property. Precisely so: that is just what we intend.

From the moment when labor can no longer be converted into capital, money, or rent, into a social power capable of being monopolized, i. e., from the moment when individual property can no longer be transformed into bourgeois property, into capital, from that moment, you say, individuality vanishes.

You must, therefore, confess that by "individual" you mean no other person than the bourgeois, than the middle-class owner of property. This person must, indeed, be swept out of the way and made impossible.

Communism deprives no man of the power to appropriate the products of society: all that it does is to deprive him of the power to subjugate the labor of others by means of such appropriation.

It has been objected that upon the abolition of private property all work will cease and universal laziness will overtake us.

According to this, bourgeois society ought long ago to have gone to the dogs through sheer idleness; for those of its members who work acquire nothing, and those who acquire anything do not work. The whole of this objection is but another expression of the tautology: that there can no longer be any wage labor when there is no longer any capital.

All objections urged against the Communistic mode of producing and appropriating material products have, in the same way, been urged against the Communistic modes of producing and appropriating intellectual products. Just as, to the bourgeois, the disappearance of class property is the disappearance of production itself, so the disappearance of class culture is to him identical with the disappearance of all culture.

That culture, the loss of which he laments, is, for the enormous majority, a mere training to act as a machine.

But don't wrangle with us so long as you apply, to our intended abolition of bourgeois property, the standard of your bourgeois notions of freedom, culture, law, etc. Your very ideas are but the outgrowth of the conditions of your bourgeois production and bourgeois property, just as your jurisprudence is but the will of your class made into a law for all, a will whose essential character and direction are determined by the economical conditions of existence of your class.

The selfish misconception that induces you to transform into eternal laws of nature and of reason the social forms springing from your present mode of production and form of property—historical relations that rise and disappear in the progress of production—this misconception you share with every ruling class that has preceded you. What you see clearly in the case of ancient property, what you admit in the case of feudal property, you are of course forbidden to admit in the case of your own bourgeois form of property.

Abolition of the family! Even the most radical flare up at this infamous proposal of the Communists.

On what foundation is the present family, the bourgeois family, based? On capital, on private gain. In its completely developed form this family exists only among the bourgeoisie. But this state of things finds its complement in the practical absence of the family among the proletarians, and in public prostitution.

The bourgeois family will vanish as a matter of course when its complement vanishes, and both will vanish with the vanishing of capital.

Do you charge us with wanting to stop the exploitation of children by their parents? To this crime we plead guilty.

But, you will say, we destroy the most hallowed of relations when we replace home education by social.

And your education! Is not that also social, and determined by the social conditions under which you educate; by the intervention, direct or indirect, of society by means of schools, etc.? The Communists have not invented the intervention of society in education; they do but seek to alter the character of that intervention, and to rescue education from the influence of the ruling class.

The bourgeois clap-trap about the family and education, about the hallowed correlation of parent and child, become all the more disgusting, the more, by the action of Modern Industry, all family ties among the proletarians are torn asunder and their children transformed into simple articles of commerce and instruments of labor.

But you communists would introduce community of women, screams the whole bourgeoisie chorus.

The bourgeois sees in his wife a mere instrument of production. He hears that the instruments of production are to be exploited in common, and, naturally, can come to no other conclusion, than that the lot of being common to all will likewise fall to the women.

He has not even a suspicion that the real point aimed at is to do away with the status of women as mere instruments of production.

For the rest, nothing is more ridiculous than the virtuous indignation of our bourgeois at the community of women which, they pretend, is to be openly and officially established by the Communists. The Communists have no need to introduce community of women; it has existed almost from time immemorial.

Our bourgeois, not content with having the wives and daughters of their proletarians at their disposal, not to speak of common prostitutes, take the greatest pleasure in seducing each others' wives.

Bourgeois marriage is in reality a system of wives in common, and thus, at the most, what the Communists might possibly be reproached with, is that they desire to introduce, in substitution for a hypocritically concealed, an openly legalized community of women. For the rest, it is self-evident that the abolition of the present system of production must bring with it the abolition of the community of women springing from that system, *i. e.,* of prostitution both public and private.

The Communists are further reproached with desiring to abolish countries and nationalities.

The working men have no country. We cannot take from them what they don't possess. Since the proletariat must first of all acquire political supremacy, must rise to be the leading class of the nation, must constitute itself the nation, it is, so far, itself national, though not in the bourgeois sense of the word.

National differences and antagonisms between peoples are daily more and more vanishing, owing to the development of the bourgeoisie, to freedom of commerce, to the world-market, to uniformity in the mode of production and in the conditions of life corresponding thereto.

The supremacy of the proletariat will cause them to vanish still faster. United action, of the leading civilized countries at least, is one of the first conditions for the emancipation of the proletariat.

In proportion as the exploitation of one individual by another is put an end to, the exploitation of one nation by another will also be put an end to. In proportion as the antagonism between classes within the nation vanishes, the hostility of one nation to another will come to an end.

18. Huey P. Newton

A Functional Definition of Politics

Politics is war without bloodshed. War is politics with bloodshed. Politics has its particular characteristics which differentiate it from war. When the peaceful means of politics are exhausted and the people do not get what they want, politics are continued. Usually it ends up in physical conflict which is called war, which is also political.

Because we lack political power, Black people are not free. Black reconstruction failed because Black people did not have political and military power. The masses of Black people at the time were very clear on the definition of political power. It is evident in the songs of Black people at that time. In the songs it was stated that on the Day of Jubilee we'd have forty acres and two mules. This was promised Black people by the Freedman's Bureau. This was freedom as far as the Black masses were concerned.

The Talented Tenth at the time viewed freedom as operative in the political arena. Black people did operate more educated than most of the Whites in the south. They had been educated in France, Canada and England, and were very qualified to serve in the political arena. But yet, Black Reconstruction failed.

When one operates in the political arena, it is assumed that he has power or represents power; he is symbolic of a powerful force. There are approximately three areas of power in the political area: economic power, land power (feudal power) and military power. If Black people at the time had received forty acres and two mules, we would have developed a powerful force. Then we would have chosen a representative to represent us in this political arena. Because Black people did not receive the forty acres and two mules it was absurd to have a representative in the political arena.

When White people send a representative into the political arena, they have a powerful force or power base that they represent. When White people, through their representatives, do not get what they

178

want, there is always a political consequence. This is evident in the fact that when the farmers are not given an adequate price for their crops the economy will receive a political consequence. They will let their crops rot in the field; they will not cooperate with other sectors of the economy. To be political, you must have a political consequence when you do not receive your desires—otherwise you are non-political.

When Black people send a representative, he is some-what absurd because he represents no political power. He does not represent land power because we do not own any land. He does not represent economic or industrial power because Black people do not own the means of production. The only way he can become political is to represent what is commonly called a military power—which the BLACK PANTHER PARTY FOR SELF-DEFENSE calls Self-Defense Power. Black people can develop Self-Defense Power by arming themselves from house to house, block to block, community to community, throughout the nation. Then we will choose a political representative and he will state to the power structure the desires of the Black masses. If the desires are not met, the power structure will receive a political consequence. We will make it economically non-profitable for the power structure to go on with its oppressive ways. We will then negotiate as equals. There will be a balance between the people who are economically powerful and the people who are potentially economically destructive.

The White racist oppresses Black people not only for racist reasons but because it is also economically profitable to do so. Black people must develop a power that will make it non-profitable for racist to go on oppressing us. If the White racist imperialist in ameriKKKa continue to wage war against all people of color throughout the world and also wage a civil war against Blacks here in ameriKKKa, it will be conomically impossible for him to survive. We must develop a strategy that will make his war campaigns non-profitable. This racist United States operates with the motive of profit. He lifts the gun and escalates the war for profit reasons. We will make him lower the guns because they will no longer serve his profit motive.

Every man is born, therefore he has a right to live, a right to share in the wealth. If he is denied the right to work then he is denied the right to live. If he can't work, he deserves a high standard of living, regardless of his education or skill. It should be up to the administrators of the economic system to design a program for providing work of livelihood for his people. To deny a man this is to deny him life. The controllers of the economic system are obligated to furnish each man with a livelihood. If they cannot do this or if they will not do this, they do not deserve the position of administrators. The means of production should be taken away from them and placed in the people's hands, so that the people can organize them in such a way as to provide themselves with a livelihood. The people will choose capable administrators motivated by their sincere interest in the people's welfare and not the interest of private property. The people will choose managers to control the means of production and the land that is rightfully theirs. Until the people control the land and the means of production, there will be no peace. Black people must control the destiny of their community.

Because Black people desire to determine their own destiny, they are constantly inflicted with brutality from the occupying army, embodied in the police department. There is a great similarity between the occupying army in Southeast Asia and the occupation of our communities by the racist police. The armies are there not to protect the people of South Vietnam, but to brutalize and oppress them for the interest of the selfish imperial power.

The police should be the people of the community in uniform. There should be no division or conflict of interest between the people and the police. Once there is a division, then the police become the enemy of the people. The police should serve the interest of the people, and be one and the same. When this principle breaks down, then the police become an occupying army. When historically one race has oppressed another and policemen are recruited from the oppressor race to patrol the communities of the oppressed people, an intolerable contradiction exist.

The racist dog policemen must withdraw immediately from our communities, cease their wanton murder and brutality and torture of Black people, or face the wrath of the armed people.

The Good, The True, The Beautiful, in Law

Now in law, as in all other disciplines, there are to be discovered major lines of guidance which can be stated, which focus the problems of policy for seeing, and which indicate the lines along which their solution is to run. Such "general propositions" of guidance do not indeed "decide concrete cases" by any deductive process, because their edges are unclear, because, also, two or more of them can commonly overlap a situation in conflicting ways. What such lines, when well stated, do, instead, is to make the nature of the controversy clear, and to point up the place and nature of the doubt or trouble, and to suggest *lines* of wise *direction* of solution, for consideration. Rules wisely built, clearly phrased, with goal and reason clear, such rules do these things for an advocate; they do these things for a counselor; they do these things for a judge; and they do them in much the same way for all three. No other type of rule does talk the same way to all three. What is in some ways even more important, rules of this right and largely unused type do these things also for the interested layman, for the law-consumer, for the law-supporter, for the man whose law our law is. Once that man can see clearly "what is up," and "where the trouble lies," and why, he can take decision against him, and realize that he has had a fair deal, though he has lost. He can take decision for him without thinking that his lawyer was just good enough to put one over. He can respect and honor the law which his ingrained—I am almost ready to say "innate"—but baffled yearning is to respect and honor.

But we technicians have become so habituated to the trees of mere authority and rule that we have forgotten how a well-run woodland, intended for a public, needs sign-posts, roads, and maps. Ours is the fault, and on us the burden of the cure. Law is complex and vast, but there are not many fields of law of which any particular citizen needs to know the guiding lines. However, where he knows his stuff, he does need and he feels need to see that the main lines of his law make sense raise sensible problems, come to decision in terms that talk and make sense in life.

This can be done for him. I have been utterly amazed, this past year, after wrestling through the squashy mud of sales law for two decades, at discovering how much sense, for a non-sales lawyer or for a businessman, could come out of rather minor reformulations, once one or another underlying idea got itself out into the clear to be looked at. I find the same thing, wherever I have worked, or have watched the relevant work of others.[1] Technicalities we cannot get rid of. What we can do, is to make the technicalities take shape and meaning *around* communicable lines of sense.

Today, this is best bodied forth in legislation, when well drawn, with lines of policy that any interested man can understand made clear, with technical detail left then to be handled flexibly by administrative regulation. I sing no paean. Much of the ensuing administrative regulation makes my hackles rise at its sheer unintelligibility in the worst manner of legal garbage. But we are on our way, and have been, for some time.

The new Sales Act can serve to point the argument.[2] I suggest it not merely because I happen to be more familiar with it, but peculiarly because I want to avoid any misconstruction to the effect that in the foregoing I am becoming mushy, mystical, or vague, or that I am over-looking a lawyer's job of phrasing clearly, to give clean guidance to a fellow-craftsman. Quite the contrary. I stand on the proposition that the new Sales Act has as its job not only to make its sense and purposes far clearer to the non-specialist and to the interested layman than does the older phrasing of the legal rules, but that it must also give to counsel and to court a sharper and a more predictable guidance. I am not arguing that Pollock was wholly right when he opined that almost any rule of law could be translated into English which an ordinary man could understand. I am arguing that he was to my knowledge partly right, and that so far as he was right—and that needs testing, case by case—so far as he was right, it is a sad thing for the law of any people to leave the translation unattempted. It is a dire thing for the law of a democracy.

It will be observed that I have been concerned in this matter only indirectly with Justice. Justice plays in, and importantly; for it is well for a man to have some direct inkling of his rights, and knowledge goes far in many cases to shape expectation. It is, perhaps, even better that he

---

1. Consider the Beckwith A.B.A. Committee's work in getting the draft regulations reformulated into relative accessibility of meaning.
2. UNIFORM COMMERCIAL CODE, Art. II.

should have some understanding of why what he manages to get can decently be considered an approximation of Justice. But above all it is a good, above and beyond Justice, for the citizen to meet his law and call it friend—or to see why he wants it different, if he does.

The present inaccessibility of knowledge of the rules, and worse, of even the main lines that organize the rules, plays twice into the other barrier, that of uncertainty and expense. Inaccessibility of knowledge increases both the labor cost and the uncertainty of advice. It does the same, one may add, for decision. By consequence, for the law-consumer, it puts a premium on peculiarly skilled or experienced advice or advocacy in the particular field. To pick the certainly right lawyer is to pay for that same and rare kind of lawyer. To pick the wrong one is to lose. To just pick is to gamble on a roulette-number—but with the possibility of winning reduced to one to one. It is a queer drift that has come upon us here. Let me say only this, with Teufelsdröckh: "If Access to Rights must be over a Bridge of Lawyers, and if Lawyers must also live, then there is Thinking to be done about how to keep little Rights, or the Rights of little Men, from being squeezed out of all Chance of Realization by the Charges at the Tollgate." The small claims court is a noble institution—a beginning, reaching toward a good which, this time, is one phase of Justice. Let me say also that the type of legislative Justice which one most hopes for here is merely that type of enabling legislation which would empower a bar, as an organized unit, to take up the problem of truly bringing home—of making known and making accessible to every man—that "Equal Justice under the Law, Within," which from the beginning of our government has been the proclaimed counterpart of "Defense, Without." Indeed the drift has been queer which, as to Defense, Without, can give us a Defense Administration, taxes, bond issues, and conscription, as a substitute for Minute Men; but which, as to Equal Justice under the Law, Within, can leave the thing to bank account, or charity, or accident. I have profound admiration for the work of Legal Aid societies. And still, I seem to see here a problem for the Good.

[Another] point of technical need I want to mention touches again upon that Good which is law's contact with law's people. Savigny may not have phrased a bull's-eye with his idea of the necessary conditioning of all law by the people's *right-way-of-life,* yet right law which touches people must live *in* them. If law does not so live, it goes first technical; it goes then formal and remote. Remote law is not law to love, but law to dodge, or else to use. Remote law is law quite all right to evade, or to defraud; it is law which puts pressure on men to reach or fix officials; it is law which is a burden or a bludgeon; it is law which is the cynical tool of pressure-groups. One can almost say: it should be. Remote law is not your law and not my law, it is *their* law, that *they* put over on us, and it is up to us to put a counter over if we can. Remote law gets the treatment it deserves. I have but little quarrel with what it gets. My quarrel is instead with law's getting, with law's remaining, thus remote. My quarrel is therefore with technicians' ways which let it get remote.

Once, lawsuits were fought out over the winter about three feet of ground or some petty fifteen-dollar sum. They may have engendered as much bitterness among neighbors as they allayed, but they made law a living institution *in* the people. Once, despite its due measure of technicality, the scheme of the legal system was close enough to every day experience to let every man have some first understanding of what it was all about. One learned to follow lawyers' work, when court sat, as the modern American has learned to follow the tactics of baseball. American judicial opinions, moreover, had as a major original function to account not to a bar only, but to a people. Once, too, almost every lawyer lived a rounded life in a rounded community with a rounded practice, and he was known as wise, not as a black magician; was known as learned, not as merely shrewd; was known as a leader and a friend, first, as a technician, only second.

These things are largely lost, by drift and circumstance. By vision and rethinking, one fair part of them can be recaptured. But it does not recapture them merely to set up an administrative agency to do the veteran's or the laborer's legal work *for* him, or what have you more. When I watch the care, the skill, the patience, with which the Tennessee Valley Authority is knitting the active co-operation of the beneficiary into every least job undertaken for his benefit, I see a lesson in democratic government which carries over into all the work of law.[3] A man's rights must be accessible, but to be right rights, they must call also for some share on his part in initiating or in working out their procurement, their fulfillment. Else law remains remote, the government becomes an enemy or a dairy-cow, and the morale of official, citizen, and group alike bogs in morass, and pressure-groups become a by-word.

Do not mistake me. I have no quarrel with pressure-groups as such. They can voice need for all-of-us, as well as wish and selfish interest of their own. But the balance to pressure-groups is not and never will be *merely* other pressure-groups. The further needed balance lies in a citizenry alive, aware, and not habituated to "let George do it all."

3. One has a tragedy in American government when Eisenhower feels necessity, at the same time, to express to Gordon Clapp his feeling that Clapp has been one of our major public servants—*and* to replace him as Chairman of the T.V.A.

Again, do not mistake me. For I have little use for empty cries for change of heart. My argument is that manageable changes in the legal techniques of the legal craftsmen, in phrasing their rules of law and in working with them, in managing their mediation of rights to the law-consumer, in rightly setting up the organs of justiciation or of administration—my argument is that such *manageable changes in legal techniques can bring law home again to law's people.* As means, or as end, I know no greater single good for law.

For when it comes to ultimate substance of the Good, I repeat that I can find no clarity, nor any conviction of reason or of deduction as to specific matters, from the broad ultimates others have found clear. I put my faith rather, as to substance, in a means: in that on-going process of effort to come closer to the Good, that on-going process of check-up and correction, and further check-up and correction, which is the method and the very life of case-law. "Reason acting on experience"—better: "Reason at work upon experience, to find and state *explicit guidance for the future;* Reason, responsibly and explicitly accounting for *why* a rule or principle seems reasonable; Reason, re-examining in the light of reasonableness, on further experience, any and every prior ruling or prior reason given, and then reshaping, reformulating, redirecting, each time need may appear in further reason." That is the common law at its high best: the Grand Style. Perhaps because I know nothing better, perhaps because Judicial Justice has been so much discussed, let me leave it at that. But do not let me leave it at that without insisting that when law ceases to be remote, when law comes home, then a process works out among the citizenry of a democracy which is the exact analogue of the common law judicial sequence of self-correction, of judicial review of prior judicial decision—which is, indeed, its twin and needed brother.

If now, you ask me what guarantee I can offer that my own faith about the Good in this institution of our law is better than another's— what does Reason show me to warrant this particular faith of mine against mistake—I have no answer. Under the common law tradition, be a man judge, citizen, or scholar, They That Come After have as their office to correct him. When the machinery of work is healthy, and formalism does not hide on-going reason, They That Come After do their office of correction. . . .

Violence versus Non-Violence

Sermon on the Mount

And there followed him great multitudes of people from Galilee and *from* Dĕcăpŏlĭs, and *from* Jerusalem, and *from* Judæa, and *from* beyond Jordan.

CHAPTER 5

And seeing the multitudes, he went up into a mountain: and when he was set, his disciples came unto him:

2 And he opened his mouth, and taught them, saying,

3 Blessed *are* the poor in spirit: for theirs is the kingdom of heaven.

4 Blessed *are* they that mourn: for they shall be comforted.

5 Blessed *are* the meek: for they shall inherit the earth.

6 Blessed *are* they which do hunger and thirst after righteousness: for they shall be filled.

7 Blessed *are* the merciful: for they shall obtain mercy.

8 Blessed *are* the pure in heart: for they shall see God.

9 Blessed *are* the peacemakers: for they shall be called the children of God.

10 Blessed *are* they which are persecuted for righteousness' sake: for theirs is the kingdom of heaven.

11 Blessed are ye, when *men* shall revile you, and persecute *you,* and shall say all manner of evil against you falsely, for my sake.

12 Rejoice, and be exceeding glad: for great *is* your reward in heaven: for so persecuted they the prophets which were before you.

13 Ye are the salt of the earth: but if the salt have lost his savour, wherewith shall it be salted? it is thenceforth good for nothing, but to be cast out, and be trodden under foot of men.

14 Ye are the light of the world. A city that is set on an hill cannot be hid.

15 Neither do men light a candle, and put it under a bushel, but on a candlestick; and it giveth light unto all that are in the house.

16 Let your light so shine before men, that they may see your good works, and glorify your Father which is in heaven.

17 Think not that I am come to destroy the law, or the prophets: I am not come to destroy, but to fulfil.

18 For verily I say unto you, Till heaven and earth pass, one jot or one tittle shall in no wise pass from the law, till all be fulfilled.

19 Whosoever therefore shall break one of these least commandments, and shall teach men so, he shall be called the least in the kingdom of heaven: but whosoever shall do and teach *them,* the same shall be called great in the kingdom of heaven.

20 For I say unto you, That except your righteousness shall exceed *the righteousness* of the scribes and Pharisees, ye shall in no case enter into the kingdom of heaven.

21 Ye have heard that it was said by them of old time, Thou shalt not kill; and whosoever shall kill shall be in danger of the judgment:

22 But I say unto you, That whosoever is angry with his brother without a cause shall be in danger of the judgment: and whosoever shall say to his brother, Rá-cǎ, shall be in danger of the council: but whosoever shall say, Thou fool, shall be in danger of hell fire.

23 Therefore if thou bring thy gift to the altar, and there rememberest that thy brother hath ought against thee;

24 Leave there thy gift before the altar, and go thy way; first be reconciled to thy brother, and then come and offer thy gift.

25 Agree with thine adversary quickly, whiles thou art in the way with him; lest at any time the adversary deliver thee to the judge, and the judge deliver thee to the officer, and thou be cast into prison.

26 Verily I say unto thee, Thou shalt by no means come out thence, till thou hast paid the uttermost farthing.

27 Ye have heard that it was said by them of old time, Thou shalt not commit adultery:

28 But I say unto you, That whosoever looketh on a woman to lust after her hath committed adultery with her already in his heart.

29 And if thy right eye offend thee, pluck it out, and cast *it* from thee: for it is profitable for thee that one of thy members should perish, and not *that* thy whole body should be cast into hell.

30 And if thy right hand offend thee, cut it off, and cast *it* from thee: for it is profitable for thee that one of thy members should perish, and not *that* thy whole body should be cast into hell.

31 It hath been said, Whosoever shall put away his wife, let him give her a writing of divorcement:

32 But I say unto you, That whosoever shall put away his wife,

saving for the cause of fornication, causeth her to commit adultery: and whosoever shall marry her that is divorced committeth adultery.

33 Again, ye have heard that it hath been said by them of old time, Thou shalt not forswear thyself, but shalt perform unto the Lord thine oaths:

34 But I say unto you, Swear not at all; neither by heaven; for it is God's throne:

35 Nor by the earth; for it is his footstool: neither by Jerusalem; for it is the city of the great King.

36 Neither shalt thou swear by thy head, because thou canst not make one hair white or black.

37 But let your communication be, Yea, yea; Nay, nay: for whatsoever is more than these cometh of evil.

38 Ye have heard that it hath been said, An eye for an eye, and a tooth for a tooth:

39 But I say unto you, That ye resist not evil: but whosoever shall smite thee on thy right cheek, turn to him the other also.

40 And if any man will sue thee at the law, and take away thy coat, let him have *thy* cloke also.

41 And whosoever shall compel thee to go a mile, go with him twain.

42 Give to him that asketh thee, and from him that would borrow of thee turn not thou away.

43 Ye have heard that it hath been said, Thou shalt love thy neighbour, and hate thine enemy.

44 But I say unto you, Love your enemies, bless them that curse you, do good to them that hate you, and pray for them which despitefully use you, and persecute you;

45 That ye may be the children of your Father which is in heaven: for he maketh his sun to rise on the evil and on the good, and sendeth rain on the just and on the unjust.

46 For if ye love them which love you, what reward have ye? do not even the publicans the same?

47 And if ye salute your brethren only, what do ye more *than others?* do not even the publicans so?

48 Be ye therefore perfect, even as your Father which is in heaven is perfect.

CHAPTER 6

Take heed that ye do not your alms before men, to be seen of them: otherwise ye have no reward of your Father which is in heaven.

2 Therefore when thou doest *thine* alms, do not sound a trumpet

before thee, as the hypocrites do in the synagogues and in the streets, that they may have glory of men. Verily I say unto you, They have their reward.

3 But when thou doest alms, let not thy left hand know what thy right hand doeth:

4 That thine alms may be in secret: and thy Father which seeth in secret himself shall reward thee openly.

5 And when thou prayest, thou shalt not be as the hypocrites *are:* for they love to pray standing in the synagogues and in the corners of the streets, that they may be seen of men. Verily I say unto you, They have their reward.

6 But thou, when thou prayest, enter into thy closet, and when thou hast shut thy door, pray to thy Father which is in secret; and thy Father which seeth in secret shall reward thee openly.

7 But when ye pray, use not vain repetitions, as the heathen *do:* for they think that they shall be heard for their much speaking.

8 Be not ye therefore like unto them: for your Father knoweth what things ye have need of, before ye ask him.

9 After this manner therefore pray ye: Our Father which art in heaven, Hallowed be thy name.

10 Thy kingdom come. Thy will be done in earth, as *it is* in heaven.

11 Give us this day our daily bread.

12 And forgive us our debts, as we forgive our debtors.

13 And lead us not into temptation, but deliver us from evil: For thine is the kingdom, and the power, and the glory, for ever. Ämĕn.

14 For if ye forgive men their trespasses, your heavenly Father will also forgive you:

15 But if ye forgive not men their trespasses, neither will your Father forgive your trespasses.

16 Moreover when ye fast, be not, as the hypocrites, of a sad countenance: for they disfigure their faces, that they may appear unto men to fast. Verily I say unto you, They have their reward.

17 But thou, when thou fastest, anoint thine head, and wash thy face;

18 That thou appear not unto men to fast, but unto thy Father which is in secret: and thy Father, which seeth in secret, shall reward thee openly.

19 Lay not up for yourselves treasures upon earth, where moth and rust doth corrupt, and where thieves break through and steal:

20 But lay up for yourselves treasures in heaven, where neither moth nor rust doth corrupt, and where thieves do not break through nor steal:

21 For where your treasure is, there will your heart be also.

22 The light of the body is the eye: if therefore thine eye be single, thy whole body shall be full of light.

23 But if thine eye be evil, thy whole body shall be full of darkness. If therefore the light that is in thee be darkness, how great *is* that darkness!

24 No man can serve two masters: for either he will hate the one, and love the other; or else he will hold to the one, and despise the other. Ye cannot serve God and mammon.

25 Therefore I say unto you, Take no thought for your life, what ye shall eat, or what ye shall drink; nor yet for your body, what ye shall put on. Is not the life more than meat, and the body than raiment?

26 Behold the fowls of the air: for they sow not, neither do they reap, nor gather into barns; yet your heavenly Father feedeth them. Are ye not much better than they?

27 Which of you by taking thought can add one cubit into his stature?

28 And why take ye thought for raiment? Consider the lilies of the field, how they grow; they toil not, neither do they spin:

29 And yet I say unto you, That even Solomon in all his glory was not arrayed like one of these.

30 Wherefore, if God so clothe the grass of the field, which to day is, and to morrow is cast into the oven, *shall he* not much more *clothe* you, O ye of little faith?

31 Therefore take no thought, saying, What shall we eat? or, What shall we drink? or, Wherewithal shall we be clothed?

32 (For after all these things do the Gentiles seek:) for your heavenly Father knoweth that ye have need of all these things.

33 But seek ye first the kingdom of God, and his righteousness; and all these things shall be added unto you.

34 Take therefore no thought for the morrow: for the morrow shall take thought for the things of itself. Sufficient unto the day *is* the evil thereof.

CHAPTER 7

Judge not, that ye be not judged.

2 For with what judgment ye judge, ye shall be judged: and with what measure ye mete, it shall be measured to you again.

3 And why beholdest thou the mote that is in thy brother's eye, but considerest not the beam that is in thine own eye?

4 Or how wilt thou say to thy brother, Let me pull out the mote out of thine eye; and, behold, a beam *is* in thine own eye?

5 Thou hypocrite, first cast out the beam out of thine own eye;

and then shalt thou see clearly to cast out the mote out of thy brother's eye.

6 Give not that which is holy unto the dogs, neither cast ye your pearls before swine, lest they trample them under their feet, and turn again and rend you.

7 Ask, and it shall be given you; seek, and ye shall find; knock, and it shall be opened unto you:

8 For every one that asketh receiveth; and he that seeketh findeth; and to him that knocketh it shall be opened.

9 Or what man is there of you, whom if his son ask bread, will he give him a stone?

10 Or if he ask a fish, will he give him a serpent?

11 If ye then, being evil, know how to give good gifts unto your children, how much more shall your Father which is in heaven give good things to them that ask him?

12 Therefore all things whatsoever ye would that men should do to you, do ye even so to them: for this is the law and the prophets.

13 Enter ye in at the strait gate: for wide *is* the gate, and broad *is* the way, that leadeth to destruction, and many there be which go in thereat:

14 Because strait *is* the gate, and narrow *is* the way, which leadeth unto life, and few there be that find it.

15 Beware of false prophets, which come to you in sheep's clothing, but inwardly they are ravening wolves.

16 Ye shall know them by their fruits. Do men gather grapes of thorns, or figs of thistles?

17 Even so every good tree bringeth forth good fruit; but a corrupt tree bringeth forth evil fruit.

18 A good tree cannot bring forth evil fruit, neither *can* a corrupt tree bring forth good fruit.

19 Every tree that bringeth not forth good fruit is hewn down, and cast into the fire.

20 Wherefore by their fruits ye shall know them.

21 Not every one that saith unto me, Lord, Lord, shall enter into the kingdom of heaven; but he that doeth the will of my Father which is in heaven.

22 Many will say to me in that day, Lord, Lord, have we not prophesied in thy name? and in thy name have cast out devils? and in thy name done many wonderful works?

23 And then will I profess unto them, I never knew you: depart from me, ye that work iniquity.

24 Therefore whosoever heareth these sayings of mine, and doeth

them, I will liken him unto a wise man, which built his house upon a rock:

25 And the rain descended, and the floods came, and the winds blew, and beat upon that house; and it fell not: for it was founded upon a rock.

26 And every one that heareth these sayings of mine, and doeth them not, shall be likened unto a foolish man, which built his house upon the sand:

27 And the rain descended, and the floods came, and the winds blew, and beat upon that house; and it fell: and great was the fall of it.

28 And it came to pass, when Jesus had ended these sayings, the people were astonished at his doctrine:

29 For he taught them as *one* having authority, and not as the scribes.

Passive Resistance

READER: Is there any historical evidence as to the success of what you have called soul-force or truth-force? No instance seems to have happened of any nation having risen through soul-force. I still think that the evil-doers will not cease doing evil without physical punishment.

EDITOR: The poet Tulsidas has said: "Of religion, pity, or love, is the root, as egotism of the body. Therefore, we should not abandon pity so long as we are alive." This appears to me to be a scientific truth. I believe in it as much as I believe in two and two being four. The force of love is the same as the force of the soul or truth. We have evidence of its working at every step. The universe would disappear without the existence of that force. But you ask for historical evidence. It is, therefore, necessary to know what history means. The Gujarati equivalent means; "It so happened." If that is the meaning of history, it is possible to give copious evidence. But, if it means the doings of kings and emperors, there can be no evidence of soul-force or passive resistance in such history. You cannot expect silver ore in a tin mine. History, as we know it, is a record of the wars of the world, and so there is a proverb among Englishmen that a nation which has no history, that is, no wars, is a happy nation. How kings played, how they became enemies of one another, how they murdered one another, is found accurately recorded in history, and if this were all that had happened in the world, it would have been ended long ago. If the story of the universe had commenced with wars, not a man would have been found alive today. Those people who have been warred against have disappeared as, for instance, the natives of Australia of whom hardly a man was left alive by the intruders. Mark, please, that these natives did not use soul-force in self-defense, and it does not require much foresight to know that the Australians will share the same fate as their victims. "Those that take the sword shall perish by the sword." With us the proverb is that professional swimmers will find a watery grave.

The fact that there are so many men still alive in the world shows

196

that it is based not on the force of arms but on the force of truth or love. Therefore, the greatest and most unimpeachable evidence of the success of this force is to be found in the fact that, in spite of the wars of the world, it still lives on.

Thousands, indeed tens of thousands, depend for their existence on a very active working of this force. Little quarrels of millions of families in their daily lives disappear before the exercise of this force. Hundreds of nations live in peace. History does not and cannot take note of this fact. History is really a record of every interruption of the even working of the force of love or of the soul. Two brothers quarrel; one of them repents and re-awakens the love that was lying dormant in him; the two again begin to live in peace; nobody takes note of this. But if the two brothers, through the intervention of solicitors or some other reason, take up arms or go to law—which is another form of the exhibition of brute force—their doings would be immediately noticed in the press, they would be the talk of their neighbors and would probably go down to history. And what is true of families and communities is true of nations. There is no reason to believe that there is one law for families and another for nations. History, then, is a record of an interruption of the course of nature. Soul-force, being natural, is not noted in history. READER: According to what you say, it is plain that instances of this kind of passive resistance are not to be found in history. It is necessary to understand this passive resistance more fully. It will be better, therefore, if you enlarge upon it.

EDITOR: Passive resistance is a method of securing rights by personal suffering; it is the reverse of resistance by arms. When I refuse to do a thing that is repugnant to my conscience, I use soul-force. For instance, the Government of the day has passed a law which is applicable to me. I do not like it. If by using violence I force the Government to repeal the law, I am employing what may be termed body-force. If I do not obey the law and accept the penalty for its breach, I use soul-force. It involves sacrifice of self.

Everybody admits that sacrifice of self is infinitely superior to sacrifice of others. Moreover, if this kind of force is used in a cause that is unjust, only the person using it suffers. He does not make others suffer for his mistakes. Men have before now done many things which were subsequently found to have been wrong. No man can claim that he is absolutely in the right or that a particular thing is wrong because he thinks so, but it is wrong for him so long as that is his deliberate judgment. It is therefore meet that he should not do that which he knows to be wrong, and suffer the consequence whatever it may be. This is the key to the use of soul-force.

READER: You would then disregard laws—this is rank disloyalty. We have always been considered a law-abiding nation. You seem to be going even beyond the extremists. They say that we must obey the laws that have been passed, but that if the laws be bad, we must drive out the law-givers even by force.

EDITOR: Whether I go beyond them or whether I do not is a matter of no consequence to either of us. We simply want to find out what is right and to act accordingly. The real meaning of the statement that we are a law-abiding nation is that we are passive resisters. When we do not like certain laws, we do not break the heads of law-givers but we suffer and do not submit to the laws. That we should obey laws whether good or bad is a new-fangled notion. There was no such thing in former days. The people disregarded those laws they did not like and suffered the penalties for their breach. It is contrary to our manhood if we obey laws repugnant to our conscience. Such teaching is opposed to religion and means slavery. If the Government were to ask us to go about without any clothing, should we do so? If I were a passive resister, I would say to them that I would have nothing to do with their law. But we have so forgotten ourselves and become so compliant that we do not mind any degrading law.

A man who has realized his manhood, who fears only God, will fear no one else. Man-made laws are not necessarily binding on him. Even the Government does not expect any such thing from us. They do not say: "You must do such and such a thing," but they say: "If you do not do it, we will punish you." We are sunk so low that we fancy that it is our duty and our religion to do what the law lays down. If man will only realize that it is unmanly to obey laws that are unjust, no man's tyranny will enslave him. This is the key to self-rule or home-rule.

It is a superstition and ungodly thing to believe that an act of a majority binds a minority. Many examples can be given in which acts of majorities will be found to have been wrong and those of minorities to have been right. All reforms owe their origin to the initiation of minorities in opposition to majorities. If among a band of robbers a knowledge of robbing is obligatory, is a pious man to accept the obligation? So long as the superstition that men should obey unjust laws exists, so long will their slavery exist. And a passive resister alone can remove such a superstition.

To use brute-force, to use gunpowder, is contrary to passive resistance, for it means that we want our opponent to do by force that which we desire but he does not. And if such a use of force is justifiable, surely he is entitled to do likewise by us. And so we should never come to an agreement. We may simply fancy, like the blind horse moving in a circle round a mill, that we are making progress. Those who believe that they are not bound to obey laws which are repugnant to their conscience have only the remedy of passive resistance open to them. Any other must lead to disaster.

READER: From what you say I deduce that passive resistance is a splendid weapon of the weak, but that when they are strong they may take up arms.

EDITOR: This is a gross ignorance. Passive resistance, that is, soul-force, is matchless. It is superior to the force of arms. How, then, can it be considered only a weapon of the weak? Physical-force men are strangers to the courage that is requisite in a passive resister. Do you believe that a coward can ever disobey a law that he dislikes? Extremists are considered to be advocates of brute force. Why do they, then, talk about obeying laws? I do not blame them. They can say nothing else. When they succeed in driving out the English and they themselves become governors, they will want you and me to obey their laws. And that is a fitting thing for their constitution. But a passive resister will say he will not obey a law that is against his conscience, even though he may be blown to pieces at the mouth of a cannon.

What do you think? Wherein is courage required—in blowing others to pieces from behind a cannon, or with a smiling face to approach a cannon and be blown to pieces? Who is the true warrior—he who keeps death always as a bosom-friend, or he who controls the death of others? Believe me that a man devoid of courage and manhood can never be a passive resister.

This, however, I will admit: that even a man weak in body is capable of offering this resistance. One man can offer it just as well as millions. Both men and women can indulge in it. It does not require the training of an army; it needs no jiu-jitsu. Control over the mind is alone necessary, and when that is attained, man is free like the king of the forest and his very glance withers the enemy.

Passive resistance is an all-sided sword, it can be used anyhow; it blesses him who uses it and him against whom it is used. Without drawing a drop of blood it produces far-reaching results. It never rusts and cannot be stolen. Competition between passive resisters does not exhaust. The sword of passive resistance does not require a scabbard. It is strange indeed that you should consider such a weapon to be a weapon merely of the weak. . . .

READER: From what you say, then, it would appear that it is not a small thing to become a passive resister, and, if that is so, I should like you to explain how a man may become one.

EDITOR: To become a passive resister is easy enough but it is also equally difficult. I have known a lad of fourteen years become a passive resister; I have known also sick people do likewise; and I have also known physically strong and otherwise happy people unable to take up passive resistance. After a great deal of experience it seems to me that those who want to become passive resisters for the service of the country have to observe perfect chastity, adopt poverty, follow truth, and cultivate fearlessness.

Chastity is one of the greatest disciplines without which the mind cannot attain requisite firmness. A man who is unchaste loses stamina, becomes emasculated and cowardly. He whose mind is given over to animal passions is not capable of any great effort. . . .

Just as there is necessity for chastity, so is there for poverty. Pecuniary ambition and passive resistance cannot go well together. Those who have money are not expected to throw it away, but they are expected to be indifferent about it. They must be prepared to lose every penny rather than give up passive resistance.

Passive resistance has been described in the course of our discussion as truth-force. Truth, therefore, has necessarily to be followed and that at any cost. In this connection, academic questions such as whether a man may not lie in order to save a life, etc., arise, but these questions occur only to those who wish to justify lying. Those who want to follow truth every time are not placed in such a quandary; and if they are, they are still saved from a false position.

Passive resistance cannot proceed a step without fearlessness. Those alone can follow the path of passive resistance who are free from fear, whether as to their possessions, false honor, their relatives, the government, bodily injuries or death.

These observances are not to be abandoned in the belief that they are difficult. Nature has implanted in the human breast ability to cope with any difficulty or suffering that may come to man unprovoked. These qualities are worth having, even for those who do not wish to serve the country. Let there be no mistake, as those who want to train themselves in the use of arms are also obliged to have these qualities more or less. Everybody does not become a warrior for the wish. A would-be warrior will have to observe chastity and to be satisfied with poverty as his lot. A warrior without fearlessness cannot be conceived of. It may be thought that he would not need to be exactly truthful, but that quality follows real fearlessness. When a man abandons truth, he does so owing to fear in some shape or form. The above four attributes, then, need not frighten anyone. It may be as well here to note that a physical-force man has to have many other useless qualities which a passive resister never needs. And you will find that whatever extra effort a swordsman needs is due to lack of fearlessness. If he is an embodiment of the latter, the sword will drop from his hand that very moment. He does not need its support. One who is free from hatred requires no sword. A man with a stick suddenly came face to face with a lion and instinctively raised his weapon in self-defense. The man saw that he had only prated about fearlessness when there was none in him. That moment he dropped the stick and found himself free from all fear.

The Death of Martin Luther King:
Requiem for Nonviolence

The murder of Dr. Martin Luther King came as a surprise—and surprisingly it also came as a shock. Many people, particularly those in the black community who long ago abandoned nonviolence and opted to implement the slogan of Malcolm X—"black liberation by any means necessary"—have been expecting to hear of Dr. King's death for a long time. Many even became tired of waiting. But that Dr. King would have to die was a certainty. For here was a man who refused to abandon the philosophy and the principle of nonviolence in face of a hostile and racist nation which has made it indisputably clear that it has no intention and no desire to grant a redress of the grievances of the black colonial subjects who are held in bondage.

To black militants, Dr. King represented a stubborn and persistent stumbling block in the path of the methods that had to be implemented to bring about a revolution in the present situation. And so, therefore, much hatred, much venom and much criticism was focused upon Dr. King by the black militants. And the contradiction in which he was caught up cast him in the role of one who was hated and held in contempt, both by the whites in America who did not want to free black people, and by black people who recognized the attitude of white America and who wanted to be rid of the self-deceiving doctrine of nonviolence. Still, black militants were willing to sit back and watch, and allow Dr. King to play out his role. And his role has now been played out.

The assassin's bullet not only killed Dr. King, it killed a period of history. It killed a hope, and it killed a dream.

That white America could produce the assassin of Dr. Martin Luther King is looked upon by black people—and not just those identified as black militants—as a final repudiation by white America of any hope of reconciliation, of any hope of change by peaceful and nonviolent means. So that it becomes clear that the only way for black people in this country to get the things that they want—and the things that they have a right to and that they deserve—is to meet fire with fire.

In the last few months, while Dr. King was trying to build support for his projected poor people's march on Washington, he already resembled something of a dead man. Of a dead symbol, one might say more correctly. Hated on both sides, denounced on both sides—yet he persisted. And now his blood has been spilled. The death of Dr. King signals the end of an era and the beginning of a terrible and bloody chapter that may remain unwritten, because there may be no scribe left to capture on paper the holocaust to come.

That there is a holocaust coming I have no doubt at all. I have been talking to people around the country by telephone—people intimately involved in the black liberation struggle—and their reaction to Dr. King's murder has been unanimous: the war has begun. The violent phase of the black liberation struggle is here, and it will spread. From that shot, from that blood. America will be painted red. Dead bodies will litter the streets and the scenes will be reminiscent of the disgusting, terrifying, nightmarish news reports coming out of Algeria during the height of the general violence right before the final breakdown of the French colonial regime.

America has said "No" to the black man's demand for liberation, and this "No" is unacceptable to black people. They are going to strike back, they are going to reply to the escalation of this racist government, this racist society. They are going to escalate their retaliation. And the responsibility for all this blood, for all this death, for all this suffering . . . well, it's beyond the stage of assigning blame. Black people are no longer interested in adjudicating the situation, in negotiating the situation, in arbitrating the situation. Their only interest now is in being able to summon up whatever it will take to wreck the havoc upon Babylon that will force Babylon to let the black people go. For all other avenues have been closed.

The assassin's bullet which struck down Dr. King closed a door that to the majority of black people seemed closed long ago. To many of us it was clear that that door had never been open. But we were willing to allow the hopeful others to bang upon that door for entry, we were willing to sit back and let them do this. Indeed, we had no other choice. But now all black people in America have become Black Panthers in spirit. There will, of course, be those who stand up before the masses and echo the eloquent pleas of Dr. King for a continuation of the nonviolent tactic. They will be listened to by many, but from another perspective: people will look back upon Dr. King and upon his successors with something of the emotions one feels when one looks upon the corpse of a loved one. But it is all dead now. It's all dead now. Now there is the gun and the bomb, dynamite and the knife, and they will be used liberally in America. America will bleed. America will suffer.

And it is strange to see how, with each significant shot that is fired, time is speeded up. How the dreadful days that we all somehow knew were coming seem to cascade down upon us immediately, and the dreadful hours that we thought were years away are immediately upon us, immediately before us. And all eternity is gone, blown away, washed away in the blood of martyrs.

Is the death of Dr. King a sad day for America? No. It is a day consistent with what America demands by its actions. The death of Dr. King was not a tragedy for America. America should be happy that Dr. King is dead, because America worked so hard to bring it about. And now all the hypocritical, vicious madmen who pollute the government of this country and who befoul the police agencies of this country, all of the hypocritical public announcements following the death of Dr. King are being repudiated and held in contempt, not only by black people but by millions of white people who know that had these same treacherous, political gangsters made the moves that clearly lay within their power to make, Dr. King would not be dead, nonviolence would prevail and the terror would not be upon us. These people, the police departments, the legislatures, the government, the Democratic Party, the Republican Party, those commonly referred to as the Establishment or the power structure, they can be looked upon as immediate targets and symbols of blame.

But it has been said that a people or a country gets the leaders and the government that it deserves. And here we have at the death of Dr. King a President by the name of Lyndon Baines Johnson who has the audacity to stand before this nation and mourn Dr. King and to praise his leadership and the nonviolence he espoused, while he has the blood of hundreds of thousands of people and the slaughtered conscience of America upon his hands. If any one man could be singled out as bearing responsibility for bringing about the bloodshed and violence to come, it would be Lyndon Baines Johnson. But not just Lyndon Baines Johnson. All of the greedy, profit-seeking businessmen in America, all of the conniving, unscrupulous labor leaders of America, all of the unspeakable bootlickers, the big businessmen of the civil rights movement and the average man on the streets who feels hatred instilled in his heart by this vicious and disgusting system—the blame is everywhere and nowhere.

Washington, D.C., is burning. My only thought at that is: I hope

Stokely Carmichael survives Washington. Chicago is burning, Detroit is burning and there is fire and the sound of guns from one end of Babylon to the other.

Last night I heard Lyndon Baines Johnson admonishing his people, admonishing black people to turn away from violence, and not to follow the path of the assassins. And of all the corn pone that he spouted forth one thing struck me and I felt insulted by it. He was ringing changes on a famous statement made by Malcolm X in his speech, "The Ballot or the Bullet." Malcolm X had prophesied that if the ballot did not prevail in gaining black people their liberation, then the bullet would be made to prevail. And Lyndon Johnson said last night that he was going to prove to the nation and to the American people that the ballot and not the bullet would prevail. Coming from him, it was a pure insult.

Those of us in the Black Panther Party who have been reading events and looking to the future have said that this will be the Year of the Panther, that this will be the Year of the Black Panther. And now everything that I can see leaves no doubt of that. And now there is Stokely Carmichael, Rap Brown, and above all there is Huey P. Newton. Malcolm X prophesied the coming of the gun, and Huey Newton picked up the gun, and now there is gun against gun. Malcolm X gunned down. Martin Luther King gunned down.

I am trying to put a few words on tape because I was asked to do so by the editor of this magazine, to try to give my thoughts on what the assassination of Dr. King means for the future, what is likely to follow and who is likely to emerge as a new or a prevailing leader of black people. It is hard to put words on this tape because words are no longer relevant. Action is all that counts now. And maybe America will understand that. I doubt it. I think that America is incapable of understanding *anything* relevant to human rights. I think that America has already committed suicide and we who now thrash within its dead body are also dead in part and parcel of the corpse. America is truly a disgusting burden upon this planet. A burden upon all humanity. And if we here in America . . .

Seize the Time

The Black Panther Party was called to Richmond by the Dowell family. They had heard of the Black Panther Party over in Oakland. Mark Comfort came down to the office at Fifty-sixth and Grove, and told us that the Dowell family would like us to come over because Denzil Dowell had been killed in Richmond by a Contra Costa County deputy sheriff.

We went there that day and saw the Dowell family. They began to explain all the details about how certain people had said they heard ten shots, and the papers and the local media there were saying that only two or three shots were fired. And how the coroner's office had originally told them he was shot nine or ten times, but the police department said he was only shot once or twice. How the pigs had lied about Denzil Dowell, the brother, telling about how he was trying to burglarize some place.

His brothers, Carl Dowell and George Dowell, explained how the pigs knew Denzil by name, because they had arrested him a number of times. The pigs had made threats that they were going to get Denzil. It was just a cold-blooded killing of a black man. Some pigs were trigger-happy and wanted to shoot somebody, shoot a "nigger."

They explained all this to us. Then the family took us over to the site where they killed brother Denzil Dowell, and showed us just where the bullets hit certain walls and the direction they came from, and how the pigs lied and said that he ran and jumped a fence. The blood was twenty yards away from the fence. They must have dragged his body over to the other side, and then over another fence. The blood was in two different places.

We were investigating, and a lot of black people in the black community there came out. They had noticed us Panthers, with our guns and everything. I guess there were ten or twelve of us who went out there together and went through the whole process of investigation, of looking over what had happened, and listening to the information that people were giving that contradicted all the crap that the pigs and the newspapers had run down. And the people were looking.

We were standing on the corner there in North Richmond. There were about 150 people around, some in cars, some standing across the street. Some of the younger brothers, fifteen, sixteen, some twenty years old, were asking us about the guns, and we were explaining to them about the Black Panther Party. All of a sudden, some sister hollers out, "Uh, oh . . . here come the *cops.*"

When the sister hollered, Huey jacked a round off into the chamber of his eighteen-inch shotgun with a loud click and clack. When he did that, I unhitched the strap that held the hammer down on my .45, and it clacked too. People started moving back. Some of them went across the street. Some got in their cars and drove up the street. Then the pigs came down and Huey stepped to the curb. I followed Huey and stepped to the curb, a few feet down from him. The pigs were surprised all of a sudden. They looked and noticed who was ready and standing tall for them. The pigs kept driving, drove right on off—in fact, they speeded on up and drove on away. Then the people moved on back, and some of them jumped around across the street, figuring there was going to be a shoot-out, but we just stood tall, ready to defend ourselves. We were educating the people that we would die here for them. This was the position we always took with brother Huey P. Newton.

We told the people there that we were going to have a rally that coming Saturday, on the corner of Third and Chesley, right down the street. We said we'd run down and educate them about the fact that we'd have to start using guns to defend ourselves, because the racist pig cops were coming to our community and murdering our brothers and sisters. Brother Denzil Dowell was killed, and we'd found information out about two, three other brothers who'd been shot up back in December, in North Richmond there. The brothers had been shot in the armpits, which clearly showed they had their arms over their heads. Two brothers were killed in December and around April 1 Denzil Dowell was gunned down by those pigs. Huey told them we were going to have a rally concerning this, to tell the people it was necessary for us to arm ourselves for self-defense.

We went forth to have this rally, and we got about twenty brothers together with their pieces and their uniforms. We had the rally right there on the corner of Third and Chesley. We got guns and a force to defend ourselves. "Ain't no pigs going to come down here and stop our street rally. We're going to exercise our constitutional rights to free speech. And we're going to have a rally right here on the corner." Most

of North Richmond doesn't have sidewalks at all. But for that section
on the corner there, in front of this liquor store, there's an eight- to
ten-foot sidewalk between the curb and the store. We got right out
there on the corner, and all the brothers out there in this community
saw us with the guns. We lined up all along the streets.

Imagine an intersection now. On one corner we put four, five
brothers, and they were spread out about twenty, thirty feet from each
other, coming around the corner. Across the street, we put a brother
on the corner, then two brothers down from him, thirty or forty feet
apart. Then on the corner where Huey and I were speaking, right there
in front of the liquor store, we lined that corner up going east and west.
Then we lined the other corner up as you go north and south. So the
whole intersection was lined up with Panthers, all up and down the
corners, going north, east, west, and south on both sides of the streets.
And we had our guns, shotguns, pistols, and everything.

The people began to line up and brother Huey told me to go ahead
and start blowing. So I started blowing to the brothers there, running
down to them about the ten-point platform and program, what kind of
organization we had now, about the fact that brother Denzil Dowell
had been killed by some racist dog Gestapo pigs. And the fact that we
must begin to unify and organize with guns and force. That the Black
Panther Party had come to North Richmond, and the Black Panther
Party is there to serve the people, it's going to be a black people's party.
I guess about two or three hundred people gathered around. In fact,
people in cars just stopped, and the whole section on the one side of the
street was just a line of cars. And on the other side, coming right up to
the intersection, there was another line of cars. Some cars were still
moving, by going on the other side of the street, driving up the wrong
side of the street.

I was blowing there, and then all of a sudden they start sending
some sheriffs in. The people had noticed that we were there, we were
there with our guns, we were back again. The pigs started driving down
the streets, the sheriff's pigs. Huey whispered, he said, "Run it down
about the pigs, Bobby. About how we're going to hold this street rally,
and how we're going to exercise our right of free speech. No pig's going
to stop it." And he said, "Tell them about the reason why no pig's going
to stop it. It's because we've got guns and force here to protect ourselves, to protect the people."

So I ran it down to the brothers, and pointed to the pigs, and the
pigs got nervous. I noticed one of the pigs stopped across the street and
sat there, and started listening. Four of the brothers came across the
street and surrounded the pig car, standing about nine, ten feet away

from it. One brother had a .357 Magnum, Warren Tucker had a .38 pistol hanging on him, and Reginald Forte had a 9mm pistol. One brother didn't even have a gun and he got up there too. Then the pig got nervous. He started trying to light a cigarette, but the cigarette just fell out of his hand, with all these people looking at him. The black people had guns and force, ready to deal with the pigs, and the pig couldn't take it any more, he couldn't light his cigarette he was so nervous, he just up and drove away. The people yelled and raved at the fact.

Huey P. Newton had placed the notion in their minds that we organize. I think the people respected the fact that Huey had all of the brothers organized, because he had them all stationed up and down the streets, covering the intersection, guarding the lives of the black people, while we went forth to organize the people. They respected this organization that Huey put down. Huey put down a form, a discipline, that the gun was for our protection, and not for bull jive. So the pig had to split.

Another pig was sitting there. This other pig came up in a car and some of the people's cars moved along. But one man said, "Well, I ain't moving my car. I'm going to sit here and listen." And this cop got caught in between the cars and he couldn't move and he had to sit there and listen to everything. He couldn't do nothing. And that brother didn't move his car. He had a Cadillac too, and he and his woman were sitting in the Cadillac, sitting right at the head of the intersection. So this pig's car was right in between, and he couldn't move, he just had to sit there and listen, and look at 300, that's right, he had to look at 300 mad niggers—mad at the pigs for killing Denzil Dowell. And twenty Panthers out there armed with guns, disciplined, standing thirty or forty feet apart, on every corner of the intersection. So it was tied down.

The people dug it and they said, "Right on." And Huey went on and blew to the brothers and sisters and told them how we're going to get organized and how we're going to start using guns and force in an organized and disciplined manner. In a very revolutionary manner we're going to go forth, and we're going to defend ourselves against any racist attacks. And we're going to patrol these pigs, we're going to patrol our own communities, even the old people are going to have to patrol from their homes and houses. And everybody has to have a shotgun in his home, everybody. Then George Dowell blew about how his brother, Denzil, had been murdered by the pigs. We said we were going to have another meeting over on Second Street, and Huey said we're going to block the whole street off, and ain't no pigs going to be allowed up the street . . . *at all.*

At the second Richmond rally, three or four hundred people came up. They drove their cars all inside the street, and brothers got on top of cars and top of roofs all up and down the street, from one corner to the next, and it was a pretty long block. The whole street was cluttered with cars. We were at one particular address, where I think some relative of George Dowell lived. This was right around the corner from George Dowell's mother's home. All the people came around and we had applications there for people to join the Party. I guess just about everybody out there joined the Party that day, from little young four- teen-year-olds and twelve-year-olds.

We blocked the whole street off. Brother Huey blew, I blew, brother Eldridge Cleaver came over and he blew to the people, and the people dug it, and the people filled out the applications.

One incident happened there. I noticed that one of the brothers moved some four, five guns to one of the corners. We were in the center of the block. Some more of the extra brothers had been moved down to one of the corners. The corner on the north end. The brother ex- plained to me (I was blowing at the time) that one of the pigs had come up at the corner down there, so the brothers blocked the street off. One of the pigs was sitting there. So a couple of other brothers went over to a vacant lot and stood with their M-1's and 30-.06's, looking at the pig's car. They couldn't have been thirty yards from the pigs. Stood staring right at the pigs' car, and the pigs looked around and one of them saw another brother walk up near his car, and stand there almost like at parade rest, but with his hand just a few inches from his .357 Magnum. And the pig looked at him when he got up there, then he looked at his partner, and he said, "That's a .357 Magnum he's got!" And when he said that, the pig turned his engine on and he got out of there and didn't come back.

Then a helicopter came around. We blocked off the whole street and held a people's rally, with power, gun power. Gun power's the only thing that backed it up. So all they could do was send a helicopter over, flap, flap, flapping all day long to try and bother us. This time it wasn't only the Black Panthers who came, but other people came there, with their rifles, with their guns, and with their pieces. I noticed some older brothers come out and they were shaking hands with a lot of us, and they had their pieces under their shirts. They just carried them con- cealed. And some sisters. One sister came out and jumped out of her car with an M-1. We saw the black community people getting uptight and ready. And the helicopter kept flapping over and Huey pointed up at the helicopter as it was going over and said, "Always remember that *the spirit of the people is greater than the man's technology.*" And the people said, "Right on." I remember we got way over 300 applications.

The community people got together and George Dowell's sisters and brothers and friends got together and began to have a regular session. And everyone would come to the meeting with the people of North Richmond. The brothers had their guns on. They were tired, sick and tired, and they loved brother Huey. They thought brother Huey was out of sight. He was a beautiful leader, and Huey began to instruct them on many things, on many ways they can go about dealing with the real problems. One of the sisters brought up the problem at one of the nightly sessions that one of those schoolteachers beat up and slapped down a couple of black kids in school. She wanted the Panthers, the Black Panther Party, to go to the school, and she was going to get a lot of mothers and parents to go to the junior high school where her kids went. We all got together and scheduled it for that Monday.

On Monday we took three carloads of Panthers down to the school. All of them were armed down to the gills. We got out of the cars with our guns and stood on the sidewalk. Right at the sidewalk there's a fence to the school yard. All the little black kids ran over to the fence, and all the little white kids ran away from the fence, and went and hid somewhere inside the school. Then the mothers came driving up. They went inside the school building to patrol the halls of the school. They patroled the halls during lunch period, and went and told the principal that they didn't want any more brutality upon their kids in the schools. "We're concerned citizens, and we'll whip your ass and anyone else's that we hear of slapping our children around."

After about twenty minutes, while the mothers were patroling the halls, the pigs drove up. This little, young, rookie, jive pig, trying to look mean and thinking he was bad or something, walked up to the car; the brothers were sitting there in the car, looking back at him, because Huey had trained his brothers, don't be moving in a rash manner. And they got shotguns, four motherfuckers, M-1's. He looks in the car and sees all these pieces and he moves back in a hurry. He got all nervous. "Wha' . . . wha' . . . what the guns for? What the guns for?" And I think Huey said, "We're the Black Panther Party, why?" "Uh, uh, da, da, doo, do you have any license? Do you have any driver's license?" And Huey gave him his license.

"Well, you're Huey P. Newton."

"Minister of Defense Huey P. Newton, of the Black Panther Party." And the pig was just shaking. He didn't know what to do, so he gave Huey his license back and went and got on his radio and called up another pig. They kind of hung off, away from us, looking and not knowing what to do. Shook, because there's too many niggers and too many guns down there for them.

They called up another car and the principal of the school came

out, and tried to talk to the pigs. Their cars were parked a little way out
in front of the sidewalk that leads into the door of the school, about
thirty, forty yards or so behind ours. All they could do was sit there and
wonder. And that's all they did, was sit there and wonder. We went
there with the mothers and they patroled the halls for the lunch period,
and then we left. . . .

PFLP and Acts of Violence

I.

The use of violence has, to a very great extent, been condemned by the majority of people if for no reason other than for its detrimental consequences. The bombing of buildings by the Weathermen in the United States, the killing of U.S. official Dan Mitrione in Uruguay by the Tupamaros, the killing of La Porte in Quebec by the Front for the Liberation of Quebec (FLQ), and the blowing up of airlines by the Popular Front for the Liberation of Palestine (PFLP) are some of the recent manifestations of acts of violence carried out by militant revolutionaries. News media saw to it to inform the public of the consequences of these acts of violence. Generally public opinion is appalled at the use of violence and—as in most cases when of information is not available to the public concerning the underlying reasons for these acts—they engage themselves in condemning these acts as the fabrications of "piracy," "terrorism," "assassination." Yet these people who condemn the acts of violence performed by revolutionaries condone the acts of the U.S. soldiers in Indo-China. This attitude was aptly expressed in the following words: "... What is described as "heroism" when performed by the U.S. soldiers or police, or soldiers of our allies, is described as "terrorism" when performed by Viet Cong, Weathermen groups, Black Panthers, Palestinian Guerrillas ..."[1]

A case in point, in this connection, is the recent exploit of PFLP in its successful multiple hijackings of the planes in September of 1971. People throughout the world reacted with indignation—the appellations "terrorists," "assassins," "pirates" were some of the terms used in describing the acts carried out by PFLP. All of a sudden we seem to have obliterated everything else from our sight except these acts of violence. Other acts of violence such as attacks on Panthers' Headquarters in U.S., the military exploits of U.S. troops in Indo-China did not receive the same condemnation. However, it is not the purpose of this

213

paper to explain why particular kinds of acts of violence are condemned while others, equally deserving of condemnation, are not. Rather my purpose is to explain PFLP's stand on acts of violence.

II.

The frequent use of acts of violence by PFLP has been its main specialty in the struggle toward the enemy camp. We do know by now, in addition to the recent multiple hijackings, of the various organized attacks marshalled by PFLP not only against Israeli embassies and planes outside Israel, but also against those countries who support Israel. With respect to PFLP it was often asked why acts of violence against European countries? Children? PFLP's stand on this matter stems from its analysis of the enemy camp which, according to PFLP, includes Israel, the World Zionist Movement, World Imperialism, and Arab Reaction. Some remarks concerning each individual enemy are in order.

PFLP in the struggle for liberation has first to face Israel as a political, military and economic entity with its dedicated, thoroughly trained and brilliantly led army of approximately 300,000 men. Also Israel enjoys a great ability to mobilize its masses on the assumption that it is waging a life or death battle and hence has no other alternative but to defend itself at all times. In addition to Israel's ability to quickly mobilize, PFLP is also fully cognizant of Israel's technological superiority which its less developed enemy lacked in their struggle for liberation.

In the perspective of PFLP, their struggle for liberation is not simply with Israel but also with a state whose structure is founded on the strength of the Zionist movement. Indeed Israel is an offshoot of political Zionism which, since its inception in 1896 by Theodor Herzl, has subscribed to the view that all jews in the world constitute one nation, and that Israel is a Jewish state created by Jews and exclusively for Jews. However, Zionism should not simply be viewed as providing Israel with moral support; it is fundamentally also a material supporting movement which has provided Israel with more people, money, technical knowledge, in addition of course to its world wide support through publicity and propaganda. Hence the world Zionist movement, which to a great extent was and still is responsible for the creation and maintenance of Israel, is a natural enemy for PFLP.

With respect to world imperialism, Zionism had always aligned itself with it. Through British imperialism, the Zionists fulfilled their dream with the signing of the *Balfour Declaration* on November 2,

1917, in which they were granted a "National Home" in Palestine. As far as American imperialism is concerned, its strategy was first executed by allowing U.S. officials and businessmen to bribe or blackmail various states in conceding to the U.N. partition of Palestine on November 29, 1947.[2] Following the partition and the creation of Israel on May 15, 1948, U.S. has been and still is the main moral as well as material mainstay of Israel. For instance, since the establishment of the state of Israel, some 9 million dollars of Western capital has been poured into Israel, mostly in gifts which, incidentally, are tax free. Private contributions from the U.S. totalled over 110 million dollars by 1967. In addition to all this, Israel has been the top capita recipient of U.S. aid. It has been estimated that Israel has received governmental loans exceeding 30 million dollars yearly and 650 million dollars in direct aid in one ten-year period,[3] not to say anything of President Nixon's new 500 million dollars foreign aid package for Israel.

Although Israel has no oil and hence not a prime target for U.S. investments, still U.S. uses Israel as a base to further her own interests stemming from oil in various countries. It has been estimated that nearly two billion dollars from the oil revenues flow into the United States.[4] As PFLP explains it: "the protection, reinforcement and support of Israel and the maintenance of its existence, are fundamental matters for the interest of world imperialism."[5]

So far the triumvirate of Israel, the world Zionist movement and world imperialism whose interests are closely interrelated in the Arab countries are instances of what one would label as an enemy, for colonialism-imperialism,[6] wherever it happens to be, attempts to maintain the status quo regardless of whether one calls it "law and order," "peace," "recognized and secure borders." Hence the danger that the Revolution in the Middle East presents to Israel, the world Zionist movement and imperialism is quite obvious. However, as far as Arab reaction is concerned, it would seem less obvious. Yet the classification of Arab reaction by PFLP, as one of the forces of the enemy, manifested itself on a number of occasions since the June war of 1967. Various attempts by Lebanon and Jordan were carried out with the sole intent of liquidating the guerrillas. The 1970 September civil war in Jordan is a case in point, for it clearly revealed the determination of the Jordanian government to liquidate the Palestinian resistance movement once and for all. The civil war in Jordan between the Palestinian commandoes and the Jordanian army reaffirmed one of PFLP's main points, i.e. that Arab reactionary element is as much an enemy to the revolution as Israel, world Zionist movement and imperialism are. For Arab capitalism, whose interests are represented and defended by reactionary regimes in the Arab countries, cannot stand on its own feet unless it has the full-fledged support of world imperialism.

Hence, within the movement of PFLP, there is great stress in specifying the nature of the enemy, for a clear analysis of the enemy camp is essential to any revolution in the struggle for liberation. As PFLP puts it: "It is the nature of the enemy which determines the nature of the confrontation, and here lies the danger of any superficial or unscientific look at the enemy camp and its main characteristics."[7]

The above analysis of the enemy camp does indicate some of the main reasons underlying PFLP's attacks on airlines. Hence the attacks by the PFLP on Israel's El Al airlines flown by reserve officers of the Israeli Air Force coupled with their attacks on Western airlines, be it European or American, are perfectly legitimate targets. George Habash, leader of PFLP, and in partial response to the question, "what right do you have to impose this war on Europeans?" had the following to say: "In a war it is fair to strike the enemy wherever he happens to be, and this rule leads us also to the European airfields where El Al planes land or takeoff."[8]

The other question which arose in connection with violence was: why acts of violence against civilians? The bazooka attacks on school buses, the bombing of cafeterias and supermarkets, the planting of mines in fields are prime cases in point. Again PFLP's position on this stems from its analysis not just of the enemy camp, but also from its strategy of upholding the principle of total war. In organization, as well as strategy, PFLP pursued certain specific objectives. From the outset PFLP enunciated its ultimate objective which was to bring about a liberated Palestine (now Israel) within the framework of a revolutionary and socialist Arab world. Following the six-day war of 1967, PFLP's adherence to socialist theory became more pronounced and finally presented the meaning and goal of the armed struggle in terms of Marxist-Leninist party, a broad national front, and the principle of armed struggle.[9] The revolutionary party is the party of the classes of the revolution, i.e. the workers and peasants who are the inhabitants of refugee camps, villages and poor urban districts. The Front, on the other hand, mobilizes the diverse existing national classes and other groups who are willing to join the struggle for liberation. Finally the principle of protracted armed struggle is the transformation of a guerrilla war into a people's war of liberation.

Hence PFLP's reluctance to disregard nonmilitary installations stems primarily from its initial commitment of upholding total war in its struggle for national liberation within, as well as outside, Palestine, and of attacking the enemy *wherever* he happens to be. Another point to consider became evident with the intensification of the struggle. If Israel uses napalm against Arab children, indiscriminately destroys homes in response to commandos' activities, tortures Palestinian commandos, enforces Dayan's policy of "collective neighborhood punishment," then, reasoned PFLP, the commandos simply refuse to delineate between military and nonmilitary targets. There is also the overall situation of the Arab-Israeli conflict to be taken into account. For if one takes into consideration the situation of the Palestinian Arabs since their forcible eviction by Israel in 1948, the attitude of the Israeli government toward the Palestinians, the yearly abrogation by Israel of the U.N.'s decisions to either compensate or repatriate the Palestinian Arabs, then one can understand the underlying frustration and the necessity on the part of the Palestinian commandos as a whole to see to it that their struggle for national liberation is maintained against the enemy camp. Since 1948 the Palestinians were recognized as refugees by Israel as well as the international community. The only claim that the Palestinians as refugees may impose, as far as Israel is concerned, is a humanitarian one. Israel's stand on the refugee problem throughout its existence is that the Arab states *caused* it and hence it is the duty of the Arab governments to find a solution which should consist of resettling them in various parts of the Arab world. Also Israeli authorities have never recognized the existence of the Palestinians[10]—let alone a Palestinian resistance movement. According to Israeli officials, guerrillas are "terrorists," "murderers," and "saboteurs." Often captured commandos at the hands of the Israelis are treated as criminals, notwithstanding the fact that these captured commandos might be wearing uniforms and belong to military units.

An understanding of the Arab governments attitude with respect to the Palestinian issue is also fundamental in any attempt to explain the motivating force underlying not just PFLP's action but the whole guerrilla movement. Prior to the 1967 June war, the Palestinians depended upon the various governments to find a solution to their problem. The Arab governments in turn kept promising them that a just solution is forthcoming. (One should add that they are still forecasting such a solution.) But the decisive defeat of the Arab states in June 1967 at the hands of the Israelis convinced the Palestinians that if there is ever to be a solution to the Palestinian conflict, then it has to be decided by the Palestinians themselves *via* guerrilla armed struggle. And since the June war of 1967, the Palestinian commandos, in their struggle for liberation, have exerted tremendous pressure upon the reactionary Arab governments of Jordan and Lebanon. The effectiveness of the guerrillas was put to task in September of 1970 when the civil war broke out between the guerrillas and the Jordanian army. Clearly the result of the civil war was not a military victory for either side. But it clearly demonstrated the willingness and the determination of the movement to fight against anyone who attempts to liquidate the struggle for national liberation.

From the above account one can understand, if not advocate, the necessity of resorting to acts of violence in search for one's specific objective. To recapitulate, PFLP's position of upholding total war against the enemy camp, coupled with the Israeli attitude as well as the Arab reactionary governments toward them, has compelled PFLP to resort to acts of violence in pursuit of its ultimate goal. Now we come to the question of what have acts of violence contributed to the cause of the revolution in the Middle East?

III.

The motivating political factor behind a protracted campaign of violence against the enemy is to exert economic as well as political pressure. The use of violence against Israel has so far accomplished some beneficial results:

(1) Domestically the use of violence has depressed Israeli morale. A paranoid attitude is quite prevalent among the inhabitants of Israel. Reports emanating from Israeli presses, as well as foreign correspondents in Israel, reflect the low morale among Israeli inhabitants. For instance, an American correspondent in the summer of 1969 filed the following: "Thirteen times a day Israelis stop whatever else they are doing to learn whether there have been crippling new acts of terror by their Arab enemies."[11] Another example comes from General Narkis, an Israeli analyst, who complained that "things have reached such a point that people have to be continually injected with morale boosters in order to preserve their confidence in our military strength and to prevent them from losing it altogether."[12]

(2) It has discouraged new investments, tourism and economic development in Israel. Immigration is almost at a standstill.

(3) It has solidified more and more the Palestinian resistance movement, and helped more in mobilizing the Arab masses behind the Palestinian revolution. The Arab masses responded well to the actions of the guerrillas. There is little doubt about the humiliation the Arabs received, especially the Palestinians, since 1948. Now the guerrillas gave them, so to speak, "a breath of hope" and a sense of dignity. The Palestinian refugees started believing in dying while upholding their principles rather than rotting in miserable tents. Thus the acts of vio-

lence had a tremendous effect, especially on young Arab revolutionaries who started to realize that the only way to express themselves is by backing the Palestinian revolution. Arab governments, as well as individuals who identified themselves with the Palestinian cause, contributed funds to the guerrillas. Thousands of Palestinians pledge monthly payments to the guerrillas. In Kuwait, for instance, Palestinians working in oil fields contribute monthly 3 to 5 percent of their salaries.[13]

(4) Another point to take into consideration is that through the acts of violence PFLP, in particular, wanted to demonstrate to the rest of the world that they are a power to reckon with; they felt that the only way for them to let the world notice them is to speak and act as Palestinians. A case in point is the recent multiple hijackings of planes. One of the fundamental points that PFLP's guerrillas tried to impart to their hostages was the Palestinian cause. As one hostage put it: "They think the idea of one nation with one religion is prejudiced, and they were kicked out of their homes. . . . They gave us some pamphlets. People said it was propaganda, but I believe that some of it was true."[14]

So far some positive aspects of the use of violence were discussed. But there are also negative aspects connected with the use of violence.

(1) While the use of violence did bring the cause of the Palestinians to the attention of the international community, it did also adversely affect public opinion. Usually acts of violence perpetrated by the guerrillas are viewed by the public as the fabrications of "assassins." This evaluation is quite understandable, though hardly excusable, if one does not take into consideration the underlying factors which have led guerrillas to resorting to violence. An investigation into the causes of acts of violence usually reveals illuminating factors. With the case of PFLP's guerrillas, it is quite understandable as I tried earlier to indicate in the paper. They are truly desperate people, and they are certain that efforts to negotiate a political solution is tantamount to the liquidation of the resistance movement. However, one should not conclude that the guerrillas do not take into consideration the evaluation of public opinion. In answer to the question whether the opinion of the world concerns PFLP, Habash had the following to say: "Obviously we are concerned with world opinion. When it is on your side it means you are in the right, when it is against you it means there is something wrong in what you are doing."[15]

But if PFLP is concerned with the evaluation of public opinion, why does it then perform acts such as hijackings of planes, bombing of embassies, etc.? Habash's answer to this question was: ". . . World opinion has never been either with us or against us; it has kept on ignoring

us."[16] A Middle East expert in response to the question why did the
commandos turn to skyjacking, knowing it would turn large segments
of the world opinion against them?" had the following to say: "Palestinians had to demonstrate dramatically—yes, ruthlessly—their conviction
that the only way for them to recover Palestine is by fighting, not
negotiating. As the commandos see it, nobody else but themselves is
either capable or willing to do that fighting."[17]

(2) Acts of violence could yield to the liquidation of not only PFLP
but also the rest of the guerrilla movement. Subsequent to the 1967
June war, Israel had on several occasions retaliated harshly against the
Arab states harboring guerrillas. With the increase in the use of violence
on the part of the guerrillas, Israel stepped up her attacks against the
Arab states. Such attacks had a detrimental effect in weakening the
Arab states, especially Jordan and Egypt, and ultimately it forced them
to accept the first cease-fire proposed by Secretary Rogers in August of
1970. Obviously should a peace treaty be consummated between the
Arab states and Israel, the possibility of the survival of the resistance
movement is slim; for the commandos are fully cognizant of the fact
that a political settlement with Israel would have to include, among
other things, the recognition of the state of Israel which, in turn, would
put an end to the Palestinian resistance movement. It was clear to the
commandos that Israel would not accept a peace treaty unless there was
a firm commitment by the concerned Arab governments to curb and,
if possible, to liquidate once and for all the Palestinian resistance movement. Put in a nutshell, a political solution would mean an end to the
revolutionary upsurge in Palestine as well as throughout the Arab
world. Viewed in this manner, it becomes quite evident why the commandos, especially PFLP, resorted to acts of violence. A prime factor
underlying the skyjacking in September of 1970 was not simply to
demonstrate to the world their disapproval of the peace initiative of
Secretary Rogers, but to stifle any serious talks of arriving at a political
settlement.

However, the multiple skyjackings by PFLP have incurred more
harm than good. I am not specifically concerned here with the immediate condemnation by world opinion of the actions of PFLP as "piracy,"
"lawlessness," "terrorism," etc. Rather I am more concerned with the
post effects the civil war had on the Palestinian resistance movement
in general and PFLP in particular. The hijackings in September of 1970
afforded the Jordanian army the long-awaited chance of confronting
the Palestinian guerrillas. The Jordanian government feared that its
authority had been undermined locally as well as internationally as a

result of PFLP's actions. In order to restore such authority, and acting
in the name of "law and order," the Jordanian army, at the behest of
King Hussein, launched its fierce attack against the guerrillas. The outcome of the civil war was quite detrimental to the *Palestinian National
Liberation Movement* in general and to the PFLP in particular. While,
admittedly, there were some obvious advantages, still the disadvantages outweighed the advantages. Some salient points stood out: (a)
PFLP, which prior to the civil war enjoyed full freedom of movement
throughout the Arab world, is now not allowed to function in the open.
The Jordanian government went so far as to put a price on the heads
of two commando leaders, George Habash of the PFLP and Nayef
Hawatmeh of the Democratic Popular Front for the Liberation of Palestine. (b) PFLP lost the confidence of a significant number of Palestinians
who were led to believe that PFLP's skyjackings caused the massacre
of thousands of innocent people.

The civil war had adversely affected the Palestinian National Liberation Movement as a whole: (a) The flow of funds from rich Arab states
such as Saudi Arabia had been curtailed. The Saudi Arabian Government, which feels a firm "brotherly" bond with the Hashemite Kingdom of Jordan, was prior to the civil war one of the largest sources of
outside support to the commandos. Clearly the discontinuation of funds
is bound to financially affect the Palestinian movement. (b) Al-Saiqa, a
Syrian based guerrilla group with an estimated 7,000 followers, is in
trouble as a result of General Assad's decision to restrict its operations.
Assad's predecessor—Atassi—on the other hand was sympathetic to the
cause of the commandos and had always allowed the Palestinian commandos freedom in Syria. Many Al-Saiqa commandos were forced to
leave Syria. It thus would appear that the Palestinian National Liberation Movement for the time being has lost the support of Syria which
in the past has been the best expounder of the Palestinians' pro-revolu-
tionary cause. (c) There seems to be somewhat of a disarray in the
Palestinian organization. Some authoritative Arab world presses reported that the Palestinian guerillas are "in total disarray after having
been the center of attraction and hope of the Arab masses and the peg
for the overall Arab revolution."[18] (d) It curtailed the action against
Israel as is evidenced by the lack of guerrilla activities against Israel.
The main concern of the Palestinian movement now is to secure and
establish a firm base in the Arab states.

Hence there appears to be some evidence that in its use of acts of
violence, PFLP could lead to its own destruction as well as that of the
rest of the resistance movement in the Middle East.

(3) An unfortunate consequence of the use of acts of violence is usually accompanied with the loss of innocent human beings. Indeed the chief complaint about justifying violence stems from the thoughts of the consequence generated by the performance of acts of violence.

IV. CONCLUSION

It is quite clear from what was reported earlier in the paper that PFLP's motivating factor in its use of violence was to hamstring the enemy politically as well as economically. The use of violence against the enemy camp is necessarily tied with PFLP's political objective in its determination to liberate Palestine. PFLP, too, considered itself part and parcel of the Third World movement as manifested by the various National Liberation Movements in Africa, Asia, Latin America, and North America. One common denominator among these movements is their dedication to put an end once and for all to the capitalist-imperialist system which, over the years, had oppressed and exploited them. Thus it would seem to follow that the use of violence perpetuated by the commandos of various liberation movements is closely connected with their overall objective. PFLP, along with other liberation movements, is quite aware that their revolution, if it is destined to get off the ground, should resort to the use of violence in destroying the counter-revolutionary elements that produced colonialism, racism and imperialism. They are striving to create a system in which the Third World population will be able to achieve its full potentials. So long as man is subjected to the capitalist-imperialist system, his freedom and dignity are thwarted. Hence, when PFLP blew up the planes, they were demonstrating to the Western World that their struggle is not against human beings in the West, but rather against the Western tool of oppression and exploitation as symbolized by the expensive destroyed planes.

Finally, PFLP's aspiration, which it shares with the rest of the contemporary liberation movements, stems from the burning desire to destroy the system which has exploited and oppressed them for generations, and replace it with one in which man will achieve his aspirations and start productively relating to the rest of mankind. It is in this context that the actions of the Palestinians should be analyzed. They are fighting against the laws of the imperialist world which has consistently condoned exploitation of these people. And make no mistake about it, the Palestinians do consider Israel as a colonialist-imperialist outpost in the sense of the imposition of a western force upon a non-western force.

Footnotes

1. J. Weinroth. "Some Political Uses of Violence."
2. For the most authoritative study on this see A. M. Lilienthal, *What Price Israel?* Chicago: Regnery Company, 1953, esp. Chapter 3.
3. *Workers World* (June 27, 1970), p. 8.
4. Cf. H. Sharabi, *Palestine and Israel,* New York: Pegasus, 1969, pp. 133-134.
5. *The Popular Front for the Liberation of Palestine (PFLP): A Strategy for the Liberation of Palestine,* Amman, 1969, p. 12.
6. It is important to keep in mind that to the Arabs and the people of the Third World, Israel is considered as a product of colonialism-imperialism, in the sense of a western force acting upon a non-western adversary. However, Zionism, unlike classical colonialism, distinguished itself in comtemporary history by being an *expelling* movement and this physical expulsion took place at the expense of the indigenous inhabitants of Palestine.
7. *The Popular Front for the Liberation of Palestine,* 1969, p. 18.
8. *Life* (June 12, 1970), p. 33.
9. Stated in "Doctrine of the Popular Front for the Liberation of Palestine," p. 52.
10. Recently Golda Mier for example, claimed "the Palestinians did not exist." See *London Sunday Times,* (January 15, 1969).
11. H. A. Ruskin, *The New York Times,* (July 7, 1969).
12. Quoted in Sharabi's *Palestine Guerrillas,* pp. 9-8.
13. See an account of this in *U.S. News and World Report,* (Sept. 21, 1970), p. 20.
14. Reported by *Time* (Sept. 28, 1970), p. 25.
15. See *Life* (June 12, 1970), p. 33.
16. *Ibid.*
17. *U.S. News and World Report* (Sept. 21, 1970), p. 24.
18. Reported by Mark Ethridge, Jr., Editor of *The Detroit Free Press,* on "The Palestinian Commando Movement." Reprinted in *Tallahassee Democrat* (Sunday, Dec. 6, 1970), p. 14A.

Study Questions

1. How can Socrates claim seriously that he owes allegiance directly to the laws of Athens? Are the laws anything more or less than the administration of law by particular officials, who in this case were corrupt? What implication does Socrates' argument in *Crito* have for conscientious objectors to the War in Vietnam?
2. In what sense might it be argued that protesters are in fact the strongest supporters of a government of law?
3. Should we strive for the long-range goal of reducing violence in human experience to a minimum, or is violence simply a built-in feature of human life? Can there be justified violence *and* unjustified violence? If there are no restrictions on the government's use

of violence, or if violence is simply a built-in feature of human life, then what is to be said against going out and murdering anyone you choose to in order to get whatever you want?

4. Does there appear to be an important difference between Gandhi's extreme doctrine of non-violence as a personal moral code and as a political strategy? Can you imagine a Gandhi type of massive non-violent resistance successfully carried out against the government in the U.S.?

5. Do you know anyone who literally practices the code of conduct set forth in the Sermon on the Mount (love thy enemies—turn the other cheek—give all that ye have to the poor)? Would you think such a person to be more than a little bit crazy? How, then, can our society justify calling itself a society based on Christian morals?

6. Is Cleaver right in asserting that a strategy of non-violence will not work in our society?

7. Why do Marx and Engels assert that capitalism by its very nature prevents the working man from ever having any property?

8. What significant features of class oppression can you identify in your surroundings? In concrete terms, what would a shift to a spirit of community produce in the way of making your social surroundings different from what they are now?

9. Does it seem to you that Huey Newton is talking about the same thing as are the other authors in Part II, B?

10. What prominent examples can you find of politically manipulative use of language? How dangerous do these examples appear to you?

11. Can you design a community in which it would not be possible—or at least not highly probable—that one ruling group could administer the laws in an unjust way?

12. What effect would an enforcement of Aristotle's rule of law have on the tax-loopholes used by modern corporations, and on similar practices?

13. What do you think the term "violence" really means?

14. Comment on the following statement:
The idea of "law" in our society is mostly invoked either for control and repression or else as a myth designed to delay and confuse anyone working for change in our society. The use of the idea of law may be seen in the range of activity praised as activity aimed at securing "law and order"—e.g. police dispersal of demonstrations, special disciplinary codes for college campuses, and federal "anti-riot" legislation.

15. Comment of the following statement:
One use of the idea of law is to achieve far-reaching social change.

Thus the social practices of racial discrimination, forced segregation, and sexual discrimination have been to some degree blocked
and weakened by the use or the threat of force by the federal
government as indicated by recently enacted laws. The aim of
speeding-up change through law—rather than "channeling"
efforts at change—is clearly in evidence here.

Part III

MAN VERSUS TECHNOLOGY

Introduction

The selections included on this topic raise various interesting questions that are of significance to all concerned citizens. Why does society organize scientific research? What is the role of science in society? What are the moral responsibilities of scientists? How does technology affect our lives? Should technology be controlled?

In Chapter XV (volume 1) of *Capital,* Karl Marx discusses the interrelations between the development of the machine, the development of the capitalistic mode of ownership and the dehumanization of the industrial workers. Two factors which Marx identifies as inherent in the process of machine-production are: (a) division of the industrial task into a number of smaller, repetitive tasks; (b) regimentation of the worker's movements on the job and his life-schedule in general in order to fit the rhythm appropriate to the machinery. The regimentation of the worker's job and life to fit the tempo of the machine in itself destroys the individuality of the worker. Nor is such regimentation accidental. The basic structure and motions of the work process are completely altered in machine manufacture. Moreover, the extreme division of labor makes the laborer unfit for any productive task except the most unthinking and unhealthfully repetitive work. Thus at one and the same time the worker is stultified as a human being, and made further dependent on the capitalist, having become merely a type of commodity on the labor market.

Bertrand Russell in "Demonology and Science" points out the rift between the scientifically oriented man and the nonscientifically (i.e. religious) man as a consequence of the technological advances in the medical field during the Middle Ages. Russell cites numerous examples in which he tried to indicate the inability of the religious man to adjust at the outset to the advances in medical technology. Though the religious community at present does not for the most part interfere with the technological achievements in medicine, there is still the explicit disapproval, e.g. of the Christian Catholic Church, toward the legalization of abortion or the practice of birth control—notwithstanding the economic as well as the scientific soundness of such practices. It should be noted that such disapproval usually ranges over the social and moral implications of the use of technology.

Russell's essay brings out an important point: technological advances produce a certain crisis in one's culture. In the Middle Ages, man witnessed various crises as a result of the advances in technology. In this century, we are witnessing another crisis, not necessarily motivated by the same reasons as that of the Middle Ages. The crisis we are facing at present stems from the dangers of uncontrolled technology. There exists the deep concern among scientists as well as nonscientists that technology, if not controlled by effective means, would end in undermining the quality and excellence of human existence. Indeed there is great emphasis at present on the detrimental social and moral consequences that uncontrolled technology might have on mankind. Scientists are in fact paying more attention to the consequences of their scientific achievements now than before. Hence scientists started realizing that it is not sufficient to just engage in and encourage the advancement of research. Rather there should be great emphasis on the possible long-range effects of the scientific activity. Put differently, man should not become a victim of technological progress; he should be the beneficiary recipient of its fruitful results. For technology not controlled by or for the benefit of the popular masses could only lead mankind into disaster.

The selections by Professors Rescher, Commoner, Sly, and Levy-Leblond alert us of some of the dangers of technological progress. Nicholas Rescher in his article "The Allocation of Exotic Medical Therapy" points out one crisis that arose subsequent to the recent technological development in the heart transplant operations. Given the accessibility of this "exotic life saving therapy" (ELT), Professor Rescher then raises the following question: Whose life to save? Rescher does indicate that the selection problem with respect to "whose life to save?" is not fundamentally a medical problem, but rather a philosophical one, i.e. an ethical one, pertaining to moral philosophy. After stating the problem, Professor Rescher discusses two types of criteria for making ELT selection, and certain relevant factors under each.

Barry Commoner, in his paper "Science and the Sense of Humanity," discusses one of the most pressing problems facing mankind at present, i.e. environmental pollution. Professor Commoner's main argument is that environmental pollution is not a consequence of man's overpopulation nor is it of man's consumption, but from changes in the technological methods of production. Such changes necessitated, according to Professor Commoner, the creation of faulty technology. Hence Commoner contends that our environmental crisis is a result of faulty technology and an effective solution to this crisis is summed as " . . . we must improve that technology and make it fit the demands of environmental processes."

In his paper "Technology and Population Growth," David Sly contends that there is an "inherent contradiction" between the possibilities of lowering world growth rates and reducing the threat of ecological disaster. In other words, Sly's main contention is that our supplies of renewable and nonrenewable resources are simply not sufficient to permit us to reduce people's desire to have too many children; and that, furthermore, if these supplies were sufficient, we would simply, so argues Professor Sly, annihilate ourselves through the resulting ecological disaster.

The final selection in this section is a speech by Jean Marc Levy-Leblond, a French theoretical physicist, given in January, 1970 when he accepted an academic prize for his research. Professor Levy-Leblond addresses himself to the question "of what is the role of science in our society." As a scientist, Professor Levy-Leblond has finally realized that there is more to scientific research than simply the technological by-products of such research. He is deeply convinced of the important role science plays in our social life. Yet it is his deep conviction that science and research "do not serve the purposes and groups they pretend to serve." Rather, Levy-Leblond contends that they serve to "insure the perpetuation, or at least, the survival of this social system."

The services rendered to society via the scientific activity is carried out, according to Professor Levy-Leblond, on various levels. First, on the political level, the resources of technology are used by the imperialist powers for military purposes. Second, on the economic level, the scientific production has also made its impact felt. Third, on the ideological level, science is used by the social class in power to advance its own ideas and principles. Finally, Levy-Leblond discusses the "amusing" aspect of science in its endeavor to divert the attention of mankind from serious problems.

Clearly, Professor Levy-Leblond is not arguing against science, but against the use of it by the ruling class in its calculated effort to exploit the masses. Indeed Professor Levy-Leblond is emphasizing that science be harnessed *by* the masses *for* the masses. For he is fearful that technology not controlled by or for the benefit of the masses can only be detrimental.

Machines and Labor

John Stuart Mill says in his "Principles of Political Economy": "It is questionable if all the mechanical inventions yet made have lightened the day's toil of any human being." That is, however, by no means the aim of the capitalistic application of machinery. Like every other increase in the productiveness of labour, machinery is intended to cheapen commodities, and, by shortening that portion of the working-day, in which the labourer works for himself, to lengthen the other portion that he gives, without an equivalent, to the capitalist. In short, it is a means for producing surplus-value.

In manufacture, the revolution in the mode of production begins with the labour-power, in modern industry it begins with the instruments of labour. Our first inquiry then is, how the instruments of labour are converted from tools into machines, or what is the difference between a machine and the implements of a handicraft? We are only concerned here with striking and general characteristics; for epochs in the history of society are no more separated from each other by hard and fast lines of demarcation, than are geological epochs. . . .

The machine, which is the starting-point of the industrial revolution, supersedes the workman, who handles a single tool, by a mechanism operating with a number of similar tools, and set in motion by a single motive power, whatever the form of that power may be. Here we have the machine, but only as an elementary factor of production by machinery. . . .

A real machinery system, however, does not take the place of these independent machines, until the subject of labour goes through a connected series of detail processes, that are carried out by a chain of machines of various kinds, the one supplementing the other. Here we have again the co-operation by division of labour that characterises Manufacture; only now, it is a combination of detail machines. The special tools of the various detail workmen, such as those of the beaters,

231

combers, spinners, &c., in the woollen manufacture, are now transformed into the tools of specialised machines, each machine constituting a special organ, with a special function, in the system. In those
branches of industry in which the machinery system is first introduced,
Manufacture itself furnishes, in a general way, the natural basis for the
division, and consequent organisation, of the process of production.
Nevertheless an essential difference at once manifests itself. In Manufacture it is the workmen who, with their manual implements, must,
either singly or in groups, carry on each particular detail process. If, on
the one hand, the workman becomes adapted to the process, on the
other, the process was previously made suitable to the workman. This
subjective principle of the division of labour no longer exists in production by machinery. Here, the process as a whole is examined objectively, in itself, that is to say, without regard to the question of its
execution by human hands, it is analysed into its constituent phases; and
the problem, how to execute each detail process, and bind them all into
a whole, is solved by the aid of machines, chemistry, &c. But, of course,
in this case also, theory must be perfected by accumulated experience
on a large scale. Each detail machine supplies raw material to the
machine next in order; and since they are all working at the same time,
the product is always going through the various stages of its fabrication,
and is also constantly in a state of transition, from one phase to another.
Just as in Manufacture, the direct co-operation of the detail labourers
establishes a numerical proportion between the special groups, so in an
organised system of machinery, where one detail machine is constantly
kept employed by another, a fixed relation is established between their
numbers, their size, and their speed. The collective machine, now an
organised system of various kinds of single machines, and of groups of
single machines, becomes more and more perfect, the more the process
as a whole becomes a continuous one, *i.e.,* the less the raw material is
interrupted in its passage from its first phase to its last; in other words,
the more its passage from one phase to another is effected, not by the
hand of man, but by the machinery itself. In Manufacture the isolation
of each detail process is a condition imposed by the nature of division
of labour, but in the fully developed factory the continuity of those
processes is, on the contrary, imperative. . . .

The implements of labour, in the form of machinery, necessitate
the substitution of natural forces for human force, and the conscious
application of science, instead of rule of thumb. In Manufacture, the
organisation of the social labour-process is purely subjective; it is a
combination of detail labourers; in its machinery system, Modern Industry has a productive organism that is purely objective, in which the

labourer becomes a mere appendage to an already existing material condition of production. In simple co-operation, and even in that founded on division of labour, the suppression of the isolated, by the collective, workman still appears to be more or less accidental. Machinery, with a few exceptions to be mentioned later, operates only by means of associated labour, or labour in common. Hence the co-operative character of the labour-process is, in the latter case, a technical necessity dictated by the instrument of labour itself. . . .

The starting-point of Modern Industry is, as we have shown, the revolution in the instruments of labour, and this revolution attains its most highly developed form in the organised system of machinery in a factory. Before we inquire how human material is incorporated with this objective organism, let us consider some general effects of this revolution on the labourer himself.

In so far as machinery dispenses with muscular power, it becomes a means of employing labourers of slight muscular strength, and those whose bodily development is incomplete, but whose limbs are all the more supple. The labour of women and children was, therefore, the first thing sought for by capitalists who used machinery. That mighty substitute for labour and labourers was forthwith changed into a means for increasing the number of wage-labourers by enrolling, under the direct sway of capital, every member of the workman's family, without distinction of age or sex. Compulsory work for the capitalist usurped the place, not only of the children's play, but also of free labour at home within moderate limits for the support of the family.

The value of labour-power was determined, not only by the labour-time necessary to maintain the individual adult labourer, but also by that necessary to maintain his family. Machinery, by throwing every member of that family on to the labour-market, spreads the value of the man's labour-power over his whole family. It thus depreciates his labour-power. To purchase the labour-power of a family of four workers may, perhaps, cost more than it formerly did to purchase the labour-power of the head of the family, but, in return, four days' labour takes the place of one, and their price falls in proportion to the excess of the surplus-labour of four over the surplus-labour of one. In order that the family may live, four people must now, not only labour, but expend surplus-labour for the capitalist. Thus we see, that machinery, while augmenting the human material that forms the principal object of capital's exploiting power, at the same time raises the degree of exploitation.

Machinery also revolutionises out and out the contract between the labourer and the capitalist, which formally fixes their mutual relations.

Taking the exchange of commodities as our basis, our first assumption was that capitalist and labourer met as free persons, as independent owners of commodities; the one possessing money and means of production, the other labour-power. But now the capitalist buys children and young persons under age. Previously, the workman sold his own labour-power, which he disposed of nominally as a free agent. Now he sells wife and child. He has become a slave-dealer. The demand for children's labour often resembles in form the inquiries for negro slaves, such as were formerly to be read among the advertisements in American journals. . . .

The moral degradation caused by the capitalistic exploitation of women and children has been so exhaustively depicted by F. Engels in his "Lage der Arbeitenden Klasse Englands," and other writers, that I need only mention the subject in this place. But the intellectual desolation artificially produced by converting immature human beings into mere machines for the fabrication of surplus-value, a state of mind clearly distinguishable from that natural ignorance which keeps the mind fallow without destroying its capacity for development, its natural fertility, this desolation finally compelled even the English Parliament to make elementary education a compulsory condition to the "productive" employment of children under 14 years, in every industry subject to the Factory Acts. The spirit of capitalist production stands out clearly in the ludicrous wording of the so-called education clauses in the Factory Acts, in the absence of an administrative machinery, an absence that again makes the compulsion illusory, in the opposition of the manufacturers themselves to these education clauses, and in the tricks and dodges they put in practice for evading them. "For this the legislature is alone to blame, by having passed a delusive law, which, while it would seem to provide that the children employed in factories shall be *educated*, contains no enactment by which that professed end can be secured. It provides nothing more than that the children shall on certain days of the week, and for a certain number of hours (three) in each day, be inclosed within the four walls of a place called a school, and that the employer of the child shall receive weekly a certificate to that effect signed by a person designated by the subscriber as a schoolmaster or schoolmistress." Previous to the passing of the amended Factory Act, 1844, it happened, not unfrequently, that the certificates of attendance at school were signed by the schoolmaster or schoolmistress with a cross, as they themselves were unable to write. . . .

If machinery be the most powerful means for increasing the productiveness of labour—*i.e.,* for shortening the working-time required in the production of a commodity, it becomes in the hands of capital the most powerful means, in those industries first invaded by it, for lengthening the working-day beyond all bounds set by human nature. It creates, on the one hand, new conditions by which capital is enabled to give free scope to this its constant tendency, and on the other hand, new motives with which to whet capital's appetite for the labour of others.

In the first place, in the form of machinery, the implements of labour become automatic, things moving and working independent of the workman. They are thenceforth an industrial *perpetuum mobile,* that would go on producing forever, did it not meet with certain natural obstructions in the weak bodies and the strong wills of its human attendants. The automaton, as capital, and because it is capital, is endowed, in the person of the capitalist, with intelligence and will; it is therefore animated by the longing to reduce to a minimum the resistance offered by that repellent yet elastic natural barrier, man. This resistance is moreover lessened by the apparent lightness of machine work, and by the more pliant and docile character of the women and children employed on it.

The productiveness of machinery is, as we saw, inversely proportional to the value transferred by it to the product. The longer the life of the machine, the greater is the mass of the products over which the value transmitted by the machine is spread, and the less is the portion of that value added to each single commodity. The active lifetime of a machine is, however, clearly dependent on the length of the working-day, or on the duration of the daily labour-process multiplied by the number of days for which the process is carried on.

The wear and tear of a machine is not exactly proportional to its working-time. And even if it were so, a machine working 16 hours daily for 7-1/2 years, covers as long a working period as, and transmits to the total product no more value than, the same machine would if it worked only 8 hours daily for 15 years. But in the first case the value of the machine would be reproduced twice as quickly as in the latter, and the capitalist would, by the use of the machine, absorb in 7-1/2 years as much surplus-value as in the second case he would in 15.

The material wear and tear of a machine is of two kinds. The one arises from use, as coins wear away by circulating, the other from non-use, as a sword rusts when left in its scabbard. The latter kind is due to the elements. The former is more or less directly proportional, the latter to a certain extent inversely proportional, to the use of the machine.

But in addition to the material wear and tear, a machine also undergoes, what we may call a moral depreciation. It loses exchange-value, either by machines of the same sort being produced cheaper than it, or by better machines entering into competition with it. In both cases, be the machine ever so young and full of life, its value is no longer determined by the labour actually materialised in it, but by the labour-time requisite to reproduce either it or the better machine. It has, therefore, lost value more or less. The shorter the period taken to reproduce its total value, the less is the danger of moral depreciation; and the longer the working-day, the shorter is that period. When machinery is first introduced into an industry, new methods of reproducing it more cheaply follow blow upon blow, and so do improvements, that not only affect individual parts and details of the machine, but its entire build. It is, therefore, in the early days of the life of machinery that this special incentive to the prolongation of the working-day makes itself felt most acutely. . . .

If, then, the capitalistic employment of machinery, on the one hand, supplies new and powerful motives to an excessive lengthening of the working-day, and radically changes, as well the methods of labour, as also the character of the social working organism, in such a manner as to break down all opposition to this tendency, on the other hand it produces, partly by opening out to the capitalist new strata of the working-class, previously inaccessible to him, partly by setting free the labourers it supplants, a surplus working population, which is compelled to submit to the dictation of capital. Hence that remarkable phenomenon in the history of Modern Industry, that machinery sweeps away every moral and natural restriction on the length of the working-day. Hence, too, the economic paradox, that the most powerful instrument for shortening labour-time, becomes the most unfailing means for placing every moment of the labourer's time and that of his family, at the disposal of the capitalist for the purpose of expanding the value of his capital. "If," dreamed Aristotle, the greatest thinker of antiquity, "if every tool, when summoned, or even of its own accord, could do the work that befits it, just as the creations of Dædalus moved of themselves, or the tripods of Hephæstos went of their own accord to their sacred work, if the weavers' shuttles were to weave of themselves, then there would be no need either of apprentices for the master workers, or of slaves for the lords." And Antipatros, a Greek poet of the time of Cicero, hailed the invention of the water-wheel for grinding corn, an invention that is the elementary form of all machinery, as the giver of freedom to female slaves, and the bringer back of the golden age. Oh! those heathens! They understood, as the learned Bastiat, and before him the still wiser MacCulloch have discovered, nothing of Political Economy and Christianity. They did not, for example, comprehend that machinery is the surest means of lengthening the working-day. They perhaps excused the slavery of one on the ground that it was a means to the full development of another. But to preach slavery of the masses, in order that a few crude and half-educated parvenus, might become "eminent spinners," "extensive sausage-makers," and "influential shoe-black dealers," to do this, they lacked the bump of Christianity.

The immoderate lengthening of the working-day, produced by machinery in the hands of capital, leads to a reaction on the part of society, the very sources of whose life are menaced; and, thence, to a normal working-day whose length is fixed by law. Thenceforth a phenomenon that we have already met with, namely, the intensification of labour, develops into great importance. Our analysis of absolute surplus-value had reference primarily to the extension or duration of the labour, its intensity being assumed as given. We now proceed to consider the substitution of a more intensified labour for labour of more extensive duration, and the degree of the former.

It is self-evident, that in proportion as the use of machinery spreads, and the experience of a special class of workmen habituated to machinery accumulates, the rapidity and intensity of labour increase as a natural consequence. Thus in England, during half a century, lengthening of the working-day went hand in hand with increasing intensity of factory labour. Nevertheless the reader will clearly see, that where we have labour, not carried on by fits and starts, but repeated day after day with unvarying uniformity, a point must inevitably be reached, where extension of the working-day and intensity of the labour mutually exclude one another, in such a way that lengthening of the working-day becomes compatible only with a lower degree of intensity, and a higher degree of intensity, only with a shortening of the working-day. So soon as the gradually surging revolt of the working-class compelled Parliament to shorten compulsorily the hours of labour, and to begin by imposing a normal working-day on factories proper, so soon consequently as an increased production of surplus-value by the prolongation of the working-day was once for all put a stop to, from that moment capital threw itself with all its might into the production of relative surplus-value, by hastening on the further improvement of machinery. At the same time a change took place in the nature of relative surplus-value. Generally speaking, the mode of producing relative surplus-value consists in raising the productive power of the workman, so as to enable him to produce more in a given time with the same expenditure of labour. Labour-time continues to transmit as before the same value to the total product, but this unchanged amount of exchange-value is spread over more use-values; hence the value of each single commodity sinks. Otherwise, however, so soon as the compulsory shortening of the hours of labour takes place. The immense impetus it gives to the development of productive power, and to economy in the means of production, imposes on the workman increased expenditure of labour in a given time, heightened tension of labour-power, and closer filling up of the pores of the working-day, or condensation of labour to a degree that is attainable only within the limits of the shortened working-day. This condensation of a greater mass of labour into a given period thenceforward counts for what it really is, a greater quantity of labour. In addition to a measure of its extension, *i.e.,* duration, labour now acquires a measure of its intensity or of the degree of its condensation or density. The denser hour of the ten hours' working-day contains more labour, *i.e.,* expended labour-power, than the more porous hour of the twelve hours' working-day. The product therefore of one of the former hours has as much or more value than has the product of 1-1/5 of the latter hours. Apart from the increased yield of relative surplus-value through the heightened productiveness of labour, the same mass of value is now produced for the capitalist say by 3-1/3 hours of surplus-labour, and 6-2/3 hours of necessary labour, as was previously produced by four hours of surplus-labour and eight hours of necessary labour. . . .

Demonology and Science

DEMONOLOGY AND MEDICINE

The scientific study of the human body and its diseases has had to contend—and to some extent still has to contend—with a mass of superstition, largely pre-Christian in origin, but supported, until quite modern times, by the whole weight of ecclesiastical authority. Disease was sometimes a divine visitation in punishment of sin, but more often the work of demons. It could be cured by the intervention of saints, either in person or through their holy relics; by prayer and pilgrimages; or (when due to demons) by exorcism and by treatment which the demons (and the patient) found disgusting.

For much of this, support could be found in the gospels; the rest of the theory was developed by the Fathers, or grew naturally out of their doctrines. St. Augustine maintained that "all diseases of Christians are to be ascribed to these demons; chiefly do they torment flesh-baptized Christians, yea, even the guiltless new-born infants." It must be understood that, in the writings of the Fathers, "demons" mean heathen deities, who were supposed to be enraged by the progress of Christianity. The early Christians by no means denied the existence of the Olympian gods, but supposed them servants of Satan—a view which Milton adopted in "Paradise Lost." Gregory Nazianzen maintained that medicine is useless, but the laying on of consecrated hands is often effective; and similar views were expressed by other Fathers.

Belief in the efficacy of relics increased throughout the Middle Ages, and is still not extinct. The possession of valued relics was a source of income to the church and city in which they were, and brought into play the same economic motives which roused the Ephesians against St. Paul. Belief in relics often survives exposure. For example, the bones of St. Rosalia, which are preserved in Palermo, have for many centuries been found effective in curing disease; but when examined by a profane anatomist they turned out to be the bones of a goat. Nevertheless the

239

cures continued. We now know that certain kinds of diseases can be cured by faith, while others cannot; no doubt "miracles" of healing do occur, but in an unscientific atmosphere legends soon magnify the truth, and obliterate the distinction between the hysterical diseases which can be cured in this way, and the others which demand a treatment based upon pathology.

The growth of legend in an atmosphere of excitement is a matter of which there were extraordinary examples during the War, such as the Russians who were supposed to have passed through England to France during the first weeks. The origin of such beliefs, when it can be traced, is valuable as a help to the historian in judging what to believe in apparently unquestionable historical testimony. We may take, as an unusually complete instance, the supposed miracles of St. Francis Xavier, the friend of Loyola, and the first and most eminent of Jesuit missionaries in the East.[1]

St. Francis spent many years in India, China and Japan, and at last met his death in 1552. He and his companions wrote many long letters, still extant, giving accounts of their labours, but in none of them, so long as he was still alive, is there any claim to miraculous powers. Joseph Acosta—the same Jesuit who was so puzzled by the animals of Peru—expressly asserts that these missionaries were not aided by miracles in their efforts to convert the heathen. But soon after Xavier's death accounts of miracles began to appear. He was said to have had the gift of tongues, although his letters are full of the difficulties of the Japanese language and the paucity of good interpreters. It was said that, on one occasion when his companions were thirsty at sea, he transformed salt water into fresh. When he lost a crucifix in the sea, a crab restored it to him. According to a later version, he threw the crucifix overboard to still a tempest. In 1622, when he was canonized, it became necessary to prove, to the satisfaction of the Vatican authorities, that he had performed miracles, for without such proof no one can become a saint. The Pope officially guaranteed the gift of tongues, and was specially impressed by the fact that Xavier made lamps burn with holy water instead of oil. This was the same Pope—Urban VIII—who found what Galileo said incredible. The legend continued to grow, until, in the biography published by Father Bouhours in 1682, we learn that the saint, during his lifetime, raised fourteen persons from the dead. Catholic writers still credit him with miraculous powers; thus Father Coleridge, of the Society of Jesus, reaffirmed the gift of tongues in a biography published in 1872.

1. This subject has been admirably treated in White's *Warfare of Science with Theology,* to which I am much indebted.

From this example it is evident how little reliance can be placed upon accounts of marvels in periods when the documents are less numerous than in the case of St. Francis Xavier.

Miraculous cures were believed in by Protestants as well as Catholics. In England, the king's touch cured what was known as "the king's evil," and Charles II, that saintly monarch, touched about 100,000 persons. His Majesty's surgeon published an account of sixty cures thus effected, and another surgeon himself saw (so he says) hundreds of cures due to the king's touch, many of them in cases which had defied the ablest surgeons. There was a special service in the Prayer Book provided for occasions when the king exercised his miraculous powers of healing. These powers duly descended to James II, William III, and Queen Anne, but apparently they were unable to survive the Hanoverian succession.

Plagues and pestilences, which were common and terrible in the Middle Ages, were attributed sometimes to demons, sometimes to the wrath of God. A method of averting God's anger, which was much recommended by the clergy, was the gift of lands to the Church. In 1680, when the plague raged at Rome, it was ascertained that this was due to the anger of St. Sebastian, who had been unduly neglected. A monument was raised to him, and the plague ceased. In 1522, at the height of the renaissance, the Romans at first made a wrong diagnosis of the plague then afflicting the city. They thought it was due to the anger of the demons, i.e. of the ancient gods, and therefore sacrificed an ox to Jupiter in the Colosseum. This proving of no avail, they instituted processions to propitiate the Virgin and the saints, which, as they ought to have known, proved far more efficacious.

The Black Death, in 1348, caused outbreaks of superstition of various sorts in various places. One of the favourite methods of appeasing God's anger was the destruction of Jews. In Bavaria, twelve thousand are reckoned to have been killed; in Erfurt, three thousand; in Strasburg, two thousand were burnt; and so on. The Pope alone protested against these mad pogroms. One of the most singular effects of the Black Death was in Siena. It had been decided to enlarge the cathedral very greatly, and a considerable amount of the work had already been done. But the inhabitants of Siena, oblivious of the fate of other places, supposed, when the plague came, that it was a special visitation to the sinful Sienese, to punish them for their pride in wishing to have such a magnificent cathedral. They stopped the work, and the unfinished structure remains to this day as a monument of their repentance.

Not only were superstitious methods of combating disease universally believed to be effective, but the scientific study of medicine was

severely discouraged. The chief practitioners were Jews, who had
derived their knowledge from the Mohammedans; they were suspected
of magic, a suspicion in which they perhaps acquiesced, since it increased their fees. Anatomy was considered wicked, both because it
might interfere with the resurrection of the body, and because the
Church abhorred the shedding of blood. Dissection was virtually forbidden, in consequence of a misunderstood Bull of Boniface VIII. Pope
Pius V, in the latter half of the sixteenth century, renewed earlier
decrees by ordering physicians first to call in the priest, on the ground
that "bodily infirmity frequently arises from sin," and to refuse further
treatment if the patient did not confess to the priest within three days.
Perhaps he was wise, in view of the backward condition of medicine in
those days.

The treatment of mental disorders, as may be imagined, was peculiarly superstitious, and remained so longer than any other branch of
medicine. Insanity was regarded as due to diabolical possession—a view
for which authority could be found in the New Testament. Sometimes
a cure could be effected by exorcism, or by touching a relic, or by a holy
man's command to the demon to come forth. Sometimes elements
which savour of magic were mixed with religion. For example: "When
a devil possesses a man, or controls him from within with disease, a
spew-drink of lupin, bishopswort, henbane, garlic. Pound these
together, add ale and holy water."

In such methods there was no great harm, but presently it came to
be thought that the best way to drive out the evil spirit was to torture
it, or to humiliate its pride, since pride was the source of Satan's fall.
Foul odours were used, and disgusting substances. The formula of exorcism became longer and longer, and more and more filled with obscenities. By such means, the Jesuits of Vienna, in 1583, cast out 12,652
devils. When, however, such mild methods failed, the patient was
scourged; if the demon still refused to leave him, he was tortured. For
centuries, innumerable helpless lunatics were thus given over to the
cruelty of barbarous gaolers. Even when the superstitious beliefs by
which cruelty had originally been inspired were no longer accepted,
the tradition survived that the insane should be treated harshly. Prevention of sleep was a recognized method; castigation was another.
George III, when mad, was beaten, though no one supposed him more
possessed of a devil than when sane.

Closely connected with the mediaeval treatment of insanity was
the belief in witchcraft. The Bible says: "Thou shalt not suffer a witch
to live" (Exod. xxii. 18). Because of this text and others, Wesley maintained that "the giving up of witchcraft is in effect the giving up of the

Bible." I think he was right.[2] While men still believed in the Bible, they did their best to carry out its commands as regards witches. Modern liberal Christians, who still hold that the Bible is ethically valuable, are apt to forget such texts and the millions of innocent victims who have died in agony because, at one time, men genuinely accepted the Bible as a guide to conduct.

The subject of witchcraft and the larger subject of magic and sorcery are at once interesting and obscure. Anthropologists find a distinction between magic and religion even in very primitive races; but their criteria, though no doubt suited to their own science, are not quite those required when we are interested in the persecution of necromancy. Thus Rivers, in his very interesting book about Melanesia, *Medicine, Magic and Religion* (1924), says: "When I speak of magic, I shall mean a group of processes in which man uses rites which depend for their efficacy on his own power, or on powers believed to be inherent in, or the attributes of, certain objects and processes which are used in these rites. Religion, on the other hand, will comprise a group of processes, the efficacy of which depends on the will of some higher power, some power whose intervention is sought by rites of supplication and propitiation." This definition is suitable when we are dealing with people who, on the one hand, believe in the strange power of certain inanimate objects such as sacred stones, and, on the other hand, regard all non-human spirits as superior to man. Neither of these is quite true of mediaeval Christians or Mohammedans. Strange powers, it is true, were attributed to the philosopher's stone and the elixir of life, but these could almost be classed as scientific: they were sought by experiment, and their expected properties were scarcely more wonderful than those which have been found in radium. And magic, as understood in the Middle Ages, constantly invoked the aid of spirits, but of evil spirits. Among the Melanesians, the distinction of good and evil spirits does not seem to exist, but in Christian doctrine it was essential. Satan, as well as the Deity, could work miracles; but Satan worked them to help wicked men, while the Deity worked them to help good men. This distinction, as appears from the Gospels, was already familiar to the Jews of the time of Christ, since they accused Him of casting out devils by the help of Beelzebub. Sorcery and witchcraft, in the Middle Ages, were primarily, though not exclusively, ecclesiastical offences, and their peculiar sinfulness lay in the fact that they involved an alliance with the infernal powers. Oddly enough, the Devil could sometimes be induced

2. Unless we accept this view, waged against belief in witchcraft when it was decaying, that the word in Exodus translated "witch" really means "poisoner." And even this does not dispose of the witch of Endor.

to do things which would have been virtuous if done by anyone else. In Sicily, there are (or recently were) puppet plays which have come down in unbroken tradition from mediaeval times. In 1908 I saw one of these at Palermo, dealing with the wars between Charlemagne and the Moors. In this play the Pope, before a great battle, secured the Devil's help, and during the battle the Devil was seen in the air giving victory to the Christians. In spite of this excellent result, the Pope's action was wicked, and Charlemagne was duly shocked by it—though he took advantage of the victory.

It is held nowadays by some of the most serious students of witch-craft that it was a survival, in Christian Europe, of pagan cults and the worship of pagan deities who had become identified with the evil spirits of Christian demonology. While there is much evidence that elements of paganism became amalgamated with magic rites, there are grave difficulties in the way of attributing witchcraft mainly to this source. Magic was a crime punishable in pre-Christian antiquity; there was a law against it in the Twelve Tables in Rome. So far back as the year 1100 B.C., certain officers, and certain women of the harem of Rameses III, were tried for making a waxen image of that king and pronouncing magic spells over it with a view to causing his death. Apuleius, the writer, was tried for magic in A.D. 150, because he had married a rich widow, to the great annoyance of her son. Like Othello, however, he succeeded in persuading the Court that he had used only his natural charms.

Sorcery was not, originally, considered a peculiarly feminine crime. The concentration on women began in the fifteenth century, and from then until late in the seventeenth century the persecution of witches was widespread and severe. Innocent VIII, in 1484, issued a Bull against witchcraft, and appointed two inquisitors to punish it. These men, in 1489, published a book, long accepted as authoritative, called *Malleus Maleficarum,* "the hammer of female malefactors." They maintained that witchcraft is more natural to women than to men, because of the inherent wickedness of their hearts. The commonest accusation against witches, at this time, was that of causing bad weather. A list of questions to women suspected of witchcraft was drawn up, and suspects were tortured on the rack until they gave the desired answers. It is estimated that in Germany alone, between 1450 and 1550, a hundred thousand witches were put to death, mostly by burning.

Some few bold rationalists ventured, even while the persecution was at its height, to doubt whether tempests, hail-storms, thunder and lightning were really caused by the machinations of women. Such men were shown no mercy. Thus towards the end of the sixteenth century

Flade, Rector of the University of Trèves, and Chief Judge of the Electoral Court, after condemning countless witches, began to think that perhaps their confessions were due to the desire to escape from the tortures of the rack, with the result that he showed unwillingness to convict. He was accused of having sold himself to Satan, and was subjected to the same tortures as he had inflicted upon others. Like them, he confessed his guilt, and in 1589 he was strangled and then burnt.

Protestants were quite as much addicted as Catholics to the persecution of witches. In this matter James I was peculiarly zealous. He wrote a book on Demonology, and in the first year of his reign in England, when Coke was Attorney-General and Bacon was in the House of Commons, he caused the law to be made more stringent by a statute which remained in force until 1736. There were many prosecutions, in one of which the medical witness was Sir Thomas Browne, who declared in *Religio Medici*: "I have ever believed, and do now know, that there are witches; they that doubt them do not only deny them, but spirits, and are obliquely and upon consequence a sort, not of infidels, but of atheists." In fact, as Lecky points out, "a disbelief in ghosts and witches was one of the most prominent characteristics of scepticism in the seventeenth century. At first it was nearly confined to men who were avowedly free thinkers."

In Scotland, where the persecution of witches was much more severe than in England, James I had great success in discovering the causes of the tempests which had beset him on his voyage from Denmark. A certain Dr. Fian confessed, under torture, that the storms were produced by some hundreds of witches who had put to sea in a sieve from Leith. As Burton remarks in his *History of Scotland* (Vol. VII, p. 116): "The value of the phenomenon was increased by a co-operative body of witches on the Scandinavian side, the two affording a crucial experiment on the laws of demonology." Dr. Fian immediately withdrew his confession, whereupon the torture was greatly increased in severity. The bones of his legs were broken in several pieces, but he remained obdurate. Thereupon James I, who watched the proceedings, invented a new torture: the victim's finger-nails were pulled off, and needles thrust in up to the heads. But, as the contemporary record says: "So deeply had the devil entered into his heart, that hee utterly denied all that which he before avouched." So he was burnt.[3]

The law against witchcraft was repealed in Scotland by the same Act of 1736 which repealed it in England. But in Scotland the belief was still vigorous. A professional text-book of law, published in 1730, says:

3. See Lecky, *History of Rationalism in Europe*, Vol. I, p. 114.

"Nothing seems plainer to me than that there may be and have been witches, and that perhaps such are now actually existing; which I intend, God willing, to clear in a larger work concerning the criminal law." The leaders of an important secession from the Established Church of Scotland published, in 1736, a statement on the depravity of the age. It complained that not only were dancing and the theatre encouraged, but "of late the penal statutes against witches have been repealed, contrary to the express letter of the law of God—'Thou shalt not suffer a witch to live.' "[4] After this date, however, the belief in witchcraft rapidly decayed among educated people in Scotland.

There is a remarkable simultaneity in the cessation of punishments for witchcraft in Western countries. In England, the belief was more firmly held among Puritans than among Anglicans; there were as many executions for witchcraft during the Commonwealth as during all the reigns of the Tudors and Stuarts. With the Restoration, scepticism on the subject began to be fashionable; the last execution certainly known to have taken place was in 1682, though it is said that there were others as late as 1712. In this year, there was a trial in Hertfordshire, instigated by the local clergy. The judge disbelieved in the possibility of the crime, and directed the jury in that sense; they nevertheless convicted the accused, but the conviction was quashed, which led to vehement clerical protests. In Scotland, where the torture and execution of witches had been much commoner than in England, it became rare after the end of the seventeenth century; the last burning of a witch occurred in 1722 or 1730. In France, the last burning was in 1718. In New England, a fierce outbreak of witch-hunting occurred at the end of the seventeenth century, but was never repeated. Everywhere the popular belief continued, and still survives in some remote rural areas. The last case of the kind in England was in 1863 in Essex, when an old man was lynched by his neighbours as a wizard. Legal recognition of witchcraft as a possible crime survived longest in Spain and Ireland. In Ireland the law against witchcraft was not repealed until 1821. In Spain a sorcerer was burnt in 1780.

Lecky, whose *History of Rationalism* deals at length with the subject of witchcraft, points out the curious fact that belief in the possibility of black magic was not defeated by arguments on this subject, but by the general spread of belief in the reign of law. He even goes so far as to say that, in the specific discussion of witchcraft, the weight of argument was on the side of its upholders. This is perhaps not surprising when we remember that the Bible could be quoted by the upholders, while the other side could hardly venture to say that the Bible was not

4. Burton, *op. cit.,* Vol. VIII, p. 410.

always to be believed. Moreover, the best scientific minds did not occupy themselves with popular superstitions, partly because they had more positive work to do, and partly because they feared to rouse antagonism. The event showed that they were right. Newton's work caused men to believe that God had originally created nature and decreed nature's laws so as to produce the results that He intended without fresh intervention, except on great occasions, such as the revelation of the Christian religion. Protestants held that miracles occurred during the first century or two of the Christian era, and then ceased. If God no longer intervened miraculously, it was hardly likely that He would allow Satan to do so. There were hopes of scientific meteorology, which would leave no room for old women on broomsticks as the causes of storms. For some time it continued to be thought impious to apply the concept of natural law to lightning and thunder, since these were specially acts of God. This view survived in the opposition to lightning conductors. Thus when, in 1755, Massachusetts was shaken by earthquakes, the Rev. Dr. Price, in a published sermon, attributed them to the "iron points invented by the sagacious Mr. Franklin," saying: "In Boston are more erected than elsewhere in New England, and Boston seems to be more dreadfully shaken. Oh! there is no getting out of the mighty hand of God." In spite of this warning, the Bostonians continued to erect the "iron points," and earthquakes, nevertheless, did not increase in frequency. From the time of Newton onward, such a point of view as that of the Rev. Dr. Price was increasingly felt to savour of superstition. And as the belief in miraculous interference with the course of nature died out, the belief in the possibility of witchcraft necessarily also disappeared. The evidence for witchcraft has never been refuted; it has simply ceased to seem worth examining.

Throughout the Middle Ages, as we have seen, the prevention and cure of disease were attempted by methods which were either superstitious or wholly arbitrary. Nothing more scientific was possible without anatomy and physiology, and these, in turn, were not possible without dissection, which the Church opposed. Vesalius, who first made anatomy scientific, succeeded in escaping official censure for a while because he was physician to the Emperor Charles V, who feared that his health might suffer if he were deprived of his favourite practitioner. During Charles V's reign, a conference of theologians, being consulted about Vesalius, gave it as their opinion that dissection was not sacrilege. But Philip II, who was less of a valetudinarian, saw no reason to protect a suspect; Vesalius could obtain no more bodies for dissection. The Church believed that there is in the human body one indestructible bone, which is the nucleus of the resurrection body; Vesalius, on being questioned, confessed that he had never found such a bone. This was bad, but perhaps not bad enough. The medical disciples of Galen—who had become as great an obstacle to progress in medicine as Aristotle in physics—pursued Vesalius with relentless hostility, and at length found an opportunity to ruin him. While, with the consent of the relatives, he was examining the corpse of a Spanish grandee, the heart—or so his enemies said—was observed to show some signs of life under the knife. He was accused of murder, and denounced to the Inquisition. By the influence of the king, he was allowed to do penance by a pilgrimage to the Holy Land; but on his way home he was shipwrecked, and although he reached land he died of exhaustion. But his influence survived; one of his pupils, Fallopius, did distinguished work, and the medical profession gradually became convinced that the way to find out what there is in the human body is to look and see.

Physiology developed later than anatomy, and may be taken as becoming scientific with Harvey (1578–1657), the discoverer of the circulation of the blood. Like Vesalius, he was a Court physician—first to James I and then to Charles I—but unlike Vesalius he suffered no persecution, even when Charles I had fallen. The intervening century had made opinion on medical subjects much more liberal, especially in Protestant countries. In Spanish universities, the circulation of the blood was still denied at the end of the eighteenth century, and dissection was still no part of medical education.

The old theological prejudices, though much weakened, reappeared when awakened by any startling novelty. Inoculation against smallpox aroused a storm of protest from divines. The Sorbonne pronounced against it on theological grounds. One Anglican clergyman published a sermon in which he said that Job's boils were doubtless due to inoculation by the Devil, and many Scottish ministers joined in a manifesto saying that it was "endeavouring to baffle a Divine judgment." However, the effect in diminishing the death-rate from smallpox was so notable that theological terrors failed to outweigh fear of the disease. Moreover, in 1768 the Empress Catherine had herself and her son inoculated, and though perhaps not a model from an ethical point of view, she was considered a safe guide in matters of worldly prudence.

The controversy had begun to die down when the discovery of vaccination revived it. Clergymen (and medical men) regarded vaccination as "bidding defiance to Heaven itself, even to the will of God"; in Cambridge, a university sermon was preached against it. So late as 1885, when there was a severe outbreak of smallpox in Montreal, the Catholic part of the population resisted vaccination, with the support of their clergy. One priest stated: "If we are afflicted with smallpox, it is because we had a carnival last winter, feasting the flesh, which has offended the Lord." "The Oblate Fathers, whose church was situated in the very heart of the infected district, continued to denounce vaccination; the faithful were exhorted to rely on devotional exercises of various sorts; under the sanction of the hierarchy a great procession was ordered with a solemn appeal to the Virgin, and the use of the rosary was carefully specified."[5]

Another occasion for theological intervention to prevent the mitigation of human suffering was the discovery of anaesthetics. Simpson, in 1847, recommended their use in childbirth, and was immediately reminded by the clergy that God said to Eve: "In sorrow shalt thou bring forth children" (Gen. iii. 16). And how could she sorrow if she was under the influence of chloroform? Simpson succeeded in proving that there was no harm in giving anaesthetics to *men,* because God put Adam into a deep sleep when He extracted his rib. But male ecclesiastics remained unconvinced as regards the sufferings of *women,* at any rate in childbirth. It may be noted that in Japan, where the authority of Genesis is not recognized, women are still expected to endure the pains of labour without any artificial alleviation. It is difficult to resist the conclusion that, to many men, there is something enjoyable in the sufferings of women, and therefore a propensity to cling to any theological or ethical code which makes it their duty to suffer patiently, even when there is no valid reason for not avoiding pain. The harm that theology has done is not to *create* cruel impulses, but to give them the sanction of what professes to be a lofty ethic, and to confer an apparently sacred character upon practices which have come down from more ignorant and barbarous ages.

The intervention of theology in medical questions is not yet at an end; opinions on such subjects as birth control, and the legal permission of abortion in certain cases, are still influenced by Bible texts and ecclesiastical decrees. See, for instance, the encyclical on marriage issued a few years ago by Pope Pius XI. Those who practise birth control, he says, "sin against nature and commit a deed which is shameful and intrinsically vicious. Small wonder, therefore, if Holy Writ bears witness that the divine Majesty regards with greatest detestation this horrible crime and at times has punished it with death." He goes on to quote St. Augustine on Genesis xxxviii. 8-10. No further reasons for the condemnation of birth control are thought necessary. As for economic arguments, "we are deeply touched by the sufferings of those parents who, in extreme want, experience great difficulty in rearing their chil-

5. White, *op. cit.,* Vol. II, p. 60.

dren," but "no difficulty can arise that justifies the putting aside of the law of God which forbids all acts intrinsically evil." As regards the interruption of pregnancy for "medical or therapeutic" reasons, i.e., when it is considered necessary in order to save the woman's life, he considers that this affords no justification. "What could ever be a sufficient reason for excusing in any way the direct murder of the innocent? Whether inflicted upon the mother or upon the child, it is against the precept of God and the law of nature: 'Thou shalt not kill.' " He goes on at once to explain that this text does not condemn war or capital punishment, and concludes: "Upright and skilful doctors strive most praiseworthily to guard and preserve the lives of both mother and child; on the contrary, those show themselves most unworthy of the noble medical profession who encompass the death of one or the other, through a pretence of practising medicine or through motives of misguided pity." Thus not only is the doctrine of the Catholic Church derived from a text, but the text is considered applicable to a human embryo at even the earliest stages of development, and the reason for this latter opinion is obviously derived from belief that the embryo possesses what theology calls a "soul."[6] The conclusions drawn from such premises may be right or wrong, but in either case the argument is not one which science can accept. The death of the mother, foreseen by the doctor in the cases which the Pope is discussing, is not murder, because the doctor can never be *certain* that it will occur; she might be saved by a miracle.

But although, as we have just seen, theology still tries to interfere in medicine where moral issues are supposed to be specially involved, yet over most of the field the battle for the scientific independence of medicine has been won. No one now thinks it impious to avoid pestilences and epidemics by sanitation and hygiene; and though some still maintain that diseases are sent by God, they do not argue that it is therefore impious to try to avoid them. The consequent improvement in health and increase of longevity is one of the most remarkable and admirable characteristics of our age. Even if science had done nothing else for human happiness, it would deserve our gratitude on this account. Those who believe in the utility of theological creeds would have difficulty in pointing to any comparable advantage that they have conferred upon the human race.

6. It was formerly held by theologians that the male embryo acquired a soul at the fortieth day, and the female at the eightieth. Now the best opinion is that it is the fortieth day for both sexes. See Needham, *History of Embryology,* p. 58.

The Allocation of Exotic Medical Lifesaving Therapy

THE PROBLEM

Technological progress has in recent years transformed the limits of the possible in medical therapy. However, the elevated state of sophistication of modern medical technology has brought the economists' classic problem of scarcity in its wake as an unfortunate side product. The enormously sophisticated and complex equipment and the highly trained teams of experts requisite for its utilization are scarce resources in relation to potential demand. The administrators of the great medical institutions that preside over these scarce resources thus come to be faced increasingly with the awesome choice: *Whose life to save?*

A (somewhat hypothetical) paradigm example of this problem may be sketched within the following set of definitive assumptions: We suppose that persons in some particular medically morbid condition are "mortally afflicted": It is virtually certain that they will die within a short time period (say ninety days). We assume that some very complex course of treatment (e.g., a heart transplant) represents a substantial probability of life prolongation for persons in this mortally afflicted condition. We assume that the facilities available in terms of human resources, mechanical instrumentalities, and requisite materials (e.g., hearts in the case of a heart transplant) make it possible to give a certain treatment—this "exotic (medical) lifesaving therapy," or ELT for short —to a certain, relatively small number of people. And finally we assume that a substantially greater pool of people in the mortally afflicted condition is at hand. The problem then may be formulated as follows: How is one to select within the pool of afflicted patients the ones to be given the ELT treatment in question; how to select those "whose lives are to be saved"? Faced with many candidates for an ELT process that can be made available to only a few, doctors and medical administrators con-

251

front the decision of who is to be given a chance at survival and who is, in effect, to be condemned to die.

As has already been implied, the "heroic" variety of spare-part surgery can pretty well be assimilated to this paradigm. One can foresee the time when heart transplantation, for example, will have become pretty much a routine medical procedure, albeit on a very limited basis, since a cardiac surgeon with the technical competence to transplant hearts can operate at best a rather small number of times each week and the elaborate facilities for such operations will most probably exist on a modest scale. Moreover, in "spare-part" surgery there is always the problem of availability of the "spare parts" themselves. A report in one British newspaper gives the following picture: "Of the 150,000 who die of heart disease each year [in the U.K.], Mr. Donald Longmore, research surgeon at the National Heart Hospital [in London] estimates that 22,-000 might be eligible for heart surgery. Another 30,000 would need heart and lung transplants. But there are probably only between 7,000 and 14,000 potential donors a year."[1] Envisaging this situation in which at the very most something like one in four heart-malfunction victims can be saved, we clearly confront a problem in ELT allocation.

A perhaps even more drastic case in point is afforded by long-term haemodialysis, an ongoing process by which a complex device—an "artificial kidney machine"—is used periodically in cases of chronic renal failure to substitute for a non-functional kidney in "cleaning" potential poisons from the blood. Only a few major institutions have chronic haemodialysis units, whose complex operation is an extremely expensive proposition. For the present and the foreseeable future the situation is that "the number of places available for chronic haemodialysis is hopelessly inadequate."[2]

The traditional medical ethos has insulated the physician against facing the very existence of this problem. When swearing the Hippocratic Oath, he commits himself to work for the benefit of the sick in "whatsoever house I enter."[3] In taking this stance, the physician substantially renounces the explicit choice of saving certain lives rather than others. Of course, doctors have always in fact had to face such choices on the battlefield or in times of disaster, but there the issue had to be resolved hurriedly, under pressure, and in circumstances in which the very nature of the case effectively precluded calm deliberation by the decision maker as well as criticism by others. In sharp contrast, however, cases of the type we have postulated in the present discussion arise predictably, and represent choices to be made deliberately and "in cold blood."

It is, to begin with, appropriate to remark that this problem is not fundamentally a medical problem. For when there are sufficiently many afflicted candidates for ELT then—so we may assume—there will also be more than enough for whom the purely medical grounds for ELT allocation are decisively strong in any individual case, and just about equally strong throughout the group. But in this circumstance a selection of some afflicted patients over and against others cannot *ex hypothesi* be made on the basis of purely medical considerations.

The selection problem, as we have said, is in substantial measure not a medical one. It is a problem *for* medical men, which must somehow be solved by them, but that does not make it a medical issue—any more than the problem of hospital building is a medical issue. As a problem it belongs to the category of philosophical problems—specifically a problem of moral philosophy or ethics. Structurally, it bears a substantial kinship with those issues in this field that revolve about the notorious whom-to-save-on-the-lifeboat and whom-to-throw-to-the-wolves-pursuing-the-sled questions. But whereas questions of this just-indicated sort are artificial, hypothetical, and far-fetched, the ELT issue poses a *genuine* policy question for the responsible administrators in medical institutions, indeed a question that threatens to become commonplace in the foreseeable future.

Now what the medical administrator needs to have, and what the philosopher is presumably *ex officio* in a position to help in providing, is a body of *rational guidelines* for making choices in these literally life-or-death situations. This is an issue in which many interested parties have a substantial stake, including the responsible decision maker who wants to satisfy his conscience that he is acting in a reasonable way. Moreover, the family and associates of the man who is turned away—to say nothing of the man himself—have the right to an acceptable explanation. And indeed even the general public wants to know that what is being done is fitting and proper. All of these interested parties are entitled to insist that a reasonable code of operating principles provides a defensible rationale for making the life-and-death choices involved in ELT.

THE TWO TYPES OF CRITERIA

Two distinguishable types of criteria are bound up in the issue of making ELT choices. We shall call these *Criteria of Inclusion* and *Criteria of Comparison,* respectively. The distinction at issue here requires some explanation. We can think of the selection as being made by a two-stage process: (1) the selection from among all possible candidates (by a suitable screening process) of a group to be taken under serious

consideration as candidates for therapy, and then (2) the actual singling
out, within this group, of the particular individuals to whom therapy is
to be given. Thus the first process narrows down the range of comparative choice by eliminating *en bloc* whole categories of potential candidates. The second process calls for a more refined, case-by-case
comparison of those candidates that remain. By means of the first set
of criteria one forms a selection group; by means of the second set, an
actual selection is made within this group.

Thus what we shall call a "selection system" for the choice of
patients to receive therapy of the ELT type will consist of criteria of
these two kinds. Such a system will be acceptable only when the reasonableness of its component criteria can be established.

ESSENTIAL FEATURES OF AN ACCEPTABLE ELT SELECTION SYSTEM

To qualify as reasonable, an ELT selection must meet two important "regulative" requirements: it must be *simple* enough to be readily
intelligible, and it must be *plausible,* that is, patently reasonable in a
way that can be apprehended easily and without involving ramified
subtleties. Those medical administrators responsible for ELT choices
must follow a modus operandi that virtually all the people involved can
readily understand to be acceptable (at a reasonable level of generality,
at any rate). Appearances are critically important here. It is not enough
that the choice be made in a *justifiable* way; it must be possible for
people—*plain* people—to "see" (i.e., understand without elaborate
teaching or indoctrination) that *it is justified,* insofar as any mode of
procedure can be justified in cases of this sort.

One "constitutive" requirement is obviously an essential feature of
a reasonable selection system: all of its component criteria—those of
inclusion and those of comparison alike—must be reasonable in the
sense of being *rationally defensible.* The ramifications of this requirement call for detailed consideration. But one of its aspects should be
noted without further ado: it must be *fair*—it must treat relevantly like
cases alike, leaving no room for "influence" or favoritism, etc.

THE BASIC SCREENING STAGE: CRITERIA OF INCLUSION (AND EXCLUSION)

Three sorts of considerations are prominent among the plausible
criteria of inclusion/exclusion at the basic screening stage: the constituency factor, the progress-of-science factor, and the prospect-of-success
factor.

The Constituency Factor

It is a "fact of life" that ELT can be available only in the institutional setting of a hospital or medical institute or the like. Such institutions generally have normal clientele boundaries. A veterans' hospital will not concern itself primarily with treating nonveterans, a children's hospital cannot be expected to accommodate the "senior citizen," an army hospital can regard college professors as outside its sphere. Sometimes the boundaries are geographic—a state hospital may admit only residents of a certain state. (There are, of course, indefensible constituency principles—say race or religion, party membership, or ability to pay; and there are cases of borderline legitimacy, e.g., sex.[4]) A medical institution is justified in considering for ELT only persons within its own constituency, provided this constituency is constituted upon a defensible basis. Thus the haemodialysis selection committee in Seattle "agreed to consider only those applications who were residents of the state of Washington. . . . They justified this stand on the grounds that since the basic research . . . had been done at . . . a state-supported institution—the people whose taxes had paid for the research should be its first beneficiaries."[5]

While thus insisting that constituency considerations represent a valid and legitimate factor in ELT selection, I do feel there is much to be said for minimizing their role in life-or-death cases. Indeed a refusal to recognize them at all is a significant part of medical tradition, going back to the very oath of Hippocrates. They represent a departure from the ideal arising with the institutionalization of medicine, moving it away from its original status as an art practiced by an individual practitioner.

The Progress-of-Science Factor

The needs of medical research can provide a second valid principle of inclusion. The research interests of the medical staff in relation to the specific nature of the cases at issue is a significant consideration. It may be important for the progress of medical science—and thus of potential benefit to many persons in the future—to determine how effective the ELT at issue is with diabetics or persons over sixty or with a negative RH factor. Considerations of this sort represent another type of legitimate factor in ELT selection.

A very definitely *borderline* case under this head would revolve around the question of a patient's willingness to pay, not in monetary terms, but in offering himself as an experimental subject, say by contracting to return at designated times for a series of tests substantially unrelated to his own health, but yielding data of importance to medical knowledge in general.

The Prospect-of-Success Factor

It may be that while the ELT at issue is not without *some* effectiveness in general, it has been established to be highly effective only with patients in certain specific categories (e.g., females under forty of a specific blood type). This difference in effectiveness—in the absolute or in the probability of success—is (we assume) so marked as to constitute virtually a difference in kind rather than in degree. In this case, it would be perfectly legitimate to adopt the general rule of making the ELT at issue available only or primarily to persons in this substantial-promise-of-success category. (It is on grounds of this sort that young children and persons over fifty are generally ruled out as candidates for haemodialysis.)

* * *

We have maintained that the three factors of constituency, progress of science, and prospect of success represent legitimate criteria of inclusion for ELT selection. But it remains to examine the considerations which legitimate them. The legitimating factors are in the final analysis practical or pragmatic in nature. From the practical angle it is advantageous—indeed to some extent necessary—that the arrangements governing medical institutions should embody certain constituency principles. It makes good pragmatic and utilitarian sense that progress-of-science considerations should be operative here. And, finally, the practical aspect is reinforced by a whole host of other considerations—including moral ones—in supporting the prospect-of-success criterion. The workings of each of these factors are of course conditioned by the ever-present element of limited availability. They are operative only in this context, that is, prospect of success is a legitimate consideration at all only because we are dealing with a situation of scarcity.

THE FINAL SELECTION STAGE: CRITERIA OF SELECTION

Five sorts of elements must, as we see it, figure primarily among the plausible criteria of selection that are to be brought to bear in further screening the group constituted after application of the criteria of inclusion: the relative-likelihood-of-success factor, the life-expectancy factor, the family role factor, the potential-contributions factor, and the services-rendered factor. The first two represent the *biomedical* aspect, the second three the *social* aspect.

The Relative-Likelihood-of-Success Factor

It is clear that the relative likelihood of success is a legitimate and appropriate factor in making a selection within the group of qualified patients that are to receive ELT. This is obviously one of the considerations that must count very significantly in a reasonable selection procedure.

The present criterion is of course closely related to item C of the preceding section. There we were concerned with prospect-of-success considerations categorically and *en bloc*. Here at present they come into play in a particularized case-by-case comparison among individuals. If the therapy at issue is not a once-and-for-all proposition and requires ongoing treatment, cognate considerations must be brought in. Thus, for example, in the case of a chronic ELT procedure such as haemodialysis it would clearly make sense to give priority to patients with a potentially reversible condition (who would thus need treatment for only a fraction of their remaining lives).

The Life-Expectancy Factor

Even if the ELT is "successful" in the patient's case he may, considering his age and/or other aspects of his general medical condition, look forward to only a very short probable future life. This is obviously another factor that must be taken into account.

The Family Role Factor

A person's life is a thing of importance not only to himself but to others—friends, associates, neighbors, colleagues, etc. But his (or her) relationship to his immediate family is a thing of unique intimacy and significance. The nature of his relationship to his wife, children, and parents, and the issue of their financial and psychological dependence upon him, are obviously matters that deserve to be given weight in the ELT selection process. Other things being anything like equal, the mother of minor children must take priority over the middle-aged bachelor.

The Potential Future-Contributions Factor (Prospective Service)

In "choosing to save" one life rather than another, "the society," through the mediation of the particular medical institution in question —which should certainly look upon itself as a trustee for the social interest—is clearly warranted in considering the likely pattern of future *services to be rendered* by the patient (adequate recovery assumed), considering his age, talent, training, and past record of performance. In its allocations of ELT, society "invests" a scarce resource in one person as against another and is thus entitled to look to the probable prospective "return" on its investment.

It may well be that a thoroughly egalitarian society is reluctant to put someone's social contribution into the scale in situations of the sort at issue. One popular article states that "the most difficult standard would be the candidate's value to society," and goes on to quote someone who said: "You can't just pick a brilliant painter over a laborer. The average citizen would be quickly eliminated."[6] But what if it were not a brilliant painter but a brilliant surgeon or medical researcher that was at issue? One wonders if the author of the *obiter dictum* that one "can't just pick" would still feel equally sure of his ground. In any case, the fact that the standard is difficult to apply is certainly no reason for not attempting to apply it. The problem of ELT selection is inevitably burdened with difficult standards.

Some might feel that in assessing a patient's value to society one should ask not only who if permitted to continue living can make the greatest contribution to society in some creative or constructive way, but also who by dying would leave behind the greatest burden on society in assuming the discharge of their residual responsibilities.[7] Certainly the philosophical utilitarian would give equal weight to both these considerations. Just here is where I would part ways with orthodox utilitarianism. For—though this is not the place to do so—I should be prepared to argue that a civilized society has an obligation to promote the furtherance of positive achievements in cultural and related areas even if this means the assumption of certain added burdens.[8]

The Past Services-Rendered Factor (Retrospective Service)

A person's services to another person or group have always been taken to constitute a valid basis for a claim upon this person or group —of course a moral and not necessarily a legal claim. Society's obligation for the recognition and reward of services rendered—an obligation whose discharge is also very possibly conducive to self-interest in the long run—is thus another factor to be taken into account. This should be viewed as a morally necessary correlative of the previously considered factor of *prospective* service. It would be morally indefensible of society in effect to say: "Never mind about services you rendered yesterday—it is only the services to be rendered tomorrow that will count with us today." We live in very future-oriented times, constantly preoccupied in a distinctly utilitarian way with future satisfactions. And this disinclines us to give much recognition to past services. But parity considerations of the sort just adduced indicate that such recognition should be given *on grounds of equity.* No doubt a justification for giving weight to services rendered can also be attempted along utilitarian lines. ("The reward of past services rendered spurs people on to greater future efforts and is thus socially advantageous in the long-run future.") In saying that past services should be counted "on grounds of equity" —rather than "on grounds of utility"—I take the view that even if this utilitarian defense could somehow be shown to be fallacious, I should still be prepared to maintain the propriety of taking services rendered into account. The position does not rest on a utilitarian basis and so would not collapse with the removal of such a basis.[9]

* * *

As we have said, these five factors fall into three groups: the biomedical factors *A* and *B,* the familial factor *C,* and the social factors *D* and *E.* With items *A* and *B* the need for a detailed analysis of the medical considerations comes to the fore. The age of the patient, his medical history, his physical and psychological condition, his specific disease, etc., will all need to be taken into exact account. These biomedical factors represent technical issues: they call for the physicians' expert judgment and the medical statisticians' hard data. And they are ethically uncontroversial factors—their legitimacy and appropriateness are evident from the very nature of the case.

Greater problems arise with the familial and social factors. They involve intangibles that are difficult to judge. How is one to develop subcriteria for weighing the relative social contributions of (say) an architect or a librarian or a mother of young children? And they involve highly problematic issues. (For example, should good moral character be rated a plus and bad a minus in judging services rendered?) And there is something strikingly unpleasant in grappling with issues of this sort for people brought up in times greatly inclined towards maxims of the type "Judge not!" and "Live and let live!" All the same, in the situation that concerns us here such distasteful problems must be faced, since a failure to choose to save some is tantamount to sentencing all. Unpleasant choices are intrinsic to the problem of ELT selection; they are of the very essence of the matter.[10]

But is reference to all these factors indeed inevitable? The justification for taking acount of the medical factors is pretty obvious. But why should the social aspect of services rendered and to be rendered be taken into account at all? The answer is that they must be taken into account not from the *medical* but from the *ethical* point of view. Despite disagreement on many fundamental issues, moral philosophers of the present day are pretty well in consensus that the justification of human actions is to be sought largely and primarily—if not exclusively —in the principles of utility and of justice.[11] But utility requires reference of services to be rendered and justice calls for a recognition of services that have been rendered. Moral considerations would thus demand recognition of these two factors. (This, of course, still leaves open the question of whether the point of view provides a valid basis of action: Why base one's actions upon moral principles?—or, to put it bluntly—Why be moral? The present paper is, however, hardly the place to grapple with so fundamental an issue, which has been canvassed in the literature of philosophical ethics since Plato.)

MORE THAN MEDICAL ISSUES ARE INVOLVED

An active controversy has of late sprung up in medical circles over the question of whether non-physician laymen should be given a role in ELT selection (in the specific context of chronic haemodialysis). One physician writes: "I think that the assessment of the candidates should be made by a senior doctor on the [dialysis] unit, but I am sure that it would be helpful to him—both in sharing responsibility and in avoiding personal pressure—if a small unnamed group of people [presumably including laymen] officially made the final decision. I visualize the doctor bringing the data to the group, explaining the points in relation to each case, and obtaining their approval of his order of priority.[12]

Essentially this procedure of a selection committee of laymen has for some years been in use in one of the most publicized chronic dialysis units, that of the Swedish Hospital of Seattle, Washington.[13] Many physicians are apparently reluctant to see the choice of allocation of medical therapy pass out of strictly medical hands. Thus in a recent symposium on the "Selection of Patients for Haemodialysis,"[14] Dr. Ralph Shakman writes: "Who is to implement the selection? In my opinion it must ultimately be the responsibility of the consultants in charge of the renal units ... I can see no reason for delegating this responsibility to lay persons. Surely the latter would be better employed if they could be persuaded to devote their time and energy to raise more and more money for us to spend on our patients."[15] Other contributors to this symposium strike much the same note. Dr. F. M. Parsons writes: "In an attempt to overcome ... difficulties in selection some have advocated introducing certain specified lay people into the discussions. Is it wise? I doubt whether a committee of this type can adjudicate as satisfactorily as two medical colleagues, particularly as successful therapy involves close cooperation between doctor and patient."[16] And Dr. M. A. Wilson writes in the same symposium: "The suggestion has been made that lay panels should select individuals for dialysis from among a group who are medically suitable. Though this would relieve the doctor-in-charge of a heavy load of responsibility, it would place the burden on those who have no personal knowledge and have to base their judgments on medical or social reports. I do not believe this would result in better decisions for the group or improve the doctor-patient relationship in individual cases."[17]

But no amount of flag waving about the doctor's facing up to his responsibility—or prostrations before the idol of the doctor-patient relationship and reluctance to admit laymen into the sacred precincts of the conference chambers of medical consultations—can obscure the essential fact that ELT selection is not a wholly medical problem. When there are more than enough places in an ELT program to accommodate all who need it, then it will clearly be a medical question to decide who does have the need and which among these would successfully respond. But when an admitted gross insufficiency of places exists, when there are ten or fifty or one hundred highly eligible candidates for each place in the program, then it is unrealistic to take the view that purely medical criteria can furnish a sufficient basis for selection. The question of ELT selection becomes serious as a phenomenon of scale—because, as more candidates present themselves, strictly medical factors are increasingly less adequate as a selection criterion precisely because by numerical category-crowding there will be more and more cases whose "status is much the same" so far as purely medical considerations go.

The ELT selection problem clearly poses issues that transcend the medical sphere because—in the nature of the case—many residual issues remain to be dealt with once *all* of the medical questions have been faced. Because of this there is good reason why laymen as well as physicians should be involved in the selection process. Once the medical considerations have been brought to bear, fundamental social issues remain to be resolved. The instrumentalities of ELT have been created through the social investment of scarce resources, and the interests of the society deserve to play a role in their utilization. As representatives of their social interests, lay opinions should function to complement and supplement medical views once the proper arena of medical considerations is left behind.[18] Those physicians who have urged the presence of lay members on selection panels can, from this point of view, be recognized as having seen the issue in proper perspective.

One physician has argued against lay representation on selection panels for haemodialysis as follows: "If the doctor advises dialysis and the lay panel refuses, the patient will regard this as a death sentence passed by an anonymous court from which he has no right of appeal."[19]

But this drawback is not specific to the use of a lay panel. Rather, it is a feature inherent in every *selection* procedure, regardless of whether the selection is done by the head doctor of the unit, by a panel of physicians, etc. No matter who does the selecting among patients recommended for dialysis, the feelings of the patient who has been rejected (and knows it) can be expected to be much the same, provided that he recognizes the actual nature of the choice (and is not deceived by the possibly convenient but ultimately poisonous fiction that because the selection was made by physicians it was made entirely on medical grounds).

In summary, then, the question of ELT selection would appear to be one that is in its very nature heavily laden with issues of medical research, practice, and administration. But it will not be a question that can be resolved on solely medical grounds. Strictly social issues of justice and utility will invariably arise in this area—questions going outside the medical area in whose resolution medical laymen can and should play a substantial role.

THE INHERENT IMPERFECTION (NON-OPTIMALITY) OF ANY SELECTION SYSTEM

Our discussion to this point of the design of a selection system for ELT has left a gap that is a very fundamental and serious omission. We have argued that five factors must be taken into substantial and explicit account:

A. *Relative likelihood of success.*—Is the chance of the treatment's being "successful" to be rated as high, good, average, etc.?[20]

B. *Expectancy of future life.*—Assuming the "success" of the treatment, how much longer does the patient stand a good chance (75 per cent or better) of living—considering his age and general condition?

C. *Family role.*—To what extent does the patient have responsibilities to others in his immediate family?

D. *Social contributions rendered.*—Are the patient's past services to his society outstanding, substantial, average, etc.?

E. *Social contributions to be rendered.*—Considering his age, talents, training, and past record of performance, is there a substantial probability that the patient will—*adequate recovery being assumed*—render in the future services to his society that can be characterized as outstanding, substantial, average, etc.?

This list is clearly insufficient for the construction of a reasonable selection system, since that would require not only *that these factors be taken into account* (somehow or other), but—going beyond this—would specify a *specific set of procedures for taking account of them.* The specific procedures that would constitute such a system would have to take account of the interrelationship of these factors (e.g., *B* and *E*), and to set out exact guidelines as to the relevant weight that is to be given to each of them. This is something our discussion has not as yet considered.

In fact, I should want to maintain that there is no such thing here as a single rationally superior selection system. The position of affairs seems to me to be something like this: (1) It is necessary (for reasons already canvassed) to *have* a system, and to have a system that is rationally defensible, and (2) to be rationally defensible, this system must take the factors *A–E* into substantial and explicit account. But (3) the exact manner in which a rationally defensible system takes account of these factors cannot be fixed in any one specific way on the basis of general considerations. Any of the variety of ways that give *A–E* "their due" will be acceptable and viable. One cannot hope to find within this range of workable systems some one that is *optimal* in relation to the alternatives. There is no one system that does "the (uniquely) best"—only a variety of systems that do "as well as one can expect to do" in cases of this sort.

The situation is structurally very much akin to that of rules of partition of an estate among the relations of a decedent. It is important *that there be* such rules. And it is reasonable that spouse, children, parents, siblings, etc., be taken account of in these rules. But the question of the exact method of division—say that when the decedent has neither living spouse nor living children then his estate is to be divided, dividing 60 per cent between parents, 40 per cent between siblings versus dividing 90 per cent between parents, 10 per cent between siblings—cannot be settled on the basis of any general abstract considerations of reasonableness. Within broad limits, a *variety* of resolutions are all perfectly acceptable—so that no one procedure can justifiably be regarded as "the (uniquely) best" because it is superior to all others.[21]

A POSSIBLE BASIS FOR A REASONABLE SELECTION SYSTEM

Having said that there is no such thing as *the optimal* selection system for ELT, I want now to sketch out the broad features of what I would regard as *one acceptable* system.

The basis for the system would be a point rating. The scoring here at issue would give roughly equal weight to the medical considerations (*A* and *B*) in comparison with the extra-medical considerations (*C*=family role, *D*=services rendered, and *E*=services to be rendered), also giving roughly equal weight to the three items involved here (*C, D,* and *E*). The result of such a scoring procedure would provide the essential *starting point* of our ELT selection mechanism. I deliberately say "starting point" because it seems to me that one should not follow the results of this scoring in an *automatic* way. I would propose that the actual selection should only be guided but not actually be dictated by this scoring procedure, along lines now to be explained.

THE DESIRABILITY OF INTRODUCING AN ELEMENT OF CHANCE

The detailed procedure I would propose—not of course as optimal (for reasons we have seen), but as eminently acceptable—would combine the scoring procedure just discussed with an element of chance. The resulting selection system would function as follows:

1. First the criteria of inclusion of Section IV above would be applied to constitute a *first phase selection group*—which (we shall suppose) is substantially larger than the number *n* of persons who can actually be accommodated with ELT.

2. Next the criteria of selection of Section V are brought to bear via a scoring procedure of the type described in Section VIII. On this basis a *second phase selection group* is constituted which is only *somewhat* larger—say by a third or a half—than the critical number *n* at issue.

3. If this second phase selection group is relatively homogeneous as regards rating by the scoring procedure—that is, if there are no really major disparities within this group (as would be likely if the initial group was significantly larger than *n*)—then the final selection is made by *random* selection of *n* persons from within this group.

This introduction of the element of chance—in what could be dramatized as a "lottery of life and death"—must be justified. The fact is that such a procedure would bring with it three substantial advantages.

First, as we have argued above (in Section VII), any acceptable selection system is inherently non-optimal. The introduction of the element of chance prevents the results that life-and-death choices are made by the automatic application of an admittedly imperfect selection method.

Second, a recourse to chance would doubtless make matters easier for the rejected patient and those who have a specific interest in him. It would surely be quite hard for them to accept his exclusion by relatively mechanical application of objective criteria in whose implementation subjective judgment is involved. But the circumstances of life have conditioned us to accept the workings of chance and to tolerate the element of luck (good or bad): human life is an inherently contingent process. Nobody, after all, has an absolute right to ELT—but most of us would feel that we have "every bit as much right" to it as anyone else in significantly similar circumstances. The introduction of the element of chance assures a like handling of like cases over the widest possible area that seems reasonable in the circumstances.

Third (and perhaps least), such a recourse to random selection does much to relieve the administrators of the selection system of the awesome burden of ultimate and absolute responsibility.

These three considerations would seem to build up a substantial case for introducing the element of chance into the mechanism of the system for ELT selection in a way limited and circumscribed by other weightier considerations, along some such lines as those set forth above.[22]

It should be recognized that this injection of *man-made* chance supplements the element of *natural* chance that is present inevitably and in any case (apart from the role of chance in singling out certain persons as victims for the affliction at issue). As F. M. Parsons has observed: "any vacancies [in an ELT program—specifically haemodialysis] will be filled immediately by the first suitable patients, even though their claims for therapy may subsequently prove less than those of other patients refused later."[23] Life is a chancy business and even the most rational of human arrangements can cover this over to a very limited extent at best.

Bibliography[24]

S. ALEXANDER. "They Decide Who Lives, Who Dies," *Life,* LIII (November 9, 1962), 102-25.

C. DOYLE. "Spare-Part Heart Surgeons Worried by Their Success," *Observer* (London), May 12, 1968.

J. FLETCHER. *Morals and Medicine.* London, 1955.

S. GOROVITZ. "Ethics and the Allocation of Medical Resources," *Medical Research Engineering,* V (1966), 5-7.

L. LADER. "Who Has the Right To Live?" *Good Housekeeping* (January, 1968), pp. 85 and 144-50.

J. D. N. NABARRO, F. M. PARSONS, R. SHAKMAN, and M. A. WILSON. "Selection of Patients for Haemodialysis," *British Medical Journal* (March 11, 1967), pp. 622-24.

H. M. SCHMECK, JR. "Panel Holds Life-or-Death Vote in Allotting of Artificial Kidney," *New York Times,* May 6, 1962, pp. 1, 83.

G. E. W. WOLSTENHOLME and M. O'CONNOR (eds.). *Ethics in Medical Progress.* London, 1966.

Notes

1. Christine Doyle, "Spare-Part Heart Surgeons Worried by Their Success,"
    Observer, May 12, 1968.
2. J. D. N. Nabarro, "Selection of Patients for Haemodialysis," *British Medical
    Journal* (March 11, 1967), p. 623. Although several thousand patients die
    in the U.K. each year from renal failure—there are about thirty new cases
    per million of population—only 10 per cent of these can for the foreseeable
    future be accommodated with chronic haemodialysis. Kidney transplanta-
    tion—itself a very tricky procedure—cannot make a more than minor
    contribution here. As this article goes to press, I learn that patients can be
    maintained in home dialysis at an operating cost about half that of main-
    taining them in a hospital dialysis unit (roughly an $8,000 minimum). In
    the United States, around 7,000 patients with terminal uremia who could
    benefit from haemodialysis evolve yearly. As of mid-1968, some 1,000 of
    these can be accommodated in existing hospital units. By June 1967, a
    world-wide total of some 120 patients were in treatment by home dialysis.
    (Data from a forthcoming paper, "Home Dialysis," by C. M. Conty and H.
    V. Murdaugh. See also R. A. Baillod *et al.,* "Overnight Haemodialysis in the
    Home," *Proceedings of the European Dialysis and Transplant Association,*
    VI [1965], 99 ff.).
3. For the Hippocratic Oath see *Hippocrates: Works* (Loeb ed.; London,
    1959), I, p. 298.
4. Another example of borderline legitimacy is posed by an endowment
    "with strings attached," e.g., "In accepting this legacy the hospital agrees
    to admit and provide all needed treatment for any direct descendant of
    myself, its founder."
5. Shana Alexander, "They Decide Who Lives, Who Dies," *Life,* LIII
    (November 9, 1962), 102-25 (see p. 107).
6. Lawrence Lader, "Who Has the Right To Live?" *Good Housekeeping*
    (January 1968), p. 144.
7. This approach could thus be continued to embrace the previous factor,
    that of family role, the preceding item *(C).*
8. Moreover a doctrinaire utilitarian would presumably be willing to with-
    draw a continuing mode of ELT such as haemodialysis from a patient to
    make room for a more promising candidate who came to view at a later
    stage and who could not otherwise be accommodated. I should be unwill-
    ing to adopt this course, partly on grounds of utility (with a view to the
    demoralization of insecurity), partly on the non-utilitarian ground that a
    "moral commitment" has been made and must be honored.
9. Of course the difficult question remains of the relative weight that should
    be given to prospective and retrospective service in cases where these
    factors conflict. There is good reason to treat them on a par.
10. This in the symposium on "Selection of Patients for Haemodialysis," *Brit-
    ish Medical Journal* (March 11, 1967), pp. 622-24. F. M. Parsons writes:
    "But other forms of selecting patients [distinct from first come, first served]
    are suspect in my view if they imply evaluation of man by man. What
    criteria could be used? Who could justify a claim that the life of a mayor
    would be more valuable than that of the humblest citizen of his borough?
    Whatever we may think as individuals none of us is indispensable." But
    having just set out this hard-line view he immediately backs away from it:

"On the other hand, to assume that there was little to choose between Alexander Fleming and Adolf Hitler . . . would be nonsense, and we should be naive if we were to pretend that we could not be influenced by their achievements and characters if we had to choose between the two of them. Whether we like it or not we cannot escape the fact that this kind of selection for long-term haemodialysis will be required until very large sums of money become available for equipment and services [so that *everyone* who needs treatment can be accomodated]."

11. The relative fundamentality of these principles is, however, a substantially disputed issue.

12. J. D. N. Nabarro, *op. cit.,* p. 622.

13. See Shana Alexander, *op. cit.*

14. *British Medical Journal* (March 11, 1967), pp. 622-24.

15. *Ibid.,* p. 624. Another contributor writes in the same symposium, "The selection of the few [to receive haemodialysis] is proving very difficult— a true 'Doctor's Dilemma'—for almost everybody would agree that this must be a medical decision, preferably reached by consultation among colleagues" (Dr. F. M. Parsons, *ibid.,* p. 623).

16. "The Selection of Patients for Haemodialysis," *op. cit.* (n. 10 above), p. 623.

17. Dr. Wilson's article concludes with the perplexing suggestion—wildly beside the point given the structure of the situation at issue—that "the final decision will be made by the patient." But this contention is only marginally more ludicrous than Parson's contention that in selecting patients for haemodialysis "gainful employment in a well chosen occupation is necessary to achieve the best results" since "only the minority wish to live on charity" *(ibid.).*

18. To say this is of course not to deny that such questions of applied medical ethics will invariably involve a host of medical considerations—it is only to insist that extra-medical considerations will also invariably be at issue.

19. M. A. Wilson, "Selection of Patients for Haemodialysis," *op. cit.,* p. 624.

20. In the case of an ongoing treatment involving complex procedure and dietary and other mode-of-life restrictions—and chronic haemodialysis definitely falls into this category—the patient's psychological makeup, his willpower to "stick with it" in the face of substantial discouragements— will obviously also be a substantial factor here. The man who gives up, takes not his life alone, but (figuratively speaking) also that of the person he replaced in the treatment schedule.

21. To say that acceptable solutions can range over broad limits is *not* to say that there are no limits at all. It is an obviously intriguing and fundamental problem to raise the question of the factors that set these limits. This complex issue cannot be dealt with adequately here. Suffice it to say that considerations regarding precedent and people's expectations, factors of social utility, and matters of fairness and sense of justice all come into play.

22. One writer has mooted the suggestion that: "Perhaps the right thing to do, difficult as it may be to accept, is to select [for haemodialysis] from among the medical and psychologically qualified patients on a strictly random basis" (S. Gorovitz, "Ethics and the Allocation of Medical Resources," *Medical Research Engineering,* V [1966], p. 7). Outright random selection would, however, seem indefensible because of its refusal to give weight to considerations which, under the circumstances, *deserve* to be given weight. The proposed procedure of superimposing a certain degree of

randomness upon the rational-choice criteria would seem to combine the advantages of the two without importing the worst defects of either.

23. "Selection of Patients for Haemodialysis," *op. cit.,* p. 623. The question of whether a patient for chronic treatment should ever be terminated from the program (say if he contracts cancer) poses a variety of difficult ethical problems with which we need not at present concern ourselves. But it does seem plausible to take the (somewhat anti-utilitarian) view that a patient should not be terminated simply because a "better qualified" patient comes along later on. It would seem that a quasi-contractual relationship has been created through established expectations and reciprocal understandings, and that the situation is in this regard akin to that of the man who, having undertaken to sell his house to one buyer, cannot afterward unilaterally undo this arrangement to sell it to a higher bidder who "needs it worse" (thus maximizing the over-all utility).

24. I acknowledge with thanks the help of Miss Hazel Johnson, Reference Librarian at the University of Pittsburgh Library, in connection with the bibliography.

Science and the Sense of Humanity

SCIENCE AND MORALITY

Science too often seems to separate itself from humanity. It seems to transcend the moral concerns and humanism of man. The bombing of Hiroshima, for instance, made an enormous difference in the relationship between science and morality. This issue was set down very well by Archibald MacLeish, who said:

> After Hiroshima it was obvious that the loyalty of science was not to humanity, but to truth—its own truth; and that the law of science was not the law of the good—what humanity thinks of as good, meaning moral, decent, humane—but the law of the possible. What it is possible for science to know, science must know. What it is possible for technology to do, technology will have done. The frustration—and it is a real and debasing frustration—in which we are mired today will not leave us until we believe in ourselves again, assume again the mastery of our lives, the management of our means.

Speaking in the name of humanity, Archibald MacLeish rejected science's pretensions to independence from humanity's concern. Speaking as a scientist, I wish to show that the apparent inhumanity of science is not a testimony to its inherent strength, but rather an expression of a dangerous erosion in the competence of science itself.

If we are concerned with the human meaning of science, its social usefulness, and the usefulness of the technology that it generates, we have to look past the gaudy circus of space spectaculars, past the boasts of unparalleled military force, past the claims that every human ill can be cured by some new chemical, some marvel of electronics, or some biological sleight of hand. Instead, we need to ask why, despite all the new marvels of science, the heavens reek, the waters below are foul, children die in infancy, and we are all threatened with nuclear annihilation. Having asked these questions, we need to seek answers that will restore the power of science to the service of man.

THE POLLUTION CRISIS

Something has gone wrong with what we know. An enormous array of evidence has piled up in connection with the deterioration of the quality of life and of the environment. The United States is the most technologically advanced society in the history of man. Yet the United States has amassed an appalling roster of technological mistakes which have broken down the quality of the environment: We built highways and strangled our cities with smog. For more than 40 years, we have put such massive amounts of lead into the environment that it is now beginning to reach toxic levels. Fertilizers produce more food; yet they have also turned out to be pollutants. The use of mercury in modern chemical technology has suddenly emerged as a serious cause of water pollution. Detergents were successfully synthesized, but had to be replaced because they were incompatible with the biological systems in surface waters. Nuclear weapons were massively exploded without our realizing that at the same time we were conducting a huge environmental experiment that would spread radioactivity into every living thing on the earth.

Most of these environmental mistakes have been made in the period since 1945, when the generation of youth that we are now looking at with such wonder and hope were born. That is why they are the first generation in human history to carry strontium 90 in their bones and DDT in their fat. They know that they have been born into a world in which knowledge—the highest goal of human beings—often leads to catastrophe.

We boast of a technology powerful enough to free ourselves from environment. But the very progress of technology has in fact made us more dependent on nature than ever before. For example, because we have filled the air over New York with pollutants, we are totally dependent on a good wind in order to be able to breathe relatively clean air.

SOME MISTAKEN EXPLANATIONS OF POLLUTION

How did this come about? Various explanations have been offered. Some people say that the reason why the United States is polluted is that there are too many people: People are polluters; they leave rubbish around; they produce waste; they consume enormous amounts of material.

What is known about the course of pollution in the United States, however, conflicts with this conclusion. In the period 1945-66, when most of our pollution problems developed, the population of the United States increased by approximately 43 per cent. Yet the pollution levels have increased much more than that; although estimates vary, pollution has gone up in that time from 500 to 1500 per cent! In other words, there is much more pollution in the United States than can be accounted for by the number of people.

There has got to be another reason. Some people say that pollution is due to the fact that we consume too much; we're too affluent. But if you look at the statistics on the consumption of shoes, outer garments, or cleansers, for example, you find that the per capita rate has not changed in the United States during 1945-66. We wear as many shoes and as much clothing and use as many cleansers as we did before. It is true that we now drive more than twice as many automobiles as in 1945; but smog levels have much more than doubled in that time.

POLLUTION CAUSED BY TECHNOLOGY

The pollution problem cannot be accounted for either by over-population or by overconsumption. Pollution is related, I believe, to certain very remarkable changes in production technology. While *per capita* consumption of clothing, food, and other necessities has hardly changed, the ways in which these goods are produced *have* changed. Synthetic fibers have replaced cotton and wool; synthetic detergents have replaced soap made from natural fats; food is produced on reduced acreage through the use of synthetic insecticides and chemical fertilizer.

All this "progress" has been ecologically unsound. Take, for example, the consequences of replacing cotton with plastic fibers. The earth obtains its energy from the sun. Essentially all the energy we use comes from the sun in one way or another. Green plants are capable of converting solar energy into useful products, such as the cotton fiber.

Now, if we look at the statistics, we find that cotton consumption per capita has gone down; plastic fiber consumption, on the other hand, has gone up to fill the gap. Everybody wears about the same number of shirts; but now instead of being made of cotton they're made of a synthetic fiber—a wonder of the world, a thing that advertisers can write glowing ads about.

What does this mean in terms of energy? The raw material that the plastic is made from has to be purified from petroleum. This means that we have to separate the particular molecule necessary out of the vast array of others. That requires energy. The chemical industry that makes such raw materials for plastics synthesis uses an enormous amount of energy which is produced by the combustion of fossil fuels. Yet unlike the absorption of solar energy by the cotton plant, combustion causes environmental pollution. In other words, we now make a substitute for cotton, but do it in a dirty way, by using energy that originally was trapped by fossil plants and deposited as coal and oil. And the process is wasteful; for instead of using renewable solar energy to form the fiber, we use irreplaceable fossil fuels. What has happened in the last 25 years is that we have learned to make commercially valuable substitutes for natural materials but in the process have created the drastic environmental pollution that we are now experiencing.

If we trace the consequences of attempting to produce man-made substitutes for natural activities, we find that they all lead from one pollution problem to another. For example, in nature insect pests are largely controlled by other insects. Ladybugs eat aphids; in nature aphids are kept under control in that way. But then we synthesized DDT as a supposedly better substitute for natural insect control; that leads to trouble because the pests become resistant to DDT, and the DDT kills off their natural insect enemies. At the same time, in order to synthesize the DDT, we have to produce a lot of chlorine because that is an essential constituent of it. (Chlorine is also needed to manufacture plastics, another substitute for natural materials.) To improve the production of chlorine, a technique involving mercury-containing electrolytic cells has been developed and, for every ton of chlorine that is produced, the industry has been dumping about a half pound of mercury into the rivers and lakes of the United States. A half pound of mercury is enough to bring 10 million pounds of fish up to the acceptable limit of toxicity. In the United States we are just now discovering that many fish and many surface waters have been polluted by mercury. The basic reason is that the mercury is being used to produce chlorine, in order to make DDT and plastics—which are themselves environmental pollutants.

The mercury problem came to the surface following the discovery of mercury pollution in Lake St. Clair in Canada. About 50 million dollars worth of chlorine was being produced annually by the chemical plants that were involved in polluting Lake St. Clair with mercury. When the pollution was discovered, the Canadian Government ordered a stop to sport and commercial fishing in the area and noted that this action would essentially bring to a halt the 500-million-dollar-a-year fishing and associated tourist activities. In other words, the price of making 50 million dollars worth of chlorine is perhaps 10 times as much in environmental costs.

The same thing is true of every pollution problem: We are paying for it. For example, in New York or Boston probably one-third of the air pollution is due to power plants. Setting aside the unmeasurable anguish of disease and death that's brought about by air pollution, a dollar value, amounting to about 20 dollars annually per person, can be placed on the air pollution produced by urban power plants. If we multiply that by a family of four, it means that we are paying about 80 dollars a year for electricity in costs that do not appear on the electricity bill. This cost is represented by laundry and doctors' bills and by the deterioration of building structures. Every pollution issue involves the choice of a balance between the associated benefits and hazards, and it looks as though the costs are going to be much larger than anyone thought.

Such costs occur not only in the developed countries, for these advanced countries are exporting pollution globally. For example, the Soviet Union helped the Egyptians build the Aswan Dam. Now the Aswan Dam was designed to produce power and water for irrigation. It is apparently going to be a disastrous failure. For one thing, it now looks as though there are going to be enough plants growing on the surface of Lake Nasser to evaporate almost as much water as enters the lake. In the second place, it is already clear that the dam is holding back the nutrients that used to go down the Nile and that this is preventing algae from growing in the Mediterranean, thus killing off the fishery industry there. It is also cutting down the natural fertility of the Valley of the Nile, so that Egyptian farmers now have to depend not only on irrigation but also on fertilizers. And we know from our own experience that the leaching of fertilizers is a cause of water pollution. At the same time, the new irrigation canals are bound to spread a serious liver disease. In other words, in receiving this magnificent piece of advanced technology, Egypt has also been given an ecological disaster.

OVERPOPULATION

The relationship between the population problem and environmental pollution has been badly misunderstood. As I have already pointed out, there is no evidence that overpopulation in the United States is the cause of pollution. It's not that we have too many people, or that they are using too much. It's just that we have developed the wrong kinds of technology to provide for their needs. On the other hand, we all know that the world population is growing at so rapid a rate that there is a danger that it may outrun our ability to produce food globally. But let me point out that although we have starvation, malnutrition, and famine in the world, we have it at a time when the world produces enough food to feed adequately everyone in it. Globally we are producing sufficient food to provide every inhabitant of the world with an adequate intake of calories and protein. The present problem is that it is not adequately distributed, rather than that it is not being produced. Nevertheless, looking at the shape of the global population growth curves, we know that if they continue there must be a time when there will be too many people to be supported by the total amount of food—even if it were adequately distributed.

Like environmental pollution, however, the world population problem is again a failure in which technology is involved. Demographers have learned a good deal about the connection between population growth and technology. During the development of the Industrial Revolution, rising productivity was generally accompanied by a rising population. For example, England experienced a kind of population explosion (with a growth rate of more than 1 per cent per year) from about the middle of the 18th century to about 1900. This coincided with rising agricultural and industrial productivity; the nation's wealth, resources, and human facilities increased, and as a result mortality rates dropped. Population size is, of course, the resultant of a balance between the death rate and the birth rate.

In general, demographers find that in every instance in which the population has risen sharply, it has been because the death rate dropped. They also find that in Western Europe especially, but more recently in Japan as well, following the drop in the death rate there has been a reduction in the birth rate, so that the population size begins to level off. Thus, after about 1900 the average annual increase in the English population dropped from more than 1 per cent to about 0.5 per cent. A number of demographers have explained this effect by proposing that rising technology and industrialization have given the people of those countries a confidence in the future and a sense of social security; so they don't need to have children as a kind of old-age insurance. The leveling off of the population is a kind of natural response to prosperity and social confidence. This is apparently the normal way in which human societies react to the acquisition of wealth, provided that this wealth is available to them in such a way as to give them confidence in their future.

THE IMPACT OF COLONIALISM

Part of the wealth of the Western world that made possible its rapid economic development was derived from tropical countries during the period of colonialism. And several demographic studies—for example, one dealing with the impact of Dutch colonialsim in Indonesia—indicate that overpopulation in the colonial country is a consequence of colonialism. Thus, the Dutch brought into Indonesia modern techniques that improved living conditions and reduced the mortality rate in the native population. And according to Professor Geertz, who has made a careful demographic study of this period, the Dutch apparently deliberately fostered the increase in the Indonesian population in order to increase the labor force that they needed to exploit the natural resources. For instance, in order to accomplish these ends, the Dutch promulgated a law that required the Indonesian population to pay taxes not in money or in produce but in labor.

It seems clear from these studies that the rising population in Indonesia was a consequence of the introduction of Western technology during the colonial period. However, much of the wealth acquired as a result of this increased productivity was taken from Indonesia and sent to Holland, where it enabled Holland to go through what is called the demographic transition; that is, to improve its living standard and social security and begin to level off its population. Thus the Indonesians were stimulated to develop a large population but were not then allowed to develop the material resources that, as previously indicated, are the only means of encouraging motivation to control fertility. Worse than that, since World War II many of the advanced countries have turned their backs on the tropical countries because they no longer need some of the natural resources. With the development of chlorine plants and synthetic chemicals, you do not need natural rubber from Indonesia. The result is that trade has declined, further depleting the opportunities for the economic advancement that might support motivation for population control.

Thus the tropical world has been put into the enormously inhumane position of having been encouraged to increase its population for the sake of supporting economic progress in the advanced part of the globe. Then, when their natural resources were less needed by Western countries, we turned our backs on them, having depleted the resources that they need in order to go through the normal, economically based, transition to a stable population. And now we are crying that it is a terrible problem because they are going to eat the globe out of house and home. This is a grave global problem. But we in the advanced countries of the world have the moral consolation of knowing that it's our own problem; we made it.

This, then, is the frightening picture of the consequences of the development of modern technology: In the advanced countries technology has incurred a huge debt to nature that is threatening to engulf us in environmental destruction; in the underdeveloped countries it has encouraged a huge debt in the form of what one demographer has called the major consequence of colonialism—a one-billion excess in the world population.

WRONG SOLUTIONS

Faced with this enormous problem, some people are in a panic to find solutions. They are looking for gimmicks. They are beginning to feel that almost any kind of control that we can exert on the world population problem ought to be used: We could put economic and political pressures on underdeveloped countries to force them to accept birth-control programs.

There is similar panic in some quarters for implementing increased population control in the United States, as a means of solving our own environmental crisis. Willard Wirtz, former Secretary of Labor, has recently said that because of our faulty technology, people are the polluters; therefore, he concluded, we must have fewer people. He has concluded: "A fisherman whipping a stream futilely and thinking to himself in the early morning that there are too few fish realizes that the banks get crowded, that it is equally a problem of too many fishermen. A Secretary of Labor spends his years in office trying futilely to fight unemployment by creating more jobs and only later, freed of the inhibitions of office and political restraints, faces the truth that there are too few jobs because there are too many people."

My own position, which is I believe far better in accord with the facts, is that the environmental crisis is the result of faulty technology; therefore, we must improve that technology and make it fit the demands of environmental processes. The problem of pollution is so severe that we can no longer tolerate the mistakes that our society makes, either in failing to provide sufficient jobs or in polluting the environment. Under the pressure of this kind of difficulty, some people are saying, "Well, we are doing things badly and the more people there are the worse off we are because more things are badly done. So we must get rid of people." This is like pushing people overboard rather than manning the pumps to allow a sinking ship to remain afloat: We are throwing humanity overboard rather than face the serious issues of changing the way in which we are living in the world.

This same faulty thinking is also beginning to be evident in our approach to the world population problem. It is true that we are facing a potential *global* overpopulation problem, for the reasons I have described. But it is also evident that the solution lies in economic improvement and social security. The advanced countries have an obligation to repay their debts to the former colonial countries. One way is by ending the continuing exploitation of the resources of these countries. For example, the protein deficiency in Latin America could be totally made up if the United States and Western Europe refrained from taking the South American anchovy catch and converting it into catfood and feed for chickens. Our using these anchovies for feed is one of the reasons for the profitability of our chicken industry and the low price of broilers. (Incidentally, when we feed anchovies to chickens, we waste nine-tenths of the nutritive value that would be used were they fed directly to people.) In other words, if we were to stop taking this protein away from Latin America, we would be doing much more to control their population explosion than we are by giving them birth control information. Of course, birth control is essential. Everyone ought to have the free choice to control fertility in the best available ways. But it is first essential that they have the sense of social security that would give them motivation to use birth control.

I think it would help also if nations like the United States would end political interventions in underdeveloped countries, such as in Southeast Asia and Latin America. I think, for example, that if it is true that a Guatemalan or Dominican peasant has got to feel secure about the future of his life and his children's lives in order to be motivated to control fertility, and if he has got to feel that he lives in a country that will take care of him in his old age, then surely it is not a good idea in the name of population control for the United States to bolster up dictators in those countries.

I believe that underdeveloped nations can develop population control provided that we in the advanced nations face our responsibility to pay back the debt we owe them. For we have deprived them of resources that would have enabled them to achieve the quality of life necessarily prerequisite to self-motivated control of fertility. This, I believe, is the only possible basis for a humane solution to the world population problem.

I am, frankly, appalled by some of the measures that have been suggested for world population control—measures that will deprive all of us of our sense of humanity. It has been proposed, for example, that we should apply triage to the underdeveloped countries; that is, that where, in our judgment, it is too late to save a country from famine, we should cut our losses and allow them to starve. This has been suggested for India. In the long run, it has been said, India can no longer be saved. Therefore, we ought to throw India overboard and not give it any support. I've seen proposals that we ought to stop giving medical aid to underdeveloped countries because all that does is to increase the population.

This is the kind of inhumanity developing under pressure of a problem that has been created not biologically, but socially, economically, and politically. And it seems to me that we have to turn our attention toward social, economic, and political solutions rather than trying to resolve the problems by biological solutions—which deny the humaneness of man.

A NEW SENSE OF HUMANITY

In spite of all this, I am an optimist. The world is facing a dreadful situation. But I am convinced that humane solutions can be achieved. Successful methods of controlling the environmental assault of modern technology have already been accomplished. We have a nuclear test ban treaty, which has helped to minimize to a degree one of our worst technological mistakes, namely, reliance on nuclear war as a means of "defense." This treaty was not brought about by national leaders but by men of great moral force, such as Bertrand Russell and Linus Pauling, who provided the leadership. We now understand the danger of pesticides, and again, this awareness did not originate from leaders in the Department of Agriculture. Rather, one woman, Rachel Carson, provided the leadership. The world is suddenly engulfed with a sense of the importance of the environment. But there are few, if any, government officials who can claim to have provided the leadership for the new awareness.

Mr. Nixon campaigned for the Presidency chiefly on a platform of law and order. But when he came to delivering his first State of the Union message, it was all about the environment. Why? Because in the interval the people of this country saw for themselves where the nation's problems really lie.

Let these successes remind us that the true source of humane leadership in a world gripped by crisis derives from the people themselves. To solve the great crisis engendered by our huge, unpaid debt to nature and to man, we must find, in ourselves, a renewed sense of our own humanity.

Technology and Population Growth

Demographers have traditionally viewed the relationship between population growth and technology in terms of a three stage model collectively referred to as the "demographic transition." During the first stage, it is argued that population size remains relatively stable and little if any growth occurs because of man's inability to control and manipulate his environment. More specifically, it is assumed that in primitive societies man has little control over either his fertility or mortality and that the rates of both are high. Thus while many children are born each year, many people also die (particularly infants), and a natural stability of size is maintained. Actual size during this stage is for the most part determined by available food supplies.

The most explicit characteristic of the second stage of the transition is population growth. This is viewed as resulting mainly from technological advancements in agriculture and health which tend to reduce mortality, but have a relatively negative (and perhaps even a positive) effect on fertility. The resulting decline in the mortality rate and relative stability in the fertility rate brings about a period of population growth because relatively greater numbers of people are being born than die.

Among the group of countries which we normally call the Western world, this stage came about "naturally" as a result of total societal change ("progress"), and has lasted for nearly two hundred years. Because the mortality reduction was spread out over a number of years fertility rates had the opportunity to adjust to the changes, and growth was not too rapid. However, among the underdeveloped (or less modern) countries of the world this stage has been forced on societies since the close of World War II and the wholesale importation of Western death control technology. That is, we have largely forced upon these countries the means of limiting and controlling their mortality, but have not provided them with the mechanisms to limit and control their fertility. Thus, the mortality reduction which took nearly two hundred years to achieve in the Western world, has taken only about thirty years to achieve in the less modern world. The rapid pace of change in the reduction of mortality has not given fertility rates the opportunity to reduce, and the resulting fabrication is what we have come to call the "population explosion."

As of today we have every right to be extremely pessimistic about the prospects of any of the third world countries ever seeing the third stage of the demographic transition. This stage, like the first, is characterized by relatively stable sized populations; however, in this case stability results from man's increasing technological ability to control his fertility and his desire to effectively use these technological capabilities.

The stability in size during the third stage, then, results from low fertility and low mortality—the reverse of the first stage. In this paper I will discuss some of the implications of this model focusing particularly on stages two and three. My basic theme will be that there is an inherent contradiction between the objectives of lowering the world's growth rate and reducing the threat of ecological disaster. That is, my argument is simply that our supplies of renewable and nonrenewable resources are not great enough to allow us to reduce people's desires to have too many children, and that even if they were, their ubiquitous use would simply annihilate the human race from the impending ecological disaster. To develop this argument I will focus on three relationships: 1) those between mortality and technology; 2) those between fertility and technology; and 3) those between resources, technology, and demographic behavior.

MORTALITY AND TECHNOLOGY

Around 1940 the average death rate in the underdeveloped countries was about 20-24 deaths per 1,000 persons in the population. By 1965 this average was reduced to a figure somewhere between eight and ten deaths per 1,000 population. These figures do not immediately strike the layman as staggering, but let us consider a simple example to illustrate the effect of such a change.

A population of 20 million people with a death rate of 22 per 1,000 removes about 440,000 people from its total each year, while a death rate of nine removes only about 180,000 people—a difference of 260,-000 who are not removed as a result of the change. This means that as a result of such a change a society must be capable of supporting an excess of 260,000 people simply as a result of the mortality reduction. Mortality reductions of this magnitude, as pointed out above, did occur in the Western world; however, they were accompanied by large scale expansions of the economic spheres of the Western countries, thus making it possible for the societies to support the larger numbers produced by the lesser effect of mortality. No such economic expansion has taken place in the less modern countries of the world where the rapid mortality declines have occurred during the last thirty years. Accordingly, the first point that we want to note is that while we have given these countries the means to increasing their numbers, we have not provided them with the means to support and sustain these increases at a decent standard of living. Moreover, we know that a substantial proportion of the reduction in mortality occurs at the youngest ages and that this means that we are increasing the number of potential parents to bear additional children in the future.

Two additional points, both implied above, need to be made concerning mortality and mortality change. The first is that there is little if any relationship today between the level of technological development of a society and the level of its crude death rate, and that the association between these two variables has become weaker over time. Prior to World War II declines in mortality among the less developed countries were following a pattern somewhat similar to the pattern that the Western countries experienced. That is, what mortality declines did take place were usually dependent upon changes in the level of economic well-being, and this in turn was largely dependent upon changes in the level of technology. The reason that technological level has played a very minor role in reducing mortality in the less developed countries is because the major causes of death in these countries could be eliminated by relatively simple procedures introduced and controlled by populations other than the indigenous population. For instance, in one year (1946–1947) Ceylon's expectation of life at birth was increased by nine years through the use of DDT to control the malaria carrying mosquito. Similar changes among Western countries took about fifty years to accomplish, during which time there was widespread social change. But now it is possible to reduce mortality resulting from infectious and parasitic diseases (the major causes of death in most underdeveloped countries) with little or no technological advancement by having persons from outside countries or organizations apply pesticides and public health measures.

What is important to bear in mind then is that the countries which are lowering their mortality today are doing so independent of changes in their level of technology, and that it seems likely that mortality reductions will actually decrease the possibility of this happening because of the added economic strain produced by rapid and excessive population growth.

The final point that we need to make concerning mortality and mortality change is that such changes can be effected without requiring the individuals involved to alter their behavior. In fact, the people effected need not even know that such changes are taking place to realize their benefits. This further implies that no special knowledge is required among the population to be effected by such changes, nor do they have any control over, or any personal decisions to make to be effected by changes which reduce mortality. For instance, reconsider the case of Ceylon mentioned above where dramatic reductions in mortality were achieved in a year through the use of pesticides. These chemicals were applied over large areas of the country by low flying airplanes contracted by the government. It seems that in this type of situation very few people would know what was happening, let alone understand it. The important point, however, is that large reductions in mortality can be achieved independent of both the technological level of a society and the behavior of individuals in that society.

FERTILITY AND TECHNOLOGY

The situation with respect to fertility is considerably different. First, let us note that there have been no comparable reductions in fertility such as those that have occurred in the case of mortality. For instance, among underdeveloped countries fertility rates of 34-36 per 1,000 population were common prior to World War II, and today rates ranging from 28-32 per 1,000 population are common. To illustrate the combined effect of the mortality change and the relative "nonchange" in fertility let us return to our earlier example of the population consisting of 20 million people.

With birth rates of 35 per 1,000 at the earlier time period and 30 per 1,000 today, and the mortality rates stated above this population would have added 13 more people per 1,000 to its number prior to World War II, and 22 more people per 1,000 today. In absolute numbers this means that prior to World War II the population would have increased by 260,000 each year whereas today it increases by 440,000. The latter figure is the same number of people that the population was removing prior to World War II in the absence of fertility. Thus the combined effect produces a yearly growth that is about equal to what should have been removed from the population prior to World War II. If the technological base of the society does not change, chances are that its productive capacity also will not change; thus creating a greater and greater imbalance between sustenance and population.

Moreover, unlike mortality, fertility appears to be very highly associated with the level of technology of a society, and it also appears that as the level of technology in societies increases, their fertility decreases. It is important to note that it is not the technology per se which reduces fertility, but rather it is the changes in the social structure which are brought about by modern technology which reduce fertility. This brings us to the third point, namely that to reduce fertility it is necessary to change the values and attitudes of individuals in societies, and that there is strong evidence to indicate that low fertility values and attitudes are only promoted in technologically advanced societies. In short, unlike the situation with respect to mortality, fertility can only be lowered in the face of technological advancement and changes in individual behavior. Moreover, the types of changes which need to take place in individuals to lower fertility appear to take place only when technological advances also occur.

RESOURCES, TECHNOLOGY, AND DEMOGRAPHIC BEHAVIOR

The crucial question now appears to be, What will it take to lower the fertility of the less modern countries of the world to a level comparable to that in the more modern countries of the world? Before taking up this question, I should point out that I in no way intend to imply that the fertility of the more modern countries of the world is ideal. Rather, I use it only because it can serve as a convenient reference point. In my personal opinion even the fertility of most of these countries is too high.

Most couples in the Western world want between two and four children. This, indeed, has not always been the case, but it does appear to have been the case since the development of the modern urban social structure which most of us live in. Many sociologists, psychologists, and demographers agree that it is this milieu which has given modern Western man his preference for relatively small families. As a matter of fact, one would probably be hard put to find someone who studies the population problem who does not subscribe to this point of view. Thus, the problem confronting the world today is that the only way we know of to reduce fertility is to create this same milieu in the rest of the world. Yet from a practical point of view, this is impossible. The reason that it is impossible is rather straightforward, and really undisputable: to support the roughly 20 percent of the world's population which lives in the modern urban social milieu requires about 80 percent of the world's income. Moreover, these countries consume nearly 90 percent of the world's natural resources excluding food. The U.S. alone, with only six percent of the world's population, consumes nearly 40 percent of the world's non-food resources each year.

Given these facts it should be obvious that the technologically sophisticated level of living to which we are accustomed cannot be shared with the rest of the world. The obvious solution to this problem often suggested by the liberal is that what we need to do is lower our own standard so that a more equitable distribution of world resources can be achieved. This indeed, may be one avenue of approach to the problem; however, I seriously doubt that most of us would agree to give up the luxuries to which we have become accustomed. Add to this the fact that many resource supplies have already reached critically low levels, and that if a more equitable distribution were achieved it would lower the standard of living in the "have nations" considerably, but raise the standard of living in the "have not nations" only slightly; and probably not enough to significantly alter their current levels of fertility.

If, as a result of some miracle, it is possible to bring the underdeveloped countries of the world up to our technological level it still appears that we will be doomed; not because of over-population, but because of over-pollution. What I am suggesting here is that the ecological disaster which we are facing today has resulted primarily from the behavior of only 20 percent of the world's population. The thought of what the world would be like if everyone polluted the environment as much as the "have nations" staggers the imagination. The dilemma which we face today, then, is one of lowering fertility, yet the only way which we know to do this places us in just as serious a situation as not lowering it. Remembering that our goal is reducing the rate of growth (a function of both fertility and mortality) there seems to be a third alternative. That involves accepting the current levels of mortality as well as that of death control technology. Also this involves diverting the funds currently being spent on developing and finding cures for diseases and the extension of life. These funds in turn would be used to find new ways of lowering fertility and developing a technology which allows us to exploit new resources at lower levels of pollution. Such a move by itself could not save us, but could, if coupled with an attempt to develop a more equitable distribution of resources and a de-emphasis of bigness as goodness.

Address to the Academie des Sciences

It is with much satisfaction that I receive, today, the Thibaud Prize awarded by your academy. And I experience a special pleasure, whose nature I hope to make you understand, in being able to thank you in person. In fact this prize is useful and valuable to me for several reasons; in particular it has given me the chance to think more deeply about my situation as a research scientist, as well as the possibility of giving some of my conclusions today.

It is impossible, in fact, to receive such a prize without asking oneself several questions: why this reward; what meritorious thing have I done; in whose eyes? And more generally, what and whom does my scientific activity serve? Why do I do research, what are my personal motivations? Why does society organize scientific research, what is the role of science in our society? These questions have more and more often been asked in scientific circles as well as outside of them, especially since the great movement of May 1968 which placed everything in question.

There exist a series of "natural" responses to all of these questions. Isn't it, in fact, absolutely evident that science plays a fundamental role in the evolution of society today and is the essential motor of its progress? That the scientific researcher has thus become the necessary agent for the happiness of humanity and takes in this thought his primary motivations and his greatest satisfactions? One recognizes here the themes of an incessant lecture (sometimes in more subtle forms although it is really there), heard from grade school to the university, pushed as much by the most conservative as well as by some revolutionary voices.

There are, however, good reasons to entertain the most serious doubts as to the validity of these responses. Consider first of all the relationship between fundamental research and the progress of society. Two of the most expensive and prestigious branches of modern science are, without doubt, high energy particle physics and space physics. But where are their contributions to general progress? High energy physicists, almost unanimously, have no difficulty in admitting that no application is expected from their domain. As to the much extolled spin-offs of space research I only know of heat-proof ovenware and other similar gadgets. Of course it is easier for me to talk of these things than my own work, for which you are rewarding me today, which furnishes a brilliant example of "pure" research, that is to say gratuitous and without much other interest than to excite the curiosity of some twenty specialists in the whole world.

Of course there are some fields where one glimpses some enormous possibilities for application: medicine or agronomy, for examples, in which there seem to be some technical solutions for the problems of sickness and hunger which are the problems of the great majority of humanity. But the social structures are exactly such that these technical solutions can't be put to work. When one thinks only of the scandal of crowded hospitals, of the lack of mass health care, of the super-profits of the drug industry and of the lack of support for medical research in France—to say nothing of the problems of the countries which have just escaped from colonial domination. And if, in fact, technical progress does lead to an increase in industrial productivity there is no known case where this has led directly to the amelioration of the living conditions of the masses. It takes a hard, never-ending, social struggle to force the ruling class not to use for their own exclusive profit the new possibilities created by modern science. Thus the modernization of industry is most often translated into lay-offs for the workers. So between 1958 and 1968 techniques and industrial productivity increased prodigiously—but it took the great strike of May–June 1968 to enable all workers to obtain some improvement in their working conditions—improvements which immediately began to be trimmed down, little by little, by the bosses.

These doubts about the progressive function of science lead to some others about the motivations of the scientists. Certainly a greater and greater number of them are becoming aware of this situation and some come to these conclusions, but too often they take refuge in an ethic of knowledge for knowledge's sake, where science becomes its own goal (for example look at the inaugural lecture of J. Monod at the College de France). Here, without doubt, is the last resort of those who refuse to look at the facts in their face.

However, in fact, far from advancing the idea that science and research have no value I am convinced that they are very useful. Only they don't, at all, serve the purposes and groups they pretend to serve.

Scientific activity cannot, anymore than any other activity, be separated from the totality of the social system in which it is practised. As with the others it is principally oriented so as to insure the perpetuation or, at least, the survival of this system. The mechanisms by which it assumes this role are complex but one can, nevertheless, distinguish several types of relations.

First, on the *political* level, it is evident that the imperialist powers use the resources of modern technology to the utmost in order to obtain weapons destined to guarantee their power. Undoubtedly the most numerous and coherent applications of scientific research in the last few years have been in this military domain. But, despite the blackmail of atomic terror, the use and effectiveness of these applications remain limited. One need only look at the victorious resistance of the Vietnamese People to American aggression in order to persuade oneself that technology and science are not sufficient to guarantee military and political power. Furthermore, these military applications principally use some relatively old discoveries and not the fundamental scientific research of today which, above all, interests me here.

Next, on the *economic* level one knows the increasingly important role played by fundamental research in the budgets of the developed capitalist countries. Can one seriously believe that such important investments would be made if they had not some use? Since, as I have already indicated, these investments are not, in general, meant to lead to more or less technical applications it must be that they are, in themselves, a necessity of the system. In fact, one sees here yet another means which modern capitalism uses to try to cure its old crises of cyclical overproduction. Scientific production, not leading to mass consumption, can thus play a role as an economic regulator (equally true for the arms race, as well). The proof is given by the sudden budget restrictions on research in periods of recession: the faucet is closed after the bowl has overflowed and the level sinks! On the other hand, in a period of economic prosperity scientific research is a fabulous source of super-profits for certain industries, for example electronics. Thus these monopolies find a particularly discreet way to pocket public funds, that is to say funds which the state extorts from the mass of workers. But I pass rapidly over these economic aspects which it would be worthwhile to study more closely.

I now want to mention the crucial *ideological* role of science. One can advance the idea that after religion, followed by the classical humanities, it is today science which increasingly underlies and structures the forms of ideology imposed by the social class in power—that is, the bourgeoisie. Then is science used to give a mask of objectivity and technical expertise to the domination of this class; to capitalism; to exploitation? Oh no, we are only speaking to you about operations research, management, etc. The so-called scientific eminents take for themselves a mission of public relations for the system: Leprince-Ringuet comes on television full of worldly platitudes (but in his own laboratory he ferociously crushes the technician's strike) the Nobel Laureates Kaslet and Monod spread warnings of left intellectuals, never mentioning the technocratic agents of capitalism such as Louis Armand. Science serves to justify the whole apparatus of the social hierarchy by giving it its "objective" criteria. This hierarchy supposedly no longer reflects the class divisions of society but only the aptitudes and competencies of individuals. And indeed it is clever to replace Latin by modern mathematics as an instrument of social selection in secondary schools: the results are the same but the mechanism is, temporarily, a little less evident.

Finally, the last service rendered to this society by science is to direct the new circus games with which they attempt to amuse the crowd and to divert them from serious questions. How else can the race to the moon be explained; the robots which scoop up its dust, at a price of billions of dollars, which represent, in fact, the sweat and blood of billions of people to whom one throws this spectacle as fodder?

In the light of these remarks on the true role played by science, the scientist, the "scholar" appears as the agent of these mechanisms of enslavement. Whether or not he is conscious of the forces in whose services he works he is, in any event, necessarily complicit. In fact, all of the motivations referring to external use that I cited above: whether it's a matter of technical progress; or of the happiness of mankind; or even of the ethic of science for the sake of science, are all mere hypocrisy in the face of these facts. Actually, in research as in everything else it is the race for power which inspires scientists. Whether it's inside the scientific community itself, or on the scale of society in general, one always finds the ideology of elitism at work. Today a university scientific career is a very good starting place for certain government positions. And why not speak very vulgarly about the many material advantages that scientists derive from their profession: in addition to stable employment and a comfortable salary they add, in proportion to their position in the hierarchy, free trips to foreign countries (and even remuneration for them since the expenses of these trips are always overvalued), and sometimes considerable additional benefits such as contracts with industry, positions as scientific consultants and non-negligible prizes such as the one you gave me today. For what other reason did I put myself forward as a candidate for this prize?

And so I find the answers to the questions that I asked at the beginning. Why scientific prizes other than to reward those who have best carried out the role assigned to them by this society: to propagate and publicize the idea of a politically neutral and socially progressive science; to accept and amplify the ideology of elitism and expertise, and thus to aid the ruling class to mask the mechanism of exploitation and oppression on which this society is founded. And naturally, the more the researcher is "pure" and unconscious of this role, the better he plays it, whether the reward is in money, in individual prestige, in crumbs of power. But, as with every selection system, there are failures in the selection mechanism, and for once the money from a scientific prize will aid those who would construct a society without exploitation, without hierarchy, and without prizes.

Study Questions

1. What social classes are important in Marx's analysis of the capitalist mode of production? How did machines affect human labor?
2. Consider the symptoms of some common illness, such as pneumonia. What sort of an account would be given of those symptoms by a *demonologist* (or say a "witch doctor")? What sort of an account would be given by a (modern) physician? What sort of "cure" would each prescribe?
3. What would count as evidence against witchcraft? How would one go about proving the "guilt" of an alleged witch? Compare this with the case one would attempt to establish against an alleged rapist or murderer.
4. What would modern society probably be like had the authorities succeeded in suppressing the experiments in medical science?
5. Discuss the claim that although the selection problem, (i.e. the problem of "Whose life to save?") is a problem *for* medical men, it is a philosophical (i.e., ethical) problem. What makes it a philosophical problem, rather than a medical one?
6. First *defend,* and then *criticize* the introduction of a chance-factor in the selection process. Is this a psychological or a philosophical (or both) element? Why *must* the introduction of the element of chance be justified? Is there any alternative factor?
7. How convincing do you find the argument(s) that pollution results not from overpopulation and/or overconsumption, but from changes in technological methods of production? Does this oversimplify the problem of pollution?
8. Discuss the relation between advanced countries and under-

developed nations with respect to colonialism, as Commoner sees it. How feasible do you find his proposal that the advanced countries *ought* to strive to bring about a "sense of social security" among the peoples of underdeveloped nations? Discuss some of the difficulties such a goal would face.

9. What means, if any, are available for legislating against pollution? How effectual are existing means? Would a world-wide solution to the pollution crisis require the establishment of a Big Brother? Discuss the consequences with respect to each alternative.

10. Critically appraise Professor Levy-Leblond's claim that scientific research is primarily used to advance the interests of the ruling class.

11. How can we stabilize world population growth? Should we? Discuss what ethical problems are involved in any attempt at stabilizing world population growth.

12. What are the moral implications of reducing mortality in countries which cannot support increasing populations?

Part IV

THE SEARCH FOR FREEDOM: NATIONAL LIBERATION MOVEMENTS

Introduction

The search for freedom finds its most salient expression in national liberation movements. Prior to the Second World War, the bulk of the national movements was striving toward the eradication of colonial rule. However, subsequent to the Second World War, national liberation movements had assumed a new form. It is not just the end of colonial rule which constituted the bone of contention. Rather the liberation movements viewed their main task as a struggle against imperialism and neocolonialism. The choice of the noncapitalist path of development is quite a common feature among contemporary national liberation movements. The objective conditions of the oppressed people living under a capitalist system had compelled them to renounce such a system. The majority of these oppressed people do not benefit from their own resources. Hence their struggle is not simply for political independence, but also the search for a socialist system. Put differently, the underlying motivating factor among current national liberation movements is the burning desire to destroy the system which has produced colonialism, neocolonialism, racism. In its stead they propose to create a system in which man will achieve his full potentials, dignity, freedom, of relating productively to the world, of being capable of determining his own destiny. This is indeed what all national liberation movements are seeking.

The successful attempts of the Chinese, Algerian and Cuban wars of liberation, irrespective of their different circumstances, encouraged a series of national liberation movements. U.S. involvement and failure in Vietnam has further engendered hope among various national liberation movements in Asia, Africa and Latin America.

Che Guevara in his classic essay "Create Two, Three, Many Vietnams" emphasized the need for a concerted effort among all the oppressed people of the world to fight for their freedom by creating many Vietnams. Che quite explicitly identifies imperialism as the arch enemy of man's freedom. Hence he calls for the destruction of imperialism from the underdeveloped continents, mainly Africa, Asia and Latin America. Lin Piao's essay "Defeat U.S. Imperialism and Its Lackey's by People's War" reinforces Guevara's main point, i.e. that U.S. imperialism is the enemy of man's freedom. Hence both Piao and Guevara advocated guerrilla warfare in the attainment of one's specific objective which is primarily focused on the restoration of the rights of the people.

The current Palestinian Liberation movement is a clear example of what can happen to a group of people who have been subjected to the forces of colonialism and imperialism. For more than two decades the Palestinian Arabs have been waiting for a political settlement, but all efforts ended in vain. However, the June War of 1967 convinced the Palestinian Arabs that a revolutionary struggle was the sole alternative left to them. Accordingly, the Palestinian revolutionary movement has arisen from the conviction that only the Palestinians themselves could restore their rights. Hence what the Palestinian revolutionaries are seeking is parallel with what other liberation movements are striving for. They no longer wish to remain as a displaced people; they do not want to be treated as second-class citizens under Israeli occupation; they want to redress the wrongs inflicted upon them as a result of the occupation of Palestine (now Israel); above all they are fighting for the right of self-determination.

The Black struggle for liberation is another manifestation of oppressed people fighting colonialism, neocolonialism and white racism. In America the Black Panther Party, founded by Huey Newton in 1966, has been engaged in the struggle for liberation for the blacks in the U.S.A. Indeed the Black Panther Party, prior to the recent split between Newton and Cleaver, constituted one of the most effective Black movements for the struggle of liberation against white racism in U.S. Their ten point program clearly reflected their aspirations for freedom for the Blacks, an end to the Capitalist exploitation, adequate housing, equal opportunity for employment, etc.

In Black Africa the struggle for liberation is focused on (a) colonialism, (b) neocolonialism and (c) apartheid. Currently colonial oppression in Africa is primarily carried out by Portugal in the territories of Angola, Mozambique, Guinea and the Cape Verde Islands. Neocolonial exploitation is sustained in some African states by means of economic exploitation, the establishment of puppet regimes, military assistance, foreign advisers in charge of training special forces to combat revolutionary struggles. The struggle against apartheid is currently waged in South Africa, South West Africa and Zimbabwe (Rhodesia).

Nosipo Majeke, in his essay "Racism in South Africa," describes at length the racist practices of the white settler European minorities. Some of these apartheid policies, which are adversely affecting the nonwhite-indigenous population, involve the following: the black Africans have no voting rights, they are constantly relegated to segregated housing facilities, they are denied the right to perform any skilled work, they are forbidden from owning land that they desire, they cannot travel without permission from the authorities, they may be searched anywhere àt any time without a warrant, they can be deported at any time, they can be arrested without trial and confined to imprisonment without due process of the law, and they are not permitted to attend the leading universities.

In addition to the above, the inhuman practice of apartheid in South Africa had adversely affected the nonwhite population in the field of education, employment and health. For example, in employment the average per month paid in mining, manufacturing and electricity is as follows: whites, £123-1/2; coloreds, £27-1/2; Asians, £25; Africans, £17-1/2. (This is based on the report supplied by the South African Bureau of Statistics in the year 1967.) The enrollment at South African universities and colleges in 1967 was the following: whites, 66,569; coloreds, 1,530; Asians, 3,239; Africans, 3,836. (This is based on the report supplied by UNESCO in *Apartheid: Its Effects on Education, Science, Culture and Information.*)

In answer to the harsh policies of apartheid in South Africa, the Africans started to support the political organization known as *The African National Congress* (ANC). ANC tried at the outset to eradicate apartheid through peaceful, political negotiations. But when it became apparent to South Africans that the nonviolent struggle for liberation is not a viable option, they decided to resort to violence in their attempt to change the apartheid policies of South Africa. In addition to ANC, one also finds the *Pan Africanist Congress* (PAC)—an offshoot of ANC —engaged in conducting the struggle for liberation in South Africa.

Apartheid is also practiced in South West Africa and Zimbabwe (Rhodesia). The apartheid policies that are adversely affecting the non-white indigenous people of South Africa are equally affecting the non-white population of South West Africa and Zimbabwe. In South West Africa, two liberation movements are engaged in the struggle for liberation, the *South West African People's Organization* (SWAPO), and the *South West African National Union* (SWANU). In Zimbabwe, the *Zimbabwe African People's Union* (ZAPO) and the *Zimbabwe African National Union* (ZANU) are actively engaged in a struggle for liberation.

In his paper, "Anarchism and Third World Revolution," Stephen P. Halbrook points out that Bakuninist anarchism is the most radical form of the search for freedom; for it demands the total abolition of the state, that is, the centralized bureaucracy, military, police, big bourgeoisie, and other members of the power elite. These elements are viewed by doctrinaire anarchists, as antithetical to man's freedom. While all of Bakunin's contributions to the ideology of scientific anarchism are not covered in Halbrook's paper, still the Bakuninist principles on revolution in underdeveloped countries are set forth—particularly Bakunin's sociological analysis of the underlying forces which predestine peasant revolutions to be instinctively anarchistic in nature.

31. *Ernesto Che Guevara*

Create Two, Three, Many Vietnams

Twenty-one years have already elapsed since the end of the last world conflagration; numerous publications in every possible language celebrate this event, symbolized by the defeat of Japan. There is a climate of apparent optimism in many areas of the different camps into which the world is divided.

Twenty-one years without a world war, in these times of maximum confrontations, of violent clashes and sudden changes, appears to be a very high figure. However, without analyzing the practical results of this peace (poverty, degradation, increasing exploitation of enormous sectors of humanity) for which all of us have stated that we are willing to fight, we would do well to inquire if this peace is real.

It is not the purpose of these notes to detail the different conflicts of a local character that have been occurring since the surrender of Japan, neither do we intend to recount the numerous and increasing instances of civilian strife which have taken place during these years of apparent peace. It will be enough just to name, as an example against undue optimism, the wars of Korea and Viet Nam.

In the first of these, after years of savage warfare, the Northern part of the country was submerged in the most terrible devastation known in the annals of modern warfare: riddled with bombs; without factories, schools or hospitals; with absolutely no shelter for housing ten million inhabitants.

Under the discredited flag of the United Nations, dozens of countries under the military leadership of the United States participated in this war with the massive intervention of U.S. soldiers and the use, as cannon fodder, of the drafted South Korean population. On the other side, the army and the people of Korea and the volunteers from the People's Republic of China were furnished with supplies and technical aid by the Soviet military apparatus. The U.S. tested all sorts of weapons of destruction, excluding the thermonuclear type, but including, on a limited scale, bacteriological and chemical warfare.

In Viet Nam, the patriotic forces of that country have carried on an almost uninterrupted war against three imperialist powers: Japan, whose might suffered an almost vertical collapse after the bombs of Hiroshima and Nagasaki; France, that recovered from that defeated country its Indo-China colonies and ignored the promises it had made in harder times; and the United States, in this last phase of the struggle.

There have been limited confrontations in every continent although in Our America, for a long time, there were only incipient liberation struggles and military coups d'état until the Cuban Revolution sounded the alert, signaling the importance of this region. This action attracted the wrath of the imperialists and Cuba was finally obliged to defend its coasts, first in Playa Girón, and again during the October [Missile] Crisis.

This last incident could have unleashed a war of incalculable proportions if a US-Soviet clash had occurred over the Cuban question.

But, evidently, the focal point of all contradictions is at present the territory of the peninsula of Indo-China and the adjacent areas. Laos and Viet Nam are torn by civil wars which have ceased being such by the entry into the conflict of U.S. imperialism with all its might, thus transforming the whole zone into a dangerous powder keg ready at any moment to explode.

In Viet Nam the confrontation has assumed extremely acute characteristics. It is not our intention, either, to chronicle this war. We shall simply remember and point out some milestones.

In 1954, after the annihilating defeat of Dien Bien Phu, an agreement was signed at Geneva dividing the country into two separate zones; elections were to be held within a term of 18 months to determine who should govern Viet Nam and how the country should be reunified. The U.S. did not sign this document and started maneuvering to substitute the emperor, Bao Dai, who was a French puppet, for a man more amenable to its purposes. This happened to be Ngo Dien Diem, whose tragic end—that of an orange squeezed dry by imperialism—is well known by all.

During the months following the agreement, optimism reigned supreme in the camp of the popular forces. The last redoubts of the anti-French resistance were dismantled in the South of the country and they awaited the fulfillment of the Geneva Agreements. But the patriots soon realized there would be no elections—unless the United States felt itself capable of imposing its will in the polls, which was practically impossible even resorting to all its fraudulent methods. Once again fighting broke out in the South and gradually acquired full intensity. At present the U.S. invading army has increased to nearly half a million troops, while the puppet forces decrease in number and, above all, have totally lost their combativeness.

Almost two years ago the United States started systematically bombing the Democratic Republic of Viet Nam, in yet another attempt to overcome the resistance of the South and impose, from a position of strength, a meeting at the conference table. At first, the bombardments were more or less isolated occurrences and were represented as reprisals for alleged provocations from the North. Later on, as they increased in intensity and regularity, they became one gigantic attack carried out by the air force of the United States, day after day, for the purpose of destroying all vestiges of civilization in the Northern zones of the country. This is an episode of the infamously notorious "escalation."

The material aspirations of the Yankee world have been fulfilled to a great extent, despite the unflinching defense of the Vietnamese anti-aircraft artillery, of the numerous planes shot down (over 1,700) and of the socialist countries' aid in war supplies.

This is the sad reality: Viet Nam—a nation representing the aspirations, the hopes of a whole world of forgotten peoples—is tragically alone. This nation must endure the furious attacks of U.S. technology, with practically no possibility of reprisals in the South and only some of defense in the North—but always alone.

The solidarity of all progressive forces of the world with the people of Viet Nam today is similar to the bitter irony of the plebeians urging on the gladiators in the Roman arena. It is not a matter of wishing success to the victim of aggression, but of sharing his fate; one must accompany him to his death or to victory.

When we analyze the lonely situation of the Vietnamese people, we are overcome by anguish at this illogical fix in which humanity finds itself.

U.S. imperialism is guilty of aggression—its crimes are enormous and cover the whole world. We already know all that, gentlemen! But this guilt also applies to those who, when the time came for a definition, hesitated to make Viet Nam an inviolable part of the socialist world; running, of course, the risks of a war on a global scale—but also forcing a decision upon imperialism. The guilt also applies to those who maintain a war of abuse and maneuvering—started quite some time ago by the representatives of the two greatest powers of the socialist camp.

We must ask ourselves, seeking an honest answer: is Viet Nam isolated, or is it not? Is it not maintaining a dangerous equilibrium between the two quarrelling powers?

And what great people these are! What stoicism and courage! And what a lesson for the world is contained in this struggle! Not for a long time shall we be able to know if President Johnson ever seriously thought of bringing about some of the reforms needed by his people—to iron out the barbed class contradictions that grow each day with explosive power. The truth is that the improvements announced under the pompous title of the "Great Society" have been poured down the drain of Viet Nam.

The largest of all imperialist powers feels in its own guts the bleeding inflicted by a poor and underdeveloped country; its fabulous economy feels the strain of the war effort. Murder is ceasing to be the most convenient business for its monopolies. Defensive weapons, and never in adequate number, is all these extraordinary Vietnamese soldiers have—besides love for their homeland, their society, and unsurpassed courage. But imperialism is bogging down in Viet Nam, is unable to find a way out and desperately seeks one that will overcome with dignity this dangerous situation in which it now finds itself. Furthermore, the Four Points put forward by the North and the Five Points of the South now corner imperialism, making the confrontation even more decisive.

Everything indicates that peace, this unstable peace which bears the name for the sole reason that no world-wide conflagration has taken place, is again in danger of being destroyed by some irrevocable and unacceptable step taken by the United States.

What role shall we, the exploited people of the world, play? The peoples of the three continents focus their attention on Viet Nam and learn their lesson. Since imperialists blackmail humanity by threatening it with war, the wise reaction is not to fear war. The general tactics of the people should be to launch a constant and a firm attack on all fronts where the confrontation is taking place.

In those places where the meager peace we have has been violated, what is our duty? To liberate ourselves at any price.

The world panorama is of great complexity. The struggle for liberation has not yet been undertaken by some countries of ancient Europe, sufficiently developed to realize the contradictions of capitalism, but weak to such a degree that they are unable either to follow imperialism or to start on their own road. Their contradictions will reach an explosive stage during the forthcoming years—but their problems and, consequently, their solutions are different from those of our dependent and economically underdeveloped countries.

The fundamental field of imperialist exploitation comprises the three underdeveloped continents: America, Asia, and Africa. Every country has also its own characteristics, but each continent, as a whole, also presents a certain unity. Our America is integrated by a group of more or less homogeneous countries and in most parts of its territory

U.S. monopoly capital maintains an absolute supremacy. Puppet government or, in the best of cases, weak and fearful local rulers, are incapable of contradicting orders from their Yankee master. The United States has nearly reached the climax of its political and economic domination; it could hardly advance much; any change in the situation could bring about a setback. Its policy is to maintain that which has already been conquered. The line of action, at the present time, is limited to the brutal use of force with the purpose of thwarting the liberation movements, no matter of what type they might happen to be.

The slogan "we will not allow another Cuba" hides the possibility of perpetrating aggressions without fear of reprisal, such as the one carried out against the Dominican Republic, or before that, the massacre in Panama—and the clear warning stating that Yankee troops are ready to intervene anywhere in America where the established order may be altered, thus endangering their interests. This policy enjoys an almost absolute impunity: the OAS is a suitable mask, in spite of its unpopularity; the inefficiency of the UN is ridiculous as well as tragic; the armies of all American countries are ready to intervene in order to smash their peoples. The International of Crime and Treason has in fact been organized. On the other hand, the national bourgeoisies have lost all their capacity to oppose imperialism—if they ever had it—and they have become the last card in the pack. There are no other alternatives; either a socialist revolution or a make-believe revolution.

Asia is a continent with different characteristics. The struggle for liberation waged against a series of European colonial powers resulted in the establishment of more or less progressive governments, whose ulterior evolution has brought about, in some cases, the reaffirming of the primary objectives of national liberation and in others, a setback towards the adoption of proimperialist positions.

From the economic point of view, the United States had very little to lose and much to gain in Asia. These changes benefited their interests; the struggle for the overthrow of other neocolonial powers and the penetration of new spheres of action in the economic field is carried out sometimes directly, occasionally through Japan.

But there are special political conditions, in Asia, particularly in Indo-China, which create certain characteristics of capital importance and play a decisive role in the entire U.S. military strategy.

The imperialists encircle China through South Korea, Japan, Taiwan, South Viet Nam, and Thailand, at least.

This dual situation, a strategic interest as important as the military encirclement of the People's Republic of China and the penetration of these great markets—which they do not dominate yet—turns Asia into one of the most explosive points of the world today, in spite of its apparent stability outside of the Vietnamese war zone.

The Middle East, though geographically a part of this continent, has its own contradictions and is actively in ferment; it is impossible to foretell how far the cold war between Israel, backed by the imperialists, and the progressive countries of that zone will go. This is just another of the volcanoes threatening eruption in the world today.

Africa offers an almost virgin territory to the neocolonial invasion. There have been changes which, to some extent, forced neocolonial powers to give up their former absolute prerogatives. But when these changes are carried out without interruption, colonialism continues in the form of neocolonialism with similar effects as far as the economic situation is concerned.

The United States had no colonies in this region but is now struggling to penetrate its partners' fiefs. It can be said that following the strategic plans of U.S. imperialism, Africa constitutes its long-range reservoir; its present investments, though, are only important in the Union of South Africa and its penetration is beginning to be felt in the Congo, Nigeria and other countries where a sharp rivalry with other imperialist powers is beginning to take place (non-violent up to the present time).

So far, it does not have great interests to defend there except its assumed right to intervene in every spot of the world where its monopolies detect the possibility of huge profits or the existence of large reserves of raw materials.

All this past history justifies our concern over the possibilities of liberating the peoples within a moderate or a short period of time.

If we stop to analyze Africa we observe that in the Portuguese colonies of Guinea, Mozambique, and Angola the struggle is waged with relative intensity, with particular success in the first and with variable success in the other two. We still witness in the Congo the dispute between Lumumba's successors and the old accomplices of Tshombe, a dispute which at the present time seems to favor the latter, those who "pacified" a large area of the country for their own benefit—though the war is still latent.

In Rhodesia we have a different problem: British imperialism used every means within its reach to place power in the hands of the white minority, now in control. The conflict, from the British point of view, is absolutely unofficial; this Western power, with its habitual diplomatic cleverness—also called hypocrisy in plain language—presents a facade of displeasure before the measures adopted by the government of Ian Smith. Its crafty attitude is supported and followed by some Commonwealth countries, but is attacked by a large group of countries belonging to Black Africa, even by some that are still docile economic vassals of British imperialism.

Should the efforts of Rhodesia's black patriots to organize armed rebellion crystallize and should this movement be effectively supported by neighboring African nations, the situation in that country could become extremely explosive. But for the moment all these problems are being discussed in such innocuous organizations as the UN, the Commonwealth and the OAU.

Nevertheless, the social and political evolution of Africa does not lead us to expect a continental revolution. The liberation struggle against the Portuguese should end victoriously, but Portugal means nothing in the imperialist field. The confrontations of revolutionary importance are those which place at bay all the imperialist apparatus, though this does not mean that we should stop fighting for the liberation of the three Portuguese colonies and for the deepening of their revolutions.

When the black masses of South Africa or Rhodesia start their authentic revolutionary struggle, a new era will dawn in Africa. Or when the impoverished masses of a nation rise up to rescue their right to a decent life from the hands of the ruling oligarchies.

Up to now, army putsches have followed one another; a group of officers succeeds one another or replaces rulers who no longer serve their caste interests and those of the powers who covertly manage them —but there are no great popular upheavals. In the Congo these characteristics appeared briefly, generated by the memory of Lumumba, but they have been losing strength in the last few months.

In Asia, as we have seen, the situation is explosive. The points of friction are not only Viet Nam and Laos, where actual fighting is going on, but also Cambodia, where a direct U.S. aggression may start at any time, Thailand, Malaya, and, of course, Indonesia, where we cannot assume that the last word has been said, despite the annihilation of the Communist Party of that country carried out by the reactionaries when they took power. And also, naturally, there is the Middle East.

In Latin America armed struggle is underway in Guatemala, Colombia, Venezuela, and Bolivia and the first uprisings are appearing in Brazil. Other foci of resistance appear and are later extinguished. But almost every country of this continent is ripe for a type of struggle that, in order to achieve victory, cannot be content with anything less than establishing a government of a socialist nature.

On this continent, for all practical purposes, only one tongue is spoken (with the exception of Brazil, with whose people those who speak Spanish can easily make themselves understood, owing to the great similarity of both languages). There is also a great similarity among the classes of the different countries, and an identification exists among them, as an "international American" type, much more complete than that of other continents. Language, customs, religion, a common foreign master, unite them. The degree and forms of exploitation are similar for both the exploiters and the exploited in many of the countries of Our America. And rebellion is ripening swiftly.

We may ask ourselves: how will this rebellion come to fruition? What type will it be? We have maintained for quite some time now that, owing to the similarity of national characteristics, the struggle in Our America will achieve, in due course, continental proportions. It will be the scene of many great battles fought for the liberation of humanity.

Within the overall struggle on a continental scale, the battles which are now taking place are only episodes—but they have already furnished their martyrs, who will figure in the history of Our America as having given their necessary quota of blood in this last stage of the fight for the total freedom of Man. These names will include Major Turcios Lima, the priest Camilo Torres, Major Fabricio Ojeda, Majors Lobatón and Luis de la Puente Uceda, all outstanding figures in the revolutionary movements of Guatemala, Colombia, Venezuela, and Peru.

But the active mobilization of the people creates new leaders; César Montes and Yon Sosa raise the flag of battle in Guatemala; Fabio Vázquez and Marulanda in Colombia; Douglas Bravo in the western half of the country and Américo Martín in El Bachiller direct their respective fronts in Venezuela. New uprisings will take place in these and other countries of Our America, as has already happened in Bolivia; they will continue to grow in the midst of all the hardships inherent in this dangerous profession of the modern revolutionary. Many will perish, victims of their errors; others will fall in the hard battle ahead; new fighters and new leaders will appear in the heat of the revolutionary struggle. The people will produce their fighters and leaders in the selective process of the war itself—and Yankee agents of repression will increase. Today there are military "advisers" in all the countries where armed struggle exists, and the Peruvian army, trained and advised by the Yankees, apparently carried out a successful action against the revolutionaries in that country. But if the foci of war grow with sufficient political and military wisdom, they will become practically invincible, obliging the Yankees to send reinforcements. In Peru itself many new figures, practically unknown, are now tenaciously and firmly reorganizing the guerrilla movement. Little by little, the obsolete weapons which are sufficient for the repression of small armed bands will be exchanged

for modern armaments and the U.S. military "advisers" will be substituted by U.S. soldiers until, at a given moment, they will be forced
to send increasingly greater numbers of regular troops to ensure the
relative stability of a government whose national puppet army is disin-
tegrating before the attacks of the guerrillas. It is the road of Viet Nam;
it is the road that should be followed by the peoples of the world; it is
the road that will be followed in Our America, with the special characteristic that the armed groups may create something like Coordinating
Councils to frustrate the repressive efforts of Yankee imperialism and
contribute to the revolutionary cause.

America, a forgotten continent in the world's more recent libera-
tion struggles, which is now beginning to make itself heard through the
Tricontinental in the voice of the vanguard of its peoples, the Cuban
Revolution, has before it a task of much greater relevance: to create a
Second or a Third Viet Nam, or the Second and Third Viet Nam of the
world.

We must bear in mind that imperialism is a world system, the last
stage of capitalism—and it must be defeated in a great world confrontation. The strategic end of this struggle must be the destruction of imperialism. Our part, the responsibility of the exploited and
underdeveloped of the world, is to eliminate the foundations of imperialism: our oppressed nations, from which they extract capital, raw
materials, cheap technicians and common labor, and to which they
export new capital—instrument of domination—arms and every kind of
article, submerging us in absolute dependence.

The fundamental element of this strategic end is, then, the real
liberation of all peoples, a liberation that will be brought about in most
cases through armed struggle and will, in Our America, almost certainly
have the characteristic of becoming a Socialist Revolution.

In envisaging the destruction of imperialism, it is necessary to identify its head, which is no other than the United States of America.

We must carry out a general task which has as its tactical purpose
drawing the enemy out of his natural environment, forcing him to fight
in places where his living habits clash with the existing reality. We must
not underrate our adversary; the U.S. soldier has technical capacity and
is backed by weapons and resources of such magnitude as to render him
formidable. He lacks the essential ideological motivation which his bit-
terest enemies of today—the Vietnamese soldiers—have in the highest
degree. We will only be able to triumph over such an army by undermining its morale—and that is accomplished by causing it repeated
defeats and repeated punishment.

But this brief scheme for victory implies immense sacrifice by the people, sacrifice that should be demanded beginning today, in plain words, and which perhaps may be less painful than what they would have to endure if we constantly avoided battle in an attempt to have others pull our chestnuts out of the fire.

It is probable, of course, that the last country to liberate itself will accomplish this without armed struggle and that people may be spared the sufferings of a long and cruel war against the imperialists. But perhaps it will be impossible to avoid this struggle or its effects in a global conflagration and the last country's suffering may be the same, or even greater. We cannot foresee the future, but we should never give in to the defeatist temptation of being leaders of a nation that yearns for freedom but abhors the struggle it entails and awaits its freedom as a crumb of victory.

It is absolutely just to avoid all useless sacrifice. For that reason, it is necessary to study carefully the real possibilities that dependent America may have of liberating itself through peaceful means. For us, the answer to this question is quite clear: the present moment may or may not be the proper one for starting the struggle, but we cannot harbor any illusion, and we have no right to do so, that freedom can be obtained without fighting. And the battles will not be mere street fights with stones against teargas bombs, nor pacific general strikes; neither will they be those of a furious people destroying in two or three days the repressive superstructure of the ruling oligarchies. The struggle will be long, harsh, and its battle fronts will be the guerrilla's refuge, the cities, the homes of the fighters—where the repressive forces will go seeking easy victims among their families—among the massacred rural population, in the villages or cities destroyed by the bombardments of the enemy.

They themselves impel us to this struggle; there is no alternative other than to prepare it and decide to undertake it.

The beginnings will not be easy; they will be extremely difficult. All of the oligarchies' powers of repression, all of their capacity for brutality and demagoguery will be placed at the service of their cause. Our mission, in the first hour, will be to survive; later, we will follow the perennial example of the guerrilla, carrying out armed propaganda (in the Vietnamese sense, that is, the propaganda of bullets, of battles won or lost—but fought—against the enemy). The great lesson of the invincibility of the guerrillas will take root in the dispossessed masses. The galvanizing of the national spirit, preparation for harder tasks, for resisting even more violent repressions. Hatred as an element of struggle; relentless hatred of the enemy that impels us over and beyond the natural limitations of man and transforms us into effective, violent selective and cold killing machines. Our soldiers must be thus; a people without hatred cannot vanquish a brutal enemy. We must carry the war as far as the enemy carries it—to his home, to his centers of entertainment—in a total war. It is necessary to prevent him from having a moment of peace, a quiet moment outside his barracks or even inside; we must attack him wherever he may be, make him feel like a cornered beast wherever he may move. Then his morale will begin to fall. He will become still more savage, but we shall see the signs of decadence begin to appear.

And let us develop a true proletarian internationalism, with international proletarian armies; let the flag under which we fight be the sacred cause of redeeming humanity, so that to die under the flag of Viet Nam, of Venezuela, of Guatemala, of Laos, of Guinea, of Colombia, of Bolivia, of Brazil—to name only a few scenes of today's armed struggle—would be equally glorious and desirable for an American, an Asian, an African, or even a European.

Each drop of blood spilled in a country under whose flag one has been born is an experience for those who survive to apply later in the liberation struggle of their own countries. And each nation liberated is a step toward victory in the battle for the liberation of one's own country.

The time has come to settle our discrepancies and place everything we have at the service of the struggle.

We all know that great controversies agitate the world now fighting for freedom; no one can hide it. We also know that these controversies have reached such intensity and such bitterness that the possibility of dialogue and reconciliation seems extremely difficult, if not impossible. It is useless to search for means and ways to propitiate a dialogue which the hostile parties avoid. But the enemy is there; it strikes every day, and threatens us with new blows and these blows will unite us, today, tomorrow, or the day after. Whoever understands this first, and prepares for this necessary union will earn the people's gratitude.

Because of the virulence and the intransigence with which each cause is defended, we, the dispossessed, cannot take sides with one or the other form of manifestation of these discrepancies, even if we at times coincide with the contentions of one party or the other, or in greater measure with those of one part than with those of the other. In time of war, the expression of current differences constitutes a weakness; but as things stand at this moment, it is an illusion to hope to settle these differences by means of words. Time will erase them or give them their true explanation.

In our struggling world, all discrepancies regarding tactics and methods of action for the attainment of limited objectives should be analyzed with the respect that the opinions of others deserve. Regarding our great strategic objective, the total destruction of imperialism via armed struggle, we should be uncompromising.

Our aspirations to victory may be summed up thus: total destruction of imperialism by eliminating its firmest bulwark: imperialist domination by the United States of America. To carry out, as a tactical method, the gradual liberation of the peoples, one by one or in groups forcing the enemy into a difficult fight far from its own territory; liquidation of all of its sustaining bases, that is, its dependent territories.

This means a long war. And, we repeat once more, a cruel war. Let no one fool himself at the outstart and let no one hesitate to begin in fear of the consequences it may bring to his peoples. It is almost our sole hope for victory. We cannot elude the call of this hour. Viet Nam is pointing it out with its endless lesson of heroism, its tragic and everyday lesson of struggle and death for the attainment of final victory.

There, the imperialist soldiers encounter the discomforts of those who, accustomed to the vaunted U.S. standard of living, must face a hostile land, the insecurity of those who are unable to move without being aware of walking on enemy territory, death to those who advance beyond their fortified encampments, the permanent hostility of an entire population. All this provokes internal repercussions in the United States and propitiates the resurgence of a factor which was attenuated in the full vigor of imperialism: class struggle even within its own territory.

What a luminous, near future would be visible to us if two, three or many Viet Nams flourished throughout the world with their share of death and their immense tragedies, their everyday heroism and their repeated blows against imperialism obliging it to disperse its forces under the attack and the increasing hatred of all the people of the earth!

And if we were all capable of uniting to make our blows more solid and more infallible so that the effectiveness of every kind of support given to the struggling peoples were increased—how great and how near that future would be!

If we, those of us who, on a small point of the world map, fulfill our duty and place at the disposal of this struggle whatever little we are able to give: our lives, our sacrifice, must some day breathe our last breath in any land, not our own yet already ours, sprinkled with our blood, let it be known that we have measured the scope of our actions and that we consider ourselves no more than elements in the great army of the proletariat, but that we are proud to have learned from the Cuban Revolution, and from its maximum leader, the great lesson emanating from Cuba's attitude in this part of the world: "What do the dangers or the sacrifices of a man or a nation matter, when the destiny of humanity is at stake?"

Our every action is a battle cry against imperialism, and a call for the peoples' unity against the great enemy of mankind: the United States of America. Wherever death may surprise us, it will be welcome, provided that this, our battle cry, reach some receptive ear, that another hand be extended to take up our weapons and that other men come forward to intone our funeral dirge with the staccato of machine guns and new cries of battle and victory.

Defeat U.S. Imperialism and Its Lackeys
by People's War

Since World War II, U.S. imperialism has stepped into the shoes of German, Japanese and Italian fascism and has been trying to build a great American empire by dominating and enslaving the whole world. It is actively fostering Japanese and West German militarism as its chief accomplices in unleashing a world war. Like a vicious wolf, it is bullying and enslaving various peoples, plundering their wealth, encroaching upon their countries' sovereignty and interfering in their internal affairs. It is the most rabid aggressor in human history and the most ferocious common enemy of the people of the world. Every people or country in the world that wants revolution, independence and peace cannot but direct the spearhead of its struggle against U.S. imperialism.

Just as the Japanese imperialists' policy of subjugating China made it possible for the Chinese people to form the broadest possible united front against them, so the U.S. imperialists' policy of seeking world domination makes it possible for the people throughout the world to unite all the forces that can be united and form the broadest possible united front for a converging attack on U.S. imperialism.

At present, the main battlefield of the fierce struggle between the people of the world on the one side and U.S. imperialism and its lackeys on the other is the vast area of Asia, Africa and Latin America. In the world as a whole, this is the area where the people suffer worst from imperialist oppression and where imperialist rule is most vulnerable. Since World War II, revolutionary storms have been rising in this area, and today they have become the most important force directly pounding U.S. imperialism. The contradiction between the revolutionary peoples of Asia, Africa and Latin America and the imperialists headed by the United States is the principal contradiction in the contemporary world. The development of this contradiction is promoting the struggle of the people of the whole world against U.S. imperialism and its lackeys.

308

Since World War II, people's war has increasingly demonstrated its power in Asia, Africa and Latin America. The peoples of China, Korea, Viet Nam, Laos, Cuba, Indonesia, Algeria and other countries have waged people's wars against the imperialists and their lackeys and won great victories. The classes leading these people's wars may vary, and so may the breadth and depth of mass mobilization and the extent of victory, but the victories in these people's wars have very much weakened and pinned down the forces of imperialism, upset the U.S. imperialist plan to launch a world war, and become mighty factors defending world peace.

Today, the conditions are more favourable than ever before for the waging of people's wars by the revolutionary peoples of Asia, Africa and Latin America against U.S. imperialism and its lackeys.

Since World War II and the succeeding years of revolutionary upsurge, there has been a great rise in the level of political consciousness and the degree of organization of the people in all countries, and the resources available to them for mutual support and aid have greatly increased. The whole capitalist-imperialist system has become drastically weaker and is in the process of increasing convulsion and disintegration. After World War I, the imperialists lacked the power to destroy the new-born socialist Soviet state, but they were still able to suppress the people's revolutionary movements in some countries in the parts of the world under their own rule and so maintain a short period of comparative stability. Since World War II, however, not only have they been unable to stop a number of countries from taking the socialist road, but they are no longer capable of holding back the surging tide of the people's revolutionary movements in the areas under their own rule.

U.S. imperialism is stronger, but also more vulnerable, than any imperialism of the past. It sets itself against the people of the whole world, including the people of the United States. Its human, military, material and financial resources are far from sufficient for the realization of its ambition of dominating the whole world. U.S. imperialism has further weakened itself by occupying so many places in the world, over-reaching itself, stretching its fingers out wide and dispersing its strength, with its rear so far away and its supply lines so long. As Comrade Mao Tse-tung has said, "Wherever it commits aggression, it puts a new noose around its neck. It is besieged ring upon ring by the people of the whole world."[1]

When committing aggression in a foreign country, U.S. imperialism

1. The Statement of Chairman Mao Tse-tung in Support of the People of the Congo (Leopoldville) Against U.S. Aggression, November 28, 1964.

can only employ part of its forces, which are sent to fight an unjust war far from their native land and therefore have a low morale, and so U.S. imperialism is beset with great difficulties. The people subjected to its aggression are having a trial of strength with U.S. imperialism neither in Washington nor New York, neither in Honolulu nor Florida, but are fighting for independence and freedom on their own soil. Once they are mobilized on a broad scale, they will have inexhaustible strength. Thus superiority will belong not to the United States but to the people subjected to its aggression. The latter, though apparently weak and small, are really more powerful than U.S. imperialism.

The struggles waged by the different peoples against U.S. imperialism reinforce each other and merge into a torrential world-wide tide of opposition to U.S. imperialism. The more successful the development of people's war in a given region, the larger the number of U.S. imperialist forces that can be pinned down and depleted there. When the U.S. aggressors are hard pressed in one place, they have no alternative but to loosen their grip on others. Therefore, the conditions become more favourable for the people elsewhere to wage struggles against U.S. imperialism and its lackeys.

Everything is divisible. And so is this colossus of U.S. imperialism. It can be split up and defeated. The peoples of Asia, Africa, Latin America and other regions can destroy it piece by piece, some striking at its head and others at its feet. That is why the greatest fear of U.S. imperialism is that people's wars will be launched in different parts of the world, and particularly in Asia, Africa and Latin America, and why it regards people's war as a mortal danger.

U.S. imperialism relies solely on its nuclear weapons to intimidate people. But these weapons cannot save U.S. imperialism from its doom. Nuclear weapons cannot be used lightly. U.S. imperialism has been condemned by the people of the whole world for its towering crime of dropping two atom bombs on Japan. If it uses nuclear weapons again, it will become isolated in the extreme. Moreover, the U.S. monopoly of nuclear weapons has long been broken; U.S. imperialism has these weapons, but others have them too. If it threatens other countries with nuclear weapons, U.S. imperialism will expose its own country to the same threat. For this reason, it will meet with strong opposition not only from the people elsewhere but also inevitably from the people in its own country. Even if U.S. imperialism brazenly uses nuclear weapons, it cannot conquer the people, who are indomitable.

However highly developed modern weapons and technical equipment may be and however complicated the methods of modern warfare, in the final analysis the outcome of a war will be decided by the sustained fighting of the ground forces, by the fighting at close quarters on battlefields, by the political consciousness of the men, by their courage and spirit of sacrifice. Here the weak points of U.S. imperialism will be completely laid bare, while the superiority of the revolutionary people will be brought into full play. The reactionary troops of U.S. imperialism cannot possibly be endowed with the courage and the spirit of sacrifice possessed by the revolutionary people. The spiritual atom bomb which the revolutionary people possess is a far more powerful and useful weapon than the physical atom bomb.

Viet Nam is the most convincing current example of a victim of aggression defeating U.S. imperialism by a people's war. The United States has made South Viet Nam a testing ground for the suppression of people's war. It has carried on this experiment for many years, and everybody can now see that the U.S. aggressors are unable to find a way of coping with people's war. On the other hand, the Vietnamese people have brought the power of people's war into full play in their struggle against the U.S. aggressors. The U.S. aggressors are in danger of being swamped in the people's war in Viet Nam. They are deeply worried that their defeat in Viet Nam will lead to a chain reaction. They are expanding the war in an attempt to save themselves from defeat. But the more they expand the war, the greater will be the chain reaction. The more they escalate the war, the heavier will be their fall and the more disastrous their defeat. The people in other parts of the world will see still more clearly that U.S. imperialism can be defeated, and that what the Vietnamese people can do, they can do too.

History has proved and will go on proving that people's war is the most effective weapon against U.S. imperialism and its lackeys. All revolutionary people will learn to wage people's war against U.S. imperialism and its lackeys. They will take up arms, learn to fight battles and become skilled in waging people's war, though they have not done so before. U.S. imperialism like a mad bull dashing from place to place, will finally be burned to ashes in the blazing fires of the people's wars it has provoked by its own actions.

The Palestinian Revolution and World Liberation Movements

World Liberation Movements acquire common political and military characteristics linked to the nature of relations between the political and military forces that control our World. It is clear that the growth of Liberation Movements after the Second World War was related to the political and military polarization which divided the World into two blocs. The first bloc consists of the Western Capitalist Camp led by the United States, which tried after its victory to inherit the Colonialist heritage of the crumbling European Empires. The second bloc included the Socialist States led by the Soviet Union.

The growth of contradictions between Colonialist European powers led to the outbreak of the Second World War. It is obvious that the breakdown of the military and economic structure of the Colonialist powers as a result of the War; the growth of the Nationalist current in Asia, Africa and Latin America; the increase of political awareness among the colonized masses; and the emergence of objective political and economic conditions for challenging the Colonialist rule gave birth to many National Liberation Movements. Their growth, in quantity and quality, led to a third bloc outside the domination of the two Western and Eastern blocs.

We are not concerned here with defining the characteristics of the National Liberation Movements, rather we are concerned with them as a new political current that has gained international strength after World War II.

Most of the States known today as the Third World were subjected to a long colonialist oppression which ravished their wealth and destroyed their human and economic resources. Meanwhile the European and American Continents flourished on this ruin. The Third World States realized that their political development and economic growth were tied to their ability to liberate themselves from colonialism. These States, therefore, resorted to political and military struggle; i.e. the war of National Liberation which is dependent on mobilizing all the energies of the masses and directing them to fight the enemy. Thus the human quantity of the masses makes up for their technological backwardness and the military superiority of the enemy.

The Palestinian Revolution has declared repeatedly that it is part of the World Liberation Movements, and that it is opposing the most vicious form of Imperialist aggression in Asia since the Middle of the 19th Century. An objective and scientific study of the characteristics of the Palestinian Revolution, and an objective analysis of the nature of relations that govern the struggle affirm the following facts:

1. The Palestinian Revolution is considered one of the forces of the World National Liberation Movement. It is a vanguard of these forces because of its direct confrontation with Zionist Imperialist base in the Arab World, and its opposition to the Imperialist American aggression in the Arab East.

2. The Palestinian Revolution affirms the existence of basic contradictions between the rights of nations to freedom and life and the Imperialist desire for controlling the sources of wealth in the World.

3. The Arab Palestinian People are subjected to a barbarous and savage Colonialism of the worst kind. Zionism exploited Jewish religious thought, nationalist Fascist European Movements, Imperialist Western hostility to the Arab Liberation Movement, and made itself a Colonialist Ideology which justifies the annihilation of a people and their expulsion from their homeland. There is no doubt that Zionist Colonialism in Palestine is worse than the racist European Colonialism in South Africa and Rhodesia. The Racist Europeans do not expell the Africans from their lands, rather they practice against them a policy of isolation and oppression, hence human and economic exploitation. Israel, however, expels the Arabs of the occupied territories. Thus we can compare its Colonialism to that of the European Colonialism in the American Continent who annihilated its indigenous Indian population.

4. The Palestinian Revolution is the revolution of the masses which expresses the national aspirations of the Palestinian Arab People and their rights to freedom in their land. The instruments of the revolution are the struggling vanguard forces of the people.

5. The Palestinian Revolution is a National Liberation Movement linked to the World Liberation Movements by ties of common struggle against Imperialism. It directly opposes the guardian of Imperialist interests in the Middle East, the Zionist State.

6. The Palestinian Revolution is organically linked to the Arab Liberation Movement, for it expresses the refusal of the Arab Na-

tion to submit to any and all forms of oppression, Imperialism, and dependency.

The Palestinian Revolution has become a political and military reality in the Arab region. Through armed struggle it affirms its unity with the World National Liberation struggles. At the same time it plays its unique role which distinguishes it from other liberation struggles in the World. It stands at the gateway of Asia and Africa defending these continents against the Imperialist Invasion which is carried on by the Zionist State.

The Palestinian Revolution is a natural ally to all Movements opposing Imperialism in our age, and it interacts with all revolutionary movements in the World. It enriches its struggle by the revolutionary experiences of oppressed peoples who fight to liberate their lands and achieve freedom. At the same time, it is required to present new means for revolutionary struggle that is related to the unique conditions and political and military requirements of its own experiences. In doing so, however, it is not isolating itself from revolutionary currents in the World.

The analysis of the factors involved in the Middle East struggle reveals the existence of an American-Zionist alliance which is directed against the Arab Nation. It aims at keeping the Arab region under Imperialist control and at destroying the will of the Palestinian People and their struggle for their national and political rights. This alliance is based on the common interests of the Zionist Movement and American Imperialism. Since these interests are controlled by economic and military considerations, this alliance cannot be considered a temporary one which will end with the disappearance of the common interests between the United States and Israel. Rather it is a strategic alliance which rests on the existence of an organic link between the expansionist exploitative nature of the Zionist State and the Imperialist interests in the Arab World. The problem is not one of Jewish American vote and its influence on American Presidential elections. The relation is a symbiotic one, for the Zionist State acts as a policeman guarding the Imperialist interests in the Middle East which are threatened by any National Liberation Movement.

The Palestinian Revolution forms a direct threat against the Zionist presence in occupied Palestine, and at the same time it is a blow directed against Imperialist interests in the Arab region. Thus it is in alliance with the Arab Liberation Movement and the World Liberation Movement. The Palestinian People today are conducting a long war of national liberation, and they have the support of all nations struggling for their freedom.

What We Want,
What We Believe

1. We want freedom. We want power to determine the destiny of our Black Community.

We believe that black people will not be free until we are able to determine our destiny.

2. We want full employment for our people.

We believe that the federal government is responsible and obligated to give every man employment or a guaranteed income. We believe that if the white American businessmen will not give full employment, then the means of production should be taken from the businessmen and placed in the community so that the people of the community can organize and employ all of its people and give a high standard of living.

3. We want an end to the robbery by the CAPITALIST of our Black Community.

We believe that this racist government has robbed us and now we are demanding the overdue debt of forty acres and two mules. Forty acres and two mules was promised 100 years ago as restitution for slave labor and mass murder of black people. We will accept the payment in currency which will be distributed to our many communities. The Germans are now aiding the Jews in Israel for the genocide of the Jewish people. The Germans murdered six million Jews. The American racist has taken part in the slaughter of over fifty million black people; therefore, we feel that this is a modest demand that we make.

4. We want decent housing, fit for shelter of human beings.

We believe that if the white landlords will not give decent housing to our black community, then the housing and the land should be made into cooperatives so that our community, with government aid, can build and make decent housing for its people.

5. We want education for our people that exposes the true nature of this

315

decadent American society. **We want education that teaches us our true history and our role in the present-day society.**

We believe in an educational system that will give to our people a knowledge of self. If a man does not have knowledge of himself and his position in society and the world, then he has little chance to relate to anything else.

6. We want all black men to be exempt from military service.

We believe that Black people should not be forced to fight in the military service to defend a racist government that does not protect us. We will not fight and kill other people of color in the world who, like black people, are being victimized by the white racist government of America. We will protect ourselves from the force and violence of the racist police and the racist military, by whatever means necessary.

7. We want an immediate end to POLICE BRUTALITY and MURDER of black people.

We believe we can end police brutality in our black community by organizing black self-defense groups that are dedicated to defending our black community from racist police oppression and brutality. The Second Amendment to the Constitution of the United States gives a right to bear arms. We therefore believe that all black people should arm themselves for self-defense.

8. We want freedom for all black men held in federal, state, county and city prisons and jails.

We believe that all black people should be released from the many jails and prisons because they have not received a fair and impartial trial.

9. We want all black people when brought to trial to be tried in court by a jury of their peer group or people from their black communities, as defined by the Constitution of the United States.

We believe that the courts should follow the United States Constitution so that black people will receive fair trials. The 14th Amendment of the U.S. Constitution gives a man a right to be tried by his peer group. A peer is a person from a similar economic, social, religious, geographical, environmental, historical and racial background. To do this the court will be forced to select a jury from the black community from which the black defendant came. We have been, and are being tried by all-white juries that have no understanding of the "average reasoning man" of the black community.

10. We want land, bread, housing, education, clothing, justice and peace. And as our major political objective, a United Nations-supervised plebiscite to be held throughout the black colony in which only black colonial subjects

will be allowed to participate, for the purpose of determining the will of black people as to their national destiny.

When, in the course of human events, it becomes necessary for one people to dissolve the political bonds which have connected them with another, and to assume, among the powers of the earth, the separate and equal station to which the laws of nature and nature's God entitle them, a decent respect to the opinions of mankind requires that they should declare the causes which impel them to the separation.

We hold these truths to be self-evident, that all men are created equal; that they are endowed by their Creator with certain unalienable rights; that among these are life, liberty, and the pursuit of happiness. **That, to secure these rights, governments are instituted among men, deriving their just powers from the consent of the governed; that, whenever any form of government becomes destructive of these ends, it is the right of the people to alter or to abolish it, and to institute a new government, laying its foundation on such principles, and organizing its powers in such form, as to them shall seem most likely to effect their safety and happiness.** Prudence, indeed, will dictate that governments long established should not be changed for light and transient causes; and, accordingly, all experience hath shown, that mankind are more disposed to suffer, while evils are sufferable than to right themselves by abolishing the forms to which they are accustomed. **But, when a long train of abuses and usurpations, pursuing invariably the same object, evinces a design to reduce them under absolute despotism, it is their right, it is their duty, to throw off such government, and to provide new guards for their future security.**

Racism in South Africa

The South African government calls itself a democracy. This may be true for less than one quarter of the population who call themselves "Europeans," but for the rest who are designated as "non-Europeans," it is a police state, where the White minority holds not only economic power but absolute political power. The Act of Union between British and Boer in 1910 was itself a colour bar act, excluding non-Whites from parliament.

South Africa is a country where the enormous dividend from gold exports goes with one of the highest infant mortality rates in the world; where a boom prosperity goes with the brutality of the Sabotage Act and a new Belsen, the foul jail on Robben Island in which some of the bravest fighters for freedom are tortured.

It is a land where peace means a military budget quadrupled since 1960 with the purchase of arms from every quarter of the Western world; for the U.S., France, West Germany, Belgium, including Britain, which alone has investments worth over one billion dollars, must protect their properties, even though the excesses of the Apartheid policy under Verwoerd embarrass them. It is a land where what is claimed to be "White Christian civilization" is maintained by means of the blackest statute book on record for the destruction of human freedom, happiness and dignity.

The ferocity of the recent fascist legislation that would silence every voice of protest, whether Black or White, indicates the desperate determination of the Nationalist Government to maintain White domination. Deaf to the demands of 14 million non-Whites for equality, contemptuous of world opinion, and defiant of economic forces, it holds rigidly to its Apartheid policy The Whites cannot cope with the needs of the industrial economy so that there is the anomaly of a chronic shortage of skilled labor while non-Whites are debarred from it.

Apartheid is a new name for an old policy basic to the South African system since the days of arch-imperialist, Cecil Rhodes, namely, segregation, and nasty under any name. For it signifies racism which has always been used by imperialism to intensify economic exploitation. This is the Black man's burden in South Africa: the more than 11 million Africans, 2 million Coloureds, and 1/2 million Indians are socially and economically depressed because they suffer racial oppression. To begin with they have no vote. This lack of political rights affects every aspect of their lives, limiting their choice of work and freedom of movement, condemning them to segregated housing and inferior education.

An elaborate system of Colour-bar laws excludes them from skilled jobs and apprenticeships to certain trades; Coloureds for the most part do semi-skilled jobs, but the African worker is restricted by law to unskilled labor. In effect the highly skilled White workers are split from the non-Whites. Trade unions have little bargaining power, being divided along racial lines, and for Africans they are illegal: when the miners went on strike in 1946 the police simply shot them down. The whole system of racial laws is best understood as labour laws for the control of non-Whites, but the heaviest oppression falls on the Africans as the largest labour force vital to the economy.

The discovery of diamonds and gold opened up a vast industrial expansion in South Africa, making it today the most industrially advanced country in Africa. That is why the liberation of the oppressed in South Africa concerns the progress of the whole continent. The gold mines are the king pin of the whole economy and they would collapse without cheap Black labour.

Every government since the Act of Union—and even before it— has legislated to force Africans into the mines and farms; and from the beginning the mines dictated the depressed wage-level for Africans, and thence for all non-Whites. The mines employ migrant labour, herding Africans into compounds; by law they are not classified as "employees" and so are bereft of their rights as workers. Outnumbering White miners by nine to one, they get wages a nineteenth part of the White wage.

The landlessness of the African peasants is an essential part of the labour policy. They occupy 1/8 of the land area, the segregated "Native reserves," where man, beast and soil perish for lack of nourishment. "Give the Natives land or increase his wages, and he won't work in the mines," declared an official before a mine commission.

In the hungry reserves a network of recruiting centers channels off the required quotas of labourers to the mines and farms. Africans hate the farms even more than the mines, for there they are virtually serfs. Some farmers put up farm-jails which are well stocked, since the daily jail population for infringement of pass-laws and curfews is 67,000. Thus Africans from the cities are deployed to the fields.

Three million Africans are city-dwellers. Many of them were born in the segregated locations and work in factories and as servants. But with the post-war economic boom, the Nationalist government stepped up the regimentation of labor for the mines and farms. Africans may not as a right have their wives and children in the cities; a bitter source of discontent is the extension of the pass law to the women. If for any reason an African loses his job, within 21 days the police close the city area to him; even if born there he can be thrown out as "redundant" or "undesirable," back to the destitute reserves or into farm labour.

The Verwoerd government, having completed the violation of the rights of Africans, then extended its attack on the minimal rights of Coloureds and Indians. The Coloureds lost their last vestige of voting rights and a Group Areas Act completed the segregation of each section into racial ghettoes where poverty, crime and death reap a heavy harvest. It is Apartheid gone mad.

Verwoerd then attacked education which was already segregated into White, Coloured, and "native". The system of debased "Bantu education" is devised as indoctrination for Africans as potential labour-fodder only. As Verwoerd remarked when introducing the Bantu Education Bill; "Those who believe in equality are not fit teachers for Natives." Violent resistance to the Act caused bloodshed in the "Reserves."

All this is the war of Apartheid against human well-being. But there is another war, and it is world-wide—the war for liberation of the oppressed. The ferocity of fascist measures by the government reflects its insecurity and the mounting demands by the non-Whites for full democratic rights for all, irrespective of race. In South Africa his is a revolutionary demand.

There is nothing the White rulers fear more than unity of the oppressed, and this is what Africans, Coloureds and poor Indians are achieving under the banner of the Unity Movement. With the formation of the Unity Movement the non-Whites for the first time in their history rejected racism, inferiority and the whole system of political and social segregation. With its Ten-Point Programme for full democratic rights for all, it launched an independent struggle on a nation-wide basis, federating the various organizations of peasants, workers, teachers and civic bodies. Realizing the danger to White domination that such a movement holds, the rulers have tried by every trick of bribery, intimidation and force to destroy it.

It is in the "Native Reserves" that Verwoerd has unleashed the full force of his attempt to crush the peasants, who, though unarmed, resist every fascist measure with increasing determination. His attempt to put back the clock of history by bribing the chiefs—the Tshombes of South Africa—to impose a grotesque retribalization on a people integrated as migrant mine and factory workers into a modern industrial economy, serves only to quicken the tempo of their political development. This is nowhere more evident than in the first so-called "independent" Bantustan in the Transkei, Cape Province, where a State of Emergency has been maintained since the Pondoland revolt. Voting for elected chiefs was carried out under coercion and intimidation. The chiefs, supported by the police, are discredited as government stooges, imposing heavier taxes and enforcing recruitment for the mines. They throw thousands into jail and sometimes burn the homes and crops of those who defy them.

But the African peasants refuse to be cowed. The Transkei is a veritable cauldron of liberatory ideas: Land and Political Rights is their cry. "There shall be no peace in this land until we make the laws in Parliament, one Parliament for all," declared a peasant of Pondoland. Moreover, they reject the sabotage incidents that have been exciting the towns, the froth that too often obscures the real struggle about which so little is known—for the press is silent. They denounce as irresponsible those behind the sabotage acts. They know that a protracted struggle for liberation must have a national political organisation constituting a unified command.

Peasant committees meet in secret in defiance of every fascist decree. And they send delegates to the distant "Reserves" in other provinces—a most hazardous journey. Peasants in the Transkei in Zululand, in Natal, in the Northern Transvaal, have a new slogan: "We build a nation." Unity is the keynote. Said one peasant from the North: "The unity I saw in Pondoland is what I would like to see throughout the country. I am awed by the spirit these people showed. They are fighting for liberation, just as I am. In spite of great suffering (in the North where soldiers brutalize the people) our morale is not broken." And the word has gone round that a new organization is born, "the organization we were looking for." Its name is APDUSA.[1]

"We build APDUSA," they say. "And APDUSA is the Nation." It was in 1964 that government troops were sent into Pondoland—to crush APDUSA. The people know that the achievement of liberation

1. (APDUSA—African Peoples' Democratic Union of South Africa, affiliated to the Unity Movement).

will be a long, grim struggle. But, in their words they are prepared to die for the Nation. The oppressed people of South Africa possess the inconquerable will to liberty. They see themselves as belonging to the forward march of mankind. But their need is all the greater for the moral and material support of freedom lovers throughout the world.

Anarchism and Third World Revolution

The dominant revolutionary force in this century is the peasant rebellion fostered by national liberation movements. The first and second worlds are characterized for the most part by classes which have become conservative, stagnated, and fearful of radical change. It is the lowly peasant in the underdeveloped world who is today pushing history along. In the Third World, "a single spark can light a prairie fire"; elsewhere there are sparks—the New Left for instance—but they cannot ignite the ocean in which they live.

What is the relation of anarchism to these revolutions? The anarchist sees the State as the major enemy of mankind and insists on voluntary organization from the bottom up. To the inherent criminality of centralized government, the anarchist counterposes decentralization and life without coercion. The extent to which today's liberation movements fit into the anarchist heritage and follow anarchist ideology explicitly or implicitly is an empirical question; too long now these movements have received an a priori "Marxist" label.

Many, possibly a majority, of self-avowed anarchists condemn the Third World revolutions of the century. In the English speaking world, the only prominent anarchist organization has for years been the Anarchist Federation of Britain. Jack Robinson, long the most powerful editor of their official weekly, *Freedom,* expresses the "official" anarchist attitude thus: "The national liberation fronts we have seen in the world are in no instance determined to destroy the institution of power. All these Guevaras, Maos, Ben Bellas, Ho Chi Minhs, Castros sought to do was to impose a new system of power—their own!"[1] He criticized in detail Guevara's message to Tricontinental which advocated two, three, many Vietnams, apparently unaware of the convincing arguments the Czech writer Stanislav Budin had made to the effect that Che was a "new Bakunin," a latter day counterpart of the most famous anarchist ever, Michael A. Bakunin.[2] Only a few of the "official" anar-

323

chists recognize the true Bakunin on such matters.[3] In any case, attacks on national liberation movements are frequent. The National Liberation Front of Vietnam is condemned for its alleged "terrorism"; in such instances it appears as though the writers have copied speeches of U.S. Presidents. Also typical is their (objective) support of U.S. imperialism by slandering Ho Chi Minh on his death, mainly because Ho believed in national liberation.[5] One representative article was headlined "Biafra—Triumph of the Politicians," which again objectively supported imperialism (in this case Nigeria) in executing genocide against the Ibo; apparently the "official" anarchists did not know that the Ibo constituted the majority of Biafraians, and the Ibo had been living in anarchist communities for centuries[6] and were, by attempting to secede, exercising their ancient libertarian tendencies. The *Freedom* critic gave the following as the basis of their condemnation of liberation movements: "You cannot have nations without a state structure. Nations must have politicians; state structures must have armed forces."[7] As will be seen, this is a dubious proposition at best.

This blanket condemnation of national liberation has not always characterized the anarchists.[8] It was Peter Kropotkin, the utopian anarchist of the turn of the century, who under the cover of "internationalism" rejected the right of each people to be free. In this, as in so many other questions, Kropotkin was a revisionist from the original Bakuninist position. Seen in light of that position, today's peasant revolutions in the underdeveloped countries are in the old anarchist tradition. Indeed, this was one of the distinguishing marks between Bakunin and Marx in their rift in the First International.

The classical Marxist view of the peasantry, along with the petty bourgeoisie, was expressed in the *Communist Manifesto:* "they are reactionary, for they try to roll back the wheel of history." Thus Marx and Engels hailed the fact that:

> The bourgeoisie has subjected the country to the rule of the towns. It has created enormous cities, has greatly increased the urban population as compared with the rural, and has thus rescued a considerable part of the population from the idiocy of rural life. Just as it has made the country dependent on the towns, so it has made barbarian and semi-barbarian countries dependent on the civilised ones, nations of peasants on nations of bourgeois, the East on the West.[9]

According to Marx and Engels, the peasantry was a reactionary class which had to be eliminated by the bourgeoisie for modernization to occur.[10] It is easy to see why they extolled imperialism, because they thought takeover by capitalist countries of underdeveloped lands led to the development of the latter. For these reasons, they favored the

French conquest of Algeria, the U.S. aggression against Mexico, German takeover of Eastern Europe, British domination of India, and so forth. By the same token, they deemed national liberation movements reactionary.[11]

Bakunin opted for the liberation of all the oppressed masses, not just the industrial proletariat. He saw the underdeveloped countries as more ripe for revolution and deemed the peasantry a great revolutionary force. Defending the right of poorer countries to be free of the more materially developed, he actually fought in and helped lead the worker-peasant rebellions in Eastern Europe in 1848. He objected to Marx in these terms:

> To the Communists, or Social Democrats, of Germany, the peasantry, any peasantry, stands for reaction; and the State, any State, even the Bismarkian State, stands for revolution. ... Altogether, the Marxists cannot even think otherwise: protagonists of the State as they are, they have to damn any revolution of a truly popular sweep and character, especially a peasant revolution, which is anarchistic by nature and which marches straightforward toward the destruction of the State.[12]

Bakunin was shocked at Marx's denial of the right of nations to self-determination:

> But do you realize that with this principle one could easily justify any kind of conquest and oppression? The bourgeoisie have always fallen back upon that principle to prove their mission and their right to *govern* or, what amounts to the same thing, to exploit the world of labor. [The assertion that capitalist domination of peasant countries "is the victory of civilization over barbarism" was detestable, and] I declare to you that in international relations, as well as in the relations of one class to another, I will be on the side of those to be civilized in this manner. Together with them I will revolt against all those arrogant civilizers—whether they call themselves Germans or workers—and in rebelling against them I shall serve the cause of revolution against reaction.[13]

In the twentieth century, we have a complete reversal of roles. The avowed "Marxists" took Bakunin's line while the so-called "anarchists" adopted many of the Marxian tenets. Lenin, who adopted the normative as well as the positive aspects of Bakunin's position, was the first great example of this. He argued for the right of nations to self-determination and denied that imperialism played a civilizing role. Indeed, the revolution he led was in many respects an anti-imperialist revolution, as Russia was dominated by French, German, and British capital. In essays such as "Backward Europe and Advanced Asia" (1914) he asserted that it was the underdeveloped countries of the East which would be the revolutionary forces of the century. He was pro-peasant (the Russian Revolution itself was in many respects a peasant revolution), and for this was accused by such Marxists as Aksel'rod as being a

Bakuninist.[14] As opposed to Marx, Lenin argued that the peasants should seize the land from below and work it as they pleased. (The NEP highlighted his laissez faire attitude.) Like Bakunin, he opposed forced collectivization from above and thought that the peasants should join collectives voluntarily; Stalin, following Marx more logically, later reversed these policies. Like Bakunin, Lenin also recognized that the peasantry was an inherently anarchistic class, that peasants had an instinctive hatred for all forms of State domination.

The Russian Revolution failed to result in the anarchist society Lenin pictured in *State and Revolution* because of the imperialist invasion and the civil war the Allies financed, which led to the perpetuation of the ruling bureaucracy left over from tsarism. However, Bakuninist-Leninist ideas spread to other lands, notably China, where in the long run success was surer. In his student days, Mao Tse-tung read pamphlets on anarchism, including some by Bakunin, which led him to call himself an anarchist. Becoming an anarchist activist in Peking, he corresponded with anarchists in other towns and attempted to form anarchist societies in Hunan and other provinces.[15] While later adopting the Marxist label, he continued to espouse anarchist views. The party, following Marx, wanted to organize the industrial proletariat, but Mao insisted on organizing the peasantry, for which he was expelled from the party. The Shanghai Massacre of 1927 proved Mao correct.

In China, the peasantry had a long anarchist tradition in that it deemed the very idea of government criminal. They saw government officials only in times of tax collection or repression. The real purpose of the State had long been obvious to them. Mao became an expression of these feelings and interests. The Red Army was a peasant army, joined and supported voluntarily by peasants, and having as its object anarchist type goals: abolition of taxation, land reform, power to the people on the local level. The Bakuninist norms and prophecies of the Chinese Revolution are evident: revolution in an underdeveloped country, of which the peasantry was the chief motive force, destruction of centralized dominance by a bureaucratic elite, substitution of power in the hands of the people.

While there have been consistent Marxist-Stalinist personalities in leadership positions in China, the Maoists have ever opposed them. In the Great Leap Forward and especially in the Cultural Revolution the Bakuninist ideas reigned supreme. Both periods were characterized by the reduction or destruction of centralization and the reversion of control over people's lives into the hands of the people themselves. With the elimination of Liu Shao-chi and his authoritarian cohorts by the late sixties, the Maoist policies of voluntarism and non-coercion ruled supreme. Far from being a totalitarian super state as pictured by U.S.

propaganda, China is a great conglomeration of thousands of self-governing communes. It is basically an anarchist society.[16]

The Maoists, particularily in the period of the Cultural Revolution, which shattered the bureaucracy and abolished the centralized standing army, have followed this advice of Bakunin:

> What should revolutionary authorities—and let us try to have as few of them as possible—do in order to organize and extend the Revolution? They must not do it themselves, by revolutionary decrees, by imposing this task upon the masses; rather their aim should be that of provoking the masses to action. They must not try to impose upon the masses any organization whatever, but rather should induce the people to set up autonomous organizations. This can be done by gaining influence over the most intelligent and advanced individuals of high standing in each locality, so that these organizations will conform as much as possible to our principles. Therein lies the whole secret of our triumph.[17]

The Cuban Revolution followed similar lines. Castro's movement was denounced by the Marxist PSP* as "anarchist" because it wanted to "skip stages," i.e. it wanted to jump into a worker's revolution while the country was still underdeveloped. Fidel agreed; referring to Marx, he has said: "But we transgressed against the laws of history by making our revolution in the first place."[18] The Cuban Revolution was again a peasant revolution, a revolution which was not supposed to happen according to Marxian orthodoxy, which pictures the peasants as a reactionary class. Since the peasantry is an instinctively anarchistic class, it is natural that anarchist practices have been prominent in Cuba since 1959. An armed people has taken the place of a centralized military, and the mass-based Committees for the Defense of the Revolution have been substituted for professional police forces. Anti-bureaucratic campaigns are promoted periodically, and emphasis is against using coercion. Once more, Bakunin's predictions and norms have much greater heuristic value than Marx's.

Similarily with the Vietnamese Revolution; by classical Marxian logic, the U.S. imperialist aggression there should be hailed. It is the "civilizer" against the "barbarian"; rule of the bourgeoisie is progressive, and peasants are reactionary. Even the deaths should not be too important, as Marx supported British massacres of the people of India. But the Vietnamese people unconsciously prefer Bakunin's line: national self-determination, peasant insurrection, revolution in backward country. The NLF stresses voluntarism and peasants taking power into their own hands. One NLF partisan describes how they take over a village:

*Popular Socialist Party

We get the villagers to nominate their own administration and then encourage them to confiscate the land of the worst of the agents and any absentee landlords, distributing it to the peasants, starting with the poorest. This creates a good atmosphere from the start. We announce, in the name of the Liberation Front, the abolition of all taxes and debts and that rent will be reduced following discussions with any local landlords still around. . . . We explain that the new local administration is an organ of the National Liberation Front, not linked to any central administration, competent in local affairs only. . . . The new administrative committee immediately forms subcommittees for education, public health, economic affairs, defense and security, and people really feel they are running their own lives.[19]

Partisans elect their own officers, who are subject to immediate recall. Democracy in the army is as important as elsewhere. The North American anarchist Noam Chomsky points out that the NLF is "a structure of interlocking self-help organizations, loosely coordinated and developed through persuasion rather than force—in certain respects of a character that would have appealed to anarchist thinkers."[20] Elsewhere, Chomsky makes a similar point in reference to the Pathet Lao, the liberation front of Laos: "Refugees commonly refer to the incessant efforts of cadres to persuade, and their avoidance of force or coercion."[21]

Asia has produced brilliant theoreticians of people's war, notably Mao, Lin Piao, Ho Chi Minh, and Vo Nguygen Giap. People's war is war of the masses, it is war to drive out the imperialists while simultaneously overthrowing domestic forms of domination such as bureaucracy and landlordism. People's war has an anarchistic character in that it relies on voluntarism, decentralization, and spontaneous action by the people on the local level. Self-avowed anarchists, from Makhno's movement in the Ukraine from 1918 to 1921 to the FAI-CNT workers and peasants movement in Spain in the thirties, resorted to people's war to fight foreign aggression and abolish domestic State exploitation. The same methods have been adopted in all the popular Third World revolutions of the century, whether consciously anarchist or not. The Vietnamese have shown that it is the most efficient as well as the most democratic form of warfare known to man. It is a revolution of peasants which bypasses the stage of dictatorship of the bourgeoisie. In Giap's words:

Our revolution must go through the stage of national people's democratic revolution and advance toward the socialist revolution, bypassing the stage of capitalist development. Our military line is based on the line of a thoroughly national people's democratic revolution; it is the *line of the people's revolutionary war,* the war of a people made up mainly of peasants, which is aimed at overthrowing imperialism and feudalism, reconquering independence for the nation and giving land back to the tillers.[22]

People's war, revolutionary war of the peasant masses led by the ideology called "Marxism-Leninism-Maoism" (substituting "Bakuninism" for "Marxism" would be more correct), is the great prime mover of the twentieth century, the force which pushes history along, the only non-conservative mass movement in the world today. In this sense, the future belongs to the Third World, and the developed countries are doomed to fall in the wake of the rising peoples of the world. The dialectic at work: the developed nations are crumbling and the underdeveloped nations are ascending. The unity of opposites: the future belongs to the primitive peoples, the barbarians, the peasants. The "civilized" will be swept into the dust bin of history. The Wretched of the Earth are sacking Rome. New York belongs to yesterday and Peking to tomorrow.

What is the cause of this upsurge? Why is the developed West condemned to waste away? From whence does the invincible power of the peasant masses derive? These queries may be answered in one sentence: power in the hands of the people is more effective, more efficient, more powerful than power in the hands of an elite which the masses blindly follow. In the West the masses are brainwashed, corrupted and bribed by material goods, believers in authority. In the East the people's minds are "barbarian," unfettered by statist fetishes, pure and simple and, therefore, naturally anarchistic, anti-authoritarian, clean and fresh. The East wind prevails over the West wind because instinctively anarchistic peasant masses possess self-initiative and are willing to dare to struggle, dare to win. They are unprogrammed by bureaucratic mind-control and are willing to take life and the future in their own hands. Proudhonism and Bakuninism triumph under Tito's worker's self-management and Ben Bella's autogestion, both of which resulted from peasant revolutions and were subjected to an influx of anarchist ideology from Spain and France, respectively; the world still awaits the "inevitable" rise of the industrial proletariat in the developed countries, Marx's "most advanced class."

People's war is based on these concepts. It is invincible because it is founded on the power and direct initiative of the masses. Rules of the guerrilla are: Speak politely. Pay for what you buy. Do not take a single needle or piece of thread from the masses. Replace what you damage. Always be the people's servant. Statist conventional warfare could never be carried out by such methods for the State rests on coercion; its purpose is to hold down the masses, to kill their initiative. Statist war is a boat dashing upon reefs on a stormy sea, while people's war is fish swimming in tranquil waters. "The guerrilla is the masses in arms"; Kwame Nkrumah knows what people's war is. In his *Handbook of Revolutionary Warfare* he attacks bureaucraticism and elitism, while calling for a local, voluntary militia system which serves, not subjugates, the masses. He opposes hierarchy and servile obedience and argues that the African liberation struggle "must be based on the immense, revolutionary potential of the peasantry."[23] To the list of those classified as "neo-Bakuninist" like Régis Debray (who is objectively as anti-Marxist as they come) and Franz Fanon (whose work appears as if it was copied from Bakunin's selected works),[24] it is clear why Nkrumah should also be added.

Africa, the dark continent of "stupid natives": the world belongs to these jungle fighters. Africa is the land of stateless societies, sabotaged by imperialist penetration. Amilcar Cabral, leader of the liberation front of Guinea, sees the power of the peasant Balantes as most invincible since they have no defined form of state organization. "What is more, these groups without any defined organization put up much more resistance against the Portuguese than the others, and they have maintained intact their tradition of resistance to colonial penetration. This is the group that we found most ready to accept the idea of national liberation."[25] Cabral has attacked all forms of elitism and emphasized that voluntarism and power at the base must reign supreme.[26] Similarily, in the fifties it was the traditionally anarchist Kibuyu which formed the vanguard of the Mau Mau peasant revolution in Kenya.[27]

Elsewhere in Africa, not to mention Asia or Latin America, the pattern is the same. And in the Mid East the prominent Palestinian Arab liberation groups—notably Fatah, the Popular Front, and especially the Democratic Popular Front—have organized around anarchistic type issues and in anarchistic fashion. They recognize, as do their brothers in Vietnam, Uruguay, North American ghettos, and elsewhere, that the enemy of their people is the institution of centralized power, the enslavement by an elite of the popular masses. They see themselves as peoples fighting U.S. imperialism and its lackeys everywhere. Implicitly if not explicitly they are fighting the international State, the most stalwart bulwark of which is the U.S. government. The U.S. government and its running dogs in Moscow, Madrid, Bonn, Buenos Aires, Saigon, and everywhere else are confronted by the invincible might of people's war. U.S. imperialism is the highest manifestation of statism man has ever been faced with and is the great enemy of the world. Great will be its downfall. And great will be the triumph of the popular masses.

Notes

1. Robinson, "National-Liberation—A Front?" *Freedom* (London), Dec. 13, 1969, p. 3.
2. Budin, "Dva, tři . . . další Vietnamy?" *Reportér* (Prague), May 19, 1967, pp.

22-3. Judging from the July 24, 1967 entry in his Bolivian diary, Che seemed complimented.

3. One who does is Fidel Miró, "Reconciliación de Marx y Bakunin?" *Reconstruir* (Buenos Aires), May–June 1970.

4. *Freedom,* Nov. 29, 1969.

5. *Freedom,* Sept. 16, 1969, p. 3.

6. Cf. Margery Perham, *Native Administration in Nigeria* (Oxford University Press, 1937), Ch. XV.

7. *Freedom,* Jan. 10, 1970.

8. Even today, there is a minority, usually non-communist anarchists, who favor national liberation. Cf. for instance "Ernesto Che Guevara, RIP," *Left and Right,* Autumn 1967 and "National Liberation," *Libertarian Forum,* Sept. 1, 1969.

9. Marx and Engels, *Selected Works* (New York: International Publishers, 1969), p. 39.

10. Cf. further David Mitrany, *Marx Against the Peasant* (University of Carolina Press, 1951).

11. Cf. Engel's attack on Bakunin in Marx and Engels, *The Russian Menace to Europe* (Glencoe: The Free Press, 1952) and more generally Shlomo Avineri (ed.), *Karl Marx on Colonialism and Modernization* (Garden City, New York: Doubleday and Co., 1968) and Horace B. Davis, *Nationalism and Socialism* (New York: Monthly Review Press, 1967).

12. G. P. Maximoff (ed.), *Bakunin* (New York: Free Press, 1953), p. 204.

13. *Ibid.,* p. 402.

14. Jonathan Frankel, Introduction to Vladimir Akimov, *On the Dilemmas of Russian Marxism 1895–1903* (Cambridge University Press, 1969), pp. 66-7 and 74. The Marxist scholar George Lichtheim develops this point in his "What is Left of Communism?" *Foreign Affairs,* Oct. 1967, especially pp. 84-5.

15. Edgar Snow, *Red Star Over China* (New York: Grove Press, 1961), p. 151; A. Rumiantsev, "Maoism and the Anti-Marxist Nature of Maoist Philosophy," *Chinese Studies in History and Philosophy,* Summer 1969, p. 79.

16. Cf. further Stephen P. Halbrook, "The Anarchism of Mao Tse-tung," *Libertarian Analysis,* Spring 1971.

17. Maximoff, p. 398.

18. Quoted in K. S. Karol, "Castro on the Contradictions in Cuba," *Ramparts,* Dec. 1970, p. 44.

19. Wilfred Burchett, *Vietnam Will Win!* (New York: Guardian, 1970), pp. 58-9.

20. Chomsky, *American Power and the New Mandarins* (New York: Random House, 1969), pp. 136-7.

21. Chomsky, "The Executive War in Laos," *Liberation,* Dec. 1970, p. 14.

22. "The Political and Military Line of Our Party," n.d., *The Military Art of People's War: Selected Writings of General Vo. Nguyen Giap* (New York: Monthly Review Press, 1970), p. 163.

23. International Publishers ed. (1969), p. 76.

24. Cf. Paul Avrich, "The Legacy of Bakunin," *The Russian Review,* April 1970; Lewis Coser, "Nechaev in the Andes," *Dissent,* Jan.–Feb. 1968; and Jolfe Rosse, "A Different Sort of Pragmatism," *Anarchy* (London), Jan. 1969.

25. Cabral, *Revolution in Guinea* (New York: Monthly Review Press, 1969), pp. 56-61.

26. Cf. Paul Hodges, "Liberating Guiné," *Anarchy,* June 1970, pp. 192-6.
27. Cf. Donald L. Barnett and Karari Njama, *Mau Mau From Within* (New York: Monthly Review Press, 1966), pp. 42 ff. This work explodes the British propaganda that Mau Mau was atavistic.

Study Questions

1. Che Guevara has been criticized for supposedly being violence prone and a terrorist. Why does he want to create "two, three, many Vietnams"? If many Vietnams are created, who, in the final analysis, must be held responsible for all the violence and deaths —guerrillas like Che or their exploiters?

2. What does Piao mean by "people's war," as opposed to conventional war? Why does he think U.S. imperialism, which resorts to conventional war, can be defeated by people's war in the Third World?

3. List the goals of the Palestinian Revolution. Why is the attainment of these goals dependent on international factors? Discuss the factors ranging from U.S. military aid to Israel to the effect of the Vietnamese Revolution on all Third World areas, including the Middle East.

4. Are the objectives of the Black Panthers realistic? Do the Black Panthers represent a danger to U.S. social structure? Eldridge Cleaver has described Bakunin's "Revolutionary Catechism" (printed in Part V) as his "bible." Discuss why you think he finds Bakunin so relevant.

5. In the case of South Africa, could you say that on the part of whites, racism is reactionary, but that on the part of blacks racism can be revolutionary? That is, is it just for blacks in South Africa to engage in a revolutionary war against the white European minorities?

6. What do the following concepts mean to you (a) imperialism, (b) colonialism, (c) neocolonialism, (d) racism, (e) capitalism, (f) exploitation.

7. Critically appraise the following:

   "With a lot of blacks, there's quite a bit of resentment along with their dissent, and possibly rightfully so. But we can't all of a sudden get down on our knees and turn everything over to the leadership of the blacks. I believe in white supremacy until the blacks are educated to a point of responsibility. I don't believe in giving authority and positions of leadership and judgment to irresponsible people." (John Wayne, *Playboy,* May 1971, p. 80)

8. Third World peoples believe that so long as exploitation of man exists, freedom is impossible. Assuming that exploitation of man is

a hindrance to the attainment of freedom, are there then other factors to be taken into consideration?

9. According to the American press, the Third World liberation movements are totalitarian Communist conspiracies; in addition, U.S. officials such as J. Edgar Hoover picture anarchism as causeless and unjustified violence, and further argue that absolute freedom is enjoyed by all U.S. citizens. Contrast this world view with the one which asserts that the only real freedom is anarchism and that only the Third World is approaching this unlimited freedom, and then give the underlying assumptions of each. Which view corresponds more to reality?

10. Give a critical evaluation of the following:

> "With rare exceptions, national liberation fronts are said to be rhetorical in their intellectual appeal and misled by such rhetoric into believing that the U.S. is their principal enemy. They are said to be incurably romantic and adventuristic in their expectations of defeating U.S. military power or circumscribing its sphere of influence. They are said to be communist conspiracies, bent on overthrowing either military regimes friendly to the U.S. or legitimate and popularly elected governments." (In *NLF: National Liberation Fronts,* edited by D. C. Hodges and Robert Elias Abu Shanab, Morrow Company, forthcoming)

Part V

THE GOOD LIFE

Introduction

This section presents various views on what constitutes the good life. In some of the selections, (e.g. Bakunin's "The Revolutionary Catechism," Huxley's "The Doors of Perception"), it is not very explicit what these thinkers view as the good life. In other selections—such as the ones by Plato and Fromm — views on what constitutes the good life are more explicit. Yet whether explicitly or implicitly stated there is undoubtedly enough material on hand to enable the reader to get a diversified perspective of some views concerning the good life.

For example, the ancient thinker Confucius made the observation that all men desire happiness, irrespective of the marked difference in the manner they define it. The good life, to Confucius, consisted in acting in perfect harmony with the dictates of the moral law. Such a law is to be found everywhere; however, its attainment is difficult. As Confucius remarked: the finding of the central clue to our moral being which unites us to the universal moral order is the highest human attainment.

Plato, in the dialogue *Philebus,* is concerned with what is good?, or what is the good life? Plato in this dialogue is not concerned with the *form* good as discussed in earlier Platonic dialogues. The main question is whether *pleasure* or *knowledge* is the good. At the end of the dialogue one is told that the good for man, or the best life, must include both pleasure and knowledge; but of the two knowledge must prevail. The Arab philosopher, al-Farabi, presents the view that the good life can only be attained in the ideal state. Indeed, according to al-Farabi, the sole aim of the ideal state is the attainment of true happiness. The other states which al-Farabi discusses are considered imperfect in that they reveal certain characteristics which render the attainment of the good life impossible.

Aldous Huxley and Erich Fromm offer the reader some interesting observations on what constitutes the good life. Several years before the topic of unconventional drugs became a political football in our current society, Aldous Huxley sought to analyze the role of drug-experience in human life. Huxley argues that drug-experiences are an inherent need for human beings, because of our ordinary, daily burden of verbal consciousness and behavior. The ability of human beings to cognize the world in verbally abstract terms is, of course, the means to man's civilized progress. However, constantly abstract living leads ultimately to the habit of pursuing sterile activity merely because such activity has been formally organized in some way. Drugs are man's means to achieve a revitalizing trip to the non-verbally perceived world. Thus, for Huxley, life is not complete and hence not good without some form of drug-experience. Huxley refers to this experience as "applied religion," and he notes the hypocritical tension in our culture between the drug use that *is* permitted (notably alcohol and tobacco) and the dull, drug-less churches which we grudgingly tolerate. Furthermore, he stresses that modern science could easily produce a chemical drug whose effect can be entirely harmless, measured, and marvelously pleasurable.

From his experience as a psychoanalyst and a student of human history, Erich Fromm concludes that wars, poverty, murders, alcoholism neurosis etc. which typify our society are the result of the perversion of human nature by a sick society. In calling our society "sick," Fromm does *not* wish merely to call attention to our disregard for air-pollution and murder in the streets. Rather, he insists that our basic way of life is sick, i.e., the average person is forced every day of his life to live out a totally meaningless existence. Creative, individual behavior will be punished by an economic marketplace that has little to do with real human needs or by a governmental bureaucracy that is totally unresponsive to the wishes of the people it rules. In the conclusion of his book, *The Sane Society,* Fromm outlines a practical, material way in which society can be reorganized so that the good life for man becomes an everyday commonplace. Society may be reorganized so that all real decisions are made within hundreds of thousands of town-meeting contexts, and the decisions of these meetings communicated to all other communities by modern electronic devices. The concept of social security can be extended to the point that a person who wants to change his life will be given the real opportunity to do so, e.g. a stipend from the state for two or three years while he or she gets the necessary education for a new job. Fromm bases his proposals in part on his theory of human nature, and in part on observations of actual communities in

Europe which have been organized along such lines. His ultimate point of argument is that man is not in any way inherently lazy or deceitful. In his view, a society with a genuinely socialistic structure will be a society in which people produce more, suffer less, and enjoy life for the first time in modern history. Thus happiness in such a society would, according to Fromm, result from the experience and enjoyment of being productive, and from the use of the powers of love and reason which would enable man to relate in a useful way to humanity.

The final three selections in this part are focused on what we would call "The good life via the revolutionary way." Bakunin had enormous appetites and they reveal what the good life was for him. He talked the night through, read a great deal, drank brandy like it was going out of style, ate and smoked a lot. However, his most enormous appetite was for absolute and unlimited freedom for man, not curtailed or defined by the arbitrary decrees of ruling elites. So much did he adore anarchy and despise the State that the most important thing in his life became the theory and practice of the Social Revolution which would completely destroy the past. Clearly the good life, to Bakunin, was the Revolution. It was a good life to theorize on the Revolution; it was a better life to form secret societies and agitate the masses; it was the best life to actually engage in revolutionary struggle, as Bakunin did in France in 1848, East Europe in the same year, Germany in 1849, and back to France in 1870-71 and Italy in 1874.

The selections from Hoffman and Rubin set forth the goals of the "yippie movement." The slogan, "Do your own thing," is a close approximation of what constitutes the good life to both Hoffman and Rubin. Hoffman presents some instructions, which if heeded, would lead toward the creation of a free society. Indeed, a free society, to Hoffman, is one in which happiness prevails. The goals embodied in "Revolution Towards a Free Society: Yippie" portray the kind of life that the yippie movement is striving for.

Rubin would also agree with Hoffman's fundamental principles about what constitutes the good life. The selection "Scenario for the Future/Yippieland," taken from Rubin's concluding chapter of his book *Do It*, envisages the goals of the future life, i.e. "yippieland."

The Good Life

I

The ordinance of God is what we call the law of our being. To fulfil the law of our being is what we call the moral law. The moral law when reduced to a system is what we call religion.

The moral law is a law from whose operation we cannot for one instant in our existence escape. A law from which we may escape is not the moral law. Wherefore it is that the moral man watches diligently over what his eyes cannot see and is in fear and awe of what his ears cannot hear.

There is nothing more evident than that which cannot be seen by the eyes and nothing more palpable than that which cannot be perceived by the senses. Wherefore the moral man watches diligently over his secret thoughts.

When the passions, such as joy, anger, grief, and pleasure, have not awakened, that is our true self, or moral being. When these passions awaken and each and all attain due measure and degree, that is the moral order. Our true self or moral being is the great reality (*lit.* great root) of existence, and moral order is the universal law in the world.

When true moral being and moral order are realised, the universe then becomes a cosmos and all things attain their full growth and development.

II

Confucius remarked: "The life of the moral man is an exemplification of the universal moral order. The life of the vulgar person, on the other hand, is a contradiction of the universal moral order.

"The moral man's life is an exemplification of the universal order, because he is a moral person who unceasingly cultivates his true self or moral being. The vulgar person's life is a contradiction of the universal

339

order, because he is a vulgar person who in his heart has no regard for, or fear of, the moral law."

The fool hath said in his heart, There is no God.

III

Confucius remarked: "To find the central clue to our moral being which unites us to the universal order, that indeed is the highest human attainment. People are seldom capable of it for long."

IV

Confucius remarked: "I know now why there is no real moral life. The wise mistake moral law for something higher than what it really is; and the foolish do not know enough what moral law really is. I know now why the moral law is not understood. The noble natures want to live too high, high above their moral ordinary self; and ignoble natures do not live high enough, *i.e.,* not up to their moral ordinary true self." . . .

XI

Confucius remarked: "There are men who seek for some abstruse meaning in religion and philosophy and live a life singular in order that they may leave a name to posterity. This is what I never would do."

"There are again good men who try to live in conformity with the moral law, but who, when they have gone half way, throw it up. I never could give it up."

"Lastly, there are truly moral men who unconsciously live a life in entire harmony with the universal moral order and who live unknown to the world and unnoticed of men without any concern. It is only men of holy, divine natures who are capable of this."

XII

The moral law is to be found everywhere, and yet it is a secret.

The simple intelligence of ordinary men and women of the people may understand something of the moral law; but in its utmost reaches there is something which even the wisest and holiest of men cannot understand. The ignoble natures of ordinary men and women of the people may be able to carry out the moral law; but in its utmost reaches even the wisest and holiest of men cannot live up to it.

Great as the Universe is, man with the infinite moral nature in him is never satisfied. For there is nothing so great but the mind of the moral man can conceive of something still greater which nothing in the world can hold. There is nothing so small but the mind of moral man can conceive of something still smaller which nothing in the world can split.

The Book of Songs says:

"The hawk soars to the heavens above and fishes dive to the depths below."

That is to say, there is no place in the highest heavens above nor in the deepest waters below where the moral law does not reign.

Emerson says: "The moral law lies at the centre of Nature and radiates to the circumference. It is the pith and marrow of every substance, every relation and every process."

The moral law takes its rise in the relation between man and woman; but in its utmost reaches it reigns supreme over heaven and earth. . . .

XIII

Confucius remarked: "The moral law is not something away from the actuality of human life. When men take up something away from the actuality of human life as the moral law, that is not the moral law."

The Kingdom of God is within you.

The Book of Songs says:
"In hewing an axe handle, the pattern is not far off."

"Thus, when we take an axe handle in our hand to hew the other and glance from one to the other there is still some distance between them as compared with the relation between the moral law and the man himself. Wherefore the moral man in dealing with men appeals to the common human nature and changes the manner of their lives and nothing more.

"When a man carries out the principles of conscientiousness and reciprocity he is not far from the moral law. What you do not wish others should do unto you, do not do unto them.

"There are four things in the moral life of a man, not one of which I have been able to carry out in my life. To serve my father as I would expect my son to serve me: that I have not been able to do. To serve my sovereign as I would expect a minister under me to serve me: that I have not been able to do. To act towards my elder brother as I would expect my younger brother to act towards me: that I have not been able to do. To be the first to behave towards friends as I would expect them to behave towards me: that I have not been able to do.

"In the discharge of the ordinary duties of life and in the exercise of care in ordinary conversation, whenever there is shortcoming, never fail to strive for improvement, and when there is much to be said, always say less than what is necessary; words having respect to actions and actions having respect to words. Is it not just this thorough genuineness and absence of pretence which characterises the moral man?"

XIV

The moral man conforms himself to his life circumstances; he does not desire anything outside of his position.

Finding himself in a position of wealth and honour, he lives as becomes one living in a position of wealth and honour. Finding himself in a position of poverty and humble circumstances, he lives as becomes one living in a position of poverty and humble circumstances. Finding himself in uncivilized countries, he lives as becomes one living in uncivilized countries. Finding himself in circumstances of danger and difficulty, he acts according to what is required of a man under such circumstances. In one word, the moral man can find himself in no situation in life in which he is not master of himself.

In a high position he does not domineer over his subordinates. In a subordinate position he does not court the favours of his superiors. He puts in order his own personal conduct and seeks nothing from others; hence he has no complaint to make. He complains not against God nor rails against men.

Thus it is that the moral man lives out the even tenor of his life, calmly waiting for the appointment of God, whereas the vulgar person takes to dangerous courses, expecting the uncertain chances of luck.

Confucius remarked: "In the practice of archery we have something resembling the principle in a moral man's life. When the archer misses the centre of the target he turns round and seeks for the cause of his failure within himself." . . .

XXI

The intelligence which comes from the direct apprehension of truth is intuition. The apprehension of truth which comes from the exercise of intelligence is the result of education. Where there is truth, there is intelligence; where there is intelligence, there is truth.

XXII

It is only he, in the world, who possesses absolute truth who can get to the bottom of the law of his being. He who is able to get to the bottom of the law of his being will be able to get to the bottom of the law of being of other men. He who is able to get to the bottom of the law of being of men will be able to get to the bottom of the laws of physical nature. He who is able to get to the bottom of the laws of physical nature will be able to influence the forces of creation of the Universe. He who can influence the forces of creation of the Universe is one with the Powers of the Universe.

XXIII

The next order of the process of man's mind is to attain to the apprehension of a particular branch of knowledge. In every particular branch of knowledge there is truth. Where there is truth, there is substance. Where there is substance, there is reality. Where there is reality, there is intelligence. Where there is intelligence, there is power. Where there is power, there is influence. Where there is influence, there is creative power. It is only he who possesses absolute truth in the world who can create.

XXIV

It is an attribute of the possession of absolute truth to be able to foreknow. When a nation or family is about to flourish, there are sure to be lucky omens. When a nation or family is about to perish, there are sure to be signs and prodigies. These things manifest themselves in the instruments of divination and in the agitation of the human body. When happiness or calamity is about to come, it can be known beforehand. When it is good, it can be known beforehand. When it is evil, it can also be known beforehand. Therefore he who possesses absolute truth is like a spiritual being.

XXV

Truth means the realisation of our being; and moral law means the law of our being. Truth is the beginning and end (the substance) of existence. Without truth there is no existence. It is for this reason that the moral man values truth.

Truth is not only the realisation of our own being: it is that by which things outside of us have an existence. The realisation of our being is moral sense. The realisation of things outside of us is intellect. These, moral sense and intellect, are the powers or faculties of our being. They combine the inner or subjective and outer or objective use of the power of the mind. Therefore with truth everything done is right.

XXVI

Thus absolute truth is indestructible. Being indestructible, it is eternal. Being eternal, it is self-existent. Being self-existent, it is infinite. Being infinite, it is vast and deep. Being vast and deep, it is transcendental and intelligent. It is because it is vast and deep that it contains all existence. It is because it is transcendental and intelligent that it embraces all existence. It is because it is infinite and eternal that it fills all existence. In vastness and depth it is like the Earth. In transcendental intelligence it is like Heaven. Infinite and eternal, it is Infinitude itself.

Such being the nature of absolute truth, it manifests itself without being evident; it produces effects without action; it accomplishes its ends without being conscious.

The principle in the course and operation of nature may be summed up in one word: it exists for its own sake without any double or ulterior motive. Hence the way in which it produces things is unfathomable.

Nature is vast, deep, high, intelligent, infinite, and eternal. The heaven appearing before us is only this bright, shining spot; but when taken in its immeasurable extent, the sun, moon, stars, and constellations are suspended in it, and all things are embraced under it. The earth, appearing before us, is but a handful of soil; but taken in all its breadth and depth, it sustains mighty Himalayas without feeling their weight; rivers and seas dash against it without causing it to leak. The mountain appearing before us is only a mass of rock; but taken in all the vastness of its size, grass and vegetation grow upon it, birds and beasts dwell on it, and treasures of precious stones are found in it. The water appearing before us is but a ladleful of liquid; but taken in all its unfathomable depths, the largest crustaceans, fishes, and reptiles are produced in them, and all useful products abound in them.

In the Book of Songs it is said:

"The ordinance of God,
How inscrutable it is and goes on for ever."

That is to say, this is the attribute of God.
It is again said:

"How excellent it is,
The moral perfection of King Wen."

That is to say, this is the characteristic of the nobleness of the Emperor
Wen. Moral perfection also never dies.

XXVII

Oh, how great is the divine moral law in man! Vast and illimitable,
it gives birth and life to all created things. It towers high up to the very
heavens. How wonderful and great it is! All the institutions of human
society and civilisation—laws, customs, and usages—have their origin
there. All these institutions wait for the man before they can be put into
practice. Hence it is said: Unless there be highest moral power, the
highest moral law cannot be realised.

Wherefore the moral man, while honouring the greatness and
power of his moral nature, yet does not neglect inquiry and pursuit of
knowledge. While widening the extent of his knowledge, he yet seeks
to attain utmost accuracy in the minutest details. While seeking to
understand the highest things, he yet lives a plain, ordinary life in
accordance with the moral order. Going over what he has already
acquired, he keeps adding to it new knowledge. Earnest and simple, he
respects and obeys the laws and usages of social life.

Therefore, when in a position of authority, he is not proud; in a
subordinate position, he is not insubordinate. When there is moral social
order in the country, what he speaks will be of benefit to the nation; and
when there is no moral social order in the country his silence will ensure
forbearance for himself.

In the Book of Songs it is said:

"With wisdom and good sense,
He guards his life from harm."

That is the description of the moral man.

Confucius remarked: "A man who is foolish, and yet is fond of using
his own judgment; who is in humble circumstances, and yet is fond of
assuming authority; who, while living in the present age, reverts to the
ways of antiquity: such a man is one who will bring calamity upon
himself."

To no one but the supreme head of the empire does it belong to
disturb the established religious and social institutions, to introduce
new forms of government, to change the form and use of language. At
the present day throughout the empire carriage wheels all have the
same standard form and size, all writing is written with the same char-

acters, and in all the relations of life all recognise the same established principles.

Although a man may occupy the position of the supreme head of the empire, yet, unless he possesses the moral qualities fitting him for the task, he may not take upon himself to make changes in the established moral and religious institutions. Although one may possess the moral qualities fitting him for the task, yet, unless he occupies the position of the supreme head of the empire, he may not take upon himself to make changes in the established moral and religious institutions.

Confucius remarked: "I have tried to understand the moral and religious institutions of the Hsia dynasty, but what remains of those institutions in the present state of Ch'i is not sufficient to give me a clue. I have studied the moral and religious institutions of the Yin dynasty; the remains of them are still preserved in the present state of Sung. I have studied the moral and religious institutions of the present Chow dynasty, which are now in use. In practice I follow the forms of the present Chow dynasty."

XXVIII

To attain to the sovereignty of the world, there are three important things necessary; they may perhaps be summed up in one: blamelessness of life.

However excellent a system of moral truths appealing to super-natural authority may be, it is not verifiable by experience; what is not verifiable by experience cannot command credence; and what cannot command credence the people will never obey. However excellent a system of moral truths appealing merely to worldly authority may be it does not command respect; what does not command respect cannot command credence; and what cannot command credence the people will never obey.

Therefore every system of moral laws must be based upon the man's own consciousness. It must be verified by the common experience of men. Examined into by comparing it with the teachings of acknowledged great and wise men of the past, there must be no divergence. Applying it to the operations and processes of nature in the physical universe, there must be no contradiction. Confronted with the spiritual powers of the universe a man must be able to maintain it without any doubt. He must be prepared to wait a hundred generations after him for the coming of a man of perfect divine nature to confirm it without any misgiving. The fact that he is able to confront the

spiritual powers of the universe without any doubt, shows that he understands the will of God. The fact that he is prepared to wait a hundred
generations after him for the man of perfect divine nature without
changes in the established moral and religious institutions. Although
one may possess the moral qualities fitting him for the task, yet, unless
he occupies the position of the supreme head of the empire, he may not
take upon himself to make changes in the established moral and religious institutions.

Pleasure versus Knowledge

* * *

Pro. I think that I partly understand you, Socrates, but I should like to have a clearer notion of what you are saying.

Soc. I may illustrate my meaning by the letters of the alphabet, Protarchus, which you were made to learn as a child.

Pro. How do they afford an illustration?

Soc. The sound which passes through the lips whether of an individual or of all men is one and yet infinite.

Pro. Very true.

Soc. And yet not by knowing either that sound is one or that sound is infinite are we perfect in the art of speech, but the knowledge of the number and nature of sounds is what makes a man a grammarian.

Pro. Very true.

Soc. And the knowledge which makes a man a musician is of the same kind.

Pro. How so?

Soc. Sound is one in music as well as in grammar?

Pro. Certainly.

Soc. And there is a higher note and a lower note, and a note of equal pitch:—may we affirm so much?

Pro. Yes.

Soc. But you would not be a real musician if this was all that you knew; though if you did not know this you would know almost nothing of music.

Pro. Nothing.

Soc. But when you have learned what sounds are high and what low, and the number and nature of the intervals and their limits or proportions, and the systems compounded out of them, which our fathers discovered, and have handed down to us who are their descendants under the name of harmonies; and the affections corresponding to them in the movements of the human body, which when measured by numbers ought, as they say, to be called rhythms and measures; and they tell us that the same principle should be applied to every one and many;—when, I say, you have learned all this, then, my dear friend, you are perfect; and you may be said to understand any other subject, when you have a similar grasp of it. But the infinity of kinds and the infinity of individuals which there is in each of them, when not classified, creates in every one of us a state of infinite ignorance; and he who never looks for number in anything, will not himself be looked for in the number of famous men.

Pro. I think that what Socrates is now saying is excellent, Philebus.

Phi. I think so too, but how do his words bear upon us and upon the argument?

Soc. Philebus is right in asking that question of us, Protarchus.

Pro. Indeed he is, and you must answer him.

Soc. I will; but you must let me make one little remark first about these matters; I was saying, that he who begins with any individual unity, should proceed from that, not to infinity, but to a definite number, and now I say conversely, that he who has to begin with infinity should not jump to unity, but he should look about for some number representing a certain quantity, and thus out of all end in one. And now let us return for an illustration of our principle to the case of letters.

Pro. What do you mean?

Soc. Some god or divine man, who in the Egyptian legend is said to have been Theuth, observing that the human voice was infinite, first distinguished in this infinity a certain number of vowels, and then other letters which had sound, but were not pure vowels (i.e. the semivowels); these too exist in a definite number; and lastly, he distinguished a third class of letters which we now call mutes, without voice and without sound, and divided these, and likewise the two other classes of vowels and semivowels, into the individual sounds, and told the number of them, and gave to each and all of them the name of letters; and observing that none of us could learn any one of them and not learn them all, and in consideration of this common bond which in a manner united them, he assigned to them all a single art and this he called the art of grammar or letters.

Phi. The illustration, Protarchus, has assisted me in understanding the original statement, but I still feel the defect of which I just now complained.

Soc. Are you going to ask, Philebus, what this has to do with the argument?

Phi. Yes, that is a question which Protarchus and I have been long asking.

Soc. Assuredly you have already arrived at the answer to the question which, as you say, you have been so long asking?

Phi. How so?

Soc. Did we not begin by enquiring into the comparative eligibility of pleasure and wisdom?

Phi. Certainly.

Soc. And we maintain that they are each of them one?

Phi. True.

Soc. And the precise question to which the previous discussion desires an answer is, how they are one and also many [i.e. how they have one genus and many species], and are not at once infinite, and what number of species is to be assigned to either of them before they pass into infinity.

Pro. That is a very serious question, Philebus, to which Socrates has ingeniously brought us round, and please to consider which of us shall answer him; there may be something ridiculous in my being unable to answer, and therefore imposing the task upon you, when I have undertaken the whole charge of the argument, but if neither of us were able to answer, the result methinks would be still more ridiculous. Let us consider, then, what we are to do:—Socrates, if I understood him rightly, is asking whether there are not kinds of pleasure, and what is the number and nature of them, and the same of wisdom.

Soc. Most true, O son of Callias; and the previous argument showed that if we are not able to tell the kinds of everything that has unity, likeness, sameness, or their opposites, none of us will be of the smallest use in any enquiry.

Pro. That seems to be very near the truth, Socrates. Happy would the wise man be if he knew all things, and the next best thing for him is that he should know himself. Why do I say so at this moment? I will tell you. You, Socrates, have granted us this opportunity of conversing with you, and are ready to assist us in determining what is the best of human goods. For when Philebus said that pleasure and delight and enjoyment and the like were the chief good, you answered—No, not those, but another class of goods; and we are constantly reminding ourselves of what you said, and very properly, in order that we may not forget to examine and compare the two. And these goods, which in your opinion are to be designated as superior to pleasure, and are the true objects of pursuit, are mind and knowledge and understanding and art, and the like. There was a dispute about which were the best, and we playfully threatened that you should not be allowed to go home until the question was settled; and you agreed, and placed yourself at our disposal. And now, as children say, what has been fairly given cannot be taken back; cease then to fight against us in this way.

Soc. In what way?

Phi. Do not perplex us, and keep asking questions of us to which we have not as yet any sufficient answer to give; let us not imagine that a general puzzling of us all is to be the end of our discussion, but if we are unable to answer, do you answer, as you have promised. Consider, then, whether you will divide pleasure and knowledge according to their kinds; or you may let the matter drop, if you are able and willing to find some other mode of clearing up our controversy.

Soc. If you say that, I have nothing to apprehend, for the words 'if you are willing' dispel all my fear; and, moreover, a god seems to have recalled something to my mind.

Phi. What is that?

Soc. I remember to have heard long ago certain discussions about pleasure and wisdom, whether awake or in a dream I cannot tell; they were to the effect that neither the one nor the other of them was the good, but some third thing, which was different from them, and better than either. If this be clearly established, then pleasure will lose the victory, for the good will cease to be identified with her:—Am I not right?

Pro. Yes.

Soc. And there will cease to be any need of distinguishing the kinds of pleasures, as I am inclined to think, but this will appear more clearly as we proceed.

Pro. Capital, Socrates; pray go on as you propose.

Soc. But, let us first agree on some little points.

Pro. What are they?

Soc. Is the good perfect or imperfect?

Pro. The most perfect, Socrates, of all things.

Soc. And is the good sufficient?

Pro. Yes, certainly, and in a degree surpassing all other things.

Soc. And no one can deny that all percipient beings desire and hunt after good, and are eager to catch and have the good about them, and care not for the attainment of anything which is not accompanied by good.

Pro. That is undeniable.

Soc. Now let us part off the life of pleasure from the life of wisdom, and pass them in review.

Pro. How do you mean?

Soc. Let there be no wisdom in the life of pleasure, nor any pleasure in the life of wisdom, for if either of them is the chief good, it cannot be supposed to want anything, but if either is shown to want anything, then it cannot really be the chief good.

Pro. Impossible.

Soc. And will you help us to test these two lives?

Pro. Certainly.

Soc. Then answer.

Pro. Ask.

Soc. Would you choose, Protarchus, to live all your life long in the enjoyment of the greatest pleasures?

Pro. Certainly I should.

Soc. Would you consider that there was still anything wanting to you if you had perfect pleasure?

Pro. Certainly not.

Soc. Reflect; would you not want wisdom and intelligence and forethought, and similar qualities? would you not at any rate want sight?

Pro. Why should I? Having pleasure I should have all things.

Soc. Living thus, you would always throughout your life enjoy the greatest pleasures?

Pro. I should.

Soc. But if you had neither mind, nor memory, nor knowledge, nor true opinion, you would in the first place be utterly ignorant of whether you were pleased or not, because you would be entirely devoid of intelligence.

Pro. Certainly.

Soc. And similarly, if you had no memory you would not recollect that you had ever been pleased, nor would the slightest recollection of the pleasure which you feel at any moment remain with you; and if you had no true opinion you would not think that you were pleased when you were; and if you had no power of calculation you would not be able to calculate on future pleasure, and your life would be the life, not of a man, but of an oyster or 'pulmo marinus.' Could this be otherwise?

Pro. No.

Soc. But is such a life eligible?

Pro. I cannot answer you, Socrates; the argument has taken away from me the power of speech.

Soc. We must keep up our spirits;—let us now take the life of mind and examine it in turn.

Pro. And what is this life of mind?

Soc. I want to know whether any one of us would consent to live, having wisdom and mind and knowledge and memory of all things, but having no sense of pleasure or pain, and wholly unaffected by these and the like feelings?

Pro. Neither life, Socrates, appears eligible to me, nor is likely, as I should imagine, to be chosen by any one else.

Soc. What would you say, Protarchus, to both of these in one, or to one that was made out of the union of the two?

Pro. Out of the union, that is, of pleasure with mind and wisdom?

Soc. Yes, that is the life which I mean.

Pro. There can be no difference of opinion; not some but all would surely choose this third rather than either of the other two, and in addition to them.

Soc. But do you see the consequence?

Pro. To be sure I do. The consequence is, that two out of the three lives which have been proposed are neither sufficient nor eligible for man or for animal.

Soc. Then now there can be no doubt that neither of them has the good, for the one which had would certainly have been sufficient and perfect and eligible for every living creature or thing that was able to live such a life; and if any of us had chosen any other, he would have chosen contrary to the nature of the truly eligible, and not of his own free will, but either through ignorance or from some unhappy necessity.

Pro. Certainly that seems to be true.

Soc. And now have I not sufficiently shown that Philebus' goddess is not to be regarded as identical with the good?

Phi. Neither is your 'mind' the good, Socrates, for that will be open to the same objections.

Soc. Perhaps, Philebus, you may be right in saying so of my 'mind'; but of the true, which is also the divine mind, far otherwise. However, I will not at present claim the first place for mind as against the mixed life; but we must come to some understanding about the second place. For you might affirm pleasure and I mind to be the cause of the mixed life; and in that case although neither of them would be the good, one of them might be imagined to be the cause of the good. And I might proceed further to argue in opposition to Philebus, that the element which makes this mixed life eligible and good, is more akin and more similar to mind than to pleasure. And if this is true, pleasure cannot be truly said to share either in the first or second place, and does not, if I may trust my own mind, attain even to the third.

Pro. Truly, Socrates, pleasure appears to me to have had a fall; in fighting for the palm, she has been smitten by the argument, and is laid low. I must say that mind would have fallen too, and may therefore be thought to show discretion in not putting forward a similar claim. And if pleasure were deprived not only of the first but of the second place, she would be terribly damaged in the eyes of her admirers, for not even to them would she still appear as fair as before.

Soc. Well, but had we not better leave her now, and not pain her by applying the crucial test, and finally detecting her?

Pro. Nonsense, Socrates.

Soc. Why? because I said that we had better not pain pleasure, which is an impossibility?

Pro. Yes, and more than that, because you do not seem to be aware that none of us will let you go home until you have finished the argument. . . .

The Contrasts of the Ideal State

The contrasts of the ideal state are: ignorant state *(jāhiliyā)*, vicious state *(fāsiqa)*, transformed state *(mubaddala* or *mutabāddala)*, and erring state *(dālla)*. Also to be contrasted to it are the misfortunate people of the cities.

The ignorant state is that whose inhabitants do not know happiness and never thought of it. If they are guided to it, they will not evaluate it or believe in it. However, they know of the good which is apparently assumed to be so; and those things which are assumed to be the goal in life are: good health, enjoyment of the senses, honor and greatness. And to the inhabitants of the ignorant state, everyone of these things is considered happiness. And, for them, the ultimate happiness is a combination of all those things. And the opposite [of this condition] is unhappiness as exemplified by poor health, poverty, non-enjoyment of the senses, and lack of honor.

It [ignorant state] is divided into state of necessity *(darūrīya)* whose inhabitants aim at the necessities of life, such as food, drinks, clothing, lodging and carnal gratification; and they help each other in securing their object.

The transformed state is that whose inhabitants intend to assist each other to attain prosperity, for it is the goal in life.

The plutocratic state[1] is that whose inhabitants aim at enjoying the pleasures of eating, drinking, and carnal gratification. All in all, these enjoyments include the pleasure of the senses, imagination, and the preference for amusement in every way and respect.

The timocratic state (karāma) is that whose inhabitants intend to assist each other in order to be honored, praised, mentioned, remem-

---

*In Collaboration with Fouad Tahan. Taken from Farabi's *Treatise on the Opinions of the Citizens of the Ideal State,* Chapter 29.

1. The Arabic words used in the text were: *khissa* (greedy, vile, debased) and *shaqwa* (desire, lust, appetite). 'Plutocratic state' would capture what Farabi intended in this passage.

bered and made famous among other nations verbally as well as in action. They excel either among others or among each other: i.e. each one [excels] according to how much he is liked or according to that which he is capable of obtaining.

The tyrannical state (taghallub) is that whose inhabitants aim at conquering and overcoming others and being able not to be overcome or defeated by them. And their efforts are crowned with success from overcoming them only.

The democratic state (jamā'iya) is that whose inhabitants aim to be free, everyone of them does whatever pleases him, and nothing is originally prohibited from them.

The rulers of the ignorant states are in accordance with the number of these [mentioned] states; and each one of them takes care and manages the state with which he is empowered in order to fulfill his wishes and desires. The worries of the ignorant states which can be made to be the goals are those which we previously mentioned.

The vicious state is that whose opinions are like those of the ideal state and they [its inhabitants] know happiness, God, the angels, the Active Intellect, and anything the ideal state may know and believe. But their actions are like the actions of the ignorant states.

The transformed state is that whose opinions and actions were once like the opinions and actions of the ideal state, but it has undergone a change and other opinions later gained entry and caused a change in the actions of others. And the erring state is that whose inhabitants assume this happiness after life. It is believed that they hold corrupt opinions about God, the angels and the Active Intellect. These opinions are not good for them even if they only are considered as imitations and fantacies. Their first ruler is the one who imagines to be inspired without actually being so, but uses tricks, deceptions and illusions [in order to lead his people astray].

The rulers of these states are to be contrasted with the rulers of the ideal state; also their leadership is to be contrasted with that of the ideal, and likewise everything else about them. And the rulers of the ideal states who rule one after another at different times are all as one soul and as one ruler who rules throughout all times. Hence if a group of them agree once either in one state or in many states, then their group would be as one ruler, and their souls as one soul. And likewise people of every class, when ruling at different times, will be as one soul throughout all times. Also if at one time there is a certain group from a certain class and it [group] is in one state or many states and if their souls are [viewed as] one, then that [particular] class will be either a *ruling* class or a *serving* class.

And to the inhabitants of the ideal state, there are many common things to learn and do and other things from the areas of knowledge and action which concern every class and everyone of them. However every one of them falls within the range of happiness by these two [ways]: i.e. by that which is common to him and to others and by that which concerns the members of that class of which he is one of them. Thus if every one of them does accordingly, then his actions will make him gain a good, virtuous, spiritual form, and the more he continues adhering to it, the more his form will become strong and virtuous. As the continuation of doing good actions from the actions of writing will make man skillful in writing, and as long as he continues doing these actions, the craft behind these actions will become stronger and better. And then power and virtue will increase by purifying these actions, and the pleasure which follows that spiritual form will be increased; and the joy of man's soul and his love for them will increase, too. And this is the condition of the actions by which he obtains happiness. For the more one obtains from them, the more they are purified and repeated. Then the soul, whose function is to be happy, becomes stronger, better and more perfect until it reaches the stage of perfection where it will not be in need of matter, and occurs free of it. Hence it will neither decay by means of the decay of matter, nor if it did survive will it be in need of matter.

And if it occurs free of matter, not attached to any corporeal, then the accidents which occur to the corporeals from the point of being corporeals will be denied and then it is neither possible to say that it moves or rests. Hence it should only be given the attributes which fit that which is not a corporeal. And whenever man thinks of something that may be given as an attribute to a corporeal, then this should be denied of the separable souls. And to understand this condition, its concept is difficult and unusual. Also anything that may be attached to it and is an accident to it in comparison to the corporeal will be denied of it. And since these souls were separated from the souls which were in different primary matters and since it has been explained that the spiritual forms follow the mixtures of bodies—some more and others less—and since every spiritual form results from the mixture of the body in which it was in, then it is necessary to be different because of the difference among them. And since the changes of bodies are indefinite, then the changes of the souls are also indefinite.

The Doors of Perception

An hour later, with ten more miles and the visit to the World's Biggest Drug Store safely behind us, we were back at home, and I had returned to that reassuring but profoundly unsatisfactory state known as "being in one's right mind."

That humanity at large will ever be able to dispense with Artificial Paradises seems very unlikely. Most men and women lead lives at the worst so painful, at the best so monotonous, poor and limited that the urge to escape, the longing to transcend themselves if only for a few moments, is and has always been one of the principal appetites of the soul. Art and religion, carnivals and saturnalia, dancing and listening to oratory—all these have served, in H. G. Wells's phrase, as Doors in the Wall. And for private, for everyday use there have always been chemical intoxicants. All the vegetable sedatives and narcotics, all the euphorics that grow on trees, the hallucinogens that ripen in berries or can be squeezed from roots—all, without exception, have been known and systematically used by human beings from time immemorial. And to these natural modifiers of consciousness modern science has added its quota of synthetics—chloral, for example, and benzedrine, the bromides and the barbiturates.

Most of these modifiers of consciousness cannot now be taken except under doctor's orders, or else illegally and at considerable risk. For unrestricted use the West has permitted only alcohol and tobacco. All the other chemical Doors in the Wall are labeled Dope, and their unauthorized takers are Fiends.

We now spend a good deal more on drink and smoke than we spend on education. This, of course, is not surprising. The urge to escape from selfhood and the environment is in almost everyone almost all the time. The urge to do something for the young is strong only in parents, and in them only for the few years during which their children go to school. Equally unsurprising is the current attitude towards drink and smoke. In spite of the growing army of hopeless alcoholics, in spite of the hundreds of thousands of persons annually maimed or killed by drunken drivers, popular comedians still crack jokes about alcohol and its addicts. And in spite of the evidence linking cigarettes with lung cancer, practically everybody regards tobacco smoking as being hardly less normal and natural than eating. From the point of view of the rationalist utilitarian this may seem odd. For the historian, it is exactly what you would expect. A firm conviction of the material reality of Hell never prevented medieval Christians from doing what their ambition, lust or covetousness suggested. Lung cancer, traffic accidents and the millions of miserable and misery-creating alcoholics are facts even more certain than was, in Dante's day, the fact of the Inferno. But all such facts are remote and unsubstantial compared with the near, felt fact of a craving, here and now, for release or sedation, for a drink or a smoke.

Ours is the age, among other things, of the automobile and of rocketing population. Alcohol is incompatible with safety on the roads, and its production, like that of tobacco, condemns to virtual sterility many millions of acres of the most fertile soil. The problems raised by alcohol and tobacco cannot, it goes without saying, be solved by prohibition. The universal and ever-present urge to self-transcendence is not to be abolished by slamming the currently popular Doors in the Wall. The only reasonable policy is to open other, better doors in the hope of inducing men and women to exchange their old bad habits for new and less harmful ones. Some of these other, better doors will be social and technological in nature, others religious or psychological, others dietetic, educational, athletic. But the need for frequent chemical vacations from intolerable selfhood and repulsive surroundings will undoubtedly remain. What is needed is a new drug which will relieve and console our suffering species without doing more harm in the long run than it does good in the short. Such a drug must be potent in minute doses and synthesizable. If it does not possess these qualities, its production, like that of wine, beer, spirits and tobacco will interfere with the raising of indispensable food and fibers. It must be less toxic than opium or cocaine, less likely to produce undesirable social consequences than alcohol or the barbiturates, less inimical to heart and lungs than the tars and nicotine of cigarettes. And, on the positive side, it should produce changes in consciousness more interesting, more intrinsically valuable than mere sedation or dreaminess, delusions of omnipotence or release from inhibition.

To most people, mescalin is almost completely innocuous. Unlike alcohol, it does not drive the taker into the kind of uninhibited action which results in brawls, crimes of violence and traffic accidents. A man under the influence of mescalin quietly minds his own business. Moreover, the business he minds is an experience of the most enlightening kind, which does not have to be paid for (and this is surely important) by a compensatory hangover. Of the long-range consequences of regular mescalin taking we know very little. The Indians who consume peyote buttons do not seem to be physically or morally degraded by the habit. However, the available evidence is still scarce and sketchy.*

Although obviously superior to cocaine, opium, alcohol and tobacco, mescalin is not yet the ideal drug. Along with the happily transfigured majority of mescalin takers there is a minority that finds in the drug only hell or purgatory. Moreover, for a drug that is to be used, like alcohol, for general consumption, its effects last for an inconveniently long time. But chemistry and physiology are capable nowadays of practically anything. If the psychologists and sociologists will define the ideal, the neurologists and pharmacologists can be relied upon to discover the means whereby that ideal can be realized or at least (for perhaps this kind of ideal can never, in the very nature of things, be fully realized) more nearly approached than in the wine-bibbing past, the whisky-drinking, marijuana-smoking and barbiturate-swallowing present.

The urge to transcend self-conscious selfhood is, as I have said, a principal appetite of the soul. When, for whatever reason, men and women fail to transcend themselves by means of worship, good works and spiritual exercises, they are apt to resort to religion's chemical surrogates—alcohol and "goof pills" in the modern West, alcohol and opium in the East, hashish in the Mohammedan world, alcohol and marijuana in Central America, alcohol and coca in the Andes, alcohol and the barbiturates in the more up-to-date regions of South America. In *Poisons Sacrés, Ivresses Divines* Philippe de Félice has written at

---

*In his monograph, *Menomini Peyotism,* published (December,1952) in the Transactions of the American Philosophical Society, Professor J. S. Slotkin has written that "the habitual use of Peyote does not seem to produce any increased tolerance or dependence. I know many people who have been Peyotists for forty to fifty years. The amount of Peyote they use depends upon the solemnity of the occasion; in general they do not take any more Peyote now than they did years ago. Also, there is sometimes an interval of a month or more between rites, and they go without Peyote during this period without feeling any craving for it. Personally, even after a series of rites occurring on four successive weekends, I neither increased the amount of Peyote consumed nor felt any continued need for it." It is evidently with good reason that "Peyote has never been legally declared a narcotic, or its use prohibited by the federal government." However, "during the long history of Indian-white contact, white officials have usually tried to suppress the use of Peyote, because it has been conceived to violate their own mores. But these attempts have always failed." In a footnote Dr. Slotkin adds that "it is amazing to hear the fantastic stories about the effects of Peyote and the nature of the ritual, which are told by the white and Catholic Indian officials in the Menomini Reservation. None of them have had the slightest first-hand experience with the plant or with the religion, yet some fancy themselves to be authorities and write official reports on the subject."

length and with a wealth of documentation on the immemorial connection between religion and the taking of drugs. Here, in summary or in
direct quotation, are his conclusions. The employment for religious
purposes of toxic substances is "extraordinarily widespread. . . . The
practices studied in this volume can be observed in every region of the
earth, among primitives no less than among those who have reached a
high pitch of civilization. We are therefore dealing not with exceptional
facts, which might justifiably be overlooked, but with a general and, in
the widest sense of the word, a human phenomenon, the kind of phenomenon which cannot be disregarded by anyone who is trying to
discover what religion is, and what are the deep needs which it must
satisfy."

Ideally, everyone should be able to find self-transcendence in some
form of pure or applied religion. In practice it seems very unlikely that
this hoped for consummation will ever be realized. There are, and
doubtless there always will be, good churchmen and good church-
women for whom, unfortunately, piety is not enough. The late G. K.
Chesterton, who wrote at least as lyrically of drink as of devotion, may
serve as their eloquent spokesman.

The modern churches, with some exceptions among the Protestant
denominations, tolerate alcohol; but even the most tolerant have made
no attempt to convert the drug to Christianity, or to sacramentalize its
use. The pious drinker is forced to take his religion in one compartment,
his religion-surrogate in another. And perhaps this is inevitable. Drinking cannot be sacramentalized except in religions which set no store on
decorum. The worship of Dionysos or the Celtic god of beer was a loud
and disorderly affair. The rites of Christianity are incompatible with
even religious drunkenness. This does no harm to the distillers, but is
very bad for Christianity. Countless persons desire self-transcendence
and would be glad to find it in church. But, alas, "the hungry sheep look
up and are not fed." They take part in rites, they listen to sermons, they
repeat prayers; but their thirst remains unassuaged. Disappointed, they
turn to the bottle. For a time at least and in a kind of way, it works.
Church may still be attended; but it is no more than the Musical Bank
of Butler's *Erewhon.* God may still be acknowledged; but He is God
only on the verbal level, only in a strictly Pickwickian sense. The effective object of worship is the bottle and the sole religious experience is
that state of uninhibited and belligerent euphoria which follows the
ingestion of the third cocktail.

We see, then, that Christianity and alcohol do not and cannot mix.
Christianity and mescalin seem to be much more compatible. This has
been demonstrated by many tribes of Indians, from Texas to as far north

as Wisconsin. Among these tribes are to be found groups affiliated with the Native American Church, a sect whose principal rite is a kind of Early Christian agape, or love feast, where slices of peyote take the place of the sacramental bread and wine. These Native Americans regard the cactus as God's special gift to the Indians, and equate its effects with the workings of the divine Spirit.

Professor J. S. Slotkin, one of the very few white men ever to have participated in the rites of a Peyotist congregation, says of his fellow worshipers that they are "certainly not stupefied or drunk. . . . They never get out of rhythm or fumble their words, as a drunken or stupefied man would do. . . . They are all quiet, courteous and considerate of one another. I have never been in any white man's house of worship where there is either so much religious feeling or decorum." And what, we may ask, are these devout and well-behaved Peyotists experiencing? Not the mild sense of virtue which sustains the average Sunday churchgoer through ninety minutes of boredom. Not even those high feelings, inspired by thoughts of the Creator and the Redeemer, the Judge and the Comforter, which animate the pious. For these Native Americans, religious experience is something more direct and illuminating, more spontaneous, less the homemade product of the superficial, self-conscious mind. Sometimes (according to the reports collected by Dr. Slotkin) they see visions, which may be of Christ Himself. Sometimes they hear the voice of the Great Spirit. Sometimes they become aware of the presence of God and of those personal shortcomings which must be corrected if they are to do His will. The practical consequences of these chemical openings of doors into the Other World seem to be wholly good. Dr. Slotkin reports that habitual Peyotists are on the whole more industrious, more temperate (many of them abstain altogether from alcohol), more peaceable than non-Peyotists. A tree with such satisfactory fruits cannot be condemned out of hand as evil.

In sacramentalizing the use of peyote, the Indians of the Native American Church have done something which is at once psychologically sound and historically respectable. In the early centuries of Christianity many pagan rites and festivals were baptized, so to say, and made to serve the purposes of the Church. These jollifications were not particularly edifying; but they assuaged a certain psychological hunger and, instead of trying to suppress them, the earlier missionaries had the sense to accept them for what they were, soul-satisfying expressions of fundamental urges, and to incorporate them into the fabric of the new religion. What the Native Americans have done is essentially similar. They have taken a pagan custom (a custom, incidentally, far more elevating and enlightening than most of the rather brutish carousals and mummeries adopted from European paganism) and given it a Christian significance.

Though but recently introduced into the northern United States, peyote-eating and the religion based upon it have become important symbols of the red man's right to spiritual independence. Some Indians have reacted to white supremacy by becoming Americanized, others by retreating into traditional Indianism. But some have tried to make the best of both worlds, indeed of all the worlds—the best of Indianism, the best of Christianity, and the best of those Other Worlds of transcendental experience, where the soul knows itself as unconditioned and of like nature with the divine. Hence the Native American Church. In it two great appetites of the soul—the urge to independence and self-determination and the urge to self-transcendence—were fused with, and interpreted in the light of, a third—the urge to worship, to justify the ways of God to man, to explain the universe by means of a coherent theology.

> Lo, the poor Indian, whose untutored mind
> Clothes him in front, but leaves him bare behind.

But actually it is we, the rich and highly educated whites, who have left ourselves bare behind. We cover our anterior nakedness with some philosophy—Christian, Marxian, Freudo-Physicalist—but abaft we remain uncovered, at the mercy of all the winds of circumstance. The poor Indian, on the other hand, has had the wit to protect his rear by supplementing the fig leaf of a theology with the breechclout of transcendental experience.

I am not so foolish as to equate what happens under the influence of mescalin or of any other drug, prepared or in the future preparable, with the realization of the end and ultimate purpose of human life: Enlightenment, the Beatific Vision. All I am suggesting is that the mescalin experience is what Catholic theologians call "a gratuitous grace," not necessary to salvation but potentially helpful and to be accepted thankfully, if made available. To be shaken out of the ruts of ordinary perception, to be shown for a few timeless hours the outer and the inner world, not as they appear to an animal obsessed with survival or to a human being obsessed with words and notions, but as they are apprehended, directly and unconditionally, by Mind at Large—this is an experience of inestimable value to everyone and especially to the intellectual. For the intellectual is by definition the man for whom, in Goethe's phrase, "the word is essentially fruitful." He is the man who feels that "what we perceive by the eye is foreign to us as such and need not impress us deeply." And yet, though himself an intellectual and one of the supreme masters of language, Goethe did not always agree with his own evaluation of the word. "We talk," he wrote in middle life, "far too much. We should talk less and draw more. I personally should like to renounce speech altogether and, like organic Nature, communicate everything I have to say in sketches. That fig tree, this little snake, the cocoon on my window sill quietly awaiting its future—all these are momentous signatures. A person able to decipher their meaning properly would soon be able to dispense with the written or the spoken word altogether. The more I think of it, there is something futile, mediocre, even (I am tempted to say) foppish about speech. By contrast, how the gravity of Nature and her silence startle you, when you stand face to face with her, undistracted, before a barren ridge or in the desolation of the ancient hills." We can never dispense with language and the other symbol systems; for it is by means of them, and only by their means, that we have raised ourselves above the brutes, to the level of human beings. But we can easily become the victims as well as the beneficiaries of these systems. We must learn how to handle words effectively; but at the same time we must preserve and, if necessary, intensify our ability to look at the world directly and not through that half opaque medium of concepts, which distorts every given fact into the all too familiar likeness of some generic label or explanatory abstraction.

Literary or scientific, liberal or specialist, all our education is predominantly verbal and therefore fails to accomplish what it is supposed to do. Instead of transforming children into fully developed adults, it turns out students of the natural sciences who are completely unaware of Nature as the primary fact of experience, it inflicts upon the world students of the humanities who know nothing of humanity, their own or anyone else's.

Gestalt psychologists, such as Samuel Renshaw, have devised methods for widening the range and increasing the acuity of human perceptions. But do our educators apply them? The answer is, No.

Teachers in every field of psycho-physical skill, from seeing to tennis, from tightrope walking to prayer, have discovered, by trial and error, the conditions of optimum functioning within their special fields. But have any of the great Foundations financed a project for co-ordinating these empirical findings into a general theory and practice of heightened creativeness? Again, so far as I am aware, the answer is, No.

All sorts of cultists and queer fish teach all kinds of techniques for achieving health, contentment, peace of mind; and for many of their hearers many of these techniques are demonstrably effective. But do we see respectable psychologists, philosophers and clergymen boldly descending into those odd and sometimes malodorous wells, at the bottom of which poor Truth is so often condemned to sit? Yet once more the answer is, No.

And now look at the history of mescalin research. Seventy years ago men of first-rate ability described the transcendental experiences which come to those who, in good health, under proper conditions and in the right spirit, take the drug. How many philosophers, how many theologians, how many professional educators have had the curiosity to open this Door in the Wall? The answer, for all practical purposes, is, None.

In a world where education is predominantly verbal, highly educated people find it all but impossible to pay serious attention to anything but words and notions. There is always money for, there are always doctorates in, the learned foolery of research into what, for scholars, is the all-important problem: Who influenced whom to say what when? Even in this age of technology the verbal humanities are honored. The non-verbal humanities, the arts of being directly aware of the given facts of our existence, are almost completely ignored. A catalogue, a bibliography, a definitive edition of a third-rate versifier's *ipsissima verba,* a stupendous index to end all indexes—any genuinely Alexandrian project is sure of approval and financial support. But when it comes to finding out how you and I, our children and grandchildren, may become more perceptive, more intensely aware of inward and outward reality, more open to the Spirit, less apt, by psychological malpractices, to make ourselves physically ill, and more capable of controlling our own autonomic nervous system—when it comes to any form of non-verbal education more fundamental (and more likely to be of some practical use) than Swedish drill, no really respectable person in any really respectable university or church will do anything about it. Verbalists are suspicious of the non-verbal; rationalists fear the given, non-rational fact; intellectuals feel that "what we perceive by the eye (or in any other way) is foreign to us as such and need not impress us deeply." Besides, this matter of education in the non-verbal humanities will not fit into any of the established pigeonholes. It is not religion, not neurology, not gymnastics, not morality or civics, not even experimental psychology. This being so the subject is, for academic and ecclesiastical purposes, non-existent and may safely be ignored altogether or left, with a patronizing smile, to those whom the Pharisees of verbal orthodoxy call cranks, quacks, charlatans and unqualified amateurs.

"I have always found," Blake wrote rather bitterly, "that Angels have the vanity to speak of themselves as the only wise. This they do with a confident insolence sprouting from systematic reasoning."

Systematic reasoning is something we could not, as a species or as individuals, possibly do without. But neither, if we are to remain sane, can we possibly do without direct perception, the more unsystematic the better, of the inner and outer worlds into which we have been born. This given reality is an infinite which passes all understanding and yet admits of being directly and in some sort totally apprehended. It is a transcendence belonging to another order than the human, and yet it may be present to us as a felt immanence, an experienced participation. To be enlightened is to be aware, always, of total reality in its immanent otherness—to be aware of it and yet to remain in a condition to survive as an animal, to think and feel as a human being, to resort whenever expedient to systematic reasoning. Our goal is to discover that we have always been where we ought to be. Unhappily we make the task exceedingly difficult for ourselves. Meanwhile, however, there are gratuitous graces in the form of partial and fleeting realizations. Under a more realistic, a less exclusively verbal system of education than ours, every Angel (in Blake's sense of that word) would be permitted as a sabbatical treat, would be urged and even, if necessary, compelled to take an occasional trip through some chemical Door in the Wall into the world of transcendental experience. If it terrified him, it would be unfortunate but probably salutary. If it brought him a brief but timeless illumination, so much the better. In either case the Angel might lose a little of the confident insolence sprouting from systematic reasoning and the consciousness of having read all the books.

Near the end of his life Aquinas experienced Infused Contemplation. Thereafter he refused to go back to work on his unfinished book. Compared with *this,* everything he had read and argued about and written—Aristotle and the Sentences, the Questions, the Propositions, the majestic Summas—was no better than chaff or straw. For most intellectuals such a sit-down strike would be inadvisable, even morally wrong. But the Angelic Doctor had done more systematic reasoning than any twelve ordinary Angels, and was already ripe for death. He had earned the right, in those last months of his mortality, to turn away from merely symbolic straw and chaff to the bread of actual and substantial Fact. For Angels of a lower order and with better prospects of longevity, there must be a return to the straw. But the man who comes back through the Door in the Wall will never be quite the same as the man who went out. He will be wiser but less cocksure, happier but less self-satisfied, humbler in acknowledging his ignorance yet better equipped to understand the relationship of words to things, of systematic reasoning to the unfathomable Mystery which it tries, forever vainly, to comprehend.

The Sane Society

Happiness is another, and one of the more popular concepts by which mental health is defined today. As the formula runs in the *Brave New World:* "everybody is happy nowadays."

What is meant by happiness? Most people today would probably answer the question by saying that to be happy is to have "fun," or "to have a good time." The answer to the question, "What is fun?" depends somewhat on the economic situation of the individual, and more, on his education and personality structure. Economic differences, however, are not as important as they may seem. The "good time" of society's upper strata is the fun model for those not yet able to pay for it while earnestly hoping for that happy eventuality—and the "good time" of society's lower strata is increasingly a cheaper imitation of the upper strata's, differing in cost, but not so much in quality.

What does this fun consist in? Going to the movies, parties, ball games, listening to the radio and watching television, taking a ride in the car on Sundays, making love, sleeping late on Sunday mornings, and traveling, for those who can afford it. If we use a more respectable term, instead of the word "fun," and "having a good time," we might say that the concept of happiness is, at best, identified with that of pleasure. Taking into consideration our discussion of the problem of consumption, we can define the concept somewhat more accurately as the pleasure of unrestricted consumption, push-button power and laziness.

From this standpoint, happiness could be defined as the opposite of sadness or sorrow, and indeed, the average person defines happiness as a state of mind which is free from sadness or sorrow. This definition, however, shows that there is something profoundly wrong in this concept of happiness. A person who is alive and sensitive cannot fail to be sad, and to feel sorrow many times in his life. This is so, not only because of the amount of unnecessary suffering produced by the imperfection of our social arrangements, but because of the nature of human existence, which makes it impossible not to react to life with a good deal of pain and sorrow. Since we are living beings, we must be sadly aware of the necessary gap between our aspirations and what can be achieved in our short and troubled life. Since death confronts us with the inevitable fact that either we shall die before our loved ones or they before us —since we see suffering, the unavoidable as well as the unnecessary and wasteful, around us every day, how can we avoid the experience of pain and sorrow? The effort to avoid it is only possible if we reduce our sensitivity, responsiveness and love, if we harden our hearts and withdraw our attention and our feeling from others, as well as from ourselves.

If we want to define happiness by its opposite, we must define it not in contrast to *sadness,* but in contrast to *depression.*

What is depression? It is the inability to feel, it is the sense of being dead, while our body is alive. It is the inability to experience joy, as well as the inability to experience sadness. A depressed person would be greatly relieved if he could feel sad. A state of depression is so unbearable because one is incapable of feeling anything, either joy or sadness. If we try to define happiness in contrast to depression, we approach Spinoza's definition of joy and happiness as that state of intensified vitality that fuses into one whole our effort both to understand our fellow men and be one with them. Happiness results from the experience of productive living, and the use of the powers of love and reason which unite us with the world. Happiness consists in our touching the rock bottom of reality, in the discovery of our self and our oneness with others as well as our difference from them. Happiness is a state of intense inner activity and the experience of the increasing vital energy which occurs in productive relatedness to the world and to ourselves.

It follows that happiness cannot be found in the state of inner passivity, and in the consumer attitude which pervades the life of alienated man. Happiness is to experience fullness, not emptiness which needs to be filled. The average man today may have a good deal of fun and pleasure, but in spite of this, he is fundamentally depressed. Perhaps it clarifies the issue if instead of using the word "depressed" we use the word "bored." Actually there is very little difference between the two, except a difference in degree, because boredom is nothing but the experience of a paralysis of our productive powers and the sense of un-aliveness. Among the evils of life, there are few which are as painful as boredom, and consequently every attempt is made to avoid it.

It can be avoided in two ways; either fundamentally, by being productive, and in this manner experiencing happiness, or by trying to avoid its manifestations. The latter attempt seems to characterize the chasing after fun and pleasure in the average person today. He senses his depression and boredom, which becomes manifest when he is alone with himself or with those closest to him. All our amusements serve the purpose of making it easy for him to run away from himself and from the threatening boredom by taking refuge in the many ways of escape which our culture offers him; yet covering up a symptom does not do away with the conditions which produce it. Aside from the fear of physical illness, or of being humiliated by the loss of status and prestige, the fear of boredom plays a paramount role among the fears of modern man. In a world of fun and amusement, he is afraid of boredom, and glad when another day has passed without mishap, another hour has been killed without his having become aware of the lurking boredom.

From the standpoint of normative humanism we must arrive at a different concept of mental health; the very person who is considered healthy in the categories of an alienated world, from the humanistic standpoint appears as the sickest one—although not in terms of individual sickness, but of the socially patterned defect. Mental health, in the humanistic sense, is characterized by the ability to love and to create, by the emergence from the incestuous ties to family and nature, by a sense of identity based on one's experience of self as the subject and agent of one's powers, by the grasp of reality inside and outside of ourselves, that is, by the development of objectivity and reason. The aim of life is to live it intensely, to be fully born, to be fully awake. To emerge from the ideas of infantile grandiosity into the conviction of one's real though limited strength; to be able to accept the paradox that every one of us is the most important thing there is in the universe— and at the same time not more important than a fly or a blade of grass. To be able to love life, and yet to accept death without terror; to tolerate uncertainty about the most important questions with which life confronts us—and yet to have faith in our thought and feeling, inasmuch as they are truly ours. To be able to be alone, and at the same time one with a loved person, with every brother on this earth, with all that is alive; to follow the voice of our conscience, the voice that calls us to ourselves, yet not to indulge in self hate when the voice of conscience was not loud enough to be heard and followed. The mentally healthy person is the person who lives by love, reason and faith, who respects life, his own and that of his fellow man.

The alienated person, as we have tried to describe him in this chapter, cannot be healthy. Since he experiences himself as a thing, an investment, to be manipulated by himself and by others, he is lacking in a sense of self. This lack of self creates deep anxiety. The anxiety engendered by confronting him with the abyss of nothingness is more terrifying than even the tortures of hell. In the vision of hell, *I* am punished and tortured—in the vision of nothingness I am driven to the border of madness—because I cannot say "I" anymore. If the modern age has been rightly called the age of anxiety, it is primarily because of this anxiety engendered by the lack of self. Inasmuch as "I am as you desire me"—I am *not;* I am anxious, dependent on approval of others, constantly trying to please. The alienated person feels inferior whenever he suspects himself of not being in line. Since his sense of worth is based on approval as the reward for conformity, he feels naturally threatened in his sense of self and in his self-esteem by any feeling, thought or action which could be suspected of being a deviation. Yet, inasmuch as he *is* human and not an automaton, he cannot help deviating, hence he must feel afraid of disapproval all the time. As a result he has to try all the harder to conform, to be approved of, to be successful. Not the voice of his conscience gives him strength and security but the feeling of not having lost the close touch with the herd.

Another result of alienation is the prevalence of a feeling of guilt. It is, indeed, amazing that in as fundamentally irreligious a culture as ours, the sense of guilt should be so widespread and deep-rooted as it is. The main difference from, let us say, a Calvinistic community, is the fact that the feeling of guilt is neither very conscious, nor does it refer to a religiously patterned concept of sin. But if we scratch the surface, we find that people feel guilty about hundreds of things; for not having worked hard enough, for having been too protective—or not protective enough—toward their children, for not having done enough for Mother, or for having been too kindhearted to a debtor; people feel guilty for having done good things, as well as for having done bad things; it is almost as if they had to find something to feel guilty about.

What could be the cause of so much guilt feeling? It seems that there are two main sources which, though entirely different in themselves, lead to the same result. The one source is the same as that from which the feelings of inferiority spring. Not to be like the rest, not to be totally adjusted, makes one feel guilty toward the commands of the great It. The other source of guilt feeling is man's own conscience; he senses his gifts or talents, his ability to love, to think, to laugh, to cry, to wonder and to create, he senses that his life is the one chance he is given, and that if he loses this chance he has lost everything. He lives in a world with more comfort and ease than his ancestors ever knew— yet he senses that, chasing after more comfort, his life runs through his fingers like sand. He cannot help feeling guilty for the waste, for the lost chance. This feeling of guilt is much less conscious than the first one, but one reinforces the other, the one often serving as a rationalization for the other. Thus, alienated man feels guilty for being himself, and for not being himself, for being alive and for being an automaton, for being a person and for being a thing.

Alienated man is unhappy. Consumption of fun serves to repress the awareness of his unhappiness. He tries to save time, and yet he is eager to kill the time he has saved. He is glad to have finished another day without failure or humiliation, rather than to greet the new day with the enthusiasm which only the "I am I" experience can give. He is lacking the constant flow of energy which stems from productive relatedness to the world.

Having no faith, being deaf to the voice of conscience, and having a manipulating intelligence but little reason, he is bewildered, disquieted and willing to appoint to the position of a leader anyone who offers him a total solution.

Can the picture of alienation be connected with any of the established pictures of mental illness? In answering this question we must remember that man has two ways of relating himself to the world. One in which he sees the world as he needs to see it in order to manipulate or use it. Essentially this is sense experience and common-sense experience. Our eye sees that which we have to see, our ear hears what we have to hear in order to live; our common sense perceives things in a manner which enables us to act; both senses and common sense work in the service of survival. In the matter of sense and common sense and for the logic built upon them, things are the same for all people because the laws of their use are the same.

The other faculty of man is to see things from within, as it were; subjectively, formed by *my* inner experience, feeling, mood.[1] Ten painters paint the same tree in one sense, yet they paint ten different trees in another. Each tree is an expression of their individuality while also being the same tree. In the dream we see the world entirely from within; it loses its objective meaning and is transformed into a symbol of our own purely individual experience. The person who dreams while awake, that is, the person who is in touch only with his inner world and who is incapable of perceiving the outer world in its objective-action context, is insane. The person who can only experience the outer world photographically, but is out of touch with his inner world, with himself, is the alienated person. Schizophrenia and alienation are complementary. In both forms of sickness one pole of human experience is lacking. If both poles are present, we can speak of the productive person, whose

1. See a more detailed discussion of this point in E. Fromm, *The Forgotten Language,* Rinehart & Company, Inc., New York, 1952.

very productiveness results from the polarity between an inner and an outer form of perception.

Our description of the alienated character of contemporary man is somewhat one-sided; there are a number of positive factors which I have failed to mention. There is in the first place still a humanistic tradition alive, which has not been destroyed by the in-human process of alienation. But beyond that, there are signs that people are increasingly dissatisfied and disappointed with their way of life and trying to regain some of their lost selfhood and productivity. Millions of people listen to good music in concert halls or over the radio, an ever-increasing number of people paint, do gardening, build their own boats or houses, indulge in any number of "do it yourself" activities. Adult education is spreading, and even in business the awareness is growing that an executive should have reason and not only intelligence.[2]

But promising and real as all these trends are, they are not enough to justify an attitude which is to be found among a number of very sophisticated writers who claim that criticisms of our society, such as the one which has been offered here, are dated and old-fashioned; that we have already passed the peak of alienation and are now on our way to a better world. Appealing as this type of optimism is, it is nevertheless only a more sophisticated form of the defense of the status quo, a translation of the praise of the American Way of Life into the concepts of a cultural anthropology which, enriched by Marx and Freud, has "gone beyond" them and is reassuring man that there is no reason for serious worry.

---

2. An impressive example of this new trend is the course in literature and philosophy for junior executives of the Bell Telephone Co., under the directorship of Professors Morse Peckham and Rex Crawford at the University of Pennsylvania.

The Revolutionary Catechism, 1869

THE DUTIES OF THE REVOLUTIONARY TOWARD HIMSELF

1. The revolutionary is a doomed man. He has no personal interests, no business affairs, no emotions, no attachments, no property and no name. Everything in him is wholly absorbed in the single thought and the single passion for revolution.

2. The revolutionary knows that in the very depths of his being, not only in words but also in deeds, he has broken all the bonds which tie him to the social order and the civilized world with all its laws, moralities and customs and with all its generally accepted conventions. He is their implacable enemy, and if he continues to live with them it is only in order to destroy them more speedily.

3. The revolutionary despises all doctrinairism and refuses to accept the mundane sciences, leaving them for future generations. He knows only one science: the science of destruction. For this reason, but only for this reason, he will study physics, mechanics, chemistry, and perhaps medicine. For the same reason, all day and all night he studies the vital science of human beings, their characteristics and circumstances, and all the phenomena of the present social order. The object is perpetually the same: the surest and quickest way of destroying the whole filthy order.

4. The revolutionary despises public opinion. He despises the existing social morality and hates all its manifestations. For him, morality is everything which contributes to the triumph of the revolution. Immoral and criminal is everything that stands in its way.

5. The revolutionary is a dedicated man, merciless toward the State and toward the educated classes; and he can expect no mercy from them. Between him and them there exists, declared or concealed, a relentless and irreconcilable war to the death. He must accustom himself to torture.

6. Hard with himself, he must be hard toward others. All the

gentle and enervating sentiments of kinship, love, friendship, gratitude and even honor must be suppressed in him and give place to the cold and single-minded passion for revolution. For him there exists only one pleasure, one consolation, one reward, one satisfaction—the success of the revolution. Night and day he must have but one thought, one aim —merciless destruction. Striving coldbloodedly and indefatigably toward this end, he must be prepared to destroy himself and to destroy with his own hands everything that stands in the path of the revolution.

7. The nature of the true revolutionary excludes all sentimentality, romanticism, infatuation and exaltation, and also all private hatred and revenge. Revolutionary passion, practiced at every moment of the day until it becomes a habit, is to be employed with cold calculation. At all times and in all places the revolutionary must obey, not his personal impulses, but only those which serve the cause of the revolution.

THE RELATIONS OF THE REVOLUTIONARY TOWARD HIS REVOLUTIONARY COMRADES

8. The revolutionary can have no friendship or affection except for those who have proved by their actions that they, like him, are agents of the revolution. The degree of friendship, devotion and obligation toward such a comrade is determined solely by the degree of his usefulness to the cause of total revolutionary destruction.

9. It is superfluous to speak of solidarity among revolutionaries; the whole strength of the revolutionary cause is based on it. Comrades who possess the same revolutionary passion and understanding should, as much as possible, deliberate all important matters together and come to unanimous conclusions. When the plan is finally decided upon, then the revolutionary must rely solely on himself. In carrying out acts of destruction each one should act alone, never running to another for advice and assistance unless the situation dictates such a course.

10. All revolutionaries should have under their command second-or-third-degree revolutionaries: that is, they must be able to control those who are not yet completely initiated. These lower members of the revolutionary order should be regarded as part of the common revolutionary capital placed at their disposal. This capital should, of course, be spent as economically as possible in order to derive from it the greatest possible profit. The revolutionary regards himself as capital consecrated to the triumph of the revolution; however, he may not personally and alone dispose of that capital without the unanimous consent of the fully initiated comrades.

11. When a comrade is in danger and the question arises whether

he should be saved or not saved, the decision must not be arrived at on the basis of sentiment, but solely in the interests of the revolutionary cause. Therefore it is necessary to weigh carefully the usefulness of the comrade against the expenditure of revolutionary forces necessary to save him, and the decision must be made accordingly.

THE RELATIONS OF THE REVOLUTIONARY TOWARD SOCIETY

12. The new member, having given proof of his loyalty not by words but by deeds, can be received into the society only by the unanimous agreement of all the members.

13. The revolutionary enters the world of the state, of the privileged classes, of the so-called civilization, and he lives in this world only for the purpose of bringing about its speedy and total destruction. He is not a revolutionary if he has any sympathy for this world. He should not hesitate to destroy any position, any place, or any man in this world. He must hate everyone and everything in it with an equal hatred. All the worse for him if he has any relations with parents, friends or lovers; he is no longer a revolutionary if he is swayed by these relationships.

14. Since he aims at implacable revolution, the revolutionary may and frequently must live within society while pretending to be completely different from what he really is, for he must penetrate everywhere, into high society as well as the middle classes, into the houses of commerce, the churches and the palaces of the aristocracy, and into the worlds of the bureaucracy and literature and the military; he must be found among the members of the Third Division and even in the Winter Palace of the Tsar.

15. This filthy social order can be divided into several categories. The first category comprises those who must be condemned to death without delay. Comrades should compile a list of those to be condemned according to the relative gravity of their crimes, always remembering what is useful for the success of the revolution; and the executions should be carried out according to the prepared order.

16. When a list of those who are condemned is made and the order of execution is prepared, no private sense of outrage should be considered, nor is it necessary to pay attention to the hatred provoked by these people among the comrades or the people. Hatred and the sense of outrage may even be useful in so far as they incite the masses to revolt. It is necessary to be guided only by the relative usefulness of these executions for the sake of the revolution. Above all, those who are especially inimical to the revolutionary organization must be destroyed; their violent and sudden deaths will produce the utmost panic in the

government, depriving it of its will to action by removing the cleverest and most energetic supporters.

17. The second group comprises those who will be spared for the time being in order that, by a series of monstrous acts, they may drive the people into inevitable revolt.

18. The third category consists of a great many brutes in high positions distinguished neither by their cleverness nor their energy, while enjoying riches, influence, power and high positions by virtue of their rank. These must be exploited in every possible way; they must be implicated and embroiled in our affairs, their dirty secrets must be ferreted out, and they must be transformed into slaves. Their power, influence and connections, their wealth and their energy will form an inexhaustible treasure and a precious help in all our undertakings.

19. The fourth category comprises ambitious officeholders and liberals of various shades of opinion. The revolutionary must pretend to collaborate with them, obediently following them. But he shall do this more successfully in order to bring them under his power, so as to reveal their secrets and completely compromise them. Then no path of retreat will be open to them, and they can be used to create disorder in the state.

20. The fifth category consists of those doctrinaires, conspirators and revolutionists who cut a great figure on paper or in their cliques. They must be constantly driven into ambiguous positions; they must be compelled to come out into the open and assume real and dangerous tasks. As a result the majority of them will disappear, while a minority will become genuine revolutionaries.

21. The sixth category is extremely important: women. They can be divided into three main groups. First, those frivolous, thoughtless and vapid women, whom we shall use as we use the third and fourth category of men. Second, women who are ardent, capable and devoted, but who do not belong to us because they have not yet achieved a passionless and austere revolutionary understanding; these must be used like the men of the fifth category. Finally, there are the women who are completely on our side: those who are wholly dedicated and who have accepted our program in its entirety. *We should regard these women as the most valuable of our treasures; without their help we would never succeed.*

THE DUTIES OF THE SOCIETY TOWARD THE PEOPLE

22. The Society has no aim other than the complete liberation and happiness of the masses, namely the laborers. Convinced that their emancipation and achievement of this happiness can only come about

as a result of an all-destroying popular revolt, the Society will use all its resources and energy toward increasing and intensifying the evils and miseries of the people until at least their patience is exhausted and they are driven to a general uprising.

23. By a popular revolution the Society does not mean an orderly revolt according to the classic western model—a revolt which always stops short of attacking the rights of property and the traditional social systems of so-called civilization and morality. The western concept of revolution has always meant only the exchanging of one form of political organization for another, thus creating the so-called revolutionary state. The only form of revolution beneficial to the people is one which destroys from top to bottom every idea of the state, exterminating all the state traditions, institutions and classes in Russia.

24. With this end in view, the Society therefore refuses to impose on the people any new organization from above. The future organization will doubtless spring up from the movement and life of the people; but this is a matter for future generations to decide. Our task is terrible, total, universal and merciless destruction.

25. Therefore, in drawing closer to the people, we must above all make common cause with those elements of the masses which, since the foundation of the state of Muscovy, have never ceased to protest, not only in words but in deeds, against everything directly or indirectly connected with the state: against the nobility, the bureaucracy, the priests, world of guilds, and the parasitic kulaks. We must unite with the adventurous tribes of brigands, who are the only genuine revolutionaries of Russia.

26. To weld the people into one single invincible and all-destructive force—this is our aim, our conspiracy and our task.*

*Edited and translated by Stephen P. Halbrook with the assistance of Thomas Egan. From Y. Steklov, *Mikhail Bakunin* (Moscow, 1927), Vol. III, pp. 468-473; M. Koralensky, *Russkaya Revolutsia v Sudebnykh Protsessakh i Memuarakh* (Moscow, 1925), pp. 37-41.

While at one time there was some unwarranted speculation that Nechayev, a follower of Bakunin, contributed weightily to the authorship of the *Catechism,* this view has been long untenable even though the document continues to be identified with Nechayev for no good reason. Cf. B. P. Kozmin, *P.N. Tkachev i revolyutsionnoye dvizhenie 1860–kh 99* (Moscow, 1922). The modern Bakunin scholars, notably Max Nomad, E. H. Carr, and Franco Venturi reach the same conclusion.

Revolution for the Hell of It

MAINTAIN A SENSE OF HUMOR. People who take themselves too seriously are power-crazy. If they win it will be haircuts for all. BEWARE OF POWER FREAKS.

* * * *

ALWAYS USE THE SYMBOLS, PROPS, DRESS AND LANGUAGE OF THE PEOPLE YOU ARE WORKING WITH. Never impose your language on people you wish to reach. If you are working on the street do not talk of imperialism, participatory democracy, or affinity groups. Save that for college seminars. Talk to the guys about getting fucked by the boss, having a say in things, getting laid, and gangs. How would you like to be known as the kid who got kicked out of your affinity group?

* * * *

IN A REVOLUTION, AS IN POOL HUSTLING, ONE SHOULD USE ONLY AS MUCH FORCE AS IS NECESSARY TO PROVE ONE'S POINT, NO MORE, NO LESS. The reason the U.S. Government will lose in Vietnam and that Daley lost in Chicago is because they overact. As the militarists would put it, they adopt a policy of overkill. When that happens they begin to devour themselves. Incidents such as police clubbing Hugh Hefner are not unlike B52's bombing American Marines with napalm. Neither the NLF nor the Yippies work that way, we never eat our own.

* * * *

WE CAN ONLY HAVE A REVOLUTION BASED ON TRUST. One day in Chicago I got a message from a group in Minneapolis that one of my closest friends was an FBI agent. They furnished me with background material and an alias he was supposed to have used there and in Milwaukee. That night I saw him and called him by his alias. "Hey Scott," I said. He didn't respond. I went up to him and handed him the note I had received. "Burn it," I said. He gave me some LSD that night

378

and it was outasight. It could have been poison, I guess. No brother will ever give you poison, even by accident. Continually search for and surround yourself with brothers, it is your best means of survival.

* * * *

THE FIRST DUTY OF A REVOLUTIONIST IS NOT TO GET CAUGHT. I discovered how to survive in the midst of chaos in Chicago. Use disguises, use different names, when you want to take care of business ditch your followers, bodyguards, reporters and establish good alibis. Reject all references to yourself as a leader. If you have to exert leadership let it be natural, arising out of the situation rather than your past history. The enemy always goes after the leaders. You should adopt the attitude that survival is the principal goal of the vanguard. You should avoid going to jail at all costs. If you are caught and put in jail, it is your revolutionary duty to escape. Going to jail presents people with the model of masochistic theater. Getting killed is the risk involved in living a revolutionary life to the fullest. I prefer death to prison.

* * * *

THE FIRST LINE OF DEFENSE IS TO TURN ON THE ENEMY. Middle-of-the-roaders, cops, mothers, everybody should be hustled into the revolution. Under the uniform (the opposite of our costumes) of a cop exists a naked human being. Cops don't like to work, and have sex hang-ups just like everybody else. Ask one why he bothers working for a wife and kids that don't respect him. Ask him if he's getting laid enough. Take a lesson from Tokyo Rose, she was a damn good pool-hustler. When you are trying to turn people onto the FREE society the first question you ask, even if you don't verbalize it, is: "What do you want?" What if the person answers "I want to kick the shit out of kids like you"? Build him a boxing ring.

* * * *

NEVER EXPLAIN WHAT YOU ARE DOING. This wastes a good deal of time and rarely gets through. Show them through your action, if they don't understand it, fuck 'em, maybe you'll hook them with the next action.

* * * *

RUN, DON'T WALK, TO THE NEAREST REVOLUTION. Wear out your shoes, get used to being exhausted. Eat only what you need and stay healthy if possible.

* * * *

WHEN YOU MEET A BROTHER, NEVER PREACH TO HIM. Only exchange information such as date, time, place, and so on. Always re-

spect the style of a brother. If he is doing your thing, you should not
even waste time talking to him. Never preach to the already committed.

* * * *

ALWAYS CREATE ART AND DESTROY PROPERTY. Become a work
of art. Art is the only thing worth dying for.

* * * *

NEVER FORGET THAT OURS IS THE BATTLE AGAINST A MA-
CHINE NOT AGAINST PEOPLE. If, however, people behave like
machines, treat them as such. If a machine slips on a banana peel we
all laugh. If a person slips on a banana peel we help him off the ground.
Our job is to line the streets of the country with banana peels.

* * * *

REMEMBER THAT THE PEOPLE YOU ARE TRYING TO REACH
OFTEN KNOW MORE THAN YOU. Learn from them. Last winter I
spoke at a high school in Port Washington, New York. Two kids from
junior high school, age fourteen and fifteen snuck into the room to listen
to the rap. At the end the kids came up and told me I didn't know much.
I asked them what they were into. "We sleep outside each night prepar-
ing ourselves for guerrilla fighting in the suburbs," they responded. One
of the kids had been arrested four times in demonstrations and was
about to be suspended for refusing to get a haircut. I went to school that
day to Port Washington.

REVOLUTION TOWARDS A FREE SOCIETY: YIPPIE!*
By A. Yippie

1. An immediate end to the War in Vietnam and a restructuring
of our foreign policy which totally eliminates aspects of military, economic, and cultural imperialism. The withdrawal of all foreign based
troops and the abolition of the military draft.

2. Immediate freedom for Huey Newton of the Black Panthers
and all other black people. Adoption of the community control concept

*This is a personal statement. There are no spokesmen for the Yippies. We suggest to all
reporters that they ask each and every Yippie in Lincoln Park why they have come to
Chicago. We are all our own leaders. We realize this list of demands is inconclusive, they
are not really demands. For people to make demands of the Democratic Party is an
exercise in wasted wish-fulfillment. If we have a demand it is simply and emphatically
that they, along with their fellow inmates in the Republican Party cease to exist. We
demand a society built along the alternative community in Lincoln Park, a society based
on humanitarian cooperation and equality, a society which allows and promotes the
creativity present in all people and especially our youth.

in our ghetto areas. An end to the cultural and economic domination of minority groups.

3. The legalization of marihuana and all other psychedelic drugs. The freeing of all prisoners currently in prison on narcotics charges.

4. A prison system based on the concept of rehabilitation rather than punishment.

5. A judicial system which works toward the abolition of all laws related to crimes without victims. That is, retention only of laws relating to crimes in which there is an unwilling injured party, i.e. murder, rape, assault.

6. The total disarmament of all the people beginning with the police. This includes not only guns, but such brutal devices as tear gas, MACE, electric prods, blackjacks, billy clubs, and the like.

7. The Abolition of Money. The abolition of pay housing, pay media, pay transportation, pay food, pay education, pay clothing, pay medical help, and pay toilets.

8. A society which works toward and actively promotes the concept of "full-unemployment." A society in which people are free from the drudgery of work. Adoption of the concept "Let the Machines do it."

9. A conservation program geared towards preserving our natural resources and committed to the elimination of pollution from our air and water.

10. A program of ecological development that will provide incentives for the decentralization of our crowded cities and encourage rural living.

11. A program which provides not only free birth control information and devices but also abortions when desired.

12. A restructured educational system which provides the student power to determine his course of study and allows for student participation in over-all policy planning. Also an educational system which breaks down its barriers between school and community. A system which uses the surrounding community as a classroom so that students may learn directly the problems of the people.

13. The open and free use of the media. A program which actively supports and promotes cable television as a method of increasing the selection of channels available to the viewer.

14. An end to all censorship. We are sick of a society which has no hesitation about showing people committing violence and refuses to show a couple fucking.

15. We believe that people should fuck all the time, anytime, whomever they wish. This is not a program demand but a simple recognition of the reality around us.

16. A political system which is more streamlined and responsive to the needs of all the people regardless of age, sex or race. Perhaps a national referendum system conducted via television or a telephone voting system. Perhaps a decentralization of power and authority with many varied tribal groups. Groups in which people exist in a state of basic trust and are free to choose their tribe.

17. A program that encourages and promotes the arts. However, we feel that if the Free Society we envision were to be fought for and achieved, all of us would actualize the creativity within us. In a very real sense we would have a society in which every man would be an artist.

* * * *

It is for these reasons that we have come to Chicago. It is for these reasons that many of us may fight and die here. We recognize this as the vision of the founders of this nation. We recognize that we are America. We recognize that we are Free Men. The present day politicians and their armies of automatons have selfishly robbed us of our birthright. The evilness they stand for will go unchallenged no longer. Political Pigs, your days are numbered. We are the Second American Revolution. We shall win. Yippie!

Scenario for the Future/Yippieland

Every high school and college in the country will close with riots and sabotage and cops will circle the campuses, standing shoulder to shoulder. The schools belong to the pigs.

Millions of young people will surge into the streets of every city, dancing, singing, smoking pot, fucking in the streets, tripping, burning draft cards, stopping traffic.

The Pentagon will send troops to fight spreading guerrilla wars in Laos, Thailand, Indonesia, India, the Congo, Bolivia, South Africa, Brazil, France.

High government officials will defect to the yippies.

The State Department will discover its highest ranks infested with the yippie symps. Black cops will join the black-and-white liberation army in the streets.

High school students will seize radio, TV and newspaper offices across the land.

Police stations will blow up.

Revolutionaries will break into jails and free all the prisoners.

Clerical workers will ax their computers and put chewing gum into the machines.

Army platoons and the National Guard will desert to the revolution, bringing their guns with them.

Workers will seize their factories and begin running them communally, without profit.

Shorthairs will become longhairs overnight.

Yippie helicopter pilots will bomb police positions with LSD-gas.

The Pentagon will strafe yippie bases, and we'll shoot the planes out of the sky.

Kids will lock their parents out of their suburban homes and turn them into guerilla bases, storing arms.

We'll break into banks and join the bank tellers in taking all the money and burning it in gigantic bonfires in the middle of the city.

Previous revolutions aimed at seizure of the state's highest authority, followed by the takeover of the means of production. The Youth International Revolution will begin with mass breakdown of authority, mass rebellion, total anarchy in every institution in the Western world. Tribes of longhairs, blacks, armed women, workers, peasants and students will take over.

The yippie dropout myth will infiltrate every structure of Amerika. The revolution will shock itself by discovering that it has friends everywhere, friends just waiting for The Moment.

At community meetings all over the land, Bob Dylan will replace The National Anthem.

There will be no more jails, courts or police.

The White House will become a crash pad for anybody without a place to stay in Washington.

The world will become one big commune with free food and housing, everything shared.

All watches and clocks will be destroyed.

Barbers will go to rehabilitation camps where they will grow their hair long.

There will be no such crime as "stealing" because everything will be free.

The Pentagon will be replaced by an LSD experimental farm.

There will be no more schools or churches because the entire world will become one church and school.

People will farm in the morning, make music in the afternoon and fuck wherever and whenever they want to.

Study Questions

1. What goals, according to Fromm, a sane society should seek? What problems can you foresee in Fromm's sketch for an ideal society?
2. Will Plato, Al-Farabi, Huxley, Fromm, Hoffman and Rubin subscribe to the view that the good life consists in one's indulgence in sex?
3. What kind of life would you lead if you were to adopt the Confucian code of ethics?
4. Evaluate the following: Hoffman and Rubin's recommendations concerning the good life are simply *hedonistic* in nature and that one is better off to adopt the Confucian way of life.
5. Do you believe that religious theories concerning the good life are

superior or inferior to the ones considered in the selections? Which
theory has had the most influence on you?

6. Huxley, in his novel *Brave New World,* portrays the society of the
future as one in which the government controls the population by
giving them daily doses of pleasurable drugs. How, then, would
Huxley reconcile this warning with his recommendation of drugs
(in our selection)? Are any drugs conducive to happiness?

7. To Bakunin the good life was passionate destruction, rational and
unrelenting commitment to long run ideals, and concentration on
non-personal objects. Contrast this with Jerry Rubin's idea of the
good life.

8. Do you find Hoffman's "advice" good? Are the principles that Rubin and Hoffman advocate the same as the ones advocated by most
"radicals" in the U.S.? If not, what would you say these radicals
consider as the good life?

9. Al-Farabi believed that the good life (happiness) can only be attained in what he calls the "ideal state." On the other hand, Jerry
Rubin advocates that the good life is to be attained in what he calls
the "yippieland." Could it be then that Al-Farabi and Rubin are
advocating similar views concerning the good life?

10. What do you consider to be the main factors with respect to the
good life?